# PLURAL OWNERSHIP

# Plural Ownership

ROGER J. SMITH

OXFORD
UNIVERSITY PRESS

# OXFORD
UNIVERSITY PRESS

Great Clarendon Street, Oxford OX2 6DP

Oxford University Press is a department of the University of Oxford.
It furthers the University's objective of excellence in research, scholarship,
and education by publishing worldwide in

Oxford  New York

Auckland  Cape Town  Dar es Salaam  Hong Kong  Karachi
Kuala Lumpur  Madrid  Melbourne  Mexico City  Nairobi
New Delhi  Shanghai  Taipei  Toronto

With offices in

Argentina  Austria  Brazil  Chile  Czech Republic  France  Greece
Guatemala  Hungary  Italy  Japan  South Korea  Poland  Portugal
Singapore  Switzerland  Thailand  Turkey  Ukraine  Vietnam

Published in the United States
by Oxford University Press Inc., New York

British Library Cataloguing in Publication Data

Data available

Library of Congress Cataloging in Publication Data

Smith, Roger J. (Roger John), 1948-
Plural ownership / Roger J. Smith.
    p. cm.
  ISBN 0–19–829852–8 (alk. paper)
1.  Joint tenancy—England.  2.  Joint tenancy—Wales.  3.  Joint ownership of personal
property—England.  4.  Joint ownership of personal property—Wales.  I.  Title.
  KD878.S635 2005
  346.4204′2—dc22

                                                        2004027323
        ISBN 0–19–829852–8      EAN 978–0–19–829852–6

        1  3  5  7  9  10  8  6  4  2

Typeset by Newgen Imaging Systems (P) Ltd., Chennai, India
Printed in Great Britain
on acid-free paper by
Biddles Ltd., King's Lynn

# *Preface*

It was Professor Peter Birks who originally suggested that I should write this book. It was by a cruel twist of fate that the principal draft was completed within a day of his untimely death in July 2004. Given the towering nature of his own scholarship, it is easy to overlook the degree to which he encouraged the work of many others. I certainly owe much to him.

As is more fully explained in the first Chapter, *Plural Ownership* covers both successive and concurrent interests in all forms of property. However, the main focus lies in the areas which have attracted the greatest attention and litigation in recent decades: concurrent interests in land and their statutory regulation. This involves a mixture of the old and the new. The basic law of concurrent interests is based on forms of co-ownership going back for many centuries. There is a veritable mountain of authority, with many technical rules and distinctions. The challenge for the modern lawyer is to consider whether this complexity can be reduced or eliminated. The radical solution would be to abolish the beneficial joint tenancy. This would do away with virtually all the complexity of the old law, but it must be asked whether this enormous benefit would be accompanied by unacceptable disadvantages for co-owners.

The new part of the law is the trust of land employed by the Trusts of Land and Appointment of Trustees Act 1996. Although aspects of the trust of land have origins in the 1925 legislation (or earlier), many changes were introduced in 1996. The legislation has resulted in a significant number of articles in legal journals and, recently, a steady flow of judicial decisions. The time is ripe to assess the working of the new legislation and to ask whether it provides a satisfactory platform for the regulation of both concurrent and successive interests in land for the coming decades.

Although these areas form the backbone of the book, there is also treatment of successive interests in land and the recognition of plural ownership in chattels. The former involves much old learning, though thankfully little of it is of much relevance today. By contrast, plural ownership in chattels is curiously undeveloped: even rights equivalent to leases (outside the scope of *Plural Ownership*) are highly controversial.

Many thanks to Pearson Education Ltd for kind permission to include material first published in Roger J. Smith, *Property Law*.

Roger J. Smith
Oxford
August 2004

# *Contents*

*Table of Cases*                                                                        viii
*Table of Legislation, Overseas Statutes and Statutory Instruments*        xvii

## PART I  INTRODUCTION

1.  Plural Ownership                                                                     3

## PART II  FORMS OF PLURAL
## OWNERSHIP OF LAND

2.  Successive Interests in Land                                                        11
3.  Co-Ownership: Requirements and Forms                                       22
4.  Termination of Co-Ownership; Severance                                      47
5.  Joint Tenancy and Tenancy in Common Reviewed                          83

## PART III REGULATION OF PLURAL
## OWNERSHIP OF LAND

6.  Regulation: Introduction and Scope                                             93
7.  Occupation: Rights, Control, and Consequences                           118
8.  Powers of Trustees: Extent, Exercise, and Control                         142
9.  Protection of Purchasers                                                          184

## PART IV OTHER PROPERTY

10. Plural Ownership of Property Other Than Land                           207

*Index*                                                                                    219

# Table of Cases

88, Berkeley Road, Re [1971] Ch 648 . . . . . . . . . . . . . . . . . . . . . . . . . . . . . . . . . . . . . . . . . . . . . . . . . . 52
90 Thornhill Road, Re [1970] Ch 261 . . . . . . . . . . . . . . . . . . . . . . . . . . . . . . . . . . . . . . . . . . . . . . . 155
Abacus Trust Co (Isle of Man) *v* Barr [2003] Ch 409 . . . . . . . . . . . . . . . . . . . . . . . . . . . . . . . . . . . 167
Abbey National BS *v* Cann [1991] 1 AC 56 . . . . . . . . . . . . . . . . . . . . . . . . . . . . . . . . . . . . . . . . . . . 136
Abbey National plc *v* Moss (1993) 26 HLR 249 . . . . . . . . . . . . . . . . . . . . 161, 162, 163, 171, 175
Abbott and Barwick *v* Price [2003] EWHC 2760 (Ch) . . . . . . . . . . . . . . . . . . . . . . . . 133, 135, 136
Abela *v* Public Trustee [1983] 1 NSWLR 308 . . . . . . . . . . . . . . . . . . . . . . . . . . . . . . . . . . 69, 72, 73
Aberconway's ST, Re [1953] Ch 647 . . . . . . . . . . . . . . . . . . . . . . . . . . . . . . . . . . . . . . . . . . . . . . . . . 101
Acklom, Re [1929] 1 Ch 195 . . . . . . . . . . . . . . . . . . . . . . . . . . . . . . . . . . . . . . . . . . . . . . . . . . . . . . . 101
AG Securities *v* Vaughan [1990] 1 AC 417 . . . . . . . . . . . . . . . . . . . . . . 23, 24, 25, 28, 29, 30, 44–5
Ahmed *v* Kendrick (1987) 56 P&CR 120 . . . . . . . . . . . . . . . . . . . . . . . . . . . . . . . . . . . . . . . . . . . . . 61
Alefounder's WT, Re [1927] 1 Ch 360 . . . . . . . . . . . . . . . . . . . . . . . . . . . . . . . . . . . . . . . . . . . . . . . 103
Alliance and Leicester plc *v* Slayford (2000) 33 HLR 743 . . . . . . . . . . . . . . . . . . . . 171, 175, 187
Allingham, Re [1932] VLR 469 . . . . . . . . . . . . . . . . . . . . . . . . . . . . . . . . . . . . . . . . . . . . . . . . . . . . . . 73
Anon (1560) 2 Dyer 187a . . . . . . . . . . . . . . . . . . . . . . . . . . . . . . . . . . . . . . . . . . . . . . . . . . . . . . . . . . . 64
Antoniades *v* Villiers [1990] 1 AC 417 . . . . . . . . . . . . . . . . . . . . . . . . . . . . . . . . . . . . . . . . . . . . 23, 25
Arkwright *v* IRC [2004] WTLR 181; reversed [2004] STC 1323 . . . . . . . . . . . . . . . . . . . . . . . 163
Armstrong, Re [1920] 1 IR 239 . . . . . . . . . . . . . . . . . . . . . . . . . . . . . . . . . . . . . . . . . . . . . . . . . . . . . . 64
Ashburn Anstalt *v* Arnold [1989] Ch 1 . . . . . . . . . . . . . . . . . . . . . . . . . . . . . . . . . . . . . . . . . . . 5, 116
Att-Gen of Hong Kong *v* Reid [1994] 1 AC 324 . . . . . . . . . . . . . . . . . . . . . . . . . . . . . . . . . . . . . 117
Att-Gen *v* Magdalen College, Oxford (1854) 18 Beav 223; reversed 6 HLC 189 . . . . . . . . . . . . 135
Austin *v* Austin (1908) 27 NZLR 1099 . . . . . . . . . . . . . . . . . . . . . . . . . . . . . . . . . . . . . . . . . . . 70, 72
Austin *v* Keele (1987) 61 ALJR 605 . . . . . . . . . . . . . . . . . . . . . . . . . . . . . . . . . . . . . . . . . . . . . . . . . 117
Aveling *v* Knipe (1815) 19 Ves 441 . . . . . . . . . . . . . . . . . . . . . . . . . . . . . . . . . . . . . . . . . . . . . . . 35, 43
Backhouse, Re [1921] 2 Ch 51 . . . . . . . . . . . . . . . . . . . . . . . . . . . . . . . . . . . . . . . . . . . . . . . . . . . . . . 213
Bagot's Settlement, Re [1894] 1 Ch 177 . . . . . . . . . . . . . . . . . . . . . . . . . . . . . . . . . . . . . . . . . . . . . . 121
Bailey *v* Barnes [1894] 1 Ch 25 . . . . . . . . . . . . . . . . . . . . . . . . . . . . . . . . . . . . . . . . . . . . . . . . . . . . 202
Bailey, Re [1977] 1 WLR 278 . . . . . . . . . . . . . . . . . . . . . . . . . . . . . . . . . . . . . . . . . . . . . . . . . . 168, 169
Baker *v* Barclays Bank Ltd [1955] 1 WLR 822 . . . . . . . . . . . . . . . . . . . . . . . . . . . . . . . . . . . . . . . 218
Bank of Baroda *v* Dhillon [1998] 1 FLR 524 . . . . . . . . . . . . . . . . . . . . . . . . . . . . . . 61, 173, 175
Bank of British Columbia *v* Nelson (1979) 17 BCLR 223 . . . . . . . . . . . . . . . . . . . . . . . . . . . . . . . 73
Bank of Credit and Commerce International (Overseas) Ltd *v* Akindele [2001] Ch 437 . . . . . . . 195
Bank of Ireland Home Mortgages Ltd *v* Bell [2001] 2 FLR 809. . . . . . . . . . . . . . 61, 161, 177, 178
Bankers Trust Co *v* Namdar (1997) 14 February . . . . . . . . . . . . . . . . . . . . . . . . . . . . . . . . . . . . . . 176
Barca *v* Mears [2004] EWHC 2170 (Ch) . . . . . . . . . . . . . . . . . . . . . . . . . . . . . . . . . . . . . . . 169, 172
Barclay *v* Barclay [1970] 2 QB 677 . . . . . . . . . . . . . . . . . . . . . . . . . . . . . . . . . . . . . . . . . . . . . . . . . 121
Barclays Bank plc *v* Hendricks [1996] 1 FLR 258 . . . . . . . . . . . . . . . . . . . . . . . . . . . . . . . . 170, 175
Barclays Bank plc *v* O'Brien [1994] 1 AC 180 . . . . . . . . . . . . . . . . . . . . . . . . . . . . . . . . . . . . 61, 189
Barrett *v* Morgan [2000] 2 AC 264 . . . . . . . . . . . . . . . . . . . . . . . . . . . . . . . . . . . . . . . . . . . . . . . . . . 65
Barrowcliff, Re [1927] SASR 147 . . . . . . . . . . . . . . . . . . . . . . . . . . . . . . . . . . . . . . . . . . . . . . . . . . . . . 77
Barton *v* Morris [1985] 1 WLR 1257 . . . . . . . . . . . . . . . . . . . . . . . . . . . . . . . . . . . . . . . . . . . . . . . . 36
Basham, Re [1986] 1 WLR 1498 . . . . . . . . . . . . . . . . . . . . . . . . . . . . . . . . . . . . . . . . . . . . . . . . . . . . 116
Bath and Wells Diocesan Board of Finance *v* Jenkinson [2003] Ch 89 . . . . . . . . . . . . . . . . . . . . . 14
Beale's ST, Re [1932] 2 Ch 15 . . . . . . . . . . . . . . . . . . . . . . . . . . . . . . . . . . . . . . . . . . . . . . . . . . . . . . 148
Bedson *v* Bedson [1965] 2 QB 666 . . . . . . . . . . . . . . . . . 39, 49, 59, 62, 121, 124, 138, 162, 164, 166

Bennett *v* Houldsworth (1911) 104 LT 304 . . . . . . . . . . . . . . . . . . . . . . . . . . . . . . . . . . . . . . . . 31
Berdal *v* Burns [1990] WAR 140 . . . . . . . . . . . . . . . . . . . . . . . . . . . . . . . . . . . . . . . . . . . . . . 69
Bernard *v* Josephs [1982] Ch 391 . . . . . . . . . . . . . . . . . . . . . . . . . . . . . . . . . . . . . 37, 134, 165
Binions *v* Evans [1972] Ch 359 . . . . . . . . . . . . . . . . . . . . . . . . . . . . . . . . . . . . . . . . . . . . . 109
Binning *v* Binning (1895) 13 R 654. . . . . . . . . . . . . . . . . . . . . . . . . . . . . . . . . . . . . . . . . . . . 32
Birmingham Midshires Mortgage Services Ltd *v* Sabherwal (1999) 80 P&CR 256 . . . 117, 185, 197
Biviano *v* Natoli (1998) 43 NSWLR 695 . . . . . . . . . . . . . . . . . . . . . . . . . . . . . . . . . . . . . . . 134
Booth *v* Alington (1857) 3 Jur (NS) 835. . . . . . . . . . . . . . . . . . . . . . . . . . . . . . . . . . . . . . 31, 32
Boston's WT, Re [1956] Ch 395. . . . . . . . . . . . . . . . . . . . . . . . . . . . . . . . . . . . . . . . . . . . . . 101
Bourne, Re [1906] 1 Ch 113 . . . . . . . . . . . . . . . . . . . . . . . . . . . . . . . . . . . . . . . . . . . . . . . . 199
Brandon *v* Robinson (1811) 18 Ves 429 . . . . . . . . . . . . . . . . . . . . . . . . . . . . . . . . . . . . . . . 207
Bremner, Re [1999] 1 FLR 912 . . . . . . . . . . . . . . . . . . . . . . . . . . . . . . . . . . . . . . . . . . . . . . 170
Brice *v* Stokes (1805) 11 Ves 319 . . . . . . . . . . . . . . . . . . . . . . . . . . . . . . . . . . . . . . . . . . . . 154
Brickwood *v* Young (1905) 2 CLR 387. . . . . . . . . . . . . . . . . . . . . . . . . . . . . . . . . . . . 135, 140
Bristol & West BS *v* Ellis (1996) 73 P&CR 158. . . . . . . . . . . . . . . . . . . . . . . . . . . . . . . . . 178
Bristol Airport plc *v* Powdrill [1990] Ch 744 . . . . . . . . . . . . . . . . . . . . . . . . . . . . . . . . . . . 212
Brook *v* Badley (1868) LR 3 Ch 672 . . . . . . . . . . . . . . . . . . . . . . . . . . . . . . . . . . . . . . . . . 120
Brown *v* Oakshot (1857) 24 Beav 254. . . . . . . . . . . . . . . . . . . . . . . . . . . . . . . . . . . . . . . . . . 35
Brown *v* Raindle (1796) 3 Ves Jun 256 . . . . . . . . . . . . . . . . . . . . . . . . . . . . . . . . . . . . . . . . 58
Brown, Re [1954] Ch 39. . . . . . . . . . . . . . . . . . . . . . . . . . . . . . . . . . . . . . . . . . . . . . . . . . . . 144
Browne *v* Pritchard [1975] 1 WLR 1366. . . . . . . . . . . . . . . . . . . . . . . . . . . . . . . . . . . . . . . 164
Bryan and Heath, Re (1979) 108 DLR 3d 245 . . . . . . . . . . . . . . . . . . . . . . . . . . . . . . . . . 49, 76
Buchanan-Wollaston's Conveyance, Re [1939] Ch 738 . . . . . . . . . . . . . . . 35, 113, 155, 160, 161
Buckley *v* Barber (1851) 6 Exch 164 . . . . . . . . . . . . . . . . . . . . . . . . . . . . . . . . . . . . . . . . . . . 34
Bull *v* Bull [1955] 1 QB 234. . . . . . . . . . . . . . . . . . . . . . . . . . 26, 113, 120–1, 133, 148, 188
Burgess *v* Rawnsley [1975] Ch 429 . . . . . . . . . . . . . . . 42, 51, 53, 54, 55, 59, 68, 69, 70, 71, 72, 77
Burke *v* Burke [1974] 1 WLR 1063 . . . . . . . . . . . . . . . . . . . . . . . . . . . . . . . . . . . . . . . 163, 164
Burnaby *v* Equitable Reversionary Interest Society (1885) 28 Ch D 416. . . . . . . . . . . . . . . . . . 58
Burton *v* Camden LBC [2000] 2 AC 399 . . . . . . . . . . . . . . . . . . . . . . . . . . . . . . . . . . . . . . . . 45
Butler's Trusts, Hughes *v* Anderson, Re (1888) 38 Ch D 286 . . . . . . . . . . . . . . . . . . . . . . . . . . 59
Byford, Re [2004] 1 P&CR 159 . . . . . . . . . . . . . . . . . . . . . . . . . . . . . . . . . . . . . . . . . . 136–7, 170
Caldwell *v* Fellowes (1870) LR 9 Eq 410. . . . . . . . . . . . . . . . . . . . . . . . . . . . . . . . . . . . . . . . 58
Campbell *v* Allgood (1853) 17 Beav 623. . . . . . . . . . . . . . . . . . . . . . . . . . . . . . . . . . . . . . . . . 21
Campbell *v* Campbell (1792) 4 Bro CC 15. . . . . . . . . . . . . . . . . . . . . . . . . . . . . . . . . . . . . . . 31
Cardigan *v* Curzon-Howe (1885) 30 Ch D 531. . . . . . . . . . . . . . . . . . . . . . . . . . . . . . . . . . 100
Cartwright, Re (1889) 41 Ch D 532 . . . . . . . . . . . . . . . . . . . . . . . . . . . . . . . . . . . . . . . . . . . . 20
Cedar Holdings Ltd *v* Green [1981] Ch 129 . . . . . . . . . . . . . . . . . . . . . . . . . . . . . . . . . . 61, 62
Chalmers *v* Johns [1999] 1 FLR 392 . . . . . . . . . . . . . . . . . . . . . . . . . . . . . . . . . . . . . . . . . . 129
Chan *v* Leung [2003] 1 FLR 23 . . . . . . . . . . . . . . . . . . . . . . . . . . . . . . . 7, 123, 125, 157, 161
Chandler *v* Clark [2003] 1 P&CR 239 . . . . . . . . . . . . . . . . . . . . . . . . . . . . . . . . . . . . . . . . . 42
Chapman *v* Chapman [1954] AC 429. . . . . . . . . . . . . . . . . . . . . . . . . . . . . . . . . . . . . . . . . 145
Charles *v* Barzey [2003] 1 WLR 437 . . . . . . . . . . . . . . . . . . . . . . . . . . . . . . . . . . . . . . . . . . . 19
Charlton *v* Lester [1976] 1 EGLR 131 . . . . . . . . . . . . . . . . . . . . . . . . . . . . . . . . . . . . . 162, 163
Chattey *v* Farndale Holdings Inc (1996) 75 P&CR 298. . . . . . . . . . . . . . . . . . . . . . . . . 116, 203
Chhokar *v* Chhokar (1983) 5 FLR 313 . . . . . . . . . . . . . . . . . . . . . . . . . . . . . . . . . . . . 121, 134
Citro, Re [1991] Ch 142 . . . . . . . . . . . . . . . . . . . . . . . . 124, 137, 168–9, 170, 172, 174, 175, 176
City of London BS *v* Flegg [1986] Ch 605; reversed [1988] AC 54. . . . 40, 113, 121, 137, 157, 186,
                                                                                187–8, 191, 196, 197, 198
Claughton *v* Charalambous [1999] 1 FLR 740. . . . . . . . . . . . . . . . . . . . . . . . . . . . . . . . . . . 169
Cleaver, Re [1981] 1 WLR 939. . . . . . . . . . . . . . . . . . . . . . . . . . . . . . . . . . . . . . . . . . . . . . . . 76
Clerk *v* Clerk (1694) 2 Vern 323 . . . . . . . . . . . . . . . . . . . . . . . . . . . . . . . . . . . . . . . . . . . 31, 32

Cogan *v* Duffield (1876) 2 Ch D 44 . . . . . . . . . . . . . . . . . . . . . . . . . . . . . . . . . . . . . . . . . 38
Connolly *v* Connolly (1866) 17 Ir Ch R 208 . . . . . . . . . . . . . . . . . . . . . . . . . . . . . . . . . . . 66
Cook, Re [1948] Ch 212. . . . . . . . . . . . . . . . . . . . . . . . . . . . . . . . . . . . . . . . . . . . . . . . . . . 200
Cook's Mortgage, Re [1896] 1 Ch 923 . . . . . . . . . . . . . . . . . . . . . . . . . . . . . . . . . . . . . . . 140
Cookson *v* Bingham (1853) 17 Beav 262 . . . . . . . . . . . . . . . . . . . . . . . . . . . . . . . . . . . 24, 32
Corin *v* Patton (1990) 169 CLR 540 . . . . . . . . . . . . . . . . . . . . . . . . . . . 58, 59, 65, 69, 70
Cowcher *v* Cowcher [1972] 1 WLR 425 . . . . . . . . . . . . . . . . . . . . . . . . . . . 28, 30, 36, 49
Cowper *v* Fletcher (1865) 6 B&S 464; 13 WR 739 . . . . . . . . . . . . . . . . . . . . . . . . . . . . 64
Crawley BC *v* Ure [1996] QB 13 . . . . . . . . . . . . . . . . . . . . . . . . . . . . . . . . . . . . . . . . . . . 149
Cray *v* Willis (1729) 2 P Wms 529. . . . . . . . . . . . . . . . . . . . . . . . . . . . . . . . . . . . . . . 30, 57
Crisp *v* Mullings [1976] 2 EGLR 103 . . . . . . . . . . . . . . . . . . . . . . . . . . . . . . . . . . . . 37, 42
Crooke *v* de Vandes (1805) 11 Ves 330 . . . . . . . . . . . . . . . . . . . . . . . . . . . . . . . . . . . . . . 75
Cubitt *v* Porter (1828) 8 B&C 257 . . . . . . . . . . . . . . . . . . . . . . . . . . . . . . . . . . . . . . . . . 23
Cummins, Re [1972] Ch 62 . . . . . . . . . . . . . . . . . . . . . . . . . . . . . . . . . . . . . . . . . . . . . . . . 41
Dale, Re [1994] Ch 31. . . . . . . . . . . . . . . . . . . . . . . . . . . . . . . . . . . . . . . . . . . . . . . . . . . . . 76
Dance *v* Goldingham (1873) LR 8 Ch App 902. . . . . . . . . . . . . . . . . . . . . . . . . . . . . . 199
Daniel *v* Camplin (1845) 7 Man & G 167 . . . . . . . . . . . . . . . . . . . . . . . . . . . . . . . . . . . 28
Davies *v* Davies [1983] WAR 305 . . . . . . . . . . . . . . . . . . . . . . . . . . . . . . . . . . . . . . . . . . 70
Dearle *v* Hall (1828) 3 Russ 1 . . . . . . . . . . . . . . . . . . . . . . . . . . . . . . . . . . . . . . . . . . . . 210
Delehunt *v* Carmody (1986) 161 CLR 464 . . . . . . . . . . . . . . . . . . . . . . . . . . . . . 43, 84, 86
Dennis *v* McDonald [1982] Fam 63. . . . . . . . . . . . . . . . . . 133, 134, 135, 136, 138, 156
Dennis, Re [1996] Ch 80 . . . . . . . . . . . . . . . . . . . . . . . . . . . . . . . . . . . . . . . . . . . . . . . . . . 59
Denny, Re (1947) 177 LT 291. . . . . . . . . . . . . . . . . . . . . . . . . . . . . . . . . . . . . . . . 50, 68, 75
Densham, Re [1975] 1 WLR 1519 . . . . . . . . . . . . . . . . . . . . . . . . . . . . 42, 168, 170, 171
Diemasters Pty Ltd *v* Meadowcorp Pty Ltd [2001] NSWSC 495. . . . . . . . . . . . . . . . . . 46
Dodsworth *v* Dodsworth (1973) 228 EG 1115 . . . . . . . . . . . . . . . . . . . . . . . . . . . . . . 109
Doe d Borwell *v* Abey (1813) 1 M&S 428 . . . . . . . . . . . . . . . . . . . . . . . . . . . . . . . . . . . 46
Doe d Leicester *v* Biggs (1808) 2 Taunt 109 . . . . . . . . . . . . . . . . . . . . . . . . . . . . . . . . . . 32
Draper's Conveyance, Re [1969] 1 Ch 486 . . . . . . . . . . . . . . . . . . . . . . . . . . . 49, 51, 53, 58
Dufour *v* Pereira (1769) Dick 419 . . . . . . . . . . . . . . . . . . . . . . . . . . . . . . . . . . . . . . . . . . 77
Dunbar *v* Plant [1998] Ch 412 . . . . . . . . . . . . . . . . . . . . . . . . . . . . . . . . . . . . . . . . . 78, 79
Dunn, Re [1916] 1 Ch 97. . . . . . . . . . . . . . . . . . . . . . . . . . . . . . . . . . . . . . . . . . . . . . . . . . 31
Dyer *v* Dyer (1788) 2 Cox 92 . . . . . . . . . . . . . . . . . . . . . . . . . . . . . . . . . . . . . . . . . . . . . . 37
Earl of Chesterfield's Trusts, Re (1883) 24 Ch D 643. . . . . . . . . . . . . . . . . . . . . . . . . . . . 21
Earl Somers, Re (1895) 11 TLR 567 . . . . . . . . . . . . . . . . . . . . . . . . . . . . . . . . . . . . . . . . 100
Edwards *v* Lloyds TSB Bank plc [2004] EWHC 1745 (Ch) . . . . . . . . . . . . 61, 166, 178, 179
Edwards *v* West (1878) 7 Ch D 858. . . . . . . . . . . . . . . . . . . . . . . . . . . . . . . . . . . . . . . . . 61
Elton *v* Cavill (No 2) (1994) 34 NSWLR 289 . . . . . . . . . . . . . . . . . . . . . . . . . . . . . . . 160
Elwes *v* Brigg Gas Company (1886) 33 Ch D 562 . . . . . . . . . . . . . . . . . . . . . . . . . . . . . 20
Evers' Trust, Re [1980] 1 WLR 1327. . . . . . . . . . . . . . . . . . . . . . . . . . . . . . 161, 163, 164, 180
Eves *v* Eves [1975] 1 WLR 1338. . . . . . . . . . . . . . . . . . . . . . . . . . . . . . . . . . . . . . . . . . . . 41
Fawcett, Re [1940] Ch 402. . . . . . . . . . . . . . . . . . . . . . . . . . . . . . . . . . . . . . . . . . . . . . . . . 21
First National Bank plc *v* Achampong [2004] 1 FCR 18; [2003]
     EWCA Civ 487. . . . . . . . . . . . . . . . . . . . . . . . . . . . . . . . 61, 62, 157, 165, 166, 173, 178–9, 187
First National Securities Ltd *v* Hegerty [1985] QB 850. . . . . . . . . . . . . . . . . . . . . . . 41, 62
Fisher *v* Wigg (1701) 1 Ld Raymond 622 . . . . . . . . . . . . . . . . . . . . . . . . . . . . . . . . . . . . 30
Flannigan *v* Wotherspoon [1953] 1 DLR 768 . . . . . . . . . . . . . . . . . . . . . . . . . . . . . . 73, 74
Foley *v* Burnell (1789) 4 Bro PC 34 . . . . . . . . . . . . . . . . . . . . . . . . . . . . . . . . . . . . . . . . 213
Franklin *v* Neate (1844) 13 M&W 481. . . . . . . . . . . . . . . . . . . . . . . . . . . . . . . . . . . . . 212
Fraser *v* Kershaw (1856) 2 K&J 496 . . . . . . . . . . . . . . . . . . . . . . . . . . . . . . . . . . . . . . . 218
Freed *v* Taffel [1984] 2 NSWLR 322. . . . . . . . . . . . . . . . . . . . . . . . . . . . . . . . . . 57, 60, 70

Frewen *v* Relfe (1787) 2 Bro CC 220. . . . . . . . . . . . . . . . . . . . . . . . . . . . . . . . . . . . . . . .31, 68
Frieze *v* Unger [1960] VR 230 . . . . . . . . . . . . . . . . . . . . . . . . . . . . . . . . . . . . . . . . . . . . .65, 66
Gansloser's WT, Re [1952] Ch 30 . . . . . . . . . . . . . . . . . . . . . . . . . . . . . . . . . . . . . . . . . . . . .30
Gant *v* Laurence (1811) Wight 395 . . . . . . . . . . . . . . . . . . . . . . . . . . . . . . . . . . . . . . . . . . . .31
Gardner, Re [1924] 2 Ch 243 . . . . . . . . . . . . . . . . . . . . . . . . . . . . . . . . . . . . . . . . . . . . . . . . . .31
Gartside *v* IRC [1968] AC 553. . . . . . . . . . . . . . . . . . . . . . . . . . . . . . . . . . . . . . . . . . . . . . . .122
Gillette *v* Cotton [1979] 4 WWR 515 . . . . . . . . . . . . . . . . . . . . . . . . . . . . . . . . . . . . . . . . . .70
Ginn *v* Armstrong (1969) 3 DLR 3d 285 . . . . . . . . . . . . . . . . . . . . . . . . . . . . . . . . . . . . .70, 72
Gissing *v* Gissing [1971] AC 886 . . . . . . . . . . . . . . . . . . . . . . . . . . .4, 37, 39, 41, 42, 43, 113, 142
Goddard *v* Lewis (1909) 101 LT 528 . . . . . . . . . . . . . . . . . . . . . . . . . . . . . . . . . . . . . . . . . . . .35
Golding *v* Hands [1969] WAR 121 . . . . . . . . . . . . . . . . . . . . . . . . . . . . . . . . . . . . . . . . . . . . .70
Goodman *v* Gallant [1986] Fam 106 . . . . . . . . . . . . . . . . . . . . . . . . . . . . . . . . . . .28, 36, 39–40
Gore and Snell *v* Carpenter (1990) 60 P&CR 456 . . . . . . . . . . . . . . . . . . . . . . . . . .53, 69, 70, 72
Gorman, Re [1990] 1 WLR 616 . . . . . . . . . . . . . . . . . . . . . . . . . . . . . . . . . . . . . . . . . . . .40, 136
Gould *v* Kemp (1834) 2 My&K 304. . . . . . . . . . . . . . . . . . . . . . . . . . . . . . . . . . . . .49, 58, 64
Grainge *v* Wilberforce (1889) 5 TLR 436 . . . . . . . . . . . . . . . . . . . . . . . . . . . . . . . . . . . . . . .60
Grant *v* Edwards [1986] Ch 638 . . . . . . . . . . . . . . . . . . . . . . . . . . . . . . . . . . . . . . . . . . . . . .117
Greenfield *v* Greenfield (1979) 38 P&CR 570 . . . . . . . . . . . . . . . . . . . . . . . . . . . . .50, 63, 69, 74
Griffies *v* Griffies (1863) 8 LT NS 758. . . . . . . . . . . . . . . . . . . . . . . . . . . . . . . . . . . . . . . . .135
Griffiths *v* Williams [1978] 2 EGLR 121 . . . . . . . . . . . . . . . . . . . . . . . . . . . . . . . . . . .5, 109
Grindal *v* Hooper (1999) 96/48 LS Gaz 41. . . . . . . . . . . . . . . . . . . . . . . . . . . . . . . . . . . . .200
Haddelsey *v* Adams (1856) 22 Beav 266 . . . . . . . . . . . . . . . . . . . . . . . . . . . . . . . . . . . . . . . .46
Hagger, Re [1930] 2 Ch 190. . . . . . . . . . . . . . . . . . . . . . . . . . . . . . . . . . . . . . . . . . . . . . . . . . .76
Halifax Mortgage Services Ltd *v* Muirhead (1997) 76 P&CR 418. . . . . . . . . . . . . . . . . . . . .175
Hall *v* Public Trustee (2003) 150 ACTR 8 . . . . . . . . . . . . . . . . . . . . . . . . . . . . . . . . . . . . . .58
Hall's Estate, Re [1914] P 1. . . . . . . . . . . . . . . . . . . . . . . . . . . . . . . . . . . . . . . . . . . . . . . . . . . .77
Halliday *v* Holgate (1868) LR 3 Ex 299 . . . . . . . . . . . . . . . . . . . . . . . . . . . . . . . . . . . . . . . .212
Hammersmith and Fulham LBC *v* Monk [1992] 1 AC 478. . . . . . . . . . . . . . . . . . . . . . .45, 149
Hamond *v* Jethro (1611) 2 Brown & Golds 97. . . . . . . . . . . . . . . . . . . . . . . . . . . . . . . . . . .34
Harbin *v* Barton (1595) Moo KB 395 . . . . . . . . . . . . . . . . . . . . . . . . . . . . . . . . . . . . . . . . . .64
Harbin *v* Loby (1629) Noy 157 . . . . . . . . . . . . . . . . . . . . . . . . . . . . . . . . . . . . . . . . . . . . . . . .64
Harris *v* Ferguson (1848) 16 Sim 308 . . . . . . . . . . . . . . . . . . . . . . . . . . . . . . . . . . . . . . . . . . .37
Harris *v* Goddard [1983] 1 WLR 1203 . . . . . . . . . . . . . . . . . . . . . . . . . . . . . .49, 51, 53, 70, 72
Harris *v* Harris (1995) 72 P&CR 408. . . . . . . . . . . . . . . . . . . . . . . . . . . . . . . . . . . . . .162, 163
Harrison *v* Barton (1860) 1 J&H 287 . . . . . . . . . . . . . . . . . . . . . . . . . . . . . . . . . . . . . . . .35, 37
Harvey *v* Harvey [1982] Fam 83 . . . . . . . . . . . . . . . . . . . . . . . . . . . . . . . . . . . . . . . . . . . . . .179
Harwood *v* Harwood [1991] 2 FLR 274. . . . . . . . . . . . . . . . . . . . . . . . . . . . . . . . . . . . . . . . .40
Hawkesley *v* May [1956] 1 QB 304 . . . . . . . . . . . . . . . . . . . . . . . . . . . . . . . . . . . . . . . . . . . . .58
Haye's Estate, Re [1920] 1 IR 207 . . . . . . . . . . . . . . . . . . . . . . . . . . . . . . . . . . . . . . . . . . . . . . .73
Haynes, Re (1887) 37 Ch D 306 . . . . . . . . . . . . . . . . . . . . . . . . . . . . . . . . . . . . . . . . . . . . . . .101
Hedley *v* Roberts [1977] VR 282 . . . . . . . . . . . . . . . . . . . . . . . . . . . . . . . . . . . . . . . . . . . . . . .45
Henderson *v* Eason (1851) 17 QB 701 . . . . . . . . . . . . . . . . . . . . . . . . . . . . . . . . . . . . . . . . .133
Herklots' WT, Re [1964] 1 WLR 583. . . . . . . . . . . . . . . . . . . . . . . . . . . . . . . . . . . . . . .147, 217
Hewett, Re [1894] 1 Ch 362 . . . . . . . . . . . . . . . . . . . . . . . . . . . . . . . . . . . . . . . . .57, 58, 208
Heys' Estate, Re [1914] P 192 . . . . . . . . . . . . . . . . . . . . . . . . . . . . . . . . . . . . . . . . . . . . .49, 76
Hill *v* Hickin [1897] 2 Ch 579 . . . . . . . . . . . . . . . . . . . . . . . . . . . . . . . . . . . . . . . . . . . . . . .135
Hill, Re [1902] 1 Ch 807 . . . . . . . . . . . . . . . . . . . . . . . . . . . . . . . . . . . . . . . . . . . . . . . . . . . . .213
Holliday, Re [1981] Ch 405. . . . . . . . . . . . . . . . . . . . . . . . . . . . . . . . . . . . . . . . . . . . . .169, 170
Hope's WT, Re [1929] 2 Ch 136 . . . . . . . . . . . . . . . . . . . . . . . . . . . . . . . . . . . . . . . . . . . . . . .217
House, Re [1929] 2 Ch 166 . . . . . . . . . . . . . . . . . . . . . . . . . . . . . . . . . . . . . . . . . . . . . . . . . . .112
Howard *v* Duke of Norfolk (1681) 2 Swans 454 . . . . . . . . . . . . . . . . . . . . . . . . . . . . . . . . .207

Hulton, Re (1890) 62 LT 200. . . . . . . . . . . . . . . . . . . . . . . . . . . . . . . . . . . . . . . . . . . . . . . 34
Hunter *v* Babbage [1994] 2 FLR 806. . . . . . . . . . . . . . . . . . . . . . . . . . . . . 53, 54, 69, 70, 72, 73
Huntingford *v* Hobbs [1993] 1 FLR 736 . . . . . . . . . . . . . . . . . . . . . . . . . . . . . . . . . . . . . 37, 40
Hyde *v* Parrat (1695) 1 P Wms 1; 2 Vern 331 . . . . . . . . . . . . . . . . . . . . . . . . . . . . . . . . . . 214
Hypo-Mortgage Services Ltd *v* Robinson [1997] 2 FLR 71. . . . . . . . . . . . . . . . . . . . . . . . . . 191
IRC *v* Bernstein [1961] Ch 399 . . . . . . . . . . . . . . . . . . . . . . . . . . . . . . . . . . . . . . . . . . . . 147
IRC *v* Eversden [2002] STC 1109; affirmed (2003) 75 TC 340 . . . . . . . . . . . . . . . . . . . . 126, 128
Jackson *v* Jackson (1804) 9 Ves 591 . . . . . . . . . . . . . . . . . . . . . . . . . . . . . . . . . 34, 35, 49, 55
Jackson *v* Jackson [1971] 1 WLR 1539 . . . . . . . . . . . . . . . . . . . . . . . . . . . . . . 49, 113, 161
Jackson, Re (1887) 34 Ch D 732 . . . . . . . . . . . . . . . . . . . . . . . . . . . . . . . . . . . . . . . . . . . . 34
Jacobs *v* Seward (1872) LR 5 HL 464 . . . . . . . . . . . . . . . . . . . . . . . . . . . . . . . . . . . . 131, 133
Jefferys *v* Small (1683) 1 Vern 217 . . . . . . . . . . . . . . . . . . . . . . . . . . . . . . . . . . . . . . . . . . 34
Jones *v* Challenger [1961] 1 QB 176 . . . . . . . . . . . . . . . . . . . . 123, 137, 161, 163, 174, 175
Jones *v* Jones [1977] 1 WLR 438. . . . . . . . . . . . . . . . . . . . . . . . . . . . . . . . . . . . . . . . 133, 135
Jones, Re [1893] 2 Ch 461 . . . . . . . . . . . . . . . . . . . . . . . . . . . . . . . . . . . . . . . . . . . . . . . . 140
Joyce *v* Barker Bros (Builders) Ltd [1980] CL 2255 . . . . . . . . . . . . . . . . . . . . . . . . . . . . . . . 32
Joyce *v* Rigolli [2004] EWCA Civ 79. . . . . . . . . . . . . . . . . . . . . . . . . . . . . . . . . . . . . . . . 116
Judd *v* Brown [1998] 2 FLR 360; reversed [1999] 1 FLR 1191 . . . . . . . . . . . . . . . . . . . . . 169
K, Re [1985] Ch 85. . . . . . . . . . . . . . . . . . . . . . . . . . . . . . . . . . . . . . . . . . . . . . . . . . . 78, 79
Kemmis *v* Kemmis [1988] 1 WLR 1307 . . . . . . . . . . . . . . . . . . . . . . . . . . . . . . . . . . . . . 121
Kemp *v* Public Curator of Queensland [1969] Qd R 145 . . . . . . . . . . . . . . . . . . . . . . . . . . . 77
Kennedy *v* De Trafford [1897] AC 180 . . . . . . . . . . . . . . . . . . . . . . . . . . . . . . . . . . . . . . 132
Kenworthy *v* Ward (1853) 11 Hare 196 . . . . . . . . . . . . . . . . . . . . . . . . . . . . . . . . . . . . 29, 30
Kinch *v* Bullard [1999] 1 WLR 423. . . . . . . . . . . . . . . . . . . . . . . . . . . . . . . . . . . . . . . . . 52
Kingsford *v* Ball (1852) 2 Giff (App) i . . . . . . . . . . . . . . . . . . . . . . . . . . . . . . . . . . . . . . . . 73
Kostiuk, Re (2002) 215 DLR 4th 78. . . . . . . . . . . . . . . . . . . . . . . . . . . . . . . . . . . . . . . . . 131
L'Estrange *v* L'Estrange [1902] 1 IR 467 . . . . . . . . . . . . . . . . . . . . . . . . . . . . . . . . . . . . . . . 31
Laird *v* Laird [1999] 1 FLR 791 . . . . . . . . . . . . . . . . . . . . . . . . . . . . . . . . . . . . . . . . . . . 180
Lake *v* Craddock (1732) 3 P Wms 158 . . . . . . . . . . . . . . . . . . . . . . . . . . . . . . . . . . . . . . . 34
Lake *v* Gibson (1729) 1 Eq Cas Abr 290. . . . . . . . . . . . . . . . . . . . . . . . . . . . . . . . . 36, 37, 43
Landi, Re [1939] Ch 828 . . . . . . . . . . . . . . . . . . . . . . . . . . . . . . . . . . . . . . . . . . . . . . . . . 133
Lashbrook *v* Cock (1816) 2 Mer 70 . . . . . . . . . . . . . . . . . . . . . . . . . . . . . . . . . . . . . . . . . . 31
Leach, Re [1912] 2 Ch 422. . . . . . . . . . . . . . . . . . . . . . . . . . . . . . . . . . . . . . . . . . . . . . . . 145
Leahy *v* Att-Gen of New South Wales [1959] AC 457 . . . . . . . . . . . . . . . . . . . . . . . . . . . . . . 7
Leak *v* Macdowall (1862) 32 Beav 28 . . . . . . . . . . . . . . . . . . . . . . . . . . . . . . . . . . . . . . . . 75
Leake *v* Bruzzi [1974] 1 WLR 1528 . . . . . . . . . . . . . . . . . . . . . . . . . . . . . . . . . . . . . . 39, 136
Leake *v* Robinson (1817) 2 Mer 363 . . . . . . . . . . . . . . . . . . . . . . . . . . . . . . . . . . . . . . . . . 18
Leigh *v* Dickeson (1884) 15 QBD 60. . . . . . . . . . . . . . . . . . . . . . . . . . . . . . . . . 132, 136, 140
Leong *v* Chye [1955] AC 648. . . . . . . . . . . . . . . . . . . . . . . . . . . . . . . . . . . . . . . . . . . . . . 208
Lewen *v* Cox (1599) Cro Eliz 695 . . . . . . . . . . . . . . . . . . . . . . . . . . . . . . . . . . . . . . . . . 30, 31
Lipinski's WT, Re [1976] Ch 235. . . . . . . . . . . . . . . . . . . . . . . . . . . . . . . . . . . . . . . . . . . . 115
Lloyds Bank Plc *v* Byrne & Byrne [1993] 1 FLR 369. . . . . . . . . . . . . . . . . 62, 157, 175, 176
Lloyds Bank plc *v* Rosset [1991] 1 AC 107. . . . . . . . . . . . . . . . . . . . . . . . . . . . . . . . . . 43, 117
Lohia *v* Lohia [2001] EWCA Civ 1691; (2002) 16 Trust Law International 231 . . . . . . . . . . . . . . 19
Lord Abergavenny's Case (1607) 6 Co Rep 78b . . . . . . . . . . . . . . . . . . . . . . . . . . . . . . . . . . . 60
Lowrie, Re [1981] 3 All ER 353 . . . . . . . . . . . . . . . . . . . . . . . . . . . . . . . . . . . . . 168, 169, 174
Luke *v* Luke (1936) 36 SR NSW 310 . . . . . . . . . . . . . . . . . . . . . . . . . . . . . . . . . . . . . . . 135
Lyons *v* Lyons [1967] VR 169 . . . . . . . . . . . . . . . . . . . . . . . . . . . . . . . . . . . . . . . . 63, 67, 68
Lysaght *v* Edwards (1876) 2 Ch D 499 . . . . . . . . . . . . . . . . . . . . . . . . . . . . . . . . . . . . . . . 116
Lyster *v* Dolland (1792) 1 Ves Jr 431 . . . . . . . . . . . . . . . . . . . . . . . . . . . . . . . . . . . . . . . . . 34
M'Gregor *v* M'Gregor (1859) 1 De GF&J 63. . . . . . . . . . . . . . . . . . . . . . . . . . . . . . . . . . . 29

M'Mahon *v* Burchell (1846) 2 Ph 127 . . . . . . . . . . . . . . . . . . . . . . . . . . . . . . . . . . . . . 131, 133, 135
Malayan Credit Ltd *v* Jack Chia-MPH Ltd [1986] AC 549. . . . . . . . . . . . . . 6, 23, 24, 29, 34, 35, 36
Marriage of Badcock (1979) 5 Fam LR 672 . . . . . . . . . . . . . . . . . . . . . . . . . . . . . . . . . . . . . . 70
Marriage of Pertsoulis (1980) 6 Fam LR 39 . . . . . . . . . . . . . . . . . . . . . . . . . . . . . . . . . . 70, 73
Marryat *v* Townly (1748) 1 Ves Sen 102 . . . . . . . . . . . . . . . . . . . . . . . . . . . . . . . . . . . . . . . 31
Martin *v* Martin (1987) 54 P&CR 238. . . . . . . . . . . . . . . . . . . . . . . . . . . . . . . . . . . . . . . 31, 32
Mastron *v* Cotton [1926] 1 DLR 767 . . . . . . . . . . . . . . . . . . . . . . . . . . . . . . . . . . . . . . . . 135
Mayes *v* Mayes (1969) 210 EG 935 . . . . . . . . . . . . . . . . . . . . . . . . . . . . . . . . . . . . . . . . . . 140
Mayhew *v* Herrick (1849) 7 CB 229. . . . . . . . . . . . . . . . . . . . . . . . . . . . . . . . . . . . . . . 208, 218
Mayn *v* Mayn (1867) LR 5 Eq 150 . . . . . . . . . . . . . . . . . . . . . . . . . . . . . . . . . . . . . . . . . . . 38
Mayo, Re [1943] Ch 302 . . . . . . . . . . . . . . . . . . . . . . . . . . . . . . . . . . . . . . . . . . . . . . . . . . 155
McCormick *v* McCormick [1921] NZLR 384. . . . . . . . . . . . . . . . . . . . . . . . . . . . . . . . . . . 135
McDowell *v* Hirschfield Lipson and Rumsey [1992] 2 FLR 126 . . . . . . . . . . . . . . . . . . . . . . 72
McKee and National Trust Co Ltd, Re (1975) 56 DLR 3d 190. . . . . . . . . . . . . . . . . . . . . 60, 75
McKerrell, Re [1912] 2 Ch 648 . . . . . . . . . . . . . . . . . . . . . . . . . . . . . . . . . . . . . . . . . . . . . 209
Mee, Re (1971) 23 DLR 3d 491. . . . . . . . . . . . . . . . . . . . . . . . . . . . . . . . . . . . . . . . . . . . . . 60
Meyer *v* Riddick (1989) 60 P&CR 50. . . . . . . . . . . . . . . . . . . . . . . . . . . . . . . . . . . . . . . . 121
Middlemas *v* Stevens [1901] 1 Ch 574 . . . . . . . . . . . . . . . . . . . . . . . . . . . . . . . . . . . . . . 100
Midland Bank plc *v* Cooke [1995] 4 All ER 562 . . . . . . . . . . . . . . . . . . . . . . . . . . . . . . 41, 42
Midland Bank plc *v* Pike [1988] 2 All ER 434 . . . . . . . . . . . . . . . . . . . . . . . . . . . . . . . . . . 62
Mikeover Ltd *v* Brady [1989] 3 All ER 618 . . . . . . . . . . . . . . . . . . . . . . . . . . . . 23, 24, 25, 46
Monarch Aluminium *v* Rickman [1989] CLY 1526 . . . . . . . . . . . . . . . . . . . . . . . . . . . . . . . 63
Morgan's Lease, Re [1972] Ch 1. . . . . . . . . . . . . . . . . . . . . . . . . . . . . . . . . . . . . . . . . . . . . 105
Morley *v* Bird (1798) 3 Ves 628 . . . . . . . . . . . . . . . . . . . . . . . . . . . . . . . . . . . . . . . . 30, 32, 33
Morris *v* Barrett (1829) 3 Y&J 384 . . . . . . . . . . . . . . . . . . . . . . . . . . . . . . . . . . . . . . . . . . 35
Mortgage Corpn *v* Shaire [2001] Ch 743 . . . . . . . . . . . . . . . . . . . . . 40, 61, 139, 157, 158, 159, 160,
163, 164, 165, 166, 176–7
Mott, Re [1987] CLY 212. . . . . . . . . . . . . . . . . . . . . . . . . . . . . . . . . . . . . . . . . . . . . . . . . . 169
Mountney *v* Treharne [2003] Ch 135 . . . . . . . . . . . . . . . . . . . . . . . . . . . . . . . . . . . . . . . . 168
Moyse *v* Gyles (1700) 2 Vern 385. . . . . . . . . . . . . . . . . . . . . . . . . . . . . . . . . . . . . . . . . . . . 49
Munroe *v* Carlson (1975) 59 DLR 3d 763 . . . . . . . . . . . . . . . . . . . . . . . . . . . . . . . . . . . . . 70
Murdoch and Barry, Re (1975) 64 DLR 3d 222. . . . . . . . . . . . . . . . . . . . . . . . . . . . . . . . . 57
Murray, Ash and Kennedy *v* Hall (1849) 7 CB 441 . . . . . . . . . . . . . . . . . . . . . . . . . . . . . . . 28
Napier *v* Williams [1911] 1 Ch 361 . . . . . . . . . . . . . . . . . . . . . . . . . . . . . . . . . . . . . . . . . . 64
National Provincial Bank Ltd *v* Ainsworth [1965] AC 1175. . . . . . . . . . . . . . . . . . . . . . . . . 211
National & Provincial BS *v* Ahmed [1995] 2 EGLR 127 . . . . . . . . . . . . . . . . . . . . . . . . . . 202
National & Provincial BS *v* Lloyd [1996] 1 All ER 630. . . . . . . . . . . . . . . . . . . . . . . . . . . 178
National Westminster Bank plc *v* Malhan [2004] EWHC 847 (Ch) . . . . . . . . . . . . . 185, 190, 193
Nestlé *v* National Westminster Bank plc [2000] WTLR 795;
affirmed [1993] 1 WLR 1260 . . . . . . . . . . . . . . . . . . . . . . . . . . . . . . . . . . . . . . . . . 152
New, Re [1901] 2 Ch 534 . . . . . . . . . . . . . . . . . . . . . . . . . . . . . . . . . . . . . . . . . . . . . . . . . . 145
Nielson-Jones *v* Fedden [1975] Ch 222 . . . . . . . . . . . . . . . . . . . . 50, 51, 54, 57, 58, 68, 69, 71, 73
Noack *v* Noack [1959] VR 137 . . . . . . . . . . . . . . . . . . . . . . . . . . . . . . . . . . . . . . . . . . . . . 140
Notting Hill Housing Trust *v* Brackley [2002] HLR 212 . . . . . . . . . . . . . . . . . . . . . . . . 149–50
Oates d Hatterley *v* Jackson (1742) 2 Stra 1172 . . . . . . . . . . . . . . . . . . . . . . . . . . . . . . . . . 29
Oke *v* Rideout [1998] CLY 4876 . . . . . . . . . . . . . . . . . . . . . . . . . . . . . . . . . . . . . . . . . . . 161
On Demand Information plc *v* Michael Gerson (Finance) plc [2003] 1 AC 368 . . . . . . . . . . . . 212
Oxley *v* Hiscock [2004] 3 WLR 715 . . . . . . . . . . . . . . . . . . . . . . . . . . . . . . . . 37, 41, 43, 117
Paddington BS *v* Mendelsohn (1985) 50 P&CR 244 . . . . . . . . . . . . . . . . . . . . . . . . . . . . . 191
Palmer *v* Rich [1897] 1 Ch 134. . . . . . . . . . . . . . . . . . . . . . . . . . . . . . . . . . . . . . . . . . . 64,73
Palmer, Re [1994] Ch 316. . . . . . . . . . . . . . . . . . . . . . . . . . . . . . . . . . . . . . . . . . . . . . . . . . 59

Parfitt *v* Hember (1867) LR 4 Eq 443 . . . . . . . . . . . . . . . . . . . . . . . . . . . . . . . . . . . . . . . . . . . . . . 46
Partriche *v* Powlet (1740) 2 Atk 54 . . . . . . . . . . . . . . . . . . . . . . . . . . . . . . . . . . . . . . . . . . . . . 67, 69
Pascoe *v* Swan (1859) 27 Beav 508 . . . . . . . . . . . . . . . . . . . . . . . . . . . . . . . . . . . . . . . . . . . . . . . . . 133
Paterson *v* Paterson (1979) 108 DLR 3d 234 . . . . . . . . . . . . . . . . . . . . . . . . . . . . . . . . . . . . . . . . . 73
Patzak *v* Lytton [1984] WAR 353 . . . . . . . . . . . . . . . . . . . . . . . . . . . . . . . . . . . . . . . . . . . . . . . . . . . 73
Pavlou, Re [1993] 1 WLR 1046 . . . . . . . . . . . . . . . . . . . . . . . . . . . . . . . . . . . 59, 134, 135, 136, 140
Payne *v* Webb (1874) LR 19 Eq 26 . . . . . . . . . . . . . . . . . . . . . . . . . . . . . . . . . . . . . . . . . . . . . . . . . . 31
Pearson *v* IRC [1981] AC 753 . . . . . . . . . . . . . . . . . . . . . . . . . . . . . . . . . . . . . . . . . . . . . . . . . . . . . 122
Pechar (deceased), Re [1969] NZLR 574 . . . . . . . . . . . . . . . . . . . . . . . . . . . . . . . . . . . . . . . . . 77, 78
Perham *v* Kempster [1907] 1 Ch 373 . . . . . . . . . . . . . . . . . . . . . . . . . . . . . . . . . . . . . . . . . . . . . . . 199
Perkins *v* Baynton (1781) 1 Bro CC 118 . . . . . . . . . . . . . . . . . . . . . . . . . . . . . . . . . . . . . . . . . . 32, 33
Pettitt *v* Pettitt [1970] AC 777 . . . . . . . . . . . . . . . . . . . . . . . . . . . . . . . . . . . . 30, 37, 39, 42, 43
Petty *v* Styward (1631–1632) 1 Ch Rep 57 . . . . . . . . . . . . . . . . . . . . . . . . . . . . . . . . . . . . . . . . . . 33
Pickering *v* Wells [2002] 2 FLR 798 . . . . . . . . . . . . . . . . . . . . . . . . . . . . . . . . . . . . . . . . . . . . . . . 171
Pink *v* Lawrence (1978) 36 P&CR 98 . . . . . . . . . . . . . . . . . . . . . . . . . . . . . . . . . . . . . . . . . . . 39, 40
Pleadal's Case (1579) 2 Leon 159 . . . . . . . . . . . . . . . . . . . . . . . . . . . . . . . . . . . . . . . . . . . . . . . . . . . . 66
Power *v* Grace [1932] 2 DLR 793 . . . . . . . . . . . . . . . . . . . . . . . . . . . . . . . . . . . . . . . . . . . . . . . 65, 66
Pozzi, Re [1982] Qd R 499 . . . . . . . . . . . . . . . . . . . . . . . . . . . . . . . . . . . . . . . . . . . . . . . . . . . . . . 72, 73
Pritchard Englefield *v* Steinberg [2004] EWHC 1908 (Ch) . . . . . . . . . . . . . . . . . . . . . . . . 116, 178
Property & Bloodstock Ltd *v* Emerton [1968] Ch 94 . . . . . . . . . . . . . . . . . . . . . . . . . . . . . . . . 202
Public Trustee *v* Evans (1985) 2 NSWLR 188 . . . . . . . . . . . . . . . . . . . . . . . . . . . . . . . . . . . . . . . 77
Public Trustee *v* Grivas [1974] 2 NSWLR 316 . . . . . . . . . . . . . . . . . . . . . . . . . . . . . . . . . . . . . . 73
R *v* Williams (1735) Bunb 342 . . . . . . . . . . . . . . . . . . . . . . . . . . . . . . . . . . . . . . . . . . . . . . . . . . 30, 33
Radziej *v* Radziej [1967] 1 WLR 659; upheld [1968] 1 WLR 1928 . . . . . . . . . . . . . . . . . . . . 49
Railway Commissioners for New South Wales, Ex p (1941) 41 SR NSW 92 . . . . . . . . . . . . . . . . . 74
Rasmanis *v* Jurewitsch (1970) 70 SR NSW 407 . . . . . . . . . . . . . . . . . . . . . . . . . . . . . . . . . . 77, 78
Raval, Re [1998] 2 FLR 718 . . . . . . . . . . . . . . . . . . . . . . . . . . . . . . . . . . . . . . . . . . . . . . . . . . . . . . . 169
Rawlings *v* Rawlings [1964] P 398 . . . . . . . . . . . . . . . . . . . . . . . . . . . . . . . . . . 123, 161, 162, 163
Recher's WT, Re [1972] Ch 526 . . . . . . . . . . . . . . . . . . . . . . . . . . . . . . . . . . . . . . . . . . . . . . . . . . . . 115
Rhoden *v* Joseph 6 September 1990 . . . . . . . . . . . . . . . . . . . . . . . . . . . . . . . . . . . . . . . . . . . . . 41, 42
Rich *v* Aldred (1705) 6 Mod 216 . . . . . . . . . . . . . . . . . . . . . . . . . . . . . . . . . . . . . . . . . . . . . . . . . . 212
Richardson *v* Richardson (1845) 14 Sim 526 . . . . . . . . . . . . . . . . . . . . . . . . . . . . . . . . . . . . . . . . 31
Rigden *v* Vallier (1751) 2 Ves Sen 252 . . . . . . . . . . . . . . . . . . . . . . . . . . . . . . . . . . . . . . 33, 36, 37
Rivett *v* Rivett (1966) 200 EG 858 . . . . . . . . . . . . . . . . . . . . . . . . . . . . . . . . . . . . . . . . . . . 161, 162
Robertson *v* Fraser (1871) LR 6 Ch App 696 . . . . . . . . . . . . . . . . . . . . . . . . . . . . . . . . . . . . . . . . 31
Robichaud *v* Watson (1983) 147 DLR 3d 626 . . . . . . . . . . . . . . . . . . . . . . . . . . . . . . . . . . . . . . . 72
Robinson *v* Briggs (1853) 1 Sm & Giff 188 . . . . . . . . . . . . . . . . . . . . . . . . . . . . . . . . . . . . . . . . 199
Robinson *v* Preston (1858) 4 K&J 505 . . . . . . . . . . . . . . . . . . . . . . . . . . . . . . . . . . . . . . 36, 42, 43
Rodway *v* Landy [2001] Ch 703 . . . . . . . . . . . . . . . . . . . . . . . . . . . . 6, 48, 126, 127, 137, 158, 164
Rogers *v* Resi-Statewide Corporation Ltd (1991) 105 ALR 145 . . . . . . . . . . . . . . . . . . . . . . . . . 63
Rose, Re [1952] Ch 499 . . . . . . . . . . . . . . . . . . . . . . . . . . . . . . . . . . . . . . . . . . . . . . . . . . . . . . . . . . . 214
Rowe *v* Prance [1999] 2 FLR 787 . . . . . . . . . . . . . . . . . . . . . . . . . . . . . . . . . . . . . . . . . . . . . . . . . 208
Roy *v* Roy [1996] 1 FLR 541 . . . . . . . . . . . . . . . . . . . . . . . . . . . . . . . . . . . . . . . . . . . . . . . . . . . . . . 40
Royal Bank of Scotland plc *v* Etridge (No 2) [2002] 2 AC 773 . . . . . . . . . . . . . . . . . 62, 171, 173
Ruck *v* Barwise (1865) 2 Dr&Sm 510 . . . . . . . . . . . . . . . . . . . . . . . . . . . . . . . . . . . . . . . . . . . . . . 29
Ryan *v* Dries [2002] NSWCA 3 . . . . . . . . . . . . . . . . . . . . . . . . . . . . . . . . . . . . . . . . . . . . . . . . . . . 136
Ryves *v* Ryves (1871) LR 11 Eq 539 . . . . . . . . . . . . . . . . . . . . . . . . . . . . . . . . . . . . . . . . . . . . . . . . 31
Sainsbury *v* IRC [1970] Ch 712 . . . . . . . . . . . . . . . . . . . . . . . . . . . . . . . . . . . . . . . . . . . . . . . . . . . 122
Sammes's Case (1609) 13 Co Rep 54 . . . . . . . . . . . . . . . . . . . . . . . . . . . . . . . . . . . . . . . . . . . . . . . . . 29
Sammon, Re (1979) 94 DLR 3d 594 . . . . . . . . . . . . . . . . . . . . . . . . . . . . . . . . . . . . . . . . . . . . . . . . . 57
Samuel *v* District Land Registrar [1984] 2 NZLR 697 . . . . . . . . . . . . . . . . . . . . . . . . . . . . . . . . 57

Saunders *v* Vautier (1841) 4 Beav 115, affirmed Cr&Ph 240. . . . . . . . . . . . . . . . . . . . . . . 49, 153, 158
Saunders's Case (1599) 5 Co Rep 12a . . . . . . . . . . . . . . . . . . . . . . . . . . . . . . . . . . . . . . . . . . . . . 96
Schobelt *v* Barber (1966) 60 DLR 2d 519. . . . . . . . . . . . . . . . . . . . . . . . . . . . . . . . . . . . . . . . . . 77
Schofield *v* Graham (1969) 6 DLR 3d 88 . . . . . . . . . . . . . . . . . . . . . . . . . . . . . . . . . . . . . . . . . . 73
Schofield, Re [1918] 2 Ch 64 . . . . . . . . . . . . . . . . . . . . . . . . . . . . . . . . . . . . . . . . . . . . . . . . . 31, 49
Selous, Re [1901] 1 Ch 921 . . . . . . . . . . . . . . . . . . . . . . . . . . . . . . . . . . . . . . . . . . . . . . . . . . . . . 24
Selwyn *v* Garfit (1888) 38 Ch D 273. . . . . . . . . . . . . . . . . . . . . . . . . . . . . . . . . . . . . . . . . . . . . 202
Shannon's Transfer, Re [1967] Tas SR 245 . . . . . . . . . . . . . . . . . . . . . . . . . . . . . . . . . . . . . . . . . 63
Sharer, Re (1912) 57 SJ 60 . . . . . . . . . . . . . . . . . . . . . . . . . . . . . . . . . . . . . . . . . . . . . . . . 62, 63, 67
Sharpe, Re [1980] 1 WLR 219 . . . . . . . . . . . . . . . . . . . . . . . . . . . . . . . . . . . . . . . . . . . . . . . . . . 116
Shelley's Case (1581) 1 Co Rep 88b . . . . . . . . . . . . . . . . . . . . . . . . . . . . . . . . . . . . . . . . . . . . . . . 29
Shiloh Spinners Ltd *v* Harding [1973] AC 691 . . . . . . . . . . . . . . . . . . . . . . . . . . . . . . . . . . . . 116
Slater *v* Slater (1987) 12 Fam LR 1 . . . . . . . . . . . . . . . . . . . . . . . . . . . . . . . . . . . . . . . . 69, 70, 72
Slingsby's Case (1587) Co Rep 18b . . . . . . . . . . . . . . . . . . . . . . . . . . . . . . . . . . . . . . . . . . . . . . . 32
Smith *v* Baker [1970] 1 WLR 1160 . . . . . . . . . . . . . . . . . . . . . . . . . . . . . . . . . . . . . . . . . . . . . . 41
Smith *v* Smith (1975) 120 SJ 100 . . . . . . . . . . . . . . . . . . . . . . . . . . . . . . . . . . . . . . . . . . . 161, 162
Smith *v* Stokes (1801) 1 East 363 . . . . . . . . . . . . . . . . . . . . . . . . . . . . . . . . . . . . . . . . . . . . . . . 59
Sorensen and Sorensen, Re (1977) 90 DLR 3d 26 . . . . . . . . . . . . . . . . 60, 63, 65, 66, 70, 76
Speight *v* Gaunt (1883) 9 App Cas 1 . . . . . . . . . . . . . . . . . . . . . . . . . . . . . . . . . . . . . . . . . . . . 20
Springette *v* Defoe (1992) 65 P&CR 1 . . . . . . . . . . . . . . . . . . . . . . . . . . . . . . . . . . . . . . . . 37, 69
Squire *v* Rogers (1979) 27 ALR 330 . . . . . . . . . . . . . . . . . . . . . . . . . . . . . . . . . . . . . . . . . . . . 140
Stapylton Fletcher Ltd, Re [1994] 1 WLR 1181. . . . . . . . . . . . . . . . . . . . . . . . . . . . . . . . . . . . 208
State Bank of India *v* Sood [1997] Ch 276. . . . . . . . . . . . 184, 186, 188–9, 191, 193, 196, 197, 198
Steeds *v* Steeds (1889) 22 QBD 537 . . . . . . . . . . . . . . . . . . . . . . . . . . . . . . . . . . . . . . . . . . 33, 210
Stephens *v* Hide (1734) Cas t Talb 27 . . . . . . . . . . . . . . . . . . . . . . . . . . . . . . . . . . . . . . . . . . . . 31
Stokes *v* Anderson [1991] 1 FLR 391 . . . . . . . . . . . . . . . . . . . . . . . . . . . . . . . . . . . . . . . . . . . 117
Stone, Re [1989] 1 Qd R 351 . . . . . . . . . . . . . . . . . . . . . . . . . . . . . . . . . . . . . . . . . . . . . . . . . . . 77
Stott *v* Ratcliffe (1982) 126 SJ 310. . . . . . . . . . . . . . . . . . . . . . . . . . . . . . . . . . . . . . . . . . . . . 163
Street *v* Mountford [1985] AC 809 . . . . . . . . . . . . . . . . . . . . . . . . . . . . . . . . . . . . . . . . . . . . . . . 5
Surtees *v* Surtees (1871) LR 12 Eq 400 . . . . . . . . . . . . . . . . . . . . . . . . . . . . . . . . . . . . . . . . 31, 32
Sutcliffe *v* Howard (1869) 38 LJ Ch 472. . . . . . . . . . . . . . . . . . . . . . . . . . . . . . . . . . . . . . . . . . 31
Suttill *v* Graham [1977] 1 WLR 819. . . . . . . . . . . . . . . . . . . . . . . . . . . . . . . . . . . . . . . . 134, 136
Swan *v* Swan (1819) 8 Price 518. . . . . . . . . . . . . . . . . . . . . . . . . . . . . . . . . . . . . . . . . . . . . . . 140
Swan, Re [1915] 1 Ch 829 . . . . . . . . . . . . . . . . . . . . . . . . . . . . . . . . . . . . . . . . . . . . . . . . . 213, 214
Swift d Neale *v* Roberts (1764) 3 Burr 1488 . . . . . . . . . . . . . . . . . . . . . . . . . . . . . . . . . . . . . . 49
Sym's Case (1584) Cro Eliz 33 . . . . . . . . . . . . . . . . . . . . . . . . . . . . . . . . . . . . . . . . . . . . . . . . . . 66
Szabo *v* Boros (1967) 64 DLR 2d 48. . . . . . . . . . . . . . . . . . . . . . . . . . . . . . . . . . . . . . 49, 68, 76
Taaffe *v* Conmee (1862) 10 HLC 64 . . . . . . . . . . . . . . . . . . . . . . . . . . . . . . . . . . . . . . . . . . . . . 46
Taggart *v* Taggart (1803) 1 Sch&Lef 84. . . . . . . . . . . . . . . . . . . . . . . . . . . . . . . . . . . . . . . . . . 38
Tan Chew Hoe Neo *v* Chee Swee Cheng (1928) LR 56 Ind App 112 . . . . . . . . . . . . . . . . . . . 34, 68
Taylor *v* Neate (1888) 39 Ch D 538 . . . . . . . . . . . . . . . . . . . . . . . . . . . . . . . . . . . . . . . . . . . . 218
Teasdale *v* Sanderson (1864) 33 Beav 534. . . . . . . . . . . . . . . . . . . . . . . . . . . . . . . . . . . . . . . . 135
Tee *v* Tee & Hamilton [1999] 2 FLR 613 . . . . . . . . . . . . . . . . . . . . . . . . . . . . . . . . . . . . . . . 180
Thornley *v* Thornley [1893] 2 Ch 229 . . . . . . . . . . . . . . . . . . . . . . . . . . . . . . . . . . . . . . . . . . . 46
Thorp and the Real Property Act, Re (1963) 80 WN NSW 61. . . . . . . . . . . . . . . . . . . . . . . . . 77
Thynne, Re [1911] 1 Ch 282. . . . . . . . . . . . . . . . . . . . . . . . . . . . . . . . . . . . . . . . . . . . . . . . 16, 213
Timber Top Realty Pty Ltd *v* Mullens [1974] VR 312. . . . . . . . . . . . . . . . . . . . . . . . . . . . . . 116
Trevor-Batye's Settlement, Re [1912] 2 Ch 339 . . . . . . . . . . . . . . . . . . . . . . . . . . . . . . . . . . . . . 20
Tritton, Re (1889) 61 LT 301 . . . . . . . . . . . . . . . . . . . . . . . . . . . . . . . . . . . . . . . . . . . . . . . . . . 213
TSB Bank plc *v* Marshall [1998] 2 FLR 769 . . . . . . . . . . . . . . . . . . . . . . . . . . . . . . . . . . . . . . 175
Tulk *v* Moxhay (1848) 2 Ph 774. . . . . . . . . . . . . . . . . . . . . . . . . . . . . . . . . . . . . . . . . . . . . . . 115

Turner *v* Morgan (1803) 8 Ves 143. . . . . . . . . . . . . . . . . . . . . . . . . . . . . . . . . . . . . . . . . . . . . . . . .47
Turner *v* Wright (1869) De G F&J 234 . . . . . . . . . . . . . . . . . . . . . . . . . . . . . . . . . . . . . . . . . . . . .12
Turner, Re [1974] 1 WLR 1556 . . . . . . . . . . . . . . . . . . . . . . . . . . . . . . . . . . . . . . . . . . . . . . . . . . .168
Turton *v* Turton [1988] Ch 542 . . . . . . . . . . . . . . . . . . . . . . . . . . . . . . . . . . . . . . . . . . . . . . . . . . . .39
Ulrich *v* Ulrich [1968] 1 WLR 180 . . . . . . . . . . . . . . . . . . . . . . . . . . . . . . . . . . . . . . . . . . . . . . . . .42
United Bank of Kuwait plc *v* Sahib [1997] Ch 107 . . . . . . . . . . . . . . . . . . . . . . . . . . . . . . . . . .81
University of Manitoba *v* Sanderson Estate (1998) 155 DLR 4th 40 . . . . . . . . . . . . . . . . . . . .76
Vickers *v* Cowell (1839) 1 Beav 529. . . . . . . . . . . . . . . . . . . . . . . . . . . . . . . . . . . . . . . . . . . . . . . . .33
Walker *v* Hall (1984) 5 FLR 126 . . . . . . . . . . . . . . . . . . . . . . . . . . . . . . . . . . . . . . . . . . . .37, 39, 42
Waller *v* Waller [1967] 1 WLR 451 . . . . . . . . . . . . . . . . . . . . . . . . . . . . . . . . . .42, 151, 186, 202
Walters and Walters, Re (1977) 79 DLR 3d 122; upheld (1978) 84 DLR 3d 416n. . . . . . . . . . . .72
Ward *v* Ward (1871) LR 6 Ch App 789 . . . . . . . . . . . . . . . . . . . . . . . . . . . . . . . . . . . . . . . . . . . . .35
Ward, Re [1920] 1 Ch 334 . . . . . . . . . . . . . . . . . . . . . . . . . . . . . . . . . . . . . . . . . . . . . . . . . . . . . . . . .31
Waring *v* London & Manchester Assurance Co Ltd [1935] Ch 311 . . . . . . . . . . . . . . . . . . . . .202
Warren, Re [1932] 1 Ch 42. . . . . . . . . . . . . . . . . . . . . . . . . . . . . . . . . . . . . . . . . . . . . . . . . . . . . . . .149
Watkins *v* Cheek (1825) 2 Sim & St 199. . . . . . . . . . . . . . . . . . . . . . . . . . . . . . . . . . . . . . . . . . . .199
Watson *v* Gray (1880) 14 Ch D 192 . . . . . . . . . . . . . . . . . . . . . . . . . . . . . . . . . . . . . . . . . . . . . . . .23
Weir's ST, Re [1969] 1 Ch 657; reversed [1971] Ch 145. . . . . . . . . . . . . . . . . . . . . . . . . . . . . . .122
Weston *v* Henshaw [1950] Ch 510 . . . . . . . . . . . . . . . . . . . . . . . . . . . . . . . . . . . . . . . . . .104, 108
Wheeler *v* Horne (1740) Willes 208 . . . . . . . . . . . . . . . . . . . . . . . . . . . . . . . . . . . . . . . . . . . . . . .133
White *v* White [2001] EWCA Civ 955 . . . . . . . . . . . . . . . . . . . . . . . . . . . . . . . . . . . . . . . . . . . . .49
White *v* White [2004] 2 FLR 321 . . . . . . . . . . . . . . . . . . . . . . . . . . . . . . . . . . .164, 166, 180–1
Whiting's Settlement, Re [1905] 1 Ch 96 . . . . . . . . . . . . . . . . . . . . . . . . . . . . . . . . . . . . . . . . . . .208
Wight *v* CIR (1982) 264 EG 935. . . . . . . . . . . . . . . . . . . . . . . . . . . . . . . . . . . . . . . . . . . . . . . . . .121
Wilford's Estate, Re (1879) 11 Ch D 267. . . . . . . . . . . . . . . . . . . . . . . . . . . . . . . . . . . . .49, 68, 76
Wilkinson *v* Haygarth (1847) 12 QB 837. . . . . . . . . . . . . . . . . . . . . . . . . . . . . . . . . . . . . . . . . . .131
Wilks, Re [1891] 3 Ch 59. . . . . . . . . . . . . . . . . . . . . . . . . . . . . . . . . . . . . . . . . . . . . . . . . .68, 69, 72
Williams & Glyn's Bank Ltd *v* Boland [1979] Ch 312; affirmed
   [1981] AC 487. . . . . . . . . . . . . . . . . . . . .61, 63, 113, 117, 121, 171, 186–8, 191, 195, 202
Williams *v* Hensman (1861) 1 J&H 546 . . . . . . . . . . . . . . . . . . . . . .44, 50, 55, 65, 67, 69, 70, 79
Williams *v* Williams (1899) 81 LT NS 163. . . . . . . . . . . . . . . . . . . . . . . . . . . . . . . . . . . . . . . . . . .135
Williams *v* Williams [1976] Ch 278 . . . . . . . . . . . . . . . . . . . . . . . . . . . . . . . . . . . . . . . . . .130, 179
Wilson *v* Wilson [1963] 1 WLR 601 . . . . . . . . . . . . . . . . . . . . . . . . . . . . . . . . . . . . . . . . . . . . . . .39
Wilson *v* Wilson [1969] 1 WLR 1470. . . . . . . . . . . . . . . . . . . . . . . . . . . . . . . . . . . . . . . . . . . . . .40
Wilson *v* Bell (1843) 5 Ir Eq R 501 . . . . . . . . . . . . . . . . . . . . . . . . . . . . . . . . . . . . . . . . . . . .55, 68
Winkfield, The [1902] P 42 . . . . . . . . . . . . . . . . . . . . . . . . . . . . . . . . . . . . . . . . . . . . . . . . . . . . . . .211
Winsper *v* Perrett [2002] WTLR 927 . . . . . . . . . . . . . . . . . . . . . . . . . . . . . . . . . . . . . . . . . . . . . . .37
Wiscot's Case (1599) 2 Co Rep 60b . . . . . . . . . . . . . . . . . . . . . . . . . . . . . . . . . . . . . . . .25, 28, 57
Woodgate *v* Unwin (1831) 4 Sim 129 . . . . . . . . . . . . . . . . . . . . . . . . . . . . . . . . . . . . . . . . . . . . . . .29
Woolley, Re [1903] 2 Ch 206 . . . . . . . . . . . . . . . . . . . . . . . . . . . . . . . . . . . . . . . . . . . . . . . . . . . . . . .31
Woolnough, Re [2002] WTLR 595. . . . . . . . . . . . . . . . . . . . . . . . . . . . . . . . . . . . . . . . . . . . . . . . . .77
Wright *v* Gibbons (1949) 78 CLR 313 . . . . . . . . . . . . . . . . . . . . . . . . . . . . . . . .56, 57, 65, 66, 67
Wright *v* Johnson [2002] 2 P&CR 210 . . . . . . . . . . . . . . . . . . . . . . . . . . . . . . . . .40, 134, 137, 140
WX Investments Ltd *v* Begg [2002] 1 WLR 2849 . . . . . . . . . . . . . . . . . . . . . . . . . . . . . . . . . . . . .52
Yaxley *v* Gotts [2000] Ch 162. . . . . . . . . . . . . . . . . . . . . . . . . . . . . . . . . . . . . . . . . . . . . . . . . . . . .117
York *v* Stone (1709) 1 Salk 158 . . . . . . . . . . . . . . . . . . . . . . . . . . . . . . . . . . . . . . . . . . . . .30, 33, 62
Young, Re (1968) 70 DLR 2d 594 . . . . . . . . . . . . . . . . . . . . . . . . . . . . . . . . . . . . . . . . . . . . . . . . . . .63
Zandfarid *v* BCCI SA [1996] 1 WLR 1420 . . . . . . . . . . . . . . . . . . . . . . . . . . . . . . . . . . . . . . . . .175

# Table of Legislation, Overseas Statutes and Statutory Instruments

**A. UK Statutes**

1540 32 H VIII c 32 . . . . . . . . . . . . . . . . . . . . 25
 s 2 . . . . . . . . . . . . . . . . . . . . . . . . . . . . 25, 26
1705 4 Anne c 16
 s 27 . . . . . . . . . . . . . . . . . . . . . . . . . . . . . . 133
Administration of Estates Act 1925
 s 22 . . . . . . . . . . . . . . . . . . . . . . . . . . . . . 102
 s 33 . . . . . . . . . . . . . . . . . . . . 112, 183, 208
 ss 45–46 . . . . . . . . . . . . . . . . . . . . . . . . . 12
 s 46 . . . . . . . . . . . . . . . . . . . . . . . . . . . . . . 86
Bodies Corporate (Joint Tenancy)
 Act 1899 . . . . . . . . . . . . . . . . . . . . . . . . . 27
Charging Orders Act 1979
 s 3(4) . . . . . . . . . . . . . . . . . . . . . . . . . . . . . 62
Children Act 1989
 Sched 1 para 1(2)(d)(e) . . . . . . . . . . . . . . 180
  para 4 . . . . . . . . . . . . . . . . . . . . . . . . . 180
Commonhold and Leasehold Reform
 Act 2002 . . . . . . . . . . . . . . . . . . . . . . . . . . . 7
Contracts (Rights of Third Parties)
 Act 1999 . . . . . . . . . . . . . . . . . . . . . . . . . 139
Conveyancing Act 1881
 s 51 . . . . . . . . . . . . . . . . . . . . . . . . . . . . . . 19
Enterprise Act 2002 . . . . . . . . . . . . . . . . . . . 173
 s 261 . . . . . . . . . . . . . . . . . . . . . . . . . . . . 164
Family Law Act 1996 . . . . . . . . . 123, 129, 130,
  180, 181
 ss 30–41 . . . . . . . . . . . . . . . . . . . . . . . . . 156
 s 30 . . . . . . . . . . . . . . . . . . . . . . . . . . . . . 129
  (7) . . . . . . . . . . . . . . . . . . . . . . . . . . . . 129
 s 33 . . . . . . . . . . . . . . . . . . . . . . . . . . . . . 129
  (1)(b) . . . . . . . . . . . . . . . . . . . . . . . . . 129
 s 35 . . . . . . . . . . . . . . . . . . . . . . . . . . . . . 129
  (1)(c) . . . . . . . . . . . . . . . . . . . . . . . . . 129
 s 36 . . . . . . . . . . . . . . . . . . . . . . . . . . . . . 129
  (1)(c) . . . . . . . . . . . . . . . . . . . . . . . . . 129
 s 40 . . . . . . . . . . . . . . . . . . . . . . . . . . . . . 129
  (1)(b) . . . . . . . . . . . . . . . . . . . . . . . . . 132
 s 41 . . . . . . . . . . . . . . . . . . . . . . . . . . . . . 129
 s 62(1) . . . . . . . . . . . . . . . . . . . . . . . . . . . 129
  (3) . . . . . . . . . . . . . . . . . . . . . . . . . . . . 128

Finance Act 1969 . . . . . . . . . . . . . . . . . . . . . 109
Finance Act 1973 . . . . . . . . . . . . . . . . . . . . . 109
Finance Act 1975 . . . . . . . . . . . . . . . . . . . . . 109
Fines and Recoveries Act 1833 . . . . . . . . . . 132
Forfeiture Act 1982 . . . . . . . . . . . . . . . . . 77, 78
 s 2(5) . . . . . . . . . . . . . . . . . . . . . . . . . . . . . 79
Human Fertilisation and Embryology Act 1990
 ss 27–29 . . . . . . . . . . . . . . . . . . . . . . . . . . 17
Human Rights Act 1998 . . . . . . . . . . . . . . . 168
Inheritance (Provision for Family and
 Dependants) Act 1975
 s 9(1) . . . . . . . . . . . . . . . . . . . . . . . . . . . . . 27
Inheritance Tax Act 1984
 s 171 . . . . . . . . . . . . . . . . . . . . . . . . . . . . . . 27
Insolvency Act 1986 . . . . . . . 59, 168, 170, 172,
   173, 174, 175, 179
 s 283A . . . . . . . . . . . . . . . . . . . . . . . . . . . 170
  (6) . . . . . . . . . . . . . . . . . . . . . . . . . . . . 170
 s 313A . . . . . . . . . . . . . . . . . . . . . . . . . . . 173
 s 335A . . . . . . . . . . . . . . . . . . . . . . . . 168, 173
 ss 336–337 . . . . . . . . . . . . . . . . . . . . . 129, 168
 s 421A . . . . . . . . . . . . . . . . . . . . . . . . . . 27, 59
Insolvency Act 2000 . . . . . . . . . . . . . . . . . . . . 59
Judicature Act 1873 . . . . . . . . . . . . . . . . . . . 209
Land Charges Act 1972 . . . . . . . . . . . . . . . . 183
Land Registration Act 1925
 s 3(xv) . . . . . . . . . . . . . . . . . . . . . . . . . . . . 187
 s 18 . . . . . . . . . . . . . . . . . . . . . . . . . . . . . . 193
 s 58(3) . . . . . . . . . . . . . . . . . . . . . . . . . . . . 40
Land Registration Act 2002
 s 23 . . . . . . . . . . . . . . . . . . . . . . . . . . . 193, 194
  (1)(a) . . . . . . . . . . . . . . . . . . . . . . . . . . . 62
 s 26 . . . 106, 107, 194–6, 197–8, 199, 201–2
  (3) . . . . . . . . . . . . . . . . . . . . . . . . . 194, 195
 ss 28–29 . . . . . . . . . . . . . . . . . . . . . . . . . . 188
 s 29 . . . . . . . . . . . . . 103, 186, 193, 194, 201
 s 33(a) . . . . . . . . . . . . . . . . . . . . . . . . . . . 201
 ss 42–44 . . . . . . . . . . . . . . . . . . . . . . . . . . 187
 s 52 . . . . . . . . . . . . . . . . . . . . . . . . . . . . . 194
 s 86 . . . . . . . . . . . . . . . . . . . . . . . . . . . . . 194
 s 116 . . . . . . . . . . . . . . . . . . . . . . . . . . . . 116

Sched 3 para 2 . . . . . . . . . . . . . . . . . . . . . . . 61
Sched 3 para 2(a) . . . . . . . . . . . . . . . . . . . . 103
Landlord and Tenant (Covenants) Act 1995
    s 3(2) . . . . . . . . . . . . . . . . . . . . . . . . . . . . . . 25
Law of Property Act 1922 . . . . . . . . . . . . . . 189
Law of Property Act 1925
    Part I . . . . . . . . . . . . . . . . . 185, 186, 188, 199
    s 1 . . . . . . . . . . . . . . . . . . . . . . . . . . . 11, 98, 99
       (1) . . . . . . . . . . . . . . . . . . . . . . . . . . . 14, 112
       (2)(e) . . . . . . . . . . . . . . . . . . . . . . 5, 14, 115
       (3) . . . . . . . . . . . . . . . . . . . . . . . . . . 112, 115
       (6) . . . . . 24, 26, 27, 30, 33, 106, 112, 113
    s 2 . . . . . . . . . . 185, 188, 189, 195, 199–200
       (1)(ii) . . . . . . . . . . . . . . . . . . . . . . . 107, 189
         (iii) . . . . . . . . . . . . . . . . . . . . . . . . . . . . 189
         (iv) . . . . . . . . . . . . . . . . . . . . . . . . . . . . 189
       (2) . . . . . . . . . . . . . . . . . . . . . . . . . . . . . 190
       (3) . . . . . . . . . . . . . . . . . . . . . . . . . 116, 190
       (5) . . . . . . . . . . . . . . . . . . . . . . . . . . . . . 190
    s 7(1) . . . . . . . . . . . . . . . . . . . . . . . . . . . . 5, 14
    s 14 . . . . . . . . . . . . . . . . . . . . . . . . . . . . . . 188
    s 19 . . . . . . . . . . . . . . . . . . . . . . . . . . . . . . 114
    s 25 . . . . . . . . . . . . . . . . . . . . . 106, 110, 155
       (1) . . . . . . . . . . . . . . . . . . . . . . . . . . . . . 152
    s 26 . . . . . . . . . . . . . . . . . . . . . . . . . . . . . . 106
       (1) . . . . . . . . . . . . . . . . . . . . . . . . . . . . . 147
       (2) . . . . . . . . . . . . . . . . . . . . . . . . . 147, 148
       (3) . . . . . . . . . . . . . . . . 49, 148, 149, 198
    s 27 . . . . . . . . . . . . . . . . . . . . . . . . . . 107, 187
       (1) . . . . . . . . . . . . . . . . . 185, 189–90, 199
       (2) . . . . . . . . . . . . . . . . . . . . . . 49, 186, 195
    s 28 . . . . . . . . . . . . . . . . . . . 20, 49, 106, 143
       (3) . . . . . . . . . . . . . . . . . . . . . . . . . . . . . . 48
    s 29 . . . . . . . . . . . . . . . . . . . . . . . . . . . . . . 153
    s 30 . . . . . . . . . . . . . 107, 155, 174, 179, 180
    s 31 . . . . . . . . . . . . . . . . . . . . . . . . . . . . . . 112
    ss 34–36 . . . . . . . . . . . . . . . . . . . . . . . 120, 188
    s 34 . . . . . . . . 24, 26, 27, 30, 33, 112, 115, 120
       (1) . . . . . . . . . . . . . . . . . . . . . . . . . . 112–13
       (2) . . . . . . . . . . . . . . . . . . . 26, 108, 112–13
       (3) . . . . . . . . . . . . . . . . . . . . . . . . . . 112–13
       (3A) . . . . . . . . . . . . . . . . . . . . . . . . . . . . 112
    s 35 . . . . . . . . . . . . . . . . . . . . . . . . . . . . . . 113
    s 36 . . . . . . . . . . . . . . . . . . . . . . . . . . 112, 113
       (1) . . . . . . 50, 106, 108, 113–14, 115, 120
       (2) . . . . 49, 50, 51, 53, 54, 70, 73, 81, 209
    s 38 . . . . . . . . . . . . . . . . . . . . . . . . . . . . . . . 23
    s 53(1)(b) . . . . . . . . . . . . . . . . . . . . . . . . . . 40
       (2) . . . . . . . . . . . . . . . . . . . . . . . . . . . . . . 37
    s 60(1) . . . . . . . . . . . . . . . . . . . . . . . . . . . . . 19
       (3) . . . . . . . . . . . . . . . . . . . . . . . . . . . . . . 19

s 63 . . . . . . . . . . . . . . . . . . . . . . . . . . . . . . . . . 61
s 72(3) . . . . . . . . . . . . . . . . . . . . . . . . . . . . . . . 57
    (4) . . . . . . . . . . . . . . . . . . . . . . . . . . . . 22, 64
s 104(2) . . . . . . . . . . . . . . . . . . . . . . . . . . . . . 202
s 111 . . . . . . . . . . . . . . . . . . . . . . . . . . . . 33, 210
s 130(1) . . . . . . . . . . . . . . . . . . . . . . . . . 19, 208
s 136(1) . . . . . . . . . . . . . . . . . . . . . . . . . . . . 209
s 149(6) . . . . . . . . . . . . . . . . . . . . . . . . . . . . 5, 16
s 176 . . . . . . . . . . . . . . . . . . . . . . . . . . . . . . . 13
s 184 . . . . . . . . . . . . . . . . . . . . . . . . . . . . . . . 26
s 188 . . . . . . . . . . . . . . . . . . . . . . . . . . . . . . 218
s 196 . . . . . . . . . . . . . . . . . . . . . . . . . . . . . . . 52
    (3) . . . . . . . . . . . . . . . . . . . . . . . . . . . . 51, 52
    (4) . . . . . . . . . . . . . . . . . . . . . . . . . . . . 51, 52
s 205(1)(ii) . . . . . . . . . . . . . . . . . . . . . . . . . . 22
       (xix) . . . . . . . . . . . . . . . . . . . . . . . . . . . . 15
       (xxi) . . . . . . . . . . . . . . . . . . . . . . . . . . . 199
       (xxvii) . . . . . . . . . . . . . . . . . . . . . . . . . 5, 14
       (xxviii) . . . . . . . . . . . . . . . . . . . . . . . . . 186
       (xxix) . . . . . . . . . . . . . . . . . . . . . . . . . . 105
Sched 1, Part VI . . . . . . . . . . . . . . . . . . . . . . . 46
Law of Property (Amendment) Act 1926 . . . . . 5
    s 1 . . . . . . . . . . . . . . . . . . . . . . . . . . . . 99, 114
    s 3 . . . . . . . . . . . . . . . . . . . . . . . . . . . . . . . 486
Law of Property (Entailed Interests) Act 1932
    s 1 . . . . . . . . . . . . . . . . . . . . . . . . . . . . . . . 208
Law of Property (Joint Tenants)
    Act 1964 . . . . . . . . . . . . . . . . . . . . 200, 202
    s 2 . . . . . . . . . . . . . . . . . . . . . . . . . . . . . . . 200
    s 3 . . . . . . . . . . . . . . . . . . . . . . . . . . . . . . . 201
Law of Property (Miscellaneous Provisions)
    Act 1989
    s 2 . . . . . . . . . . . . . . . . . . . . . . . . . . . . . . . . 68
    Sched 1 para 6 . . . . . . . . . . . . . . . . . . . . . 154
Married Women's Property Act 1882
    s 1 . . . . . . . . . . . . . . . . . . . . . . . . . . . . . . . . 46
Matrimonial Causes Act . . . . . . . . . . . . 180, 181
    s 24 . . . . . . . . . . . . . . . . . . . . . . 130, 156, 179
    s 25 . . . . . . . . . . . . . . . . . . . . . . . . . . . . . . 179
Matrimonial Proceedings and Property
    Act 1970
    s 37 . . . . . . . . . . . . . . . . . . . . . . . . . . . . . . 140
Perpetuities and Accumulations Act 1964 . . . 18
    s 1 . . . . . . . . . . . . . . . . . . . . . . . . . . . . . . . . 18
    s 2(1) . . . . . . . . . . . . . . . . . . . . . . . . . . . . . . 18
    s 3 . . . . . . . . . . . . . . . . . . . . . . . . . . . . . . . . 17
    s 4 . . . . . . . . . . . . . . . . . . . . . . . . . . . . . . . . 18
       (3)–(4) . . . . . . . . . . . . . . . . . . . . . . . . . . . 18
    s 5 . . . . . . . . . . . . . . . . . . . . . . . . . . . . . . . . 18
Postal Services Act 2000
    s 125 . . . . . . . . . . . . . . . . . . . . . . . . . . . . . . 51

Sched 8 para 2 . . . . . . . . . . . . . . . . . . . . . . . 51
Powers of Attorney Act 1971
    s 1 . . . . . . . . . . . . . . . . . . . . . . . . . . . . . . 154
    s 5 . . . . . . . . . . . . . . . . . . . . . . . . . . . . . . 154
Recorded Delivery Service Act 1962
    s 1. . . . . . . . . . . . . . . . . . . . . . . . . . . . . . 51
Rentcharges Act 1977 . . . . . . . . . . . . . . . . . . . 5
Reverter of Sites Act 1987
    s 1 . . . . . . . . . . . . . . . . . . . . . . . . . . . . . 112
Sale of Goods (Amendment) Act 1995 . . . . 208
Sale of Goods Act 1979
    ss 20A, 20B. . . . . . . . . . . . . . . . . . . . . . . . 208
    ss 24, 25 . . . . . . . . . . . . . . . . . . . . . . . . . 215
Settled Estates Drainage Act 1840 . . . . . . . . . 96
Settled Land Act 1882 . . . . . . . . . . . . . . . . . . . 98
Settled Land Act 1925 . . . . . . 20, 98, 108–110,
                                     153, 181, 217
    s 1 . . . . . . . . . . . . 99, 105, 108, 112, 114, 115
        (1)(i) . . . . . . . . . . . . . . . . . . . . . . . . . . . 99
        (ii)(a) . . . . . . . . . . . . . . . . . . . . . . . . . 99
            (b) . . . . . . . . . . . . . . . . . . . . . . . . . 99
            (c) . . . . . . . . . . . . . . . . . . . . . . . . . 99
            (d) . . . . . . . . . . . . . . . . . . . . . . . . . 99
        (iii) . . . . . . . . . . . . . . . . . . . . . . . . . . . 99
        (v). . . . . . . . . . . . . . . . . . . . . . . . . . . . 99
        (7). . . . . . . . . . . . . . . . . . . . . . . . 105, 181
    s 4(3) . . . . . . . . . . . . . . . . . . . . . . . . . . . 102
    s 5 . . . . . . . . . . . . . . . . . . . . . . . . . . . . . 102
    s 7(2) . . . . . . . . . . . . . . . . . . . . . . . . . . . 102
        (4) . . . . . . . . . . . . . . . . . . . . . . . . . . . 103
        (5). . . . . . . . . . . . . . . . . . . . . . . 103, 105
    s 8(4) . . . . . . . . . . . . . . . . . . . . . . . . . . . 102
    s 9(2) . . . . . . . . . . . . . . . . . . . . . . . . . . . 102
    s 13 . . . . . . . . . . . . . . . . . . . . . . . . . . . . 103
    s 17. . . . . . . . . . . . . . . . . . . . 102, 104, 201
    s 18. . . . . . . . . . . . . . . . . . . . 103, 104, 105
        (1)(b). . . . . . . . . . . . . . . . . 101, 103, 105
            (c) . . . . . . . . . . . . . . . . . . . 103, 105
    s 19 . . . . . . . . . . . . . . . . . . . . . . . . . . . . . 99
        (1) . . . . . . . . . . . . . . . . . . . . . . . . . . . 100
        (2) . . . . . . . . . . . . . . . . . . . . . . . . . . . 110
        (4) . . . . . . . . . . . . . . . . . . . . . . . . . . . 100
    s 20 . . . . . . . . . . . . . . . . . . . . . . . . . . . . . 99
        (1) . . . . . . . . . . . . . . . . . . . . . . . . 99, 100
        (iv). . . . . . . . . . . . . . . . . . . . . . . . . . . . 5
    s 23 . . . . . . . . . . . . . . . . . . . . . . . . 103, 109
    s 24 . . . . . . . . . . . . . . . . . . . . . . . . . . . . 100
    s 26 . . . . . . . . . . . . . . . . . . . . . . . . . . . . 100
    ss 30–33 . . . . . . . . . . . . . . . . . . . . . . . . . 102
    s 30(3). . . . . . . . . . . . . . . . . . . . . . . . . . 102
    s 34 . . . . . . . . . . . . . . . . . . . . . . . . . . . . 102

s 36 . . . . . . . . . . . . . . . . . . . . . . . . . . . . . . . 99
    (4) . . . . . . . . . . . . . . . . . . . . . . . . . . . . . 113
ss 38–72 . . . . . . . . . . . . . . . . . . . . . . . 100, 143
s 38 . . . . . . . . . . . . . . . . . . . . . . . . . . . . . . 100
s 39 . . . . . . . . . . . . . . . . . . . . . . . . . . . . . . 104
s 41 . . . . . . . . . . . . . . . . . . . . . . . . . . 20, 100
s 46 . . . . . . . . . . . . . . . . . . . . . . . . . . . . . . . 21
s 47 . . . . . . . . . . . . . . . . . . . . . . . . . . . . . . . 20
s 65 . . . . . . . . . . . . . . . . . . . . . . . . . . 100, 102
s 66 . . . . . . . . . . . . . . . . . . . . . . . . . . . . . . . 20
s 67 . . . . . . . . . . . . . . . . . . . . . . . . . . 109, 217
s 68 . . . . . . . . . . . . . . . . . . . . . . . . . . . . . . 102
s 71 . . . . . . . . . . . . . . . . . . . . . . . . . . . . . . 100
s 72 . . . . . . . . . . . . . . . . . . . . . . . . . . . . . . 102
s 75(1) . . . . . . . . . . . . . . . . . . . . . . . . . . . . 101
    (2) . . . . . . . . . . . . . . . . . . . . . . . . . . . . . 101
s 95 . . . . . . . . . . . . . . . . . . . . . . . . . . 100, 104
s 98(3) . . . . . . . . . . . . . . . . . . . . . . . . . . . . 104
s 101 . . . . . . . . . . . . . . . . . . . . . . . . . 101, 102
    (5) . . . . . . . . . . . . . . . . . . . . . . . . . . . . . 104
s 102 . . . . . . . . . . . . . . . . . . . . . . . . . 100, 143
s 104 . . . . . . . . . . . . . . . . . . . . . . . . . . . . . 100
s 105(5) . . . . . . . . . . . . . . . . . . . . . . . 101, 102
s 106 . . . . . . . . . . . . . . . . . . . . . . . . . 101, 144
s 107 . . . . . . . . . . . . . . . . . . . . . . . . . . . . . 100
s 110(1) . . . . . . . . . . . . . . . . . . . . . . . 104, 105
    (2) . . . . . . . . . . . . . . . . . . . . . . . . . . . . . 103
    (5). . . . . . . . . . . . . . . . . . . . . . . . . . . . . 104
s 117(1)(iv) . . . . . . . . . . . . . . . . . . . . . . . . . 99
    (xxviii) . . . . . . . . . . . . . . . . . . . . . . . . . 99
    (xxx) . . . . . . . . . . . . . . . . . . . . . . . . . . 105
Timeshare Act 1992 . . . . . . . . . . . . . . . . . . . . . 7
Torts (Interference with Goods) Act 1977
    s 10(1)(b) . . . . . . . . . . . . . . . . . . . . . . . . 218
Trustee Act 1925 . . . . . . . . . . . . . . . . . . 215, 217
    s 17 . . . . . . . . . . . . . . . . . . . . . . . . . 187, 193
    s 25 . . . . . . . . . . . . . . . . . . . . . . . . . . . . 155
    ss 31, 32 . . . . . . . . . . . . . . . . . . . . . . . . . . 32
    s 34 . . . . . . . . . . . . . . . . . . . . . . . . . . . . 184
        (2) . . . . . . . . . . . . . . . . . . . . . . . . . . . 108
    s 57 . . . . . . . . . . . . . . . . . . . . . . . . . 145, 217
    s 63 . . . . . . . . . . . . . . . . . . . . . . . . . . . . 145
    s 69(2) . . . . . . . . . . . . . . . . . . . . . . . 147, 155
Trustee Act 2000 . . . . . . . . . . . . . . 146, 215, 217
    s 1 . . . . . . . . . . . . . . . . . . . . . . . . . . . . . 145
    s 3 . . . . . . . . . . . . . . . . . . . . . . . . . . . . . 216
    s 4 . . . . . . . . . . . . . . . . . . . . . . . . . . . . . 216
        (2) . . . . . . . . . . . . . . . . . . . . . . . . . . . 216
    s 5 . . . . . . . . . . . . . . . . . . . . . . . . . . . . . 216
    s 8 . . . . . . . . . . . . . . . . . . . . . . . . . 143, 216
        (3) . . . . . . . . . . . . . . . . . . . . . . . . . . . 143

s 9(2) . . . . . . . . . . . . . . . . . . . . . . . . . . . . . 143
s 12(3) . . . . . . . . . . . . . . . . . . . . . . . . . . . . 217
Trustee Investments Act 1961
  s 1(1) . . . . . . . . . . . . . . . . . . . . . . . . . . . . 217
Trusts of Land and Appointment of Trustees
    Act 1996
  s 1(1)(a) . . . . . . . . . . . . . . . . . . . . . . . . 4, 215
    (2)(a) . . . . . . . . . . . . . . . . . . 111, 114, 181
    (b) . . . . . . . . . . . . . . . . . . . . . . . . . . . . 111
  s 2 . . . . . . . . . . . . . . . . . . . . . . . . . . . . 98, 110
    (1) . . . . . . . . . . . . . . . . . . . . . . . . . . . . . 53
    (2) . . . . . . . . . . . . . . . . . . . . . . . . . . . . 110
    (3) . . . . . . . . . . . . . . . . . . . . . . . . . . . . 110
  s 3 . . . . . . . . 61, 98, 110, 120, 183, 185, 187
  s 4 . . . . . . . . . . . . . . . . . . . . 49, 152, 154, 155
    (1) . . . . . . . . . . . . . . . . . . . . 106, 149, 181
  s 5(1) . . . . . . . . . . . . . . . . . . . . . . . . . . . 111
  ss 6–9A . . . . . . . . . . . . . . . . . . . . . . . . . . 149
  s 6 . . . . . . . . . . . . 106, 124, 143, 144, 146–7,
      149, 152, 154, 188, 191, 194, 196, 216
    (1) . . . . . . . . . . . . . . . . . . . . . . . . . . . . 196
    (2) . . . . . . . . . . . . . 143, 151, 152, 153, 201
    (3) . . . . . . . . . . . . . . . . . . . . . . . . . . . . 143
    (5) . . . . . . . . . . . . . . . . 146, 147, 196, 198
    (6) . . . . . . . . . . . . . . . . 146, 196, 197, 198
    (7) . . . . . . . . . . . . . . . . . . . . . . . . . . . . 146
    (8) . . . . . . . . . . . . . . . . . . . . 146, 196, 197
    (9) . . . . . . . . . . . . . . . . . . . . . . . . 145, 196
  s 7 . . . . . . . . . . . . . . . . . 124, 143, 152, 154
    (3) . . . . . . . . . . . . . . . . . . . . . . . . . . . . 198
  s 8 . . . . . . . . . . 49, 124, 144, 147, 154, 155,
                    190, 192, 195, 197
    (2) . . . . . . . . . . . . . . . . . . . . . . . . . . . . 147
  s 9 . . . . . . . . . . . . 143, 149, 153–4, 155, 217
    (1) . . . . . . . . . . . . . . . . . . . . . . . . 153, 154
    (2) . . . . . . . . . . . . . . . . . . . . . . . . . . . . 154
    (3) . . . . . . . . . . . . . . . . . . . . . . . . . . . . 154
    (4) . . . . . . . . . . . . . . . . . . . . . . . . . . . . 154
    (7) . . . . . . . . . . . . . . . . . . . . . . . . . . . . 154
    (8) . . . . . . . . . . . . . . . . . . . . . . . . . . . . 154
  s 9A . . . . . . . . . . . . . . . . . . . . . . . . . . . . 154
    (6) . . . . . . . . . . . . . . . . . . . . . . . . . . . . 154
  s 10 . . . . . . . . . . . . . . . . . . . . 106, 149, 193
    (1) . . . . . . . . . . . . . . . . . . . . . . . . . . . . 148
    (3) . . . . . . . . . . . . . . . . . . . . . . . . . . . . 148
  s 11 . . . . . . . 49, 146, 148–52, 159, 167, 185,
                    196, 198, 216
    (1)(b) . . . . . . . . . . . . . . . . . . . . . . . . . . 150
    (2)(b) . . . . . . . . . . . . . . . . . . . . . . . . . . 153
    (3) . . . . . . . . . . . . . . . . . . . . . . . . . . . . 148

s 12 . . . . . . . . . 36, 48, 64, 107, 120, 122–5,
                    126, 127, 128, 129, 130,
                    137, 138, 139, 154, 157
    (1) . . . . . . . . . . . . . . . . . . . . . . . . . . 122–4
    (a) . . . . . . . . . . . . . 122–4, 125, 137, 182
    (b) . . . . . . . . . . . . . . . . . . . . 124, 138–9
    (2) . . . . . . . . . . . . . . . . . . . 123, 125, 138
  s 13 . . . . . . . . . . 36, 48, 120, 122, 123, 125,
                    126–7, 128, 129, 130, 132, 137,
                    139, 141, 146, 149, 151, 158
    (1) . . . . . . . . . . . . 126, 127, 128, 131, 139
    (2) . . . . . . . . . . . . . . . . . . . . . . . . . . . . 127
    (3) . . . . . . . . . . . . . . . . . . . . 127, 128, 137
    (4) . . . . . . . . . . . . . . . . 127, 137, 146, 151
    (a) . . . . . . . . . . . . . . . . . . . . . . . . . . . . 137
    (b) . . . . . . . . . . . . . . . . . . . . . . . . . . . . 137
    (5) . . . . . . . . . . . . . . . . . . . . . . . . 127, 137
    (6) . . . . . . 125, 131–2, 137, 138, 139, 162
    (7) . . . . . . . . . 123, 125, 126–7, 132, 139,
                    143, 156, 157
    (8) . . . . . . . . . . . . . . . . . . . . . . . . . . . . 127
  s 14 . . . . . . . . 123, 126, 127, 128, 130, 132,
      137, 138, 143, 144, 145, 147, 148,
      149, 150, 151, 153, 156–8, 161,
      167, 168, 173, 179, 180, 187, 192, 216
    (1) . . . . . . . . . . . . . . . . . . . . . . . . . . . . 157
    (2) . . . . . . . . . . . . . . . . . . . . . . . . . . . . 156
  s 15 . . . . . . . . . 127, 151, 156, 158–67, 171,
      173, 174, 175, 176, 178, 179, 180
    (1) . . . . . . . . . . . . . . . . . . . . 124, 158, 159
    (a) . . 122, 137, 159, 164, 165, 178, 181
    (b) . . . . . . 122, 137, 160, 164, 165, 178
    (c) . . . . . . . . . . . . 127, 160, 163, 165–6
    (d) . . 159, 165, 167, 171, 173, 176, 179
    (2) . . . . . . . . . . . . . . . . 149, 151, 158, 159
    (3) . . . . . . . . . 151, 153, 158–9, 176, 216
    (4) . . . . . . . . . . . . . . . . . . . . . . . . 168, 175
  s 16 . . . . . 148, 193, 194, 195, 197, 201, 203
    (1) . . . . . . . . . . . . . . . . . . . . . . . . 198, 202
    (2) . . . . . . . . . . . . . . . . 197, 198, 202, 203
    (3) . . . . . . . . . . . . 190, 193, 197, 201, 203
    (4) . . . . . . . . . . . . . . . . . . . . . . . . 104, 201
    (5) . . . . . . . . . . . . . . . . . . . . 104, 201, 203
    (7) . . . . . . . . . . . . . . . . . . . . . . . . 193, 201
  s 22 . . . . . . . . . . . . . . . . . . . . . . . . . . . . 122
  Sched 1 . . . . . . . . . . . . . . . . . . . . . . . . . . 114
    para 1 . . . . . . . . . . . . . . . . . . . . . . . . . . 114
    para 2 . . . . . . . . . . . . . . . . . . . . . . . . . . 114
    para 3 . . . . . . . . . . . . . . . . . . . . . . . . . . 114
    para 4 . . . . . . . . . . . . . . . . . . . . . . . . . . 114

para 5 . . . . . . . . . . . . . . . . . . . . . . . 19, 114
para 6 . . . . . . . . . . . . . . . . . . . . . . . . . 114
Sched 2 . . . . . . . . . . . . . . . . . . . . . . 111, 112
para 3(6) . . . . . . . . . . . . . . . . . . . . . . . 181
para 4(4) . . . . . . . . . . . . . . . . . . . . . . . 181
Sched 3, para 2(11) . . . . . . . . . . . . . . . . . . 99
para 12(3) . . . . . . . . . . . . . . . . . . . . . . . 183
Variation of Trusts Act 1958 . . . . . . . . . . . . 144
Wills Act 1837
s 33 . . . . . . . . . . . . . . . . . . . . . . . . . . . . 32
s 18A . . . . . . . . . . . . . . . . . . . . . . . . . . . 87

**B. Overseas Statutes**
Conveyancing Act 1919
(New South Wales)
s 26 . . . . . . . . . . . . . . . . . . . . . . . . . 44, 86

Joint Family Homes Act 1964
(New Zealand) . . . . . . . . . . . . . . . . . . . 172

**C. UK Statutory Instruments**
Insolvency Proceedings (Monetary Limits)
(Amendment) Order 2004
(SI 2004 No 547) . . . . . . . . . . . . . . . . . 173
Land Registration Rules 1997 (SI 1997
No 3037) . . . . . . . . . . . . . . . . . . . . . . . 40
Land Registration Rules 2003 (SI 2003 No 1417)
rr 93, 94 . . . . . . . . . . . . . . . . . . . . . . . . 187
r 99 . . . . . . . . . . . . . . . . . . . . . . . . . . . 201
Sched 1 . . . . . . . . . . . . . . . . . . . . . . . . . 40
Sched 4, Form R . . . . . . . . . . . . . . . . . . . 115
Public Trustee (Custodian Trustee)
Rules 1975 (SI 1975 No 1189) . . . . . . 186

# PART I
# INTRODUCTION

# 1

# Plural Ownership

## 1. General Scope

This Chapter establishes the scope of the book. There are many ways in which two or more people may have rights in the same property. We are not concerned with rights which do not confer full enjoyment—we are not, therefore, concerned with easements, covenants, licences, or charges. For some forms of property, we might say that we are interested in ownership, but ownership is not a concept readily applied to land in English law. Using the technical language of English land law, we are interested in estates in land.

The situations to be covered involve either successive interests, where the property will be enjoyed successively by different persons, or concurrent interests, where the property is enjoyed by two or more persons at the same time. Concurrent interests are frequently said to result in co-ownership; the two labels are used interchangeably in this book. Enjoyment is not limited to physical occupation; frequently, it involves receipt of rents paid by tenants. How do leases fit in with successive interests? Leases may be said to involve successive rights to land and a plausible case could be made for treating them as an example of successive interests. However, leases have always been treated differently from freehold estates and, as will be seen in the following Chapter,[1] it would not be appropriate to treat them in the same way as freehold estates. Leases are, of course, very important in practice and constitute a very large area of law, but to include them in this book would be impracticable. There are other ways in which equivalent results to successive or concurrent ownership can be achieved. One example is where individuals hold shares in a company, which owns land or other assets. Later in this Chapter there is a brief summary of devices which provide alternative forms of plural ownership.

Within the areas of successive and concurrent interests, we are interested in the nature and operation of the interests recognized by the law. This is fully analysed below for concurrent interests. A significant characteristic of the common law is the recognition of two forms of concurrent interests: joint tenancy and tenancy in common. The joint tenancy is special in that the interests have to be identical and, most important, the property passes to the survivors when one co-owner dies. This has led to much litigation, both as to which form of co-ownership has

---

[1] See p 15 below.

been created and as to whether joint tenancy has been converted to tenancy in common (severed). Successive interests attracted much attention in previous decades. Today, much of the complex legal analysis has either been overtaken by legislation or is of limited importance. Accordingly, the current law is briefly summarized: no attempt is made to cover the wealth of detail to be encountered in books from an earlier age.

However, most of this book deals with the regulation of successive and concurrent interests in land. Today, all such interests involve trusts of land, which are controlled by the Trusts of Land and Appointment of Trustees Act 1996. This regulation applies to both successive and concurrent interests: an important reason for covering both types of interest in this book. In particular, we look at occupation of the land, powers of management (including sale) vested in trustees, court control over those powers, and the protection of purchasers and others dealing with trustees.

This coverage does not mean that every legal issue regarding successive and concurrent interests is covered. A highly controversial topic concerns the circumstances in which constructive and resulting trusts and estoppels can give rise to interests (almost invariably concurrent interests) in the family home.[2] These principles are, indeed, not limited to the family home, though that is the context in which there is most disquiet about their operation. These issues are interesting, difficult, and controversial. However, they raise issues which are very different from the topics covered here. Equally tellingly, proper coverage of them would require a doubling the length of this book.

The regulation of trusts of land applies, of course, only to land.[3] Other forms of property are subject to no equivalent regulatory regime. Not only that, but estates are recognized only in land. It follows that much of the law differs widely, according to the form of property involved. Indeed, the law regarding assets other than land is distinctly under-developed.[4] Accordingly, other forms of property are considered separately in Chapter 10 below. This is delayed until after interests in land are considered, in order that the contrasting rules for different types of property can be most effectively compared.

## 2. Other Techniques for Recognizing Plural Ownership

### A. Leases

It has already been observed that leases over land are treated differently from successive and concurrent interests: the interests considered in this book. One

---

[2] Based on *Gissing v Gissing* [1971] AC 886; see the inconclusive 2002 Law Commission Discussion Paper on Sharing Homes (Law Com No 278).

[3] Trusts of land include mixed asset trusts (Trusts of Land and Appointment of Trustees Act 1996, s 1(1)(a)) but most of the statutory powers and rights apply only to land.

[4] Much of the analysis by commentators concentrates on commercial transactions and security interests—not the concern of plural ownership.

element of this is further discussed at that stage. Freehold estates are commonly described as family interests: they are generally held by members of the family as a result of a settlement. Leases, on the other hand, are almost invariably commercial transactions. Even when leases are granted to family members, this is more likely to be for consideration than as a gift or part of a settlement. This goes far to explain why they are treated differently: the different contexts in which they arise call for different responses.[5] However, when we refer to family and commercial interests, there is a danger of treating this dichotomy as being more conclusive than the facts justify.

Taking leases first, at one time it was common to have a lease for life. Today, we distinguish between such arrangements according to whether there is consideration or not. If there is consideration (and it does not take effect under a settlement) then it is treated as a lease, otherwise it will take effect as a life interest under a trust of land.[6] Here, at least, the family/commercial distinction is recognized, though the existence of consideration may mask the underlying reality.[7] More generally, it seems possible to have leases for a term of years without rent,[8] though the courts tend towards holding that there is a licence where the arrangement is gratuitous.[9]

Equally, there is no reason why life interests may not be created for consideration. Indeed, in the traditional marriage settlement there is likely to be consideration, though the setting is very much one of settlement rather than the simple commercial acquisition of a life interest. Examples of commercial acquisition always seems to have been exceptional. In the past, it was possible for the holder of a freehold estate to be liable to pay an annual sum: a rentcharge. This demonstrates the potential for commercial transactions to spill over into the family interest arena,[10] though rentcharges are relatively rare after the Rentcharges Act 1977.

The context of concurrent interests is one in which the relationships may be either commercial or family. Although we think of the family home as the obvious

---

[5] This is discussed at p 15 below.

[6] Law of Property Act 1925 (hereafter LPA), s 149(6); cf Settled Land Act 1925, s 20(1)(iv) (holder is tenant for life).

[7] As in *Griffiths v Williams* [1978] 2 EGLR 121, where the parties agreed to a lease determinable on death, with a nominal rent, as an alternative to a life interest. The context was one dominated by the unsuitability of a life interest because of the application of settled land. This is now obsolete, but the case remains an example of how lease and life interest can be seen as viable alternative outcomes.      [8] LPA, s 205(1)(xxvii); *Ashburn Anstalt v Arnold* [1989] Ch 1, 9–10.

[9] *Street v Mountford* [1985] AC 809.

[10] It caused a real problem for the 1925 legislation. At one time, it was common practice in certain parts of England for a rentcharge to be payable to the seller of land as part of the consideration for the sale. If it were not paid, there would be a right of re-entry. This practice was overlooked in the 1925 legislation, so that this commercial arrangement attracted the settled land regime. It required remedial legislation: LPA, s 7(1) as amended by Law of Property (Amendment) Act 1926. The fee simple subject to right of re-entry can still be legal, despite not being strictly 'absolute'; this right of re-entry is also legal (LPA, s 1(2)(e)).

example of concurrent interests today, there are modern examples of concurrent interests being employed by professional partners[11] and (less commonly) by two or more businesses.[12] The major consequences of this in the commercial setting are that the land will be controlled by the co-owners (as trustees) and that the law provides for the resolution of disputes. Both these elements are as suitable for commercial as for family situations.

It may be concluded that the real driving force behind the modern law is the suitability of the regulatory regime which applies to trusts of land. Although distinctions between family and commercial interest may assist our understanding of the situations, they do not form a safe basis for explaining the legal structures.

The above points apply to land. For chattels, the area equivalent to leases is bailment, or chattel leases. The absence of any regulatory regime for chattels in plural ownership means that distinctions between family and commercial relationships are not generally employed.

## B. Land Companies

Land companies have already received a brief mention. Instead of individuals owning land directly, they may have shares in a company, which itself has the fee simple absolute in the land. There is, of course, no reason why companies should not be used for other forms of assets as well. Companies are obviously suitable for concurrent interests, as the shareholdings determine the extent of each person's interest.[13] However, they can also be used for successive interests, for example if the shares are held in trust for successive interests. Leaving aside any taxation advantages, the effect of employing a company is to simplify the legal title: there is one single and unchanging holder of the fee simple.

It has been said that the growth of land companies was one reason for the decline in the use of the Settled Land Act settlement during the twentieth century.[14] Land companies may also be suitable in situations which have a more commercial flavour, such as investments in land and farming arrangements.[15] Where land companies are employed, the normal regulation of concurrent interests by the Trusts of Land and Appointment of Trustees Act 1996 will not apply. Any disputes will have to be resolved by use of company analyses and

---

[11] *Rodway v Landy* [2001] Ch 703 (doctors' surgery).

[12] *Malayan Credit Ltd v Jack Chia-MPH Ltd* [1986] AC 549.

[13] For an interesting analysis of the rights of shareholders as co-owners of the issued share capital, see Goode [2003] LMCLQ 379. This use of co-ownership within the corporate financial structure does not affect the proposition that the land (or other asset) is not co-owned.

[14] Grove (1961) 24 MLR 123. For other reasons, see p 108 below.

[15] Cf Grant [1987] CLP 159, 159–64 (also dealing with other techniques). Taxation considerations are likely to drive the decision whether to use a company (cf Shipwright, *Strategic Tax Planning*, G3.9). At present, companies are not commonly used as an alternative to having successive or concurrent interests in the underlying property.

procedures. However, a hybrid result may emerge whereby the company holds the land on trust, thereby attracting the 1996 Act. This would not be the natural result, but may arise in the unusual setting where a couple purchase land through the medium of a company.[16]

## C. Timeshare Agreements

Timeshare agreements involve rights to property for specified periods each year. They are rather special arrangements and do not fall naturally into any of our categories. They can take effect as discontinuous leases, though the normal structure[17] is for the use of a club. The legal title is held on trust for the members,[18] who each hold a licence to give effect their individual rights to use the property.

The use of a trust means that the arrangement triggers the Trusts of Land and Appointment of Trustees Act 1996, fully discussed in Part III below. However, so much of the law relating to timeshares[19] relates to the club structure and the licence that timeshare agreements are not further considered.

## D. Unincorporated Associations

Just as companies may hold land or other assets, so may unincorporated associations. However, it is unlikely that unincorporated associations will be deliberately chosen as method of holding assets. Rather, holding assets will be a subsidiary aspect of their activities. As explained below,[20] the assets are normally vested in trustees. Such arrangements might therefore be thought to fall within the scope of this book. However, problems affecting unincorporated associations[21] have been very different from those encountered with other forms of plural ownership. In particular, they have little or nothing to tell us about the general operation of trusts of land. Accordingly, unincorporated associations do not receive detailed treatment here.

## E. Commonhold

Commonhold, introduced by the Commonhold and Leasehold Reform Act 2002, is designed to deal with the problems of regulating ownership of flats and houses sharing common facilities. To the extent that it regulates the use of

---

[16] *Chan v Leung* [2003] 1 FLR 23.

[17] Edmonds, *International Timesharing* (3rd edn), pp 36, 44.

[18] This has to be carefully structured to avoid the perpetuity problems afflicting unincorporated associations: *Leahy v Att-Gen of New South Wales* [1959] AC 457.

[19] Entering into timeshare agreements is regulated by the Timeshare Act 1992.

[20] See p 115 below.

[21] Principally, problems relating to certainty of objects and the courts' failure to allow purpose trusts.

individual units, it is not of interest to us. However, it provides methods to control common areas, such as access roads, open areas, staircases, and perhaps roofs. The mechanism employed is ownership of the fee simple by a company, of which all the unit holders will be members. Structurally, therefore, commonhold is an example of a land company. However, there is much detailed regulation of how the company (the commonhold association) is to function and of its relationship with the unit holders. It lies well outside the scope of this book.

# PART II

# FORMS OF PLURAL
# OWNERSHIP OF LAND

# 2

# Successive Interests in Land

The law relating to successive interests in land formed a major part of land law in earlier centuries.[1] Today, the law is both simpler and less important. Reforms have removed much of the old technicality, whilst the incidence of successive interest settlements has declined over the past century.[2] The purpose of this Chapter is to describe the general structure of the law relating to successive interests, mainly to assist in understanding their regulation by modern legislation.

## 1. The Range of Successive Interests

### A. Freehold Estates

A peculiar aspect of the common law is that it recognizes estates in land rather than ownership of land, unlike civil law systems. This emphasis on estates permits flexibility in the range of rights recognized. English law is inclined to say that X, Y, and Z have estates in land, without saying that anybody owns it.[3] In the modern law, it is easier to refer to ownership now that the only legal estate recognized is the fee simple absolute in possession,[4] an estate which will normally be registered.[5] However, an enduring legacy of our history is a rich variety of equitable interests in land.

The basic building blocks are the three estates: life estate, fee tail (entail), and fee simple. These enable entitlement to land to be sliced by time: the estates are defined by reference to the time for which they may last.[6] The fee simple is, essentially, the residual right to the land. It comes closest to ownership, though it may only come into possession (that is, give a present right to enjoy the land) after the termination of another estate. Indeed, if the earlier interest were an entail,

---

[1] Together with the associated area of tenures, it takes up over a third of the treatment of real property in Blackstone, *Commentaries on the Laws of England*, Book II.

[2] This is more fully explained in Chapter 6 below.

[3] It is sometimes said that the Crown owns land, with X, Y, and Z holding (directly or indirectly) estates from the Crown: Megarry and Wade, *Law of Real Property* (6th edn), para 2-001. However, other authors stress the Crown as Lord rather than owner: Simpson, *A History of the Land Law* (2nd edn), pp 47–8.     [4] Law of Property Act 1925 (hereafter LPA), s 1.

[5] Registration is especially important in diminishing the importance of the traditional English analysis that titles are relative: there can be more than one holder of a fee simple.

[6] If the time is fixed (one year, for example) this creates a lease.

then enjoyment of the fee simple might be postponed for generations or, indeed, be defeated entirely.

The life estate is, fairly obviously, a right to enjoy the land for life. Although a life estate can be transferred, it will only last for as long as the original grantee is alive. Plainly, it is not an attractive interest to purchase or to take as security for a loan. The life estate can be granted for the life of another person, when it is called a life estate *pur autre vie*. The life estate differs from the fee simple not only in duration, but also in the freedom of the holder to manage and take benefit from the land. The holder of the fee simple[7] can, when the interest is in possession, do whatever he or she wishes with the land.[8] However, this proposition must be heavily qualified: it is obviously subject to limits resulting from nuisance, planning permission, and environmental control. Nor can things be done which interfere with proprietary interests of others in the same plot of land.[9] Life interest holders are in a very different position: they can do little more than use the land in the normal manner. This is governed by the law of waste, which precludes for example, the opening of new mines.[10]

Thus one might have a simple settlement of to A for life, remainder to B in fee simple.[11] A would enjoy the property for A's life (whether by physically occupying the land or receiving rents from tenants) whilst B would obtain effective ownership of the land on A's death. Technically, we would describe A as having a life interest in possession and B a fee simple in remainder. There is no owner of the land. If it is desired to sell the land,[12] then A and B would have to act together.

The third estate is the entail. Since the Trusts of Land and Appointment of Trustees Act 1996 (hereafter TLATA) entails can no longer be created,[13] but they form an important aspect of the history and development of modern land law. The nature of an entail is that it passes automatically from one generation to another. It passes according to traditional primogeniture principles applicable to the descent of real property on death:[14] to the eldest son, with daughters being entitled only if there is no son. It was possible to limit the passing to sons (tail male) or, more rarely, daughters (tail female). In some respects it operates in a

---

[7] But not the holder of a qualified fee simple, as it may be cut short: *Turner v Wright* (1869) De G F&J 234.

[8] Perhaps most strongly expressed by Blackstone, *Commentaries on the Laws of England*, Book II, ch 1, p 2: 'sole and despotic dominion'.

[9] Two examples may suffice. First, the rights of a holder of the fee simple may be limited by the existence of a lease. Secondly, actions cannot undertaken which would interfere with, eg, a right of way.                                                          [10] See pp 20, 96 below.

[11] If the holder of the fee simple grants a life interest to A, this leaves the grantor with a fee simple *in reversion*. Interests in remainder and interests in reversion are very similar.

[12] This employs non-technical terminology; the purchaser would wish to acquire a fee simple absolute in possession.                                                          [13] See p 114 below.

[14] These general descent rules were abandoned in 1925 in favour of property passing to all the children of the deceased: Administration of Estates Act 1925, ss 45–46. The rules applicable to entails were unaffected by this change.

similar manner to a series of life estates, but with the significant difference that it is not subject to the perpetuity rules, which make it difficult to provide for more than one future generation.[15] At first sight, it appears to be a marvellous way of tying up land indefinitely. Unless the family dies out,[16] the land will pass through generations and the remainder in fee simple will never come into possession.

However, this prospect of tying up land was thwarted by a procedure known as barring the entail. As a result of initially fictitious actions, and later the Fines and Recoveries Act 1833, it became possible to turn an entail into a fee simple. Although this may be viewed as legal alchemy, it ensured that settlements could not last indefinitely. Barring the entail could take two forms, both based on simple transfers of the land.[17] First, the tenant in tail (X) whose interest is in possession could bar the entail so as to create a fee simple absolute. The original fee simple in remainder is destroyed, as are the expectancy rights of the heirs of X. It follows that the holder of a fee tail in possession can usually[18] be treated as being equivalent to a fee simple owner. The second form of barring an entail applies where it is a remainder interest. In this case X can bar it, but not so as to affect the fee simple remainder. Those who would otherwise take under the entail (the children and remoter issue of X) are, however, defeated. This creates a *base fee*, a form of fee simple but (exceptionally) subject to a remainder if the family dies out. It sits rather awkwardly in the structure of estates: close to a fee simple absolute, but ultimately susceptible to being defeated. However, if the holder of the entail in remainder acts together with the holder of the prior life estate (which is in possession) then they can fully bar the entail.[19]

As has been mentioned, entails can no longer be created. However, existing entails continue and can still be barred. Their modern significance is very small, but they contributed much to earlier settlements and thereby to the structure of regulation that exists today.

## B. Qualified Estates

That estates may be in possession, reversion, or remainder represents just one level of variety. It is possible to qualify estates so that they may be cut short, or

---

[15] See p 17 below.

[16] It does not matter if a current holder of the entail dies without children: descent can be to any descendant of the original holder of the entail: Megarry and Wade, *Law of Real Property* (5th edn), p 77. To provide a simple example, suppose that an entail is granted to A. A has two children, the elder of whom, F, inherits the entail. If F later dies without children, the entail could pass to the younger child of A (and his or her issue) though not to nephews and nieces of A.

[17] Until LPA, s 176, it was not possible to disentail by will.

[18] The only general limit is that barring is not allowed if it is impossible for the entail to pass on death. The best example is if the issue must be those of X and Y, where X is the holder of the entail. If Y dies without issue, there never can be issue of X and Y. The entail continues for X's life, but cannot be barred.

[19] This was a crucial factor in the standard form of nineteenth-century settlement: see p 95 below.

alternatively come into effect, only if some condition is satisfied. Examples are 'To R on condition that she never smokes' (R loses her estate if she smokes) and 'To the first person to land on the moon after my death' (there is no interest until the eventual beneficiary identifies himself or herself by landing on the moon).

Here we begin to encounter some technical, but still practically important, rules. As we will see a little later, future interests are subject to the risk of being invalidated by the rule against perpetuities. However, those that can be described as being *vested in interest* are safe. An interest is vested if all that lies between it and the enjoyment is the natural termination of a prior interest. In a settlement to A for life, remainder to B in tail, remainder to C in fee simple, all three interests are vested. Even though the fee simple remainder might become *vested in possession* (ie, give present rights of enjoyment) only after many generations, this does not matter.[20] An interest is *contingent* rather than vested if it takes effect on the earlier interest's being cut short (as in the example about R's smoking), or if the identity of its holder is not yet known, or if some condition (such as obtaining a university degree) remains to be satisfied. As a matter of terminology, an interest that can be cut short is generally described as *qualified*, whereas the normal unqualified interest is *absolute*. Since 1925, qualified interests cannot generally be legal estates.[21] The interest which follows a qualified interest is generally described as contingent.

When an interest is qualified, what happens when the qualification operates? The property may either revert to the grantor (this is the default position, when no other recipient is identified) or go to a third party. When it goes back to the grantor, this may take one of two forms. The distinctions here are exceptionally technical.[22] If the qualification determines how long the interest is to last (to M so long as he remains unmarried) then it is described as a *determinable* interest, with the grantor having a *possibility of reverter*. On the other hand, if the property is apparently given absolutely, but then an attempt is made to cut it short (to P in fee simple, on condition that she does not remarry) then it is called a *conditional* interest, with the grantor having a *right of re-entry*. Given how similar these examples are and how accidentally the wording may be chosen, it is astonishing that there are substantial differences in the rules applying to these types of

---

[20] C may be long dead, but this poses no legal problems as it will pass to his estate on his death. If the settlement was created so that C can be identified only when the interest comes into possession ('remainder in fee simple to X's eldest issue living at the time when B's entail comes to an end') then it could not be vested and would fall foul of the rule against perpetuities.

[21] LPA, s 1(1). For technical reasons (see p 5, n 10 above) an exception is made for estates subject to a right of entry: s 7(1). This has very limited practical effect, as most rights of entry on a fee simple will be equitable, thereby triggering a trust and the application of TLATA. Nearly all leases may be cut short by forfeiture operating on breach. Being part of the leasehold relationship, rather than a settlement of the lease, this does not stop the lease from being legal: LPA, s 205(1)(xxvii). Rights of entry on leases are legal: LPA, s 1(2)(e).

[22] The transmissibility of the rights of the grantor raised contentious issues in the nineteenth century, recently discussed in *Bath and Wells Diocesan Board of Finance v Jenkinson* [2003] Ch 89.

qualified interests.[23] Fortunately, the details lie outside the scope of the present analysis.

It will be appreciated that the law confers considerable flexibility on those creating settlements. All sorts of events can be chosen to qualify interests, whether or not the purpose is to inhibit or encourage activities of the grantee. It should be added that any form of estate may be made qualified or contingent.

## C. Leases

It has been seen that freehold estates enable land to be enjoyed successively by different persons. In broad terms, leases are similar. A five-year lease enables the tenant to enjoy the property (to the exclusion of the landlord) for those five years. Yet we do not bring leases into the estate structure just described. This may be explained in both theoretical and practical terms.

Historically, the lease was always a lesser form of estate; indeed, its origins lie in a purely personal right. When (many centuries ago) it achieved proprietary status, this was outside the freehold estate structure. This was reflected in the long defunct rule that freehold estates could not be created out of leases, as the lease was by definition a lesser interest. To deny a life interest in a 999-year lease seems, in economic terms, very odd! More technically, freehold estates enjoyed seisin (essentially, possession) which was not available to tenants of leases. In the modern law, this is mirrored in the recognition that an estate may be in possession despite the fact that somebody else has a lease over it and is actually enjoying the land. We are prepared to view the receipt of rent, if any, as enjoyment of the land.[24]

At a practical level, a number of features combine to justify treating leases very differently from, say, a life estate. Although, like freehold estates, they exist for a slice of time, they differ because the period of time is fixed. Freehold estates involve uncertain ending (notably on death) whereas a lease requires a certain maximum period. This makes it much easier to put a commercial value on a lease (and on the freehold subject to the lease). Next, leases today are almost invariably commercial arrangements. Unless the lease is for an extended period (when the tenant may pay a significant capital sum for the lease) rent will be payable. This may be contrasted with freehold estates, where it is very unusual for payment to be made.[25] These factors lead to there being a market in the transfer of leases and of the landlord's freehold reversion. An assigned lease can be as attractive as taking a new one. If T takes a (fifteen-year) lease at full market rent, then it will not be difficult to find somebody willing to take over, say, the remaining ten years after five years have passed. The attractiveness or otherwise of the terms of the

---

[23] Megarry and Wade, *Law of Real Property* (6th edn), paras 3-062–3-075.
[24] LPA, s 205(1)(xix).     [25] See p 5 above.

lease (especially the rent payable) will be reflected in the financial deal between the tenant and the assignee. From the landlord's perspective, the lease is a source of income. Purchasers of the freehold reversion will be willing to treat it as an income-yielding investment: an attractive prospect for many. If the lease is a short one, then of course there may be attractions in taking over the land when it ends. Although life interests and remainders can be purchased, they are more difficult to value and have never attracted the sort of market which permits their full economic value to be realized.[26]

As we will see in Chapter 6 below, freehold estates were employed to create complex settlements, frequently making it difficult to sell the land or use it efficiently. Leases for fixed periods formed no part of that settlement structure. Ultimately, the settled land may be leased to tenant farmers, but this is not part of the settlement. The problems caused by complex settlements led to the modern regulatory structures controlling plural ownership. Under these structures, the fee simple absolute in possession is held by trustees, who have power to deal with it. When the land is, for example, sold by the trustees, the beneficial interests attach to the proceeds of sale rather than to the land. This is generally described as overreaching. Overreaching is neither necessary nor suitable for leases. It is not necessary, as both lease and freehold reversion can be sold and otherwise dealt with as separate interests. It is not suitable, as the whole point of leases is enjoyment of the land. If Sainsbury's take a twenty-year lease of a store, it is crucial to their plans that they can use the store for that period. Any suggestion that their right to the store could be replaced by an interest in proceeds of sale would be disastrous to their plans; it would inhibit the commercial exploitation of land. The 1925 legislation viewed freehold estates under settlements as being more of a right to an income than a right to the land. Although this approach may have underestimated the importance attached by many families to their land, the reforms were justified by the need to ensure that land could be managed effectively.

It was observed in Chapter 1 above that the line between freehold estates and leases is by no means as clear as the above analysis may suggest. The existence of a lease for life[27] is an obvious blurring of the categories. The 1925 legislation had to draw a distinction and the solution was to treat leases for life (or until marriage) as being leasehold estates if made for consideration.[28] It remains possible to create a gratuitous lease for a term of years, though this is very unusual in practice.

---

[26] They are more likely to be charged as security for a loan. The weakness of the security is reflected by high rates of interest: to take just one example, 30% in *Re Thynne* [1911] 1 Ch 282 (mortgage of reversion).

[27] Originally a freehold estate, even if rent was paid: Challis, *Real Property* (3rd edn, Sweet), p 340.

[28] LPA, s 149(6); this does not apply to leases created as part of a settlement. In order to comply with the requirement that leases have a certain maximum term, they take effect as grants for 99 years or until death or remarriage, as the case may be.

## 2. Creating Successive Interests

### A. The Rule Against Perpetuities

The rule against perpetuities has for centuries operated to prevent settlors from creating interests which may vest many years in the future. It is generally justified as balancing the interests of past generations (settlors, who wish to determine what happens to their property in the future) and the present generation (who want freedom to use their property as they wish). Linked to this are economic problems resulting from creating settlements lasting for many decades, though these problems may have been resolved by legislation (today, TLATA) which ensures that the property can be managed effectively.

The perpetuity rules are highly complex[29] and this Chapter deals only with their general effect. The central requirement is that the gift must vest within a life in being (a person alive at the time of the gift) plus a further twenty-one years. When we refer to vesting, this means vesting in interest as described above,[30] it is not a reference to vesting in possession. This distinction is crucial for those drafting settlements.

The faintest possibility of vesting outside the period was sufficient to invalidate the gift, though since 1964 it has been possible to 'wait and see' whether it does in fact vest outside the period.[31] An example will demonstrate its application. Suppose a testator provides in his will for property to go to his son, A, for life, thereafter to A's first child to reach eighteen for life, and thereafter to A's eldest great-grandchild in fee simple. At the testator's death (the relevant point in time), A is aged forty-five, with children aged fifteen and ten. A's life estate is vested and is therefore outside the rule and valid. The gift to the first child to reach eighteen is safe: a moment's thought will show that a child of A cannot reach eighteen more than twenty-one years after A's death![32] However, the gift to the grandchildren is problematic. It might be thought that the children aged ten and fifteen are lives in being and that the eldest grandchild (one of their children) will be identified by their deaths. However, that overlooks the possibility that A's children may die and that A may have a further child. In that event the new child must reach eighteen, if at all, within twenty-one years of A's death (so the second life interest is safe) but the eldest grandchild might well be identified (or even born) more than twenty-one years after A's death. The gift to the grandchild therefore falls foul

---

[29] The standard treatment is by Morris and Leach, *The Rule Against Perpetuities* (2nd edn); see also Maudsley, *The Modern Law of Perpetuities*.   [30] See p 14.

[31] Perpetuities and Accumulations Act 1964 (hereafter PAA), s 3. The Act specifies the relevant lives in being for this purpose, complicating the exercise further.

[32] The rule does not take account of modern reproductive technology. However, ss 27–9 of the Human Fertilisation and Embryology Act 1990 solve most of the problems: Law Com No 251, paras 8.32–8.35.

of the rule, though it may be saved by the wait and see provisions. In general terms, gifts to children of a living person are likely to be valid (so long as there is no age qualification greater than twenty-one years[33]) but gifts to grandchildren of living persons are likely to be void.[34] The possibilities may be regarded as preposterous by A, but that is irrelevant.[35]

The examples considered above concern gifts to individuals. A gift to a class (C's grandchildren, for example) involves a further complication. If the interest of any member of the class may vest outside the perpetuity period, then the gift is entirely void.[36] This applies where there are some members of the class whose interests are bound to vest within the period, even sometimes if their interests are vested at the time of the gift.[37] The logic is that the size of each share depends upon the number in the class, so even those with vested interests have shares which depend upon others.[38] The rule is relaxed by PAA, s 4(3)–(4) so that those whose interests in fact vest within the period are protected.

This brief summary of the rules serves as a warning that those drafting settlements must take great care not to contravene perpetuity rules. Although it is true that the worst outcomes have been mellowed by the Perpetuities and Accumulations Act 1964, many traps remain for the unwary. The more complex the trusts and the more interests are postponed to future generations, the greater the chance of invalidity. The Law Commission[39] has recommended sweeping away the present rules, replacing them with a requirement that gifts must vest within 125 years.[40] Interests not vested at that time would fail, but those that had

---

[33] PAA, s 4 saves gifts where a higher age is specified.

[34] It is necessary to add the qualification 'likely to be', as careless or careful drafting can change the picture. First, careless drafting of a gift to children. A standard trap was to make a gift to A's children vest after the death of A's spouse (who would be given a life interest). If A were unmarried at the time of the gift, then the possibility of marrying a presently unborn person, who might outlive A by 21 years, might invalidate the gift. There is a specific statutory 'fix' for this problem: PAA, s 5. Conversely, careful drafting can save gifts to grandchildren. The trust may provide that the gift to the eldest grandchild vests no later than 21 years after the deaths of A and his 2 living children. It then satisfies the rule and is valid. Such a grandchild might die before his or her interest vests in possession, but that slight risk is worth taking.

[35] A minor relaxation is that, since 1964, it is presumed that women cannot have children after reaching 55: PAA, s 2(1). Inability to have children can also be proved.

[36] *Leake v Robinson* (1817) 2 Mer 363.

[37] Gifts may be saved by a rule of construction that when the first share vests in possession then, subject to certain conditions, the class closes so that only those alive at that time may take. This complex rule is well described by Morris and Leach, *The Rule Against Perpetuities* (2nd edn), pp 109–25. If there is a gift to F's grandchildren at 21, and at the time of the gift F already has some grandchildren aged 21, then only those already born (of whatever age) can take. The purpose is to enable the minimum shares of the grandchildren over 21 to be established, so that payment can safely be made by the trustees. However, it may on occasion have the added bonus of saving the gift from the perpetuity rule, as it would in this example.

[38] Contrast a gift of £30,000 to each of the members of a class. This is valid for those whose interests must vest within the perpetuity period. It is a series of individual gifts rather than a class gift with a single fund (the latter is exemplified by '£300,000 to be shared between my grandchildren').

[39] Law Com No 251. The new rules would not, in general, apply to existing trusts.

[40] At present, settlors can opt for an 80-year period: PAA, s 1.

vested would be valid. This would be more generous than the present rules, as well as being very much easier to comprehend and apply.

## B. Words of Limitation

In past centuries, this was a highly complex area. Precise words had to be used to create a fee simple (G and his heirs) or entail (H and the heirs of her body). Failure to comply led to only a life estate being created. Indeed, even a grant 'to J in fee simple' operated to create a life estate![41] It might be added that the reference to heirs never signified that the heirs took any interest themselves. Rather, they signi-fied the type of estate taken by the grantee. As lawyers say, they were words of limitation rather than words of purchase.

The rules were relaxed during the nineteenth century and since 1925 the topic has become almost unrecognizably different from its strict origins. Today, a grant without any words of limitation passes the entirety of the transferor's estate.[42] In the usual case of the holder of a fee simple, a conveyance automatically passes the fee simple.[43] If the settlor wishes to create a life interest, then this has to be made clear. No particular words are required for this purpose: as the life estate was origin-ally the default grant, it had never required specific words.

As stated above, entails can no longer be created. Accordingly, we will not consider words of limitation for entails.[44] However, it might be noted that quite technical words were required by LPA, s 130(1) (now repealed by TLATA). The purpose in 1925 was clearly to prevent the accidental creation of entails, given that they can be misleading for those who are not fully aware of their characteristics.

The upshot is that words of limitation need no longer trouble us. There may be cases in which the grantor has failed to make it clear what estate is desired, but this will be resolved on normal construction principles, not the failure to use technical words.[45]

---

[41] Corrected by Conveyancing Act 1881, s 51; rules for wills were always more relaxed.

[42] LPA, s 60(1), 'unless a contrary intention appears in the conveyance'.

[43] A separate question, outside the scope of this analysis, is whether the grantee holds on a resulting trust for the grantor: LPA, s 60(3) and *Lohia v Lohia* [2001] EWCA Civ 1691, [24], [25]; (2002) 16 Trust Law International 231.

[44] TLATA, Sched 1, para 5 provides that a person who 'purports . . . to grant to another person an entailed interest' declares a trust for a beneficial fee simple. Does this provision require that the technical words for an entail are used? If so, and if the words would not have been sufficient to create an entail before 1996, then a legal fee simple will pass by virtue of LPA, s 60(1). This means that the absence of words of limitation still has some lingering effect in ensuring that the fee simple passes, rather than there being a para 5 declaration of trust. On the other hand, if para 5 operates without reference to words of limitation (which might cause greater uncertainty) then the para 5 trust will be more common and words of limitation irrelevant. A person subsequently taking an interest in the land would be wise to ensure that both grantor and grantee of the purported entail are parties to the disposition, thus avoiding any question as to the title.

[45] A recent example is *Charles v Barzey* [2003] 1 WLR 437 (PC).

## 3. Enjoyment of the Estates

The principal difference between the estates lies in their duration, a topic already considered. However, it was seen above that the holder of the fee simple possesses much wider powers than the holder of a life estate. One difference in their rights is illustrated by this example. Suppose a valuable prehistoric artefact is discovered whilst excavation for a new building is being undertaken. If the holder of the fee simple is excavating and finds the artefact, then he or she owns it and can sell it. On the other hand, if it is discovered by a life tenant then it belongs to the owner of the fee simple, not the tenant who discovers it.[46]

The old rules relating to waste determined what life tenants (and tenants under leases) were entitled to do and when they might be held liable for their stewardship of the land. Generally speaking, tenants are not liable for ameliorating waste (which improves the land) or permissive waste (failure to prevent the land falling into disrepair). The latter means that any duty to repair must be express.[47] On the other hand, there is liability for voluntary waste: conduct which reduces the value of the land. This includes activities which the life tenant is not entitled to do (opening new mines would be an example) as well as damaging the property (badly executed repairs are an example). The former category is especially interesting because it lays down exactly what benefits a life tenant is entitled to. In particular, the cases establish the extent of rights to minerals and timber. The final category is equitable waste. This is less principled, being 'a peculiarly flagrant branch of voluntary waste'.[48] It is significant because it is common for liability for voluntary waste to be excluded; there is still liability for the more extreme equitable waste.

These rules have a distinctly nineteenth-century feel to them. Do they possess any relevance today? As will be seen below, all new settlements take effect as trusts of land, under which trustees have unlimited management powers.[49] Any proposition that, for example, new mines cannot be opened seems overturned by this legislation. If powers are delegated to a tenant for life, then the same result must follow. Waste therefore no longer limits what trustees can do. Insofar as voluntary and equitable waste is based on the idea that the property should not be damaged, it appears that the equitable duties of trustees already cover this perfectly adequately.[50]

---

[46] The example is based on *Elwes v Brigg Gas Company* (1886) 33 Ch D 562 (prehistoric boat) where the occupier was a tenant under a lease.        [47] *Re Cartwright* (1889) 41 Ch D 532.

[48] Megarry and Wade, *Law of Real Property* (6th edn), para 3–103.

[49] In settlements governed by the Settled Land Act 1925 (not capable of being created after TLATA) the tenant for life could grant mining leases and cut timber despite the waste principles (SLA 1925, ss 41, 66). Fairness was established by requiring three-quarters of the receipts (one-quarter for existing mines) to be treated as capital (ss 47, 66). These principles were carried across to trusts for sale prior to TLATA: LPA, s 28.

[50] The traditional test is that they must act as prudent men of business: *Speight v Gaunt* (1883) 9 App Cas 1, 19; Underhill and Hayton, *Law Relating to Trusts and Trustees* (16th edn), pp 376–7. Before the 1925 legislation, Parker J had stated in *Re Trevor-Batye's Settlement* [1912] 2 Ch 339, 342: 'There is no question of waste in the ordinary sense, because it would be the duty of the trustees in case they purchased an estate to manage it in the ordinary and normal course of agricultural or timber cultivation'.

More problematic are the financial benefits of, for example, opening mines. If all the benefits were to go to the life tenant, then this would seem unduly generous, especially if the mined material were exhausted within a short period. The solution reached for settled land[51] was that three-quarters of the mining rents were treated as capital. However, there appears to be no provision for the modern trust of land. The answer cannot be found in the old law of waste, because that simply stated what could and could not be done. It had no clear solution for the destination of money received.[52]

The problem is similar to the purchase of a wasting asset, such as a short lease. In such cases the cost will be borne by capital, but the benefit may be gained by the life tenant alone. This issue was discussed by the Law Commission,[53] who concluded that the trustees should have unlimited powers and therefore maximum flexibility. It appears to be thought that general equitable duties can determine whether the power can be exercised.[54] Unfortunately, this misses the point that it may make sense to exercise powers only if there is some adjustment as between life tenant and remainderman. In some cases (such as opening mines) exercise of the power may be the only sensible course of action. At the same time, it would be unfair for the life tenant to take all the benefit. It is unfortunate that there is no guidance on how this is to be achieved, whether by way of quantum or procedure. The courts might accept that the duty on trustees to ensure a fair balance between the beneficiaries includes power to require financial adjustment. In appropriate cases, the trustees might exercise their powers only if the beneficiary who would take an unjustified benefit (such as a tenant for life if a new mine is opened) agrees to part of the rent being capitalized.[55]

Fortunately, the problem would be solved if very recent proposals by the Law Commission[56] are implemented. It is suggested that trustees should have wide powers of allocation of receipts and expenditure, to be exercised as part of their duty to balance the interests of the beneficiaries.

---

[51] See n 49 above; the same consequences applied to trusts for sale.

[52] The closest analogies come from two sources (on which see Pettit, *Equity and the Law of Trusts* (9th edn), chapter 19). First, as regards unauthorized investments held when a trust commences, a tenant for life is entitled to 4% income: *Re Fawcett* [1940] Ch 402 (the background was that unauthorized investments are likely to be risky and thereby pay a higher income). Conversely, where an asset is a reversionary interest which falls in (or is realized), an original value is calculated by discounting at a rate of 4% per annum. The difference represents income which is due to the life tenant: *Re Earl of Chesterfield's Trusts* (1883) 24 Ch D 643. Although neither is directly applicable to our problem with trusts of land, they demonstrate an approach that 4% income on the capital value is reasonable. This seems less generous than the 25% of mining lease rent permitted by the Settled Land Act 1925, s 46, though the examples are only marginally comparable.

[53] Law Com No 181, paras 10.8–10.9.

[54] In the nineteenth century these duties appeared to mimic the waste rules: *Campbell v Allgood* (1853) 17 Beav 623 (cutting timber).

[55] An analogy can be found in decisions whether to order sale of the land, when the courts may say that sale will be ordered unless the defendant agrees to something: see pp 138, n 124 (payment for occupation), and 177 (payment to creditor of co-owner) below.

[56] Law Com CP 175, paras 5.41 *et seq*.

# 3

# Co-Ownership: Requirements and Forms

What is co-ownership? What are the forms of co-ownership and rules relating to them? These are the questions considered in this Chapter.

## 1. The Meaning of Co-Ownership

In most cases it will be obvious whether there is co-ownership or not. Thus when two people together buy a house to live in as their family home and have it transferred into their joint names, it is clear that they are co-owners.

Co-ownership must be contrasted with the situation where two people enjoy separate ownerships of adjoining areas of land. Here there is no co-ownership of the combined area. It is usually clear whether or not there is co-ownership: there has been little litigation on the issue over the years. The single requirement demanded by all forms of co-ownership is *unity of possession*; this is what is missing if there is separate ownership of adjoining areas. Although unity of possession has attracted quite a lot of attention in the cases, this has related to its consequences for the rights of co-owners, rather than whether the unity exists. The essence of unity of possession is that each co-owner is entitled to possession of all the property: not just part of it. Although this is comprehensible for interests in possession in land and chattels, it must be remembered that co-ownership can apply to choses in action (including beneficial interests under trusts) and to future interests. Accordingly, we should not concentrate overly on physical occupation: unity of possession concentrates more on the nature of the rights of the co-owner. Suppose shares are held on trust for X and Y as co-owners. When we say that there is co-ownership, this entails that the entire block of shares is held on trust for X and Y, rather than that some shares are held on trust for X and others are held on trust for Y.

Even with interests in possession in land, there is no requirement that all the co-owners should remain entitled to physical possession of the whole. One obvious possibility is that they may (as freeholders) lease the land to one of their number, meaning that only that person will be entitled to occupy.[1] They remain

---

[1] For leases by co-owners to one of their number, see Law of Property Act 1925 (hereafter LPA), ss 72(4), 205(1)(ii). The effect of such leases as severing joint tenancies is considered by Fox [2000] Conv 208; see p 64 below.

co-owners of the freehold. Similarly, one of the co-owners may lease his or her interest to a third party.[2] But it is also possible that two parties may agree before the grant that one will occupy one part of the premises and the other the remainder, each bearing their proportionate part of the expenses. This was the situation in *Malayan Credit Ltd v Jack Chia-MPH Ltd*,[3] in which two companies took a lease of a floor of a building. The issue related to the form of co-ownership created (it was held to be a tenancy in common in equity): no question as to unity of possession was raised. One may ask why there should be co-ownership in such a case: at first sight, the situation would seem tailor-made for separate rights to the two parts of the floor. The answer may lie in two considerations. The first is that the case involved a lease and landlords may be hesitant about splitting premises in the way desired by the tenants. Co-ownership also possesses the distinct advantages that in a joint tenancy each co-owner is fully liable on the covenants (and therefore for the full rent)[4] and that forfeiture is likely to involve the recovery of the entire premises. The second consideration is that it is open to the co-owners to vary the arrangement in the future, without significant formalities being required.[5]

It was observed above that there has been little litigation as to whether there is unity of possession. There is one rather specialized, and today obsolete, exception. This lies in the context of party walls: walls which divide two properties. Until 1925 there were three basic possibilities.[6] The first was that the wall belongs entirely to one party; this is not of interest to us. The second and third possibilities were that the wall was held by the parties as tenants in common[7] and that each owned part of the wall.[8] The circumstances frequently failed to make it clear whether or not co-ownership of the wall was intended. Since 1925[9] there can no longer be a tenancy in common of a party wall: the statutory regime[10] introduced to regulate co-ownership was quite unsuitable for party walls. The idea that the wall might be sold to a third party is obviously a non-starter. It follows that co-ownership has, quite understandably, been driven out from the party wall area.

Leases, of course, are quite different from co-ownership. However, this does not mean that a tenant cannot be a co-owner. A very simple case is where there is a joint lease of a flat to a couple: they are joint tenants of the lease.[11] Here, of course,

---

[2] See the cases on severance in this context: p 64 below.    [3] [1986] AC 549.
[4] See *AG Securities v Vaughan* [1990] 1 AC 417, 469 (Lord Oliver), 473–4 (Lord Jauncey); *Mikeover Ltd v Brady* [1989] 3 All ER 618.
[5] An attempt to do so seems to have been the source of the dispute in *Malayan Credit*.
[6] Megarry and Wade, *Law of Real Property* (5th edn), pp 462–463. See eg *Cubitt v Porter* (1828) 8 B&C 257 and *Watson v Gray* (1880) 14 Ch D 192.
[7] The joint tenancy has never featured in this context. Apart from the fact that only rarely would there be unity of title, survivorship would be hopelessly inappropriate between neighbouring owners.
[8] In the first and third cases the non-owning party might have easements over the other's wall.
[9] LPA, s 38 (ownership of the wall is split between the parties with cross easements of support and user).
[10] Originally trust for sale; trust of land since Trusts of Land and Appointment of Trustees Act 1996 (hereafter TLATA).
[11] Although there is controversy as to exactly when there will be such an arrangement, it is undoubted that it can exist: *Antoniades v Villiers* [1990] 1 AC 417.

the co-ownership is between the two tenants and does not involve the landlord. However, other situations have caused more difficulty. In particular, the creation of tenancies in common for such a couple has been implicitly challenged. The leading case is *AG Securities v Vaughan*,[12] in which four people were separately given rights to a four-bedroomed flat; it was intended that they would agree between themselves how to allocate the rooms. Having held (entirely justifiably) that there could be no joint tenancy, the House of Lords proceeded to say that there could not be a lease and that the four must be licensees. This raises the question why there was no tenancy in common. This is a question of some difficulty because it is not immediately obvious why the four could not be tenants in common.

The question was not considered by the House of Lords, as the speeches concentrated on joint tenancy and the concept of exclusive possession. Both Lord Oliver and Lord Jauncey indicated that there was no unity of possession, but without explanation.[13] In the Court of Appeal, Sir George Waller had considered unity of possession, but in terms which related more to the relationship with the landlord than anything else.[14] Arguably, that relationship takes us back to the requirement of exclusive possession: it fails to answer the question why the four did not enjoy sufficient possession for unity of possession.

A number of possible answers present themselves. First, is there a problem with the very idea of lessees being tenants in common? The stress in *AG Securities* on the difficulty of showing exclusive possession may indicate that the House of Lords was thinking along these lines. Yet it is quite clear that lessees can be tenants in common.[15] This is obvious in the modern law as regards beneficial interests under a trust.[16] It was equally true before 1925 that lessees could be legal tenants in common.[17] This first answer must be discarded. The second possible answer is that problems may arise in accommodating the demands of the 1925 legislation, whereby there cannot be a legal tenancy in common and the estate (fee simple or lease, as the case may be) must be held as a joint tenancy on trust for the parties as tenants in common.[18] In a case such as *AG Securities*, such a trust is difficult to implement.[19] Although the lack of the four unities may not be a problem in the light of the statutory imposition of a joint tenancy, more troublesome is the likelihood that the parties would be jointly liable to pay the entire rent: an obligation that has not been undertaken.[20] This would not be a problem in the

---

[12] [1990] 1 AC 417.          [13] Ibid, 472, 474 respectively.

[14] Ibid, 436 (dissenting, but upheld by the House of Lords).

[15] A factor which calls into question some of the reasoning in *AG Securities*: Smith, *Property Law* (4th edn), p 372.

[16] *Re Selous* [1901] 1 Ch 921; *Malayan Credit Ltd v Jack Chia-MPH Ltd* [1986] AC 549. Many trusts, of course, involve assets other than land.

[17] Co Litt 199b. See eg *Cookson v Bingham* (1853) 17 Beav 262; *Encyclopaedia of Forms and Precedents* (1st edn, 1905), vol 7, p 662.          [18] LPA, ss 1(6), 34.

[19] See Sparkes (1989) 18 Anglo-American LR 151, though his solution is unconventional.

[20] See also *Mikeover Ltd v Brady* [1989] 3 All ER 618 and pp 45–6 below.

case of a joint purchase of an existing lease, as the purchasers could not limit liability in this way.[21] Where there is a grant of a long lease it is highly likely that the landlord will insist on the parties taking as joint tenants in order to avoid problems in enforcing the covenants. It is where there are short-term arrangements, as in *AG Securities*, that the landlord will be content for the liabilities to be split and, indeed, may insist on this to avoid the statutory protections for tenants (though these have been much watered down in recent years).

Perhaps the most intriguing way of explaining *AG Securities* is to observe that there was no estate which was held concurrently: it was a case in which the parties had separate agreements which were not identical. One can, of course, contrast cases in which the agreements are interdependent, so that they can be treated as a single agreement constituting a single co-owned lease.[22] This observation fits in with the 1925 legislation, which requires a trust to give effect to a tenancy in common. What would be the subject matter of the trust? Not the fee simple, as we certainly would not want to treat the freeholder's estate as being within the trust of land. If we were to say the lease, what lease would this be? One person may have a right for six months commencing 6 July and another a right for nine months commencing 13 September, quite possibly paying a different rent. It seems almost impossible to conjure up any single lease which could be held on trust by the two individuals.[23]

The reason why this is intriguing is that it raises the fundamental question of what we mean by co-ownership. Are we dealing with, first, a specific right to property which right can be said to be co-owned (as suggested in the previous paragraph), or secondly, merely a situation where two people concurrently possess rights to occupy property?[24] The well established statement that unity of possession is the sole requirement for a tenancy in common points to the latter. The clue to understanding this area may lie in the old rules for freehold estates. It seems fairly clear that there could be a tenancy in common between a holder of the fee simple and a life tenant.[25] In this context, it is difficult to point to any estate which is co-owned and this supports the idea that there could be tenancy in common where there are separate leases, or a concurrent lease and freehold estate. Although examples in the cases are difficult to find, it seems to have been assumed that such tenancies in common involving leases could exist.[26] In the modern law there is bound to be a trust of land (of the fee simple) if there is a life estate.[27] This means

[21] Cf Landlord and Tenant (Covenants) Act 1995, s 3(2).

[22] As in the co-joined appeal in *Antoniades v Villiers*.

[23] Though this explains *AG Securities*, it would not justify the failure to find a tenancy in common in the more difficult case of *Mikeover Ltd v Brady* [1989] 3 All ER 618, where the agreements were interdependent. [24] Or enjoy a chose in action.

[25] Co Litt 189a ('by one title and severall rights'; the earlier inclusion of terms of years supports the idea of a tenancy in common between freehold and leasehold estates); Blackstone, *Commentaries on the Laws of England*, vol ii, pp 191–2; *Wiscot's Case* (1599) 2 Co Rep 60b; 32 H 8, c 32. The absence of unity of estate excludes the possibility of a joint tenancy.

[26] 32 H VIII, c 32; Smith, *Law of Joint Interests* (1840), p 6; Carr, *Collective Ownership* (1907), p 31.

[27] LPA, s 1.

that, if life tenant and holder of the fee simple are tenants in common,[28] the consequences are limited: the regulatory regime of TLATA is already in place. It is in the leasehold setting that the issue becomes vital, as the lease itself does not itself create a trust of land and it is the tenancy in common which will lead to a trust of land.[29]

One suspects that these problems have not been adequately thought through. If we simply use tenancy in common as a descriptive label for situations where two persons enjoy rights of possession to the same land, then it does not matter much how the lines are drawn. As soon as legal consequences are encountered, however, severe problems arise. In the old law, were there problems where partition was claimed? Generally, the tenant would be entitled to the partitioned part only for life or the term of years (accordingly to the nature of the tenant's interest); certainly the partition would not affect a freeholder unless a party to the action.[30] Problems are more likely with the modern regulatory regime. An obvious question today is how the trust of land operates: in particular, what estate is held on trust?

It appears that the conclusion must be that unity of possession is all that was traditionally required for a tenancy in common: it was not necessary to find a proprietary interest over which the tenancy in common operated. However, it is far from clear that this can survive the 1925 legislation, at least where there is no estate (freehold or leasehold) which could sensibly and credibly be held upon trust.

## 2. Joint Tenancy and Tenancy in Common

As has been observed, modern English law recognizes two forms of co-ownership. The remainder of this Chapter is devoted to investigating the minimum require-ments for each and the principles determining whether the courts will find one or the other. There is no imperative reason for having more than one form of co-ownership and the question whether we should reform the present law is considered in Chapter 5 below, after the vexed question of severance of joint tenancies has been studied.

The major practical difference between joint tenancy and tenancy in common is that there is survivorship (*ius accrescendi*) in joint tenancy: when one joint tenant dies the property is owned by the surviving joint tenants and the estate of the deceased joint tenant gets nothing.[31] As well as being an ideal form of land

---

[28] It is not suggested that there is a tenancy in common whenever there is a fee simple and a life estate: it is viable only if the fee simple is in possession concurrently with the life estate.

[29] LPA, ss 1(6), 34(2). *Bull v Bull* [1955] 1 QB 234 illustrates the willingness of the courts to find a trust of land notwithstanding the apparently restricted scope of LPA, s 34.

[30] 32 H VIII, c 32, s 2. Cf Walker, *The Partition Acts 1868 and 1876* (2nd edn), pp 2–3.

[31] If the order of death is uncertain, the elder is presumed to have died first: LPA, s 184.

holding for trustees,[32] joint tenancy is well suited for family settings. In particular, where there is co-ownership of a family home it is natural that the surviving spouse or partner should be intended to own the property. Equally obviously, joint tenancy is not suitable in very many cases and this is reflected in the courts' preference for a tenancy in common in several types of situations.

At a more conceptual level, the nature of a joint tenancy is that each person owns the whole. It is this that explains survivorship: when one person dies he or she simply drops out of the picture. The survivors already own the whole land: there is simply one fewer person claiming ownership of the land. However, we should not get too carried away by this theory. Statute ensures that there are no advantages as regards family provision, inheritance tax, or liabilities to a creditor on the death of a joint tenant.[33] Nor does the law prevent joint tenants from transferring their notional shares *inter vivos*. By way of contrast, in a tenancy in common each person owns a share, albeit a share that has not been divided. Indeed, the 1925 legislation refers to it as 'undivided shares'.[34] That share can be left by will (or pass on intestacy) just like any other property.

## A. The Four Unities

The first unity is that of possession. As discussed above, it is the only unity required for all forms of co-ownership: it is what distinguishes co-ownership from separate ownerships of separate parts of a plot of land. However, joint tenancies require the presence of all four unities: they articulate in more detail the concept of each owning the whole. Although much of the law can be traced back at least as far as Coke, it was Blackstone who articulated the four unities as being essential.[35] These are the unities of possession, of interest, of title, and of time. We now consider what each of them requires. Later in this Chapter we consider how far they really are (and should be) legal requirements for a joint tenancy, as opposed to merely guidelines.

First, however, three points should be stressed. Though the four unities are said to be essential for a joint tenancy, it does not follow that a joint tenancy necessarily results from their presence. We shall see that both Common Law and Chancery recognized a tenancy in common in numerous cases, regardless of the four unities. The second point is that since 1925 a tenancy in common can exist only in equity. We have already seen that, for leases, the need for a legal joint tenancy may sometimes make it difficult to recognize a co-owned lease after 1925.[36] However, in most modern cases the only question is whether an equitable interest is a joint tenancy or tenancy in common. Finally, the unities are also important when a

---

[32] Since the Bodies Corporate ( Joint Tenancy) Act 1899, companies (which do not naturally die) can be joint tenants. This is especially important when companies are trustees.

[33] Inheritance (Provision for Family and Dependants) Act 1975, s 9(1); Inheritance Tax Act 1984, s 171; Insolvency Act 1986, s 421A.   [34] Eg LPA, ss 1(6), 34; cf (1944) 9 Conv 37.

[35] *Commentaries on the Laws of England*, vol ii, pp 181–2.   [36] See p 24 above.

joint tenancy is severed so as to create a tenancy in common. This aspect of the unities will be considered as part of severance in the following Chapter.

The requirement of unity of possession requires little further elaboration. It is sometimes said that each co-owner holds '*per my et per tout*',[37] meaning 'to hold the whole and nothing'.[38] What does this mean? The co-owners can be said to own the whole together, or to have rights to the whole (recognized by the right to possess the whole and by survivorship on death). Holding nothing is, perhaps, less easy to explain. It is best understood in the sense that neither has exclusive rights to any part of the land (the other also has rights of occupation) and cannot deal with the land so as to give rights to it to a third party. It remains possible for any co-owner to deal with his or her share: to sell, lease, or charge it.[39] The disponee enjoys (according to the nature of the disposition) rights as great of those of the disponor.

Unity of interest is required only for joint tenancy. It embodies the idea that the joint tenants have the same right: there cannot be a joint tenancy between a life interest and a freehold, or between a lease and a freehold estate. Unlike the conclusion tentatively reached for tenancies in common,[40] there really must be some interest which is jointly owned. This seems fairly clear from the books and the cases.[41] One point is worth mentioning in this context: it is no objection to a joint tenancy that one of the co-owners also has a different interest in the land. Accordingly, though a life interest and a fee simple cannot co-exist in a joint tenancy, it is possible to give A and B a joint life interest and A a fee simple in remainder.[42] This makes sense: unity of interest applies only to the interest which is claimed to be jointly held. Another aspect of unity of interest, which may be more troublesome in practice, is that the parties cannot hold shares of differing sizes: one cannot hold a one-third share and the other two-thirds, for example.[43] It might be thought that this does not matter if the survivor is going to get the entire property anyway. However, it is possible to sever a joint tenancy so as to create a tenancy in common (as will be seen in the following Chapter) and the size of the shares is vital at that stage.[44] Unity of interest ensures that if there are, say, three joint tenants, severance will result in each having a one-third share. Similarly, if

[37] Co Litt 186a.
[38] Co Litt 186a '*Et sic totum tenet et nihil tenet*'. See note c in the report of *Daniel v Camplin* (1845) 7 Man & G 167, 172; also note a to *Murray, Ash and Kennedy v Hall* (1849) 7 CB 441, 455.
[39] This is illustrated by a multitude of cases in the severance setting: pp 55–66 below.
[40] See p 26 above.
[41] Co Litt 189a: a tenancy in common exists where land is held 'by one title and by severall rights'; *AG Securities v Vaughan* [1990] 1 AC 417 is a modern authority.
[42] *Wiscot's Case* (1599) 2 Co Rep 60b. Greater problems arise when A and B are joint tenants of a life interest and the fee simple is later purchased by A. There is then a risk that A's life interest merges in the fee simple so that unity of interest terminates. This is discussed in the severance context: see p 57 below.
[43] *Cowcher v Cowcher* [1972] 1 WLR 425, 430. As will be seen below, unequal contribution to the purchase cost will generally induce equity to recognize a tenancy in common so that size of the contributions can be reflected in the shares in the property.
[44] *Goodman v Gallant* [1986] Fam 106.

the joint tenants are in dispute, the land may well be sold in which case each is entitled to a one-third share of the proceeds. In the case of dispute, it may well be important to sell the land and the size of the shares then becomes crucial as regards rights to the purchase money.[45] It is also possible that the parties might want different sized shares (as well as survivorship) for, say, tax reasons: this is not possible in a joint tenancy.

Unity of title means that the joint tenants must each derive their title from the same immediate source (usually a conveyance or settlement). Interestingly, it is dealt with by Coke as the primary distinguishing factor between joint tenancy and tenancy in common.[46] In practice, unity of title is rarely significant outside the severance setting. If R and S are joint tenants and S sells her interest to T, then R and T are tenants in common. R derives title from the document setting up the initial co-ownership, whereas T's title is immediately derived from the transfer by S. The joint tenancy is severed. From a theoretical perspective, it is not immediately apparent why this unity should be required. If X chooses to give property to X and Y by separate documents, it is difficult to understand why a joint tenancy must be precluded. Nevertheless, the law has been clear for centuries and must be accepted as being beyond challenge. It makes particular sense in the severance setting: the reasons for having a joint tenancy, with survivorship, between R and S (in the example above) are most unlikely to apply as between R and T.

Unity of time is the least important and most questionable unity. It means that the interests must vest at the same time. Thus if property is given to the children of F at the age of twenty-one, then it will vest at different times in the future as each child reaches that age.[47] In the cases, this is sometimes mixed up with unity of interest (some have interests in possession, others reversionary interests).[48] This enhances the doubts as to whether unity of time is a true requirement of the joint tenancy. Indeed, it has long been recognized that the requirement does not apply to uses or wills.[49] The modern equivalent to uses is the trust, so it comes as no surprise that the unity is not required where there is a trust.[50] An interesting question concerns the effect of the 1925 legislation. All co-ownership of land today has to take effect behind a trust, so what effect does this trust have upon the requirement of unity of time? At one extreme, it might be argued that unity of

---

[45] This formed the background to *Malayan Credit Ltd v Jack Chia-MPH Ltd* [1986] AC 549, in which a tenancy in common was found.      [46] Co Litt 188b *et seq.*

[47] Co Litt 188a, *Woodgate v Unwin* (1831) 4 Sim 129; *Ruck v Barwise* (1865) 2 Dr&Sm 510; *AG Securities v Vaughan* [1990] 1 AC 417, 472, 474.

[48] Turner LJ in *M'Gregor v M'Gregor* (1859) 1 De GF&J 63, 74 (commenting on *Woodgate v Unwin* (1831) 4 Sim 129 and denying that it created a universal requirement of unity of time). See Megarry and Wade, *Law of Real Property* (6th edn), para 9-006, n 25.

[49] Co Litt 188a; *Shelley's Case* (1581) 1 Co Rep 88b, 101a; *Sammes's Case* (1609) 13 Co Rep 54, 56; *Kenworthy v Ward* (1853) 11 Hare 196; *M'Gregor v M'Gregor* (1859) 1 De GF&J 63. Most cases talk about uses and devises, though there are fewer on devises. One example is *Oates d Hatterley v Jackson* (1742) 2 Stra 1172.

[50] *Kenworthy v Ward* (1853) 11 Hare 196 (made explicit, 203-4); *M'Gregor v M'Gregor* (1859) 1 De GF&J 63; Williams, *Real Property* (24th edn, 1926), p 199.

time is never relevant for the beneficial joint tenancy. Take the purported conveyance to the sons of F at twenty-one. As indicated above, this is a standard example of the absence of unity of time (assuming some sons are under that age). However, could the sons claim (on reaching twenty-one) a joint tenancy in equity? The problem, of course, is that the trust is imposed by law rather than expressly by the transferor. Dicta of the House of Lords in *AG Securities v Vaughan*[51] suggest that unity of time remains a test to be satisfied. However, this is difficult to assess because the case contains no reference to any trust and, as we have seen, appears to confuse issues of leasehold tenancy and joint tenancy. However, outside the leasehold context, it is unlikely that parties will attempt to create co-ownership (certainly not one with complex provisions which deny unity of time) unless employing an express trust or a will. It therefore seems that the practical impact of unity of time is minimal.

## B.  Words of Severance

Even if the four unities are present, it does not necessarily follow that there is a joint tenancy. Both common law and chancery courts recognized that the parties' intentions are paramount. Nearly all the cases deal with settlements, where it is the intention of the settlor which is crucial. Though it goes without saying that an express reference to tenancy in common or undivided shares will create a tenancy in common, the real question is whether an intention of a tenancy in common can be inferred. Words which lead to an inference of tenancy in common are called words of severance (signifying that each is not treated as owning the whole).

It will be seen below that there are particular circumstances in which equity has long sought to find a tenancy in common rather than a joint tenancy. Several eighteenth-century Chancery judges describe the joint tenancy as 'odious'.[52] Yet at the same time other Chancery judges were extolling the benefits of survivorship. Thus in *Cray v Willis*[53] Varny MR stated 'neither is there any thing unreasonable or unequal in the law of jointenancy'. At least in the context of the interpretation of the words employed, it is wrong to think that common law and equity took different approaches. The cases show that common law courts were ready to find a tenancy in common, given an indication from the wording employed,[54] whilst courts of equity presume a joint tenancy in the absence of any indication to the contrary.[55] A tenancy in common arises only in equity since 1925,[56] but we can

---

[51] [1990] 1 AC 417, 472, 474; see also the Court of Appeal, 432 and 436.
[52] *York v Stone* (1709) 1 Salk 158; *R v Williams* (1735) Bunb 342 (though this did not prevent survivorship from operating on the facts).                    [53] (1729) 2 P Wms 529.
[54] See eg *Lewen v Cox* (1599) Cro Eliz 695; *Fisher v Wigg* (1701) 1 Ld Raymond 622.
[55] Amongst older cases, see eg *Morley v Bird* (1798) 3 Ves 628, 631; *Kenworthy v Ward* (1853) 11 Hare 196, 204 (most of the cases concluding in favour of a joint tenancy implicitly apply this presumption). For more modern cases, see eg *Re Gansloser's WT* [1952] Ch 30; *Cowcher v Cowcher* [1972] 1 WLR 425, 430; *Pettitt v Pettitt* [1970] AC 777, 814.                    [56] LPA, ss 1(6), 34.

look to older cases both at law and in equity to determine whether effective words of severance have been used.

What words, then, are effective to create a tenancy in common? A initial point to stress is that the court may look at the disposition as a whole in order to decide whether there is a joint tenancy or tenancy in common: it is more than an automatic effect of certain words being used in the disposition.[57] However, the standard approach is to find a tenancy in common from the use of certain words, especially as the court is usually keen to avoid a joint tenancy. The following quotation from Lord Hatherley LC in *Robertson v Fraser*[58] indicates the prevalent approach:

I cannot doubt, having regard to the authorities respecting the effect of such words as 'amongst' and 'respectively,' anything which in the slightest degree indicates an intention to divide the property must be held to abrogate the idea of a joint tenancy, and to create a tenancy in common. Perhaps it would have been well if the Courts had held that in bequests, as in partnerships, every community of interest was to be considered a tenancy in common. But that has not been done. However, putting aside such words as 'alike' and 'equally'—for they may be considered more decidedly inconsistent with joint tenancy, inasmuch as the interests of joint tenants are very rarely quite equal, considering the difference that may exist in the ages of the legatees – it does not appear to me that such words as 'amongst' and 'respectively' are at all stronger than 'participate.' I have, therefore, no doubt that the word 'participate' is sufficient to indicate an intention to divide, and to create a tenancy in common.

In general, it might be said that anything which indicates division of the property, or having shares in it, is inconsistent with the very essence of joint tenancy that each owns the whole. Use of words such as 'amongst',[59] 'respectively',[60] 'equally',[61] 'divided',[62] 'between'[63] feature in most of the scores of cases on the question, often combined together. One type of case is where the working of the trust is inconsistent with a joint tenancy, as where a share is intended to survive the death of its holder.[64] Similarly, powers of maintenance[65] and, more clearly, advancement[66] may require each co-owner to have a separate share: something

---

[57] The 'general intent of the testator', as Lord Thurlow LC described it in *Frewen v Relfe* (1787) 2 Bro CC 220, 224. See eg *Clerk v Clerk* (1694) 2 Vern 323 (clear that survivorship intended, despite use of the words 'equally to be divided'); *Re Schofield* [1918] 2 Ch 64.

[58] (1871) LR 6 Ch App 696, 699, applied in *Re Woolley* [1903] 2 Ch 206 and, more recently, *Martin v Martin* (1987) 54 P&CR 238.

[59] *Campbell v Campbell* (1792) 4 Bro CC 15; *Richardson v Richardson* (1845) 14 Sim 526.

[60] Eg *Stephens v Hide* (1734) Cas t Talb 27; *Marryat v Townly* (1748) 1 Ves Sen 102; *Sutcliffe v Howard* (1869) 38 LJ Ch 472.

[61] Eg *Lewen v Cox* (1599) Cro Eliz 695; *Frewen v Relfe* (1787) 2 Bro CC 220; *Re Woolley* [1903] 2 Ch 206.      [62] *Booth v Alington* (1857) 3 Jur (NS) 835; *Payne v Webb* (1874) LR 19 Eq 26.

[63] *Lashbrook v Cock* (1816) 2 Mer 70.

[64] *Ryves v Ryves* (1871) LR 11 Eq 539; *Surtees v Surtees* (1871) LR 12 Eq 400.

[65] *Re Ward* [1920] 1 Ch 334; cf *Re Gardner* [1924] 2 Ch 243, from which it appears less likely that there will be a tenancy in common if there is a gift of capital rather than income: the income rather than the capital is affected by the power.

[66] *L'Estrange v L'Estrange* [1902] 1 IR 467; *Gant v Laurence* (1811) Wight 395; *Re Dunn* [1916] 1 Ch 97; *Bennett v Houldsworth* (1911) 104 LT 304.

inconsistent with a joint tenancy. This is particularly important because these powers are implied into all modern trusts, subject to any contrary intention.[67]

One aspect of many cases is that they depend very much on the drafting of the particular trust or will. An important factor is that survivorship is suitable for some cases but not others. If a person gives his property to his children, it may readily be thought that a joint tenancy is inappropriate: one would expect that a child's own family would be entitled to benefit from a testamentary gift.[68] On the other hand, if an elderly father leaves a house to two sons, in circumstances where they are unmarried and living in the house in late middle age, then survivorship is very natural.[69] When considering wills, the doctrine of lapse may point to a joint tenancy. Under the doctrine, a gift in a will lapses if the legatee predeceases the testator; the lapsed share falls into residue. Not infrequently, it may be desired that the surviving co-owners should share the property: this can be achieved if there is a joint tenancy.[70] However, the significance of this point is limited as lapse does not apply to a gift to a class nor (under the Wills Act 1837, s 33) to certain devises to descendants of the testator.

Occasionally, dispositions contain inconsistent wording: part indicating a joint tenancy and part a tenancy in common. An extreme example is 'as beneficial joint tenants in common in equal shares'![71] At one time, it was thought that this could be solved by the supposed rule[72] that the later of two inconsistent provisions prevailed in a will, whilst the earlier of two such provisions prevailed in an *inter vivos* disposition. Although there are some cases consistent with this 'rule',[73] it is difficult to find support for it in the present context save for a decision of Vinelott J.[74] It may be regarded as fortunate that Millett J has more recently doubted the rule and preferred to construe the document as a whole in order to elicit the true intention of the parties.[75] It might be observed that this is what courts in this context have been doing for many years, without feeling the need to resort to any rule.[76]

A final comment is that words of severance excited far more attention in the eighteenth and nineteenth centuries than they do today. Although there are a few modern cases, and fresh ones will doubtless continue to arise, family settlements are much less common than in the past. In contexts other than the family settlement, we shall see that other principles have been developed in order to find a tenancy in

[67] Trustee Act 1925, ss 31, 32.

[68] On the other hand, survivorship may work well if a child dies young: *Binning v Binning* (1895) 13 R 654.   [69] *Clerk v Clerk* (1694) 2 Vern 323 has similar facts.

[70] *Morley v Bird* (1798) 3 Ves 628, 631.

[71] *Joyce v Barker Bros (Builders) Ltd* [1980] CL 2255, noted [1980] Conv 171; also *Martin v Martin* (1987) 54 P&CR 238.

[72] See Megarry and Wade, *Law of Real Property*, 5th edn, pp 426, 529–30, describing the rule as 'quaint'. The rule is based on *Slingsby's Case* (1587) Co Rep 18b, 19a, though it provides little support.

[73] It is clearly articulated in *Doe d Leicester v Biggs* (1808) 2 Taunt 109, 113.

[74] *Joyce v Barker Bros (Builders) Ltd* [1980] CL 2255, noted [1980] Conv 171.

[75] *Martin v Martin* (1987) 54 P&CR 238.

[76] *Clerk v Clerk* (1694) 2 Vern 323; *Perkins v Baynton* (1781) 1 Bro CC 118; *Cookson v Bingham* (1853) 17 Beav 262; *Booth v Alington* (1857) 3 Jur (NS) 835; *Surtees v Surtees* (1871) LR 12 Eq 400.

common. On the other hand, it appears that the factors influencing the courts in earlier centuries are still relevant for modern society. So long as it is remembered that we are searching for the intention of the settlor or testator, and not applying earlier cases mechanically, it is appropriate to look at the earlier authorities.

## C. Equitable Preference for Tenancy in Common

It has already been seen that many Chancery judges viewed the joint tenancy as wholly inappropriate. It is described as 'odious',[77] whilst a tenancy in common is to be preferred as a 'usable interest'.[78] In settlements, we have seen that it was often possible to find a tenancy in common by reference to the wording employed. Other situations are apt to cause greater difficulty. For a start, the wording employed is less likely to be susceptible to an interpretation favouring a tenancy in common. At the same time, a joint tenancy (with survivorship) is even less likely to be appropriate outside a settlement. Where members of a family are involved (almost invariably the case in settlements), then survivorship can make sense. In most other contexts, it will be indefensible. The result was that equity implied a tenancy in common in certain types of cases. The legal title was still held as joint tenants, but equity compelled them to hold on trust for themselves as tenants in common.[79] Since 1925, the legal estate cannot be held by tenants in common,[80] so regardless of the basis for finding a tenancy in common (absence of one of the unities, words of severance, equity) we are always asking the question whether there is an *equitable* tenancy in common or joint tenancy.

### (i) Mortgages

It has long been the case that a joint mortgage is treated as creating a tenancy in common in equity.[81] The context is one of joint lenders (mortgagees) there is no equivalent rule for joint borrowers (mortgagors). It can readily be seen that that those jointly lending money are acting in a similar way to partners, another context in which a tenancy in common will be implied. If the money is contributed in unequal proportions, this makes a tenancy in common even more obvious.[82]

The single point which deserves attention is that mortgages commonly include a 'joint account clause': a declaration that the monies belong to the mortgagees on a joint account in law and in equity.[83] The purpose of this is to ensure that the

---

[77] *York v Stone* (1709) 1 Salk 158; *R v Williams* (1735) Bunb 342, 343.
[78] *Perkins v Baynton* (1781) 1 Bro CC 118.      [79] See eg *Morley v Bird* (1798) 3 Ves 628, 631.
[80] LPA, ss 1(6), 34.
[81] *Rigden v Vallier* (1751) 2 Ves Sen 252, 258; *Morley v Bird* (1798) 3 Ves 628, 631; *Vickers v Cowell* (1839) 1 Beav 529; *Steeds v Steeds* (1889) 22 QBD 537, 541.
[82] *Petty v Styward* (1631–1632) 1 Ch Rep 57.
[83] Since 1881 mortgagors receive similar protection where there is a joint account between the mortgagees: LPA, s 111. The section makes it clear that it protects the mortgagor rather than affecting the rights of the mortgagees *inter se*, so it is an even less significant pointer to an equitable tenancy in common.

mortgagor is safe in dealing with the survivor. Somewhat surprisingly,[84] the courts have sensibly held that the clause does not override the parties' clear intention to hold as tenants in common as between themselves.[85]

## (ii) Partnership and Trade

It was early accepted that survivorship is out of place as between partners: the relationship is one where it would be wholly inappropriate for the survivor to own the partnership property. This was accepted for merchants by the early seventeenth century[86] and there are many early cases applying the principle.[87] From an early time, the category has been broadly applied: the question is whether the relationship is one in which survivorship makes sense. To quote from Parke B in *Buckley v Barber*,[88] 'At a very early period the term "merchant" was very liberally construed—it was held to include shopkeepers (2 Brownl 99). The same principle of the encouragement of trade applies to manufacturers in partnership, and every other description of trade (Story, sect 342).'[89]

The breadth of the category is illustrated by the modern leading decision of the Privy Council in *Malayan Credit Ltd v Jack Chia-MPH Ltd*.[90] Two businesses took a lease of a floor in an office block, splitting the floor area between them and dividing the rent and expenses proportionately to the areas occupied. The Privy Council had no difficulty in finding that there was a tenancy in common in equity even though they could not be regarded as partners: the business concerns of the two parties were unconnected. As the judgment delivered by Lord Brightman states:[91]

It seems to their Lordships that where premises are held by two persons as joint tenants at law for their several business purposes, it is improbable that they would intend to hold as joint tenants in equity . . . . Such cases are not necessarily limited to purchasers who contribute unequally, to co-mortgagees and to partners. There are other circumstances in which equity may infer that the beneficial interest is intended to be held by the grantees as tenants in common. In the opinion of their Lordships, one such case is where the grantees hold the premises for their several individual business purposes.

Although the finding of a tenancy in common was bolstered by the way the rent and expenses were split (so that the shares were of differing sizes) it seems clear that a tenancy in common would have been found without that feature.

---

[84] Normally, a statement of the beneficial interests is conclusive: see p 38 below.

[85] *Re Jackson* (1887) 34 Ch D 732 (North J).

[86] *Hamond v Jethro* (1611) 2 Brown & Golds 97.

[87] *Jefferys v Small* (1683) 1 Vern 217; *Lake v Craddock* (1732) 3 P Wms 158; *Lyster v Dolland* (1792) 1 Ves Jr 431; *Jackson v Jackson* (1804) 9 Ves 591.

[88] (1851) 6 Exch 164, 180–1. See also *Re Hulton* (1890) 62 LT 200 (purchase of land for speculative reasons, but without any formal partnership: tenancy in common).

[89] But the fact that the individuals are described as 'merchants' is not conclusive, as they must purchase in that capacity: *Tan Chew Hoe Neo v Chee Swee Cheng* (1928) LR 56 Ind App 112 (brothers and nephew).                                                                    [90] [1986] AC 549.

[91] Ibid at 560.

This is tremendously important. Outside the family context[92] there will be few examples of beneficial joint tenancies.[93] It will be unusual to find cases in which individuals who are not in business buy property together (giving property away is rare outside a family setting). Nevertheless, some examples do arise. One would be if a group of householders were to buy adjoining land in order to prevent its development.[94] Another would be if two householders (both lacking garages for their cars) took a joint lease of a double garage. These are scarcely examples of partnership, trade, or commerce, whether considered from their joint perspective or their individual perspectives. Yet to allow survivorship to operate would be as remarkable as it would have been on the facts of *Malayan Credit*. Indeed, the more we look at *Malayan Credit*, the less significant appears the trade of the parties. It is true that it provides a link with the traditional categories, but its principal role is to establish that the parties had separate purposes for which survivorship (or any substantial idea of joint enterprise) is inappropriate. This characteristic may be equally important in many cases of individuals buying land together. In general terms, one may sympathize with Page Wood V-C[95] in his doubts whether a purchase of property should be distinguished from lending money on mortgage.

The categories of partners (broadly defined) and family settlements are not mutually exclusive. There are cases in which property was left to children and they then acted as partners in respect of it: farming land is a common example. In this context, the initial gift is generally to them as joint tenants: the partnership arises after the gift, so there is not a gift to partners. Accordingly, the question is whether their trading activities sever the joint tenancy so as to create a tenancy in common.[96] Generally the answer will be that there is a severance,[97] but in some cases simply using the land as farming land is insufficient to show a partnership or trading relationship.[98] More generally, the joint holding of property within a family setting does not necessarily lead to a tenancy common just because there is some element of trading. Thus it is possible for an uncle and nephew to hold farming land as joint tenants, as Lord Hatherley LC noted in *Ward v Ward*: 'their cultivating the property at their equal expense, and sharing the profits equally, is just what two farmers would do as to land of which they were joint tenants'.[99] Not

[92] Including both settlements and purchase of property by members of a family: *Aveling v Knipe* (1815) 19 Ves 441 (the deceased was the father-in-law of the other purchaser).
[93] *Goddard v Lewis* (1909) 101 LT 528 provides an exception, but the partnership point is inadequately considered.
[94] The fact situation in *Re Buchanan-Wollaston's Conveyance* [1939] Ch 738, though the nature of the co-ownership was not relevant.
[95] *Harrison v Barton* (1860) 1 J&H 287, 292; see also the note to *Jackson v Jackson* (1804) 9 Ves 591, 604.
[96] Severance is considered in the following Chapter, but its basis is generally that the parties have treated their relationship as one of tenancy in common. This often produces the same result as if they had purchased land during that relationship, though *Morris v Barrett* (1829) 3 Y&J 384 provides an exception.
[97] *Jackson v Jackson* (1804) 9 Ves 591 (bequest of a trade); *Brown v Oakshot* (1857) 24 Beav 254, 258. [98] *Morris v Barrett* (1829) 3 Y&J 384.
[99] (1871) LR 6 Ch App 789, 792.

surprisingly, it all depends upon the circumstances. An instructive modern case is
*Barton v Morris*,[100] in which an unmarried couple used their home as a guest
house. Even though partnership accounts were drawn up, Nicholls J sensibly held
that the true nature of the relationship was not one of partnership with separate
shares. This finding was made easier by the fact that there was an express beneficial
joint tenancy (the question being whether the business enterprise had severed it)
but the result would have been defensible in the event that the beneficial interests
had never been expressed.

One might ask whether these principles are affected by the modern trust of
land. In the nineteenth century, the paradigm situation was one where the legal
joint tenants used the premises for the purposes of the partnership. In the modern
law, does it make any difference that the user is likely to be by the trustees? As a
matter of principle, the fact that trustees carry on a trade on the premises should
be irrelevant to the nature of the beneficial interests: it is their trade rather than
that of beneficiaries. However, two factors combine to point towards a tenancy in
common. First, the trustees and beneficiaries are in many cases the same persons
(almost invariably when the land is purchased by the co-owners) and here the
old principles seem to continue to apply. Alternatively there may be a family
settlement, in which the trustees allow the beneficiaries to use the land.[101] Here
again, use of the land by the beneficiaries in the course of trade is likely to point to
a tenancy in common, this time by severance.

### (iii) Unequal Purchase

It has long been held that a tenancy in common arises where there have been
unequal contributions to the purchase of land. In a joint tenancy the (notional)
shares are equal and therefore cannot reflect the different contributions.[102] A
desire for survivorship is not inconsistent with unequal contributions, partly
because either party can subsequently sever a joint tenancy so as to create a
tenancy in common. However, it must be remembered that in a joint tenancy the
shares are equal on severance[103] and on distribution of proceeds of sale. It is here
that the joint tenancy fails to reflect the economic realities of the situation and it is
no surprise that equity finds a tenancy in common. A somewhat separate point is
that the ideas of partnership and unequal contribution frequently overlap: examples
from different periods are found in *Lake v Gibson*[104] and *Malayan Credit Ltd v
Jack Chia-MPH Ltd*.[105]

The principle has been recognized in many cases over the years.[106] Just two points
deserve attention. At one time it was thought that the unequal contribution must

---

[100] [1985] 1 WLR 1257.   [101] TLATA, ss 12, 13.
[102] Confirmed in eg *Cowcher v Cowcher* [1972] 1 WLR 425, 430.
[103] See *Goodman v Gallant* [1986] Fam 106 (p 39 below). It is suggested at 119 that unequal
shares on severance could be specified at purchase, but such provisions are very rare.
[104] (1729) 1 Eq Cas Abr 290.   [105] [1986] AC 549.
[106] *Rigden v Vallier* (1751) 2 Ves Sen 252; *Robinson v Preston* (1858) 4 K&J 505.

appear from the conveyance,[107] but this was not required by the later cases and has long been regarded as unnecessary.[108] The second point is that, unsurprisingly, the circumstances may point to a joint tenancy being intended even though the contributions are unequal. This is, of course, similar to the position in the partnership setting discussed above; it is an entirely plausible outcome in the family setting.[109]

In modern cases, however, the principle has been little considered. There is a good reason for this. The courts are used to finding a resulting trust when land is purchased, so that the beneficial interests correspond to the contributions.[110] This principle most obviously applies where land is conveyed to one of the parties, but it applies just as well where it is conveyed to the purchasers jointly. Absent any express provision for their beneficial interests,[111] the purchasers (necessarily joint tenants as regards the legal estate) will hold on trust for themselves in shares related to their contributions.[112] Where a home is purchased with a mortgage loan, the trust today is likely to be a constructive trust employing the common intention sanctioned by *Gissing v Gissing*.[113] Once there is a resulting or constructive trust in shares other than 50/50,[114] it follows that there has to be a tenancy in common: lack of unity of title means that it is impossible for there to be a beneficial joint tenancy. The point to stress is that the question in these cases is what the size of the shares should be: the issue of joint tenancy or tenancy in common is simply a consequence of the finding of the quantum of the shares.

It follows that there need be no special rule that unequal contributions give rise to a tenancy in common. The true rule is that unequal contributions are likely to give rise to a resulting (or constructive) trust in unequal shares and this can only be a tenancy in common.[115] As has been observed, unequal contributions do not necessarily lead to a tenancy in common in equity, just as other circumstances in which equity presumes a tenancy in common are not conclusive. We are dealing with the intentions of the parties, and if they intend a joint tenancy then effect will be given to this intention. This was recently recognized in *Winsper v Perrett*.[116] It was said that this intention, being oral, has to take effect as a

---

[107] Based on the formulation in *Lake v Gibson* (1729) 1 Eq Cas Abr 290 and as urged by *Sugden on Vendors and Purchasers*, p 698. See Friend and Newton [1982] Conv 213, 214–15 and Harpum [1990] CLJ 277, 298.

[108] *Rigden v Vallier* (1751) 2 Ves Sen 252; *Harrison v Barton* (1860) 1 J&H 287, 293, 295.

[109] *Harris v Ferguson* (1848) 16 Sim 308; see also below.

[110] Based on *Dyer v Dyer* (1788) 2 Cox 92.    [111] See p 38 below.

[112] *Pettitt v Pettitt* [1970] AC 777, 814 (Lord Upjohn); *Crisp v Mullins* [1976] 2 EGLR 103; *Bernard v Josephs* [1982] Ch 391 (50% shares on the facts); *Walker v Hall* (1984) 5 FLR 126, 133–4; *B v B* [1988] 2 FLR 490; *Springette v Defoe* (1992) 65 P&CR 388; *Huntingford v Hobbs* [1993] 1 FLR 736. The more recent approach as regards family homes is to apply a broad brush analysis to produce a fair result, rather than a strict mathematical calculation: *Oxley v Hiscock* [2004] 3 WLR 715 (60/40 shares).    [113] [1971] AC 886.

[114] The nature of the rights where there is a constructive trust and the shares are 50/50 is considered below, p 41.

[115] The presence of such a trust (which is exempted from formality requirements: LPA, s 53(2)) goes far to explain why the contributions need not appear from the documents: see n 108 above.

[116] [2002] WTLR 927.

constructive trust, requiring an element of detrimental reliance. Arguably, however, the court is simply finding that the presumption of a resulting trust has been rebutted on the facts, so that the original terms of the conveyance (joint tenancy) prevail. This should not require writing or detrimental reliance.[117]

### (iv) Executory Trusts

If the court is called upon to determine the detailed terms to be inserted in a trust, then a tenancy in common is often preferred.[118] Unlike the cases discussed above, this does not leave the same parties holding the legal title as joint tenants: the court is merely determining what their beneficial interests should be. Examples of this are likely to be relatively rare today, but the reasoning is to facilitate the power of advancement and it may be less likely to apply if that power is not relevant to the beneficial interests. It would be unsafe to assume, for example, that a remainder to the settlor's adult siblings would necessarily be a tenancy in common.

## 3. Joint Tenancy and Tenancy in Common in the Modern Law

One cannot but notice the extent to which this area of law is steeped in history. The basic concepts go back many centuries, whilst most of the cases are based on eighteenth- and nineteenth-century settlements. Today, the most common example of co-ownership is that of the family home. In this section, we consider how the rules operate today and the extent to which they remain defensible. Five categories for analysis might be considered: (1) the role of express provision for co-ownership; (2) the application of co-ownership in the common intention trust; (3) whether the distinction between joint tenancy and tenancy is drawn in the most appropriate place; (4) whether the joint tenancy deserves any place in the modern law; and (5) whether the courts apply appropriate criteria in deciding whether there is co-ownership of the family home. The last of these, significant and controversial as it is, lies outside the scope of the present book, which is to investigate how co-ownership operates, rather than general principles of law determining when interests will arise. The question of the future of the joint tenancy is an important one, but discussion of it is postponed until severance has been considered in the following Chapter. Accordingly, the first three categories are next investigated.

## A. Express Provision for Co-Ownership

It has been seen that a conveyance to co-owners as legal joint tenants is not determinative as to their beneficial interests. What happens if there is a statement

---

[117] See also p 40 below.
[118] *Mayn v Mayn* (1867) LR 5 Eq 150, following the Irish case of *Taggart v Taggart* (1803) 1 Sch&Lef 84; cf *Cogan v Duffield* (1876) 2 Ch D 44.

of the beneficial interests? Given that the rules are generally structured so as to give effect to the parties' intentions, one would expect the statement to be conclusive. Obviously, this has to be qualified by the requirement that the four unities must be present for a joint tenancy. It follows that an attempt to create a joint tenancy with unequal shares (no unity of interest) is doomed to inevitable failure. However, the most common scenario is that the transfer provides for a joint tenancy (not specifying shares) but one of the parties argues for a tenancy in common.

Why does that party desire a tenancy in common? Rarely does survivorship play a role. Rather, problems generally arise when the relationship breaks down and it has to be determined how much of the proceeds of sale each party is to receive. The problems are most likely to be acute if one party has contributed significantly more than the other, most especially by cash contributions with money owned before the beginning of the relationship. The leading case of *Goodman v Gallant*[119] has facts which illustrate this well. The plaintiff had a beneficial half share in the family home. When her marriage broke down, she and her new partner purchased her husband's half share. Taking a resulting trust type approach, one would expect her to have a 75 per cent share: 50 per cent originally owned and half the recently purchased share from her husband. Yet the conveyance to her and her new partner declared that they held as joint tenants. Some four or five years later that new relationship had broken down; she claimed a 75 per cent share.

Although there had been clear Court of Appeal authority that such express provision is conclusive,[120] dicta in *Bedson v Bedson*[121] cast some doubt on this. Subsequent dicta in the House of Lords[122] and decisions in the Court of Appeal[123] supported the conclusiveness of the express provision and this was confirmed by *Goodman v Gallant*. *Goodman* is a significant case because it contains a very full discussion of the issues and the cases and it settles the general issue for the future.[124] It may be seen as a beneficial result in that it provides much needed certainty and also an incentive for the parties to state, at the time of purchase, their beneficial interests.[125] This is particularly significant when one considers the enormous uncertainty and expense evidenced by cases involving claims to shares in the family home.

Yet there are some contrary arguments and, strong as the decision in *Goodman* is, it is not unqualified. The root problem is that the parties may well not appreciate what they are doing, sometimes coupled with an understandable assumption that

[119] [1986] Fam 106.     [120] *Wilson v Wilson* [1963] 1 WLR 601.

[121] [1965] 2 QB 666, 681–2 (Lord Denning MR) and 684–5 (Davies LJ); Russell LJ disagreed (p 689).

[122] *Pettitt v Pettitt* [1970] AC 777, 813 (Lord Upjohn); *Gissing v Gissing* [1971] AC 886, 905 (Lord Diplock).

[123] *Leake v Bruzzi* [1974] 1 WLR 1528; *Pink v Lawrence* (1978) 36 P&CR 98.

[124] *Turton v Turton* [1988] Ch 542, 546.

[125] Something demanded by Dillon LJ in *Walker v Hall* (1984) 5 FLR 126 and usually ensured by the modern form of transfer of registered land (see p 40 below).

their relationship will succeed and that the express provision operates only in that setting. One clear point is that the court has jurisdiction to adjust property rights on marriage breakdown, so the significance of the rule is limited in the matrimonial context. *Goodman*, of course, involved an unmarried couple. *Goodman* itself recognized that the conveyance could be rectified[126] or set aside for fraud or mistake. In practice, these exceptions are unlikely to be widely applied.

A somewhat different point concerns what is required for an effective declaration of beneficial interests. Not surprisingly, a beneficiary who is not a party to the declaration is not bound by it: an excellent example is if a couple buy property in their names with a contribution from parents.[127] On the other hand, it is not required that the beneficiary should formally execute the transfer containing the declaration. In practice it is not uncommon for purchasers not to sign a conveyance,[128] but so long as they approve the declaration then it is effective.[129] Insofar as the form of co-ownership is ultimately a matter of intention, this seems justified. Nor can it be argued that the declaration fails to comply with formality requirements,[130] as the declaration merely confirms the position as it appears from the legal title and precludes equity from drawing any other inference as to the parties' intentions.[131] But when is there a declaration of trust? In the past, it was common for transfers of registered land to contain a clause[132] that 'The transferees declare that the survivor of them can give a valid receipt for capital money arising on a disposition of the land', as this appeared on the printed form. Such a clause was not treated as a declaration of trust.[133] Although the reasoning is a little stretched,[134] the result is justified as it seems unlikely that the parties were aware of the possibility of survivorship.[135] These issues are less likely to arise today. For several years, the statutory form of transfer[136] has contained a clause which requires the nature of the landholding to be stipulated, one option being 'The Transferees are to hold

[126] *Wilson v Wilson* [1969] 1 WLR 1470 (solicitor did not appreciate that a brother was co-owner merely for a mortgage loan to be available).
[127] *City of London BS v Flegg* [1988] AC 54 (the money was not a loan to the couple).
[128] For recent comments relating to registered titles, see Law Com No 271, para 13.15.
[129] *Re Gorman* [1990] 1 WLR 616 (Vinelott J); *Roy v Roy* [1996] 1 FLR 541 (CA). If it does not reflect their intention then rectification would be available: *Pink v Lawrence* (1978) 36 P&CR 98.
[130] LPA, s 53(1)(b) (declaration of trust requires signed writing).
[131] *Roy v Roy* [1996] 1 FLR 541, 545–6. Lack of writing has never caused difficulty for the categories of mortgagees and partners, even though equity is not following the outcome at law.
[132] It ensured that a restriction (limiting the power of the survivor as a single trustee to sell) was not required under Land Registration Act 1925, s 58(3): *Mortgage Corpn v Shaire* [2001] Ch 743, 752. The presence of a restriction is an indication that a tenancy in common was intended: *Wright v Johnson* [2002] 2 P&CR 210.
[133] *Harwood v Harwood* [1991] 2 FLR 274; *Huntingford v Hobbs* [1993] 1 FLR 736; *Mortgage Corpn v Shaire* [2001] Ch 743.
[134] *Re Gorman* [1990] 1 WLR 616 was not easily distinguished.
[135] A point stressed by Neuberger J in *Mortgage Corpn v Shaire* [2001] Ch 743, 753. The same is true if the parties charge the land 'as beneficial owners' and these words are taken as merely importing covenants for title: *Harwood v Harwood* [1991] 2 FLR 274.
[136] Form TR1, introduced by Land Registration Rules 1997 (SI 1997 No 3037). See now Land Registration Rules 2003 (SI 2003 No 1417), Sched 1.

the Property on trust for themselves as joint tenants'. Selection of this option will clearly result in a beneficial joint tenancy.

In conclusion, it appears that certainty is secured by the use of an express declaration (whether of joint tenancy or tenancy in common) and that nearly all modern transfers to joint purchasers contain such a declaration. The danger, of course, remains that the significance of the declaration will be inadequately explained to the purchasers (or inadequately understood by them). In the absence of compelling evidence of such a mistake as to justify rectification, it will be difficult to oust the conclusiveness of the declaration. On balance, this does appear to be the preferable outcome.

## B. Co-Ownership and the *Gissing v Gissing* Common Intention Trust

When purchasers of the family make explicit provision for beneficial interests, it is very common for a joint tenancy to be chosen.[137] Survivorship is likely to be positively intended by spouses or those in long-term relationships. It is notorious, however, that the legal title is often held by one of the partners and the beneficial interests have to be found by employing a resulting or constructive trust (or, less commonly for concurrent interests, estoppel).[138] If the partners are found to be beneficial co-owners, are they joint tenants or tenants in common?

If, as is not uncommon, the shares are unequal, then a tenancy in common is the only possible outcome. However, it is not unusual for the shares to be found to be equal.[139] Will there then be a joint tenancy or tenancy in common? The question is rarely touched on in the manifold cases on the breakdown of relationships, simply because it is unusual for one of the parties to have died. When they are living it matters not what form of co-ownership subsists. Nor has it been significant in the modern cases on severance.[140] Nearly all these cases involve an express declaration of a beneficial joint tenancy. In the remainder, it has usually been conceded that there was a beneficial joint tenancy. Accordingly, we have to rely upon dicta in the *Gissing v Gissing* line of cases, though it must be remembered that the nature of the co-ownership is not relevant in the great majority of these cases and the point almost certainly has not been argued.

It is interesting that in two of the three cases in which one of the parties has died the court has assumed that there was a tenancy in common,[141] although there is

---

[137] Todd and Martin, *Matrimonial Property* (1972). Given the increasing purchase of property by those in less permanent relationships (or as friends) one would expect greater use of tenancies in common today. See also p 85 below.

[138] The same problems can arise if the beneficial interests are not stated in a joint purchase. However, this is unlikely today because the transfer form provides for the interests to be specified.

[139] The analysis in *Midland Bank plc v Cooke* [1995] 4 All ER 562 favours this outcome, but it is heavily criticized by *Oxley v Hiscock* [2004] 3 WLR 715.

[140] The only exception is *Rhoden v Joseph* 6 September 1990 (Kaye QC, Ch D), in which an express common intention of a joint tenancy was explicitly found.

[141] *Smith v Baker* [1970] 1 WLR 1160; *Re Cummins* [1972] Ch 62.

no discussion of the issue. The third and most recent case, *Chandler v Clark*,[142] inclines to a joint tenancy. However, *Chandler* is somewhat unusual as most of the purchase price came from funds to which the parties were jointly entitled. Beyond these three cases, most of the dicta assume that there is joint tenancy,[143] though Lord Denning has asserted the contrary.[144] It is true that a large number of cases refer to 'equal shares' as a result of contribution. Technically, these words connote a tenancy in common, but it seems that they are used in a non-technical sense to denote that the shares are not unequal in quantum. Similarly, references to property being owned jointly cannot be taken to connote a joint tenancy.[145] Of course, a tenancy in common is the most appropriate result on the breakdown of a relationship (the context of most of the cases) but this should not determine the outcome of the generality of house purchases: any joint tenancy (express or otherwise) can be severed if breakdown occurs. Just as the question is not clearly answered by the cases, it is left unclear by commentators: indeed it is rare to find the question addressed.[146]

Given this lack of clarity in the cases, does principle point to joint tenancy or tenancy in common? Four principal factors might be stressed. First, where reliance is placed upon an express common intention, then a clear intention of a particular form of co-ownership will be conclusive.[147] Secondly, where the courts rely on a pattern of sharing family assets and expenditure as a significant element in determining the parties' shares,[148] then it may be appropriate to find a joint tenancy. This can be justified because the nature of sharing fits the concept of survivorship. In addition, the situation is one where, had the parties thought about putting the beneficial co-ownership on the transfer, it is unthinkable that anything other than a joint tenancy would have been chosen. We must be careful not to impute intentions,[149] but here there is a common intention and the circumstances show what its full substance is.[150]

---

[142]   [2003] 1 P&CR 239; the question was remitted to the Master for decision.

[143]   *Pettitt v Pettitt* [1970] AC 777, 814 (Lord Upjohn); *Eves v Eves* [1975] 1 WLR 1338, 1345 (Brightman J); *Crisp v Mullings* [1976] 2 EGLR 103, 104 (Russell LJ); *Walker v Hall* (1984) 5 FLR 126, 133 (Dillon LJ); *First National Securities Ltd v Hegerty* [1985] QB 850, 853 (Bingham J). In the last 3 cases, the conveyance was to the parties as legal joint tenants. *Contra: Waller v Waller* [1967] 1 WLR 451, though it is unclear that the shares were equal (see Crane (1967) 31 Conv 141).

[144]   *Ulrich v Ulrich* [1968] 1 WLR 180, 186. This has been applied to a resulting trust arising on the failure of a purpose: *Burgess v Rawnsley* [1975] Ch 429, 438 (Lord Denning MR), 448 (Sir John Pennycuick). Outside the family home context, a resulting trust will give rise to a joint tenancy if there is equal contribution: *Robinson v Preston* (1858) 4 K&J 505, 510 (Page-Wood V-C).

[145]   See Bandali (1977) 41 Conv 243, 254–5.

[146]   For one exception, see Bandali (1977) 43 Conv 243, 254–7. Bandali considers that the cases assume a tenancy in common, though this is questionable.

[147]   See *Rhoden v Joseph* (n 140 above) and (if 'jointly' indicates a joint tenancy) *Re Densham* [1975] 1 WLR 1519.

[148]   *Midland Bank plc v Cooke* [1995] 4 All ER 562; but see n 139 above. The court was discussing the quantum of the share, not the nature of the co-ownership.

[149]   *Gissing v Gissing* [1971] AC 886.

[150]   The dangers of finding a tenancy in common in the family setting are considered at p 86 below.

Both these factors depend, to a greater or lesser extent, on common intentions either express or inferred from the relationship. What if the common intention is inferred simply from contribution?[151] Here our third factor might be introduced: if the contributions are equal, then a joint tenancy will be presumed.[152] This might well be our starting point for all cases, including those in the preceding paragraph, where the presumption is confirmed by the common intention. However, the fourth factor points in favour of the tenancy in common. Any analysis which places emphasis upon contributions as a determinant of shares (it is clear after *Gissing v Gissing*[153] that contributions are most important and that equal sharing does not result from use as family property) immediately uses analyses inconsistent with joint tenancy. We are not in the world of each owning the whole, but each having a share reflecting their contributions. In the great majority of cases this will involve post-purchase contributions in the form of mortgage instalments. We might note the test proposed by Lord Diplock: 'there is nothing inherently improbable in their acting on the understanding that the wife should be entitled to a share which was not to be quantified immediately . . . but should be left to be determined [later] on the basis of what would be fair having regard to the total contributions, direct or indirect'.[154] The stress here on shares, and in particular shares which may vary as to what fairness requires as time goes by, seems wholly inconsistent with the idea of a joint tenancy.[155]

It might therefore be thought that an analysis which takes a strong resulting trust basis is likely to lead to a tenancy in common, whereas one which is more family property oriented will result in a joint tenancy. Yet the cases scarcely support this. Lord Denning, always a proponent of family property, favoured a tenancy in common, whereas judges taking a stricter resulting trust analysis (such as Lord Upjohn in *Pettitt v Pettitt*[156]) have supported a joint tenancy.

The picture remains very confused. Absent clear contrary authority, it may be appropriate to apply to the family home the principle that joint tenancy is the presumed outcome. This may be supported because of the frequency with which those buying land as co-owners do in practice choose joint tenancy. This justification, of course, is usually inapplicable to short-term relationships and purchases by friends.

## C. The Appropriate Distinction between Tenancy in Common and Joint Tenancy

Many of the rules depend upon working out the parties' intentions and it is difficult to take objection to the principle that the intentions should

---

[151] The major category, at least until *Lloyds Bank plc v Rosset* [1991] 1 AC 107, appeared to restrict it to direct financial contributions.

[152] *Lake v Gibson* (1729) 1 Eq Cas Abr 290, 291; *Aveling v Knipe* (1815) 19 Ves 441; *Robinson v Preston* (1858) 4 K&J 505, 510. The preference for joint tenancy in cases of purchase has not gone unquestioned: see p 35 above.                                        [153] [1971] AC 886.

[154] [1971] AC 886, 909; recently applied in *Oxley v Hiscock* [2004] 3 WLR 715.

[155] This element may well serve to distinguish the Australian preference for a joint tenancy in *Delehunt v Carmody* (1986) 161 CLR 464. The context was one of an instalment purchase, in which property passed when it had been completely paid for: at that time it could be said with certainty and finality that the parties had contributed equally.                                        [156] [1970] AC 777, 814.

determine the outcome. Whether the courts have always reached the most appropriate result in specific cases may be doubted, but there is little to stop a court from finding the outcome it considers the parties to have intended. Two points deserve attention, however. The first is whether it is appropriate to continue to treat the joint tenancy as the default position. Is survivorship sufficiently special that we should require evidence that it is intended?[157] If we are dealing with non-family situations, then there is much to be said for reversing the present rule. At present, the partnership and unequal contribution rules combine to ensure that nearly all cases give rise to tenancies in common. Although this might be thought to reduce the pressure for any change, there are gaps and these would be covered by a new principle that any purchase of property gives rise to a tenancy in common (absent any intention to the contrary, of course).[158] In the contexts of family purchases, wills, and settlements, the position is much less clear. Survivorship often fits the parties' intentions very well, as shown by the popularity of joint tenancies when beneficial interests are declared.[159] To prefer a tenancy in common in such cases might well do more harm than good. Given that a tenancy in common is virtually always found in the non-family setting, this points against change.[160] These questions are related to the bigger issue of whether we should retain the beneficial joint tenancy at all, discussed in Chapter 5 below.

The second point to consider is whether the four unities should continue to be required. At a conceptual level they provide a useful explanation for numerous rules, including survivorship. They are often useful in determining whether there is a tenancy in common or a severance of a joint tenancy. Yet one cannot help feeling that the real point of a joint tenancy is survivorship. Is there any sufficient reason why the law should not permit survivorship where one of the unities is lacking? The most obvious situation in which this would be useful is where the shares are unequal in size, blocking unity of interest. The parties may want unequal shares in order to protect themselves should severance occur or the property be sold (so that a large contribution can be recognized if a relationship breaks down, for example) or for tax purposes (a person contributing 10 per cent of the cost may want survivorship, but not the inheritance tax bill for relatives that would accompany a half share[161]). Two aspects of this problem could be noted. It is not new to doubt the need for the unities: Challis observed that it is more justified by its 'captivating appearance of symmetry and exactness, than by reason of its practical utility'.[162] More recently, in *AG*

---

[157] Page-Wood VC certainly thought so: *Williams v Hensman* (1861) 1 J&H 546, 557–8. Some other jurisdictions prefer a tenancy in common, as in New South Wales (Conveyancing Act 1919, s 26; see also Sackville and Neave, *Property Law: Cases and Materials* (6th edn), para 7.4.5).

[158] See p 35 above.      [159] See n 137 above.

[160] Drafting a change so that is limited to the non-family context might well be difficult.

[161] A good illustration is an elderly person who purchases property with their only son or daughter.

[162] *Real Property* (3rd edn), p 367.

*Securities v Vaughan*[163] counsel felt able to argue that the four unities should no be treated as conclusive, even though the argument failed to persuade the House of Lords that there was joint tenancy on the facts. More recently, Lord Nicholls said of the idea that each joint tenant owns the whole:[164] 'I have to say that this esoteric concept is remote from the realities of life. It should be handled with care, and applied with caution.' This supports a movement towards a less conceptual analysis of co-ownership.

It may be that the four unities are too deeply entrenched in English property law to be dropped completely, but it may be feasible to relax them somewhat. As suggested, the main benefit would be to allow shares of different sizes to subsist within a joint tenancy.[165] It is more difficult to see how survivorship could operate if the nature of the shares is different (life interest and fee simple, for example) simply because there is no co-owned estate which could go to the survivor. As for the other unities, unity of title is generally relevant when one joint tenant sells his or her interest: the transferee holds by a title (the transfer) different from that of the other joint tenants. As will be seen in the following Chapter, this is a very well established ground of severance. Although there is much to be said for its abolition (because the other joint tenants need not be aware of it) this would have to be part of a root and branch reform of the area. The remaining unities are less troublesome. Unity of possession is required for all co-ownership, so it is not material as to the choice between joint tenancy and tenancy in common. By contrast, unity of time is a weak requirement which is rarely relevant today.

Greater stress on survivorship as the factor which distinguishes joint tenancy from tenancy in common leads to the question whether a joint tenancy possesses different incidents than a tenancy in common in any other respect.[166] It is frequently stressed that a single joint tenant cannot act alone.[167] Yet it is equally clear that one tenant in common cannot affect the other, whilst a joint tenant and a tenant in common can each act so as to affect their share.[168] There may be more in the point that in a joint tenancy obligations are owed jointly, whereas in a tenancy in common there may be separate obligations. This has been most discussed in the context of joint leases,

---

[163] [1990] 1 AC 417, 452: 'The "four unities," relied upon by the landlords, are not a doctrine of law but a textbook construction related to the joint tenancy (i.e. tenure) of a freehold interest. They originated with Blackstone as part of his passion for organising and formalising the common law. While they are not to be disregarded, neither are they to be slavishly applied and followed. They are a means of focusing on the straightforward general proposition that there comes a point at which people whose rights in something differ sufficiently cannot be said to be sharing it or jointly entitled to it.'

[164] *Burton v Camden LBC* [2000] 2 AC 399, 404–5.

[165] It might well be appropriate, however, to continue to presume a tenancy in common if the shares are unequal.

[166] One incident related to survivorship is the operation of lapse in gifts by will: p 32 above.

[167] This is at the heart of the principle applied in *Hammersmith and Fulham LBC v Monk* [1992] 1 AC 478 that the continuation of a periodic tenancy requires the concurrence of both of 2 tenants.

[168] The point is usefully discussed in *Hedley v Roberts* [1977] VR 282. A lease by one co-owner provides a good example; the controversial question whether this constitutes severance is not material for present purposes.

where it is thought that joint tenants must each be liable for the entire rent.[169] The joint tenancy may have some special features as regards third parties. Thus it appears that satisfaction of an obligation to one joint tenant may discharge that obligation, whereas the same may not apply to a tenancy in common.[170] It has also been held in Australia that the notice (or conduct) of one purchasing joint tenant affects the other, even though it would be otherwise for tenants in common.[171] It may be concluded that it is somewhat premature to assert that the incidents of joint tenancy and tenancy in common are the same apart from survivorship. Yet it is suggested that the differences are not substantial. A more convincing argument can be mounted that the four unities are outdated in their present form.

A related point is that it appears that a settlor can provide that survivorship shall operate in a tenancy in common.[172] This initially surprising proposition fits conventional analysis in that the settlor can always determine where the property is to go after death of one of the beneficiaries.[173] As the cases observe,[174] this form of survivorship cannot be precluded by severance. If we can combine survivorship with tenancy in common, is it not odd to maintain the four unities for joint tenancy?

## 4. Old Forms of Co-Ownership

A final point to note is that other forms of co-ownership were recognized in the past. Until 1925 there could also be tenancies by entireties[175] and coparcenary. Tenancy by entireties was limited to husband and wife: in essence it was a joint tenancy that could not be severed. Based on the idea that husband and wife were one person, it is inconsistent with modern notions of husband and wife having separate property rights. Coparcenary was something of a hybrid of joint tenancy and tenancy in common, with no survivorship. It was based on pre-1925 rules of descent of property on intestacy and can virtually never arise today.[176]

---

[169] See eg Smith, *Property Law* (4th edn), p 372, questioning the assumption to this effect in *Mikeover Ltd v Brady* [1989] 3 All ER 618.

[170] Cf the distinction between joint and several rights in contract: Treitel, *The Law of Contract* (11th edn), pp 577–8. Tenants in common may nevertheless undertake joint obligations: ibid, p 575, though the examples are where the obligations are undertaken separately from the initial tenancy in common.          [171] *Diemasters Pty Ltd v Meadowcorp Pty Ltd* [2001] NSWSC 495, [17].

[172] *Doe d Borwell v Abey* (1813) 1 M&S 428 (Bayley J; the other judges employ a different analysis); *Haddelsey v Adams* (1856) 22 Beav 266; *Taaffe v Conmee* (1862) 10 HLC 64. See Megarry and Wade, *Law of Real Property* (6th edn), para 9-011; cf Sparkes (1989) 18 Anglo-Am LR 151, 162, using the material to support the recognition of interests other than joint tenancies and tenancies in common.

[173] See *Parfitt v Hember* (1867) LR 4 Eq 443. This analysis is more readily employed if (as in all the cases cited) the co-owned interests are life interests.

[174] *Haddelsey v Adams* (1856) 22 Beav 266, 275; *Taafe v Conmee* (1862) 10 HLC 64, 78. This factor is less significant than it might appear, as it seems that severance of a joint tenancy can be expressly excluded: p 49 below.

[175] Married Women's Property Act 1882, s 1 prohibited new tenancies by entireties (*Thornley v Thornley* [1893] 2 Ch 229, 234); remaining ones were converted into joint tenancies by LPA, Sched 1, Part VI.          [176] For details, see Megarry and Wade, *Law of Real Property* (5th ed), pp 456–60.

# 4

# Termination of Co-Ownership; Severance

Survivorship on the death of one of two joint tenants will cause the survivor to be solely entitled. Leaving this aside, almost certainly the most common example of termination is where land subject to co-ownership is sold and the proceeds divided between the co-owners. Looking at this example reveals that we need to distinguish between two issues: when does the co-ownership *of the specific property* terminate and when does *all* co-ownership terminate. Sale of the property means that the land is no longer subject to co-ownership,[1] but the proceeds will be co-owned until they are distributed. Our interest in this Chapter is with the second issue: when is the relationship *between the parties* terminated? However, by far the main focus of the Chapter is on severance: converting a joint tenancy into a tenancy in common and thereby avoiding survivorship.

## 1. Partition

Partition is the splitting of the property between the co-owners. It results in separate ownership of the various parts, rather than concurrent ownership of the whole. In terms of the unities, it means that there is no longer unity of possession: the basic requirement for all forms of co-ownership. Splitting the proceeds between the owners following sale may be one example of partition, but the term is more commonly used where there is a division of physical assets (particularly land). In past centuries, partition was the standard and only way to terminate co-ownership when the parties failed to agree on sale.

Indeed, for several centuries a co-owner had a right to have the land physically partitioned. It ensured that disagreements as to the use of the land could be resolved and made sense for large settlements, but some very odd results could be reached. *Turner v Morgan*[2] involved the partition of a house; the court upheld an award of 'the whole stack of chimneys, all the fire-places, the only staircase in the house, and all the conveniences in the yard'. By 1868 the courts had power to order sale if it was more beneficial, but any co-owner could insist on there being sale or partition. Since 1925 sale has been the standard response to most

---

[1] Presuming that the requirements for overreaching are satisfied (see p 185 below).
[2] (1803) 8 Ves 143.

disputes; it is the only sensible outcome for disputes involving the family home, where physical division is rarely either feasible or appropriate. Partition requires agreement of all the trustees and beneficiaries: section 7 of the Trusts of Land and Appointment of Trustees Act 1996 (hereafter TLATA).[3] The power to partition applies only if there is a tenancy in common, but beneficiaries who agree to partition can easily agree to sever any equitable joint tenancy:[4] the limitation appears superfluous. Under section 14 the court can order partition if consent is refused, but such orders are very rare.

The modern case which comes closest to partition is *Rodway v Landy*.[5] It involved a doctor's surgery owned by two doctors; the question was what should happen when they fell out and their partnership was terminated. Sale was precluded by legislation relating to such property and the Court of Appeal held that the best solution was for the premises to be divided between the two doctors. In the words of Peter Gibson LJ:[6] 'It seems to me . . . self-evident that a property consisting of a ground floor which is divided by a central corridor and a second floor which can be divided into two lends itself fairly readily to division'. However, this was not an exercise of the power in section 7 to partition.[7] Rather, it was an exercise of the power to vary the occupation rights of the co-owners.[8] Nevertheless, the criteria applied by the court seem equally applicable to a decision to partition under section 7. It may be that the nature of the premises made partition an inappropriate solution to adopt as it would result in a permanent division. In addition, the court may have hesitated to override the lack of consent, which partition requires.

## 2. Severance

Severance is very different from partition. It operates as a conversion of a joint tenancy into a tenancy in common, so that co-ownership continues. Its practical importance lies in ensuring that survivorship is excluded. Though severance is possible for all joint tenancies, its major significance is where property is bought as a family home, but the relationship between the parties has broken down. In that context neither party is likely to want the other to get the property by survivorship. Following severance, the shares in the tenancy in common will be proportionate to the number of joint tenants.[9]

The observation that severance is possible for all joint tenancies deserves two comments. The first is that until 1925 there was, as between husband and wife, a form of joint tenancy that could not be severed: the tenancy by entireties.[10]

[3] This substantially re-enacts Law of Property Act 1925 (hereafter LPA), s 28(3). See also pp 152, 154 below.
[4] It is likely that an agreement to sever would be inferred from a unanimous agreement to partition, as partition is consistent only with there being a tenancy in common.
[5] [2001] Ch 703.     [6] At [35].
[7] Though frequent reference is made to partition, this is not partition under s 7.
[8] TLATA, ss 12, 13; p 126 below.     [9] See p 36 above.     [10] See p 46 above.

Its conceptual basis lay in the idea of husband and wife being one person, something which was dismantled at the end of the nineteenth century. Despite an apparently rogue suggestion by Lord Denning[11] that husband and wife still cannot sever, this is clearly not the law.[12] Quite apart from its statutory abolition, the very concept of the tenancy by entireties is not now regarded as 'sociologically acceptable'.[13] The second comment is that it appears possible for severance to be expressly excluded.[14] Although it is most unlikely that purchasers (at least those not living together) would choose to exclude severance,[15] it is more likely that a settlor might wish to ensure that no severance takes place. Nor does this seem all that odd. A settlor who is contemplating creating a non-severable joint tenancy of a fee simple could just as readily create a joint life interest with remainder to the survivor in fee simple. To insist that this cannot be achieved by a non-severable fee simple appears perverse. As will be seen very shortly below, today severance takes effect under LPA, section 36(2). Insofar as the section provides a right to sever (including the new method of a notice in writing) without any provision for a contrary intention, can this right be excluded? Given the arguments just considered, it seems preferable that all rights to sever, statutory or otherwise, should be subject to express exclusion.[16]

Whatever the form of severance, it must take place before death. Once a joint tenant dies, their interest terminates and the survivors share the property. The most important practical point is that a will cannot effect severance.[17] It remains possible for an agreement between joint tenants regarding wills to constitute severance,[18] but then it is the agreement and not the will which severs. The Law Commission did suggest at one point that a will might suffice,[19] but this idea has been viewed sceptically by commentators.[20] It has been noted that the

---

[11] *Bedson v Bedson* [1965] 2 QB 666, 678, repeated in *Jackson v Jackson* [1971] 1 WLR 1539, 1542.
[12] Russell LJ in *Bedson*, 690: 'without the slightest foundation in law or in equity'; *Radziej v Radziej* [1967] 1 WLR 659, upheld [1968] 1 WLR 1928; *Re Draper's Conveyance* [1969] 1 Ch 486; *Harris v Goddard* [1983] 1 WLR 1203.  [13] *Cowcher v Cowcher* [1972] 1 WLR 425, 430.
[14] *Jackson v Jackson* (1804) 9 Ves 591, 599 (Lord Eldon LC); *Re Schofield* [1918] 2 Ch 64 (Younger J); *White v White* [2001] EWCA Civ 955, [38] (Robert Walker LJ). Cf the doubts expressed by Butt (2001) 75 ALJ 7.
[15] Consensual severance would in any event remain possible, as all the beneficiaries acting together possess ultimate control over the property: *Saunders v Vautier* (1841) 4 Beav 115.
[16] Similar questions arise for powers conferred on trustees. These sometimes expressly allow exclusion (eg LPA, s 26(3) and today TLATA, s 11 on consultation; TLATA, s 8 on general powers) and sometimes expressly preclude exclusion (eg LPA, s 27(2) on payment to 2 trustees; TLATA, s 4 on powers to postpone sale). Where provisions are silent, see Megarry and Wade, *Law of Real Property* (5th edn), p 394 (on LPA, s 28, now repealed) and pp 124, 154 below.
[17] *Moyse v Gyles* (1700) 2 Vern 385; *Swift d Neale v Roberts* (1764) 3 Burr 1488; *Gould v Kemp* (1834) 2 My&K 304, 309.
[18] Most likely in the context of mutual wills: *Re Wilford's Estate* (1879) 11 Ch D 267; *Re Heys' Estate* [1914] P 192, 195–6; *Szabo v Boros* (1967) 64 DLR 2d 48; *Re Bryan and Heath* (1979) 108 DLR 3d 245. This area is discussed at p 75 below.
[19] Law Com WP 94, para 16.14 (1985); severance was omitted from the resulting report (Law Com No 181, para 1.3).
[20] Thompson [1987] Conv 275, 276–7; Tee [1995] Conv 105, 111–13.

person making a will could get the best of both worlds: survivorship would operate if the other died first, whereas severance would operate if the testator died first. Given that the other joint tenants might be unaware of the will, such lack of balance seems difficult to justify.[21] Another general rule is that the onus of proof lies, unsurprisingly, on the party claiming severance. In practice, this is most significant when there is a dispute as to whether there is a sufficient agreement or course of dealing.[22] Much as equity dislikes the joint tenancy, it was prepared neither to presume that there was initially a tenancy in common[23] nor to presume that there was an intention to sever.

Since 1925, joint tenancies have taken effect behind a trust;[24] in the case of a purchase the same persons will usually be both trustees and beneficiaries. Partly as a result of this change, LPA, section 36(2) makes provision for severance:

No severance of a joint tenancy of a legal estate, so as to create a tenancy in common in land, shall be permissible . . . but this subsection does not affect the right of a joint tenant to release his interest to the other joint tenants, or the right to sever a joint tenancy in an equitable interest whether or not the legal estate is vested in the joint tenants:

Provided that, where a legal estate (not being settled land) is vested in joint tenants beneficially, and any tenant desires to sever the joint tenancy in equity, he shall give to the other joint tenants a notice in writing of such desire or do such other acts or things as would, in the case of personal estate, have been effectual to sever the tenancy in equity, and thereupon the land shall be held in trust on terms which would have been requisite for giving effect to the beneficial interests if there had been an actual severance.

Three preliminary points may be noted. The first, obviously, is that the legal joint tenancy cannot be severed. This is to comply with the statutory policy[25] that in cases of concurrent ownership the legal estate shall be held by trustees as joint tenants. Accordingly, we ask only whether the equitable joint tenancy has been severed. Secondly, the existing methods of severance are retained. This appears from both of these paragraphs of the subsection. The reference to personal estate in the second paragraph is a little puzzling. It may be explained by the trust for sale employed pre-TLATA, whereby the beneficial interests were in the proceeds of sale (personalty). In addition, *Williams v Hensman*[26] (the case invariably taken as encapsulating the old rules) involved personalty, though it seems agreed that the equitable rules were the same whatever the property.[27] Accordingly, the reference to personal estate appears today to be an unnecessary

---

[21] As will be seen at p 58 below, severance sometimes operates without the other joint tenants being aware, but at least severance then operates on all the shares, regardless of who dies first.

[22] *Re Denny* (1947) 199 LT 291, 293; *Greenfield v Greenfield* (1979) 38 P&CR 570, 578.

[23] See p 30 above.

[24] LPA, s 36(1). Prior to the Trusts of Land and Appointment of Trustees Act 1996 it was a trust for sale. For more detail, see pp 106–8 and 112–14 below.

[25] See p 97 below (the same policy applies to successive interests).         [26] (1861) 1 J&H 546.

[27] *Nielson-Jones v Fedden* [1975] Ch 222, 229 (fully considered by Pritchard [1975] CLJ 28, 29–30; Megarry and Wade, *Law of Real Property* (6th edn) para 9-036, n 41).

(if probably harmless) leftover from the old trust for sale. Thirdly, there is a completely new provision for severance by written notice.

Against this background, we look next at the individual grounds for severance, splitting them between written notice and the old equitable grounds; public policy is also considered. Once the details have been considered, we consider whether a coherent and workable overall structure exists.

## A. Severance by Written Notice

In many respects this is the ideal method of severing a beneficial joint tenancy. Clearly, it allows a single joint tenant to sever contrary to the wishes of the others. However, it is required that all the other joint tenants are served with notice, so that problems of severing behind the back of other joint tenants are avoided. But why should we seek to avoid a hidden severance? Although the idea of taking the other party by surprise when they expect survivorship to operate is unappealing, what harm does it do? The context must be one where the other party (B) loses out by severance, that is, where the person severing (A) is the first to die. It is far from obvious that B has in any sense acted on the basis that there will be survivorship, the more so as A could give an effective deathbed notice of severance. Two rather different factors are more compelling. The first is that there is a danger that, without notice, the severance might be concealed if B dies first, so that A would benefit by survivorship if he or she in fact survives, whilst if A dies first his or her estate would benefit from a share by severance. There is good reason to limit any temptation to practise such fraud.[28] The second factor is not dissimilar. Without notice to the other parties, there may be a question whether severance in fact took place at all. Even without fraud, there may be evidential problems in proving severance. Written notice to the other joint tenants substantially limits such problems.

So long as a beneficiary is correctly advised, there is usually little difficulty in using this form of severance. Notice in writing must, of course, be given to the other joint tenants, but no special form of words is required. Walton J in *Nielson-Jones v Fedden*[29] stated that the notice must be irrevocable. However, it is difficult to comprehend what an irrevocable notice might be and the idea has been implicitly rejected by the Court of Appeal.[30] LPA, section 196(3) renders notices valid if 'left at the last-known place of abode or business in the United Kingdom' and notices sent by registered mail (including recorded delivery and special delivery)[31] are deemed by subsection (4) to have been delivered at the normal

---

[28] This danger was recently highlighted by Crown (2001) 117 LQR 477, 491.

[29] [1975] Ch 222, 236.

[30] *Burgess v Rawnsley* [1975] Ch 429; *Harris v Goddard* [1983] 1 WLR 1203. In particular, Lord Denning MR in *Burgess* considered the approach of Walton J (though not specifically as regards s 36(2) notices) to be erroneous. Though these cases do not directly address the revocability issue for s 36(2) notices, they endorse *Re Draper's Conveyance* [1969] 1 Ch 486, which Walton J had criticized on the basis that the notice was revocable.

[31] Recorded Delivery Service Act 1962, s 1; Postal Services Act 2000, s 125 and Sched 8, para 2.

time, unless returned.[32] It is therefore possible that a notice may be valid even if not received or read by the addressee, though the need for certainty justifies the statutory rule.

Thus in *Re 88, Berkeley Road*[33] a notice was sent by recorded delivery and received by the *sender*. Even though Plowman J held that the other person (to whom it was addressed) had not seen it, the surprising result was reached that the sender's estate could assert a valid severance. The more recent case of *Kinch v Bullard*[34] contains a more compelling analysis of the issues. In *Kinch*, the sender, the wife of the addressee, was commencing divorce proceedings. A notice of severance was delivered to the addressee's house at a time when he was in hospital following a sudden heart attack. The wife realized that it was no longer in her interests to sever: if he died she would benefit from survivorship. Accordingly, she picked up the letter as it arrived and destroyed it. The husband died without ever being aware of the notice and the question arose whether the severance was effective. Following the approach in *Re 88, Berkeley Road*, Neuberger J held that the effect of the legislation was that the notice was effective, though he recognized that the present case did not involve recorded delivery. On the facts this seems entirely proper: it is not a case where the person destroying the notice gets any benefit from the rule in LPA, section 196(3) that notices left at the premises are effective. Any requirement that the sender should continue to have an intention to sever until delivery was properly rejected: we need a clear rule to determine when a notice is effective.

However, two qualifications were considered. First, if the addressee is told of a change of intention before delivery of the letter then the notice may well be ineffective.[35] More interestingly, what would happen if the sender, having destroyed the notice, were to die first? Neuberger J considered that 'it cannot be right for the sender of a notice, who had intentionally taken steps to ensure that it did not come to the attention of the addressee, to contend that it was served on him . . . [section 196] could not be relied on by the sender as an engine of fraud.'[36] Though it is not readily compatible with *Re 88, Berkeley Road*,[37] this instinctively seems the preferable result. However, is it clear that there would be fraud? It is difficult to argue that the addressee relied upon there not being a severance, especially as we will see that severance in equity can be effective without notice. A broader concept of fraud, encompassing conduct which deliberately

---

[32] Applied in *WX Investments Ltd v Begg* [2002] 1 WLR 2849 (not in the severance context).

[33] [1971] Ch 648.        [34] [1999] 1 WLR 423.

[35] [1999] 1 WLR 423, 429. It is not clear how this is reconciled with the terms of s 196(3), though the notice has no effect until delivery. Cf postal acceptance of offers (though this possesses different features): Treitel, *The Law of Contract* (11th edn), pp 28–9.

[36] [1999] 1 WLR 423, 431. This analysis was employed in order to avoid a more general conclusion that interception nullifies the notice: the latter conclusion would have precluded the addressee from relying on the notice on the facts of the case.

[37] Unless the 'deemed to be made' wording of LPA, s 196(4) is too strong to allow the exception where recorded delivery is employed.

nullifies the statutory purpose that all joint tenants should be aware of the severance, is required.

Useful as severance by written notice is, it gives rise to two major difficulties. The first concerns the form of the notice. We have observed that no formal words are required. Whilst the absence of technicalities is to be applauded, it is less welcome that inferences of severance can be drawn from writing which is not directed towards severance. This leads to a temptation to dissect correspondence in order to see whether words supporting a severance can be found. In the relatively early case of *Re Draper's Conveyance*[38] a court summons requesting sale and division of the proceeds of the former matrimonial home was held to be a notice of severance, as severance would inevitably follow if the court ordered sale and division. Although approved by subsequent cases,[39] it has not been widely applied. In *Harris v Goddard*[40] a general request for the court to exercise its matrimonial jurisdiction was held insufficient to amount to a notice of severance. One suspects that the lawyers drafting the court applications in these cases paid no attention at all to severance and that the differing results were entirely accidental. Correspondence between the parties was considered in *Gore and Snell v Carpenter*,[41] in which an estranged couple were considering the future of two houses they owned, it being suggested that each should own one of them outright. Following the suicide of the husband, Judge Blackett-Ord held that the correspondence did not amount to a notice of severance; in particular, a proposal for severance in earlier correspondence was simply part of a package of proposals.

It is difficult to know how to react to this. From one point of view, it seems clear that joint tenancy was inappropriate for the parties following the breakdown of the marriage: it seems wrong for the court to apply a strict test for severance to succeed. On the other hand, the principal merit of severance by notice is clarity and certainty: something which could not be attributed to the circumstances of the last two cases considered above. Perhaps the decisions can be justified in terms of LPA, section 36(2), though severance by mutual agreement might have been appropriate in *Gore and Snell*.[42]

The second major area of difficulty concerns the forms of joint tenancy covered by section 36(2). It will be recalled that it reads 'where a legal estate (not being settled land) is vested in joint tenants beneficially . . .' There are three points to consider here. First, for reasons that are not obvious, it does not apply to settled land. Given that there are relatively few such settlements and none can be created after 1996,[43] this need not concern us too much. Rather more serious is the limitation to land: the reference to legal estate ensures that it does not apply to personalty.

---

[38] [1969] 1 Ch 486.

[39] *Burgess v Rawnsley* [1975] Ch 429; *Harris v Goddard* [1983] 1 WLR 1203; *Hunter v Babbage* [1994] 2 FLR 806.

[40] [1983] 1 WLR 1203; reluctantly followed in *Hunter v Babbage* [1994] 2 FLR 806.

[41] (1990) 60 P&CR 456 (Ch D). The case illustrates a classic dispute between the surviving co-owning spouse and the deceased's new partner.

[42] This was also rejected by Judge Blackett-Ord: see p 72 below.    [43] TLATA, s 2(1).

This means, for example, that if land is sold and the proceeds held by the trustees then this route to severance is barred.[44] This incomprehensible limiting of such a useful rule was discussed in *Burgess v Rawnsley*.[45] All the judges regarded it as unjustified,[46] but opinions varied as to what could be done. Lord Denning MR[47] argued that the section was declaratory of the law, so that severance by notice was already available for personalty. His ingenious argument was based on the wording of section 36(2) 'shall give . . . a notice in writing . . . or do such other acts or things as would, in the case of personal estate, have been effectual to sever'. It was urged that the word 'other' signified that a notice was of the same nature as the traditional methods of severance. Though the wording of the subsection does indeed support this analysis, Sir John Pennycuick expressed distinct doubts[48] and Browne LJ considered that the subsection played a positive and novel role.[49] Professor Hayton[50] seems right to argue that the sense of section 36(2) is that the person shall give a notice in writing or *otherwise* comply with the equitable routes to severance. To interpret it as urged by Lord Denning MR does violence to the final words of the subsection,[51] which assume that the notice in writing is not technically a severance.

The third restriction on the scope of severance by notice is that it requires that 'a legal estate . . . is vested in joint tenants beneficially'. This appears to mean that the trustees and beneficiaries must be the same persons. It will not apply where A and B hold on trust for C and D, nor (it seems) if F holds on trust for F and G, or R and S hold on trust for R, S, and T. Restricting notice in this way is almost impossible to justify, though there may be good reason for requiring notice to be given to all trustees and to beneficiaries. It might remain possible for the courts to construe LPA, section 36(2) in an imaginative fashion to avoid some elements of its unnecessary strict drafting.[52]

A quite different sort of question concerns the effect of giving notice. If there are three joint tenants, does it sever the joint tenancy as regards all three or does it merely sever the share of the party giving notice? If the latter is the case, then the other two would remain joint tenants of the remaining two-thirds, as between themselves. Although section 36(2) is not explicit, it seems that this is the more likely outcome: it produces the same result as severance by transfer of a share.[53] There seems to be no good reason why those who have not expressed a desire to sever should find that their rights *as between themselves* have been severed.

[44] Possibly (and more disastrously) it even means that notice is not possible after a *contract to sell* land: Pritchard [1995] CLJ 28, 31. However, this does not appear to be the intention of Walton J in *Nielson-Jones v Fedden* [1975] Ch 222, 229.                                    [45] [1975] Ch 429.

[46] Lord Denning MR: 'ridiculous' (ibid. 440); Sir John Pennycuick: 'quite indefensible' (ibid. 448).                                    [47] Ibid, 440.

[48] Ibid, 447–8. *Hunter v Babbage* [1994] 2 FLR 806, 814–15 (John McDonnell QC, Ch D) considers that there is support for Lord Denning from his fellow judges in the Court of Appeal.

[49] [1975] Ch 429, at 444.        [50] [1976] CLJ 20, 24.

[51] 'thereupon the land shall be held in trust on terms which would have been requisite for giving effect to the beneficial interests *if there had been an actual severance*' (emphasis added).

[52] Tee in *Land Law: Issues, Debates, Policy* (ed Tee), p 141.        [53] See p 56 below.

To conclude, severance by written notice is a very valuable form of severance. However, it is badly in need of statutory updating to remove unnecessary limits. It is more questionable whether legislation can provide clear answers to the question of what counts as a notice of severance. This must be dealt with on a case-by-case basis, though the authorities provide some guidance. There is no need for an explicit statement that the notice is to sever, but the courts will not readily spell a notice out of negotiations (even if severance is mentioned) or a general application to court in respect of the property.

## B.  Severance in Equity

In the words of Lord Denning MR,[54] uncharacteristically orthodox on this occasion, 'Nowadays everyone starts with the judgment of Sir William Page Wood V-C in *Williams v Hensman*'. The statement of principle reads:[55]

A joint-tenancy may be severed in three ways: in the first place, an act of any one of the persons interested operating upon his own share may create a severance as to that share. The right of each joint-tenant is a right by survivorship only in the event of no severance having taken place of the share which is claimed under the *jus accrescendi*. Each one is at liberty to dispose of his own interest in such manner as to sever it from the joint fund—losing, of course, at the same time, his own right of survivorship. Secondly, a joint-tenancy may be severed by mutual agreement. And, in the third place, there may be a severance by any course of dealing sufficient to intimate that the interests of all were mutually treated as constituting a tenancy in common. When the severance depends on an inference of this kind without any express act of severance, it will not suffice to rely on an intention, with respect to the particular share, declared only behind the backs of the other persons inter-ested. You must find in this class of cases a course of dealing by which the shares of all the parties to the contest have been effected, as happened in the cases of *Wilson v Bell* and *Jackson v Jackson*.

This quotation obscures the fact that there are two very different bases for sever-ance. The first is that if the four unities cease to be present, then a joint tenancy can no longer exist. This was recognized by courts of both law and equity, though since 1925 legal joint tenancies can no longer be severed. Other methods of severance owe nothing to the unities, but represent equity's dislike of the joint tenancy and its willingness to find a tenancy in common whenever possible: factors discussed in the previous Chapter.

### (i)  The Four Unities: An Act . . . Operating Upon his own Share

Amongst the unities, unity of title has played the greatest role in severance. If one joint tenant transfers his or her share, then the purchaser's immediate title will be this transfer. This is different from the title of the other joint tenant (or tenants) and accordingly unity of title breaks down: there can no longer be a joint tenancy.

---

[54]  [1975] Ch 429, 438.     [55]  (1861) 1 J&H 546, 557–8.

This is one of the most common grounds for severance and is established in countless cases.[56] In theory, one might ask how a joint tenant can transfer a share, given that joint tenants are said to hold the whole (together with the others) and nothing (separately).[57] Yet in practice this has simply not troubled the courts.[58]

One aspect of this form of severance deserves attention. Suppose that there are three joint tenants (J, K, and L) and J transfers her share to P. This clearly severs J's interest, but it leaves K and L as joint tenants as between themselves.[59] It follows that if K subsequently dies, L will take a two-thirds share and P (holding a severed share under a tenancy in common) a one-third share: at this point the joint tenancy finally terminates. This example demonstrates how joint tenancy and tenancy in common can exist alongside each other: K and L are joint tenants as between themselves, but together are tenants in common with P. We may say that there is an overarching tenancy in common with one of the interests (here the two-thirds share) being held on a joint tenancy. The essential point is that the joint tenancy is not over the land, but over the two-thirds share. It is the same if one of two initial tenants in common leaves his share to his two children as joint tenants.

This analysis raises the question whether there can be an overarching joint tenancy, with an interest under that joint tenancy being held by tenants in common. For example, could a settlor provide (admittedly improbably) that his son V shall be beneficial joint tenant with the two children (X and Y) of his deceased daughter W, the two grandchildren (X and Y) being tenants in common as between themselves? Unlike the example involving an overarching tenancy in common, this situation could not have been created by W (an original joint tenant) transferring to X and Y: that transfer would itself have severed the joint tenancy with V. Nor does it appear that the settlor can create such a situation.[60] It could work if V died first, as his share would pass to X and Y. But what if Y were the first to die? It is nonsensical to say that V would take by survivorship but that, relative to X, the interest would pass under Y's will: there cannot be two claimants to Y's share! The settlor may have intended V to take if both X and Y predeceased him, but co-ownership rules cannot distinguish between a tenancy in common between X and Y and a tenancy in common as between one of them and the other's estate. Unless we are prepared to recognize a joint tenancy where survivorship operates on V's share alone (which would anyway fail to give effect to the settlor's wishes), we seem forced to conclude that there is no unity of interest and accordingly no joint tenancy. What the settlor should have done was to create joint life interests with remainder to the survivor of V, X, and Y.

[56] Co Litt 186a, 193a–b; the link with the unities is most clearly expressed at 188b–189a.

[57] See p 28 above.

[58] *Wright v Gibbons* (1949) 78 CLR 313, 330 (Dixon J). Crown (2001) 117 LQR 477, 478 notes 'considerable logical difficulties' in the approach taken, though these difficulties have not caused trouble in practice.          [59] Co Litt 193a; *Wright v Gibbons* (1949) 78 CLR 313, 332 (Dixon J).

[60] The contrary appears to be assumed by McClean (1979) 57 Can BR 1, 2, n 7, in the context of severance by agreement. See also Mendes da Costa (1962) 3 Melb ULR 433, 441.

So far we have been considering unity of title. The other unities are less significant to severance. Unity of possession is required for all co-ownership: we have seen that termination of it results in partition. It is not relevant to our present analysis, as co-ownership continues after severance. Unity of time relates to something that is past: it cannot be later undone and hence is not relevant to severance.[61] Unity of interest may, however, be affected by subsequent events. Take two cases. In the first A and B hold on trust for C and D for life (the joint tenancy), remainder to E; C purchases E's remainder. Here the traditional approach is that there is merger of C's life interest into the remainder so that unity of interest is shattered: C has a fee and D a life interest.[62] What is the significance of this? If the life interest is for their joint lives then it will end when the first dies (regardless of what form of co-ownership is involved). By contrast, if it is for both joint lives and that of the survivor, then the estate of the deceased could share with the survivor, but only if there is severance. However, shattering the unity of interest is based on there being merger. Today, the approach to merger has changed so that it depends more upon the intent of the parties.[63] If there is any advantage to the purchaser in merger not taking place, then it is unlikely to operate. This would probably be the case if a joint remainderman purchased a life interest: the purchaser would want to keep the life interest alive so that he or she had exclusive rights to the property until the life interest holder died.[64] In the second case, F and G hold on trust for R, S, and T. R purchases T's interest. In this situation, the law does not say that R has a two-thirds share and S a one-third share (which would obviously shatter the unity of interest). Rather, the law says that R and S hold a two-thirds share jointly and R also has a one-third share. This means that (as in the example above involving K, L, and P) there will still be a joint tenancy as regards the two-thirds share.[65] It is plain that the way we characterize the effect of the purchase in each case is crucial to the operation of the unities. This characterization is not always obvious.

Severance by transfer of a share is so well established that there is little to add as regards its application to cases of outright transfer. Three points, however, deserve mention. The first is that it is possible to employ this method of severance whilst keeping the beneficial interest. For many years it has been recognized that a transfer to a third party on trust for the transferor suffices.[66] Now that statute renders it possible to convey land to oneself, it may be that this would also be an effective severance.[67]

---

[61] *Nielson-Jones v Fedden* [1975] Ch 222, 228.

[62] *Wiscot's Case* (1599) 2 Co Rep 60b; cf p 28 above.

[63] Megarry and Wade, *Law of Real Property* (6th edn), para 9-048, where the point is fully discussed; see eg *Re Fletcher* [1917] 1 Ch 339.

[64] A similar benefit may not be so readily found where a remainder is purchased by a joint life interest holder, as in the example involving C, D, and E.

[65] Co Litt 193a; *Re Hewett* [1894] 1 Ch 362; *Wright v Gibbons* (1949) 78 CLR 313, 324 (Latham CJ), 332 (Dixon J).

[66] *Cray v Willis* (1729) 2 P Wms 529; *Wright v Gibbons* (1949) 78 CLR 313, 332 (Dixon J).

[67] LPA, s 72(3); *Re Murdoch and Barry* (1975) 64 DLR 3d 222; *Re Sammon* (1979) 94 DLR 3d 594; *Freed v Taffel* [1984] 2 NSWLR 322; *Samuel v District Land Registrar* [1984]

However, it must be remembered that we are dealing with transfers of the beneficial interest rather than the legal fee simple: it is less clear that transfers to oneself will be recognized in this context.[68] Nevertheless, it seems probable that since 1925 a transfer to oneself will sever.

Secondly, equity extended severance to contracts to transfer.[69] Equity treats as done what ought to be done, so that in equity the future transferee has a different title. Now that only equitable joint tenancies can be severed, the rule operates without our having to distinguish legal and equitable severance: all we have to remember is that a contract to sell an interest (which today must be in writing) effects a severance.[70]

Finally, this method of severance (unlike all the others) requires neither the participation of the other joint tenants nor notice to them. It follows that it is possible to sever and to keep it secret. This result may be regarded as unfortunate and conducive of fraudulent activity,[71] though it is difficult to see how the other party could rely upon there being a joint tenancy: almost invariably it could be severed by written notice at any time. Despite being extremely well established (both in theory and in the case-law) this method of severance may be thought to fit uneasily with the other methods and to raise serious questions about whether, in any statutory reform, it should be retained in its present form.[72]

The scope of this first head of severance has frequently caused confusion in judicial analysis. Thus in *Hawkesley v May*[73] Havers J held that a declaration of intention to sever falls within the first head. As Walton J observed in *Nielson-Jones v Fedden*,[74] it is 'very difficult to understand the reasoning': the declaration is patently not 'an act of any one of the persons interested operating upon his own share' as required by Page-Wood V-C. Yet Walton J himself had treated an agreement to sever as shattering the unity of interest.[75] This seems equally erroneous. It may be that unity of interest is shattered as a result of the severance, but it is scarcely the immediate effect of the agreement. This appears to be part of an excessive

---

2 NZLR 697; Tooher (1998) 24 Monash ULR 422, 430–433. *Hall v Public Trustee* (2003) 150 ACTR 8 doubts this where notice is not given to the other trustee, though Butt (2004) 78 ALJ 233 demonstrates that this is unconventional.

[68] Although equity normally takes any opportunity to find a tenancy in common, note the views of Deane J mentioned in n 71 below. Note also the doubts expressed by Gray and Gray, *Elements of Land Law* (3rd edn), p 857, n 17.

[69] *Brown v Raindle* (1796) 3 Ves Jun 256; *Gould v Kemp* (1834) 2 My&K 304, 309; *Caldwell v Fellowes* (1870) LR 9 Eq 410; *Burnaby v Equitable Reversionary Interest Society* (1885) 28 Ch D 416 (even if voidable as a contract by an infant); *Re Hewett* [1894] 1 Ch 362.

[70] It should be remembered that we are dealing with sale of the beneficial interest. Sale of the legal fee simple is different (*Nielson-Jones v Fedden* [1975] Ch 222), as would be a sale of the entire co-owned beneficial interest by all the joint tenants acting together.

[71] See p 51 above. In *Corin v Patten* (1990) 169 CLR 540, 585–6, Deane J questioned whether severance should operate without notice to the other joint tenants, though he recognized that the cases support severance (see also *Hall v Public Trustee* (2003) 150 ACTR 8 regarding self-transfers).

[72] This may be linked with a wider reconsideration of the role of the four unities: see p 44 above.

[73] [1956] 1 QB 304, followed (without discussion of this point) in *Re Draper's Conveyance* [1969] 1 Ch 486. For devastating criticism, see Baker (1968) 84 LQR 462.          [74] [1975] Ch 222, 234.

[75] Ibid., at 228.

reliance by Walton J on shattering the unities, a reliance which was criticised by the Court of Appeal in *Burgess v Rawnsley*.[76] Although the four unities are some-times given prominence,[77] this is best seen as an unnatural limitation of severance in the modern law.[78]

*(a) Transfers: Less Obvious Examples* We have seen that an outright transfer clearly effects a severance, probably even if to the transferor. In this section we consider a few less obvious forms of outright transfer.

The first category to consider is where the transfer takes effect by operation of law. No distinction has been drawn between these and other transfers, with the result that severance operates in these cases just as in an express transfer. The most obvious case[79] is that of bankruptcy, where property vests in the trustee in bank-ruptcy. It has long been recognized that this gives rise to severance,[80] so that on the death of any joint tenant the trustee in bankruptcy will be able to claim the original proportionate share and no more.[81] The only question (more one of bankruptcy law[82] than of severance) concerns the date upon which the transfer takes place. Death after the appointment of the trustee in bankruptcy raises no problem, but what if the death occurs between the act of bankruptcy and the appointment? Before the Insolvency Act 1986 the vesting of property related back to the act of bankruptcy so that severance operated from that time.[83] Today, the picture is less clear as the doctrine of relation back no longer applies.[84] If there is no bankruptcy order before the death of the bankrupt, *Re Palmer*[85] holds that there is no relation back before death, so that no severance takes place. If there was a bankruptcy order before death (but no appointment of a trustee in bankruptcy), then the position is unclear.[86] However, even without severance the solvent survivor may today have to compensate the creditors.[87]

The second category of less obvious transfers concerns a declaration of trust. At first sight this appears simply not to be a transfer, but that response is too simplistic. In some Commonwealth countries it has been recognized, without

---

[76] [1975] Ch 429, especially 438. An 'unhelpful and even confusing starting point': Deane J in *Corin v Patton* (1990) 169 CLR 540, 573.

[77] Most recently, see Mason CJ and McHugh J in *Corin v Patton* (1990) 169 CLR 540, 548.

[78] Tooher (1998) 24 Monash ULR 422, 448.

[79] In the nineteenth century marriage sometimes had the same effect: *Re Butler's Trusts, Hughes v Anderson* (1888) 38 Ch D 286.

[80] In addition to the cases cited below, see Russell LJ in *Bedson v Bedson* [1965] 2 QD 666, 690.

[81] This may be advantageous or disadvantageous to the trustee in bankruptcy according to whether the bankrupt or the other joint tenant dies first. If there are three or more joint tenants then the joint tenancy (and hence survivorship) should continue to operate as between the others.

[82] See Megarry and Wade, *Law of Real Property* (6th edn), para 9-046; Tee [1995] CLJ 52.

[83] *Smith v Stokes* (1801) 1 East 363, 367; *Re Dennis* [1996] Ch 80.

[84] As recognized by Millett LJ in *Re Dennis* [1996] Ch 80, 104.

[85] [1994] Ch 316; Haley [1995] Conv 68.

[86] It was conceded in *Re Pavlou* [1993] 1 WLR 1046, 1048 that there was severance, but this predates *Re Palmer* [1994] Ch 316; cf Cretney [1995] All ER Rev 292.

[87] Insolvency Act 1986, s 421A (added by Insolvency Act 2000).

much difficulty, as a valid form of severance.[88] It may be justified because the beneficiary is just as entitled to the share as if there were a contract (when all agree that there is severance). However, this proposition becomes less clear if there are qualified rights under the declaration, so that there is no right to call for transfer of the share.[89] In England, a further argument in favour of severance arises because we are necessarily considering a beneficial joint tenancy under a trust. This raises the question whether the sub-trust constituted by the declaration has the effect of transferring the beneficial interest to the beneficiary, with the original beneficiary dropping out of the picture. This seems likely, at least if the original beneficiary has no active duties to perform,[90] and would therefore clearly constitute a severance. One objection to this form of transfer is that it might well be known only to the joint tenant declaring the trust, giving rise to possibilities of fraud.[91] This is indeed a good point, though it is a not uncommon feature of severance by shattering unities. Rather than questioning whether declarations should sever, the larger issue is whether non-notified severance should ever be recognized.

*(b) Dispositions Other than Transfers* All the dispositions discussed above are based on the underlying idea of there being a transfer; even a declaration of trust can be seen as a form of equitable transfer. Difficult questions arise when we consider other forms of disposition, some of which have received recent academic discussion.

It is quite clear that not all dispositions will sever. Where no form of estate is involved, it is clear that severance is out of the question. Thus granting a rentcharge or *profit à prendre* clearly does not sever.[92] It is easy to comprehend that the grantor's estate is fundamentally unchanged by such a grant; similarly, it would be inappropriate to regard the holder of the rentcharge or profit as a tenant in common with the other original joint tenant of the fee simple.[93]

This principle was applied in Canada[94] to deny that granting an option severs a joint tenancy. If we view an option as simply an adverse right affecting the land, this seems entirely correct. On the other hand, it can be seen as an equitable right

---

[88] In Canada, see *Re Mee* (1971) 23 DLR 3d 491; *Re Sorensen and Sorensen* (1977) 90 DLR 3d 26. Its possibility has also been recognized in Australia: *Freed v Taffel* [1984] 2 NSWLR 322, 325. Commentators have been supportive: McClean (1979) 57 Can BR 1, 13; Butt (1982) 9 Syd LR 568, 572–3.

[89] In *Re Mee* (1971) 23 DLR 3d 491, where the trust was for a son at 21, there was still held to be severance.

[90] *Grainge v Wilberforce* (1889) 5 TLR 436; the idea of the beneficiary dropping out of the picture is criticized by Green (1984) 47 MLR 385, 396–8. The issue is commonly discussed in the context of formality requirements for dispositions of equitable interests: see eg Pettit, *Equity and the Law of Trusts* (9th edn), pp 83–4.

[91] Similar to the arguments discussed at pp 51, 58 above. The danger is stressed by Crown (2001) 117 LQR 477, 491.        [92] Co Litt 185a; *Lord Abergavenny's Case* (1607) 6 Co Rep 78b.

[93] Tenants in common can, of course, have differing estates (and there can be co-ownership of rentcharges or profits). However, it seems to take the concept too far to apply it to (for example) profit and fee simple.        [94] *Re McKee and National Trust Co Ltd* (1975) 56 DLR 3d 190.

to the fee simple (or other interest jointly held), analogous to a normal estate contract. This raises the difficult question of the effect of an option. Though the area has given rise to some difficulty, the better view is that the grantor of the option does not hold the land on trust,[95] though of course the holder has an equitable interest. This supports the Canadian analysis.[96]

Dispositions which cause the greatest difficulty are those involving a right to possession: most obviously mortgages and leases. It is obvious that, without severance, these dispositions may prove worthless if the grantor dies soon thereafter. Though this problem is not limited to these dispositions, they are likely to arise in a commercial setting, involving a significant financial commitment on the part of the grantee. Before looking at specific dispositions, two points should be made. The first is that it is not simply a matter of asking whether there is severance or not: more sophisticated analyses may be available. Thus it is arguable that there may be severance solely so as to ensure that the disponee is not prejudiced by the death of the disponor, or survivorship may be suspended during the life of the disposition. These possibilities have been argued mainly for leases.

The second point is that deliberate dispositions (other than transfer) of beneficial joint tenancies are now rare.[97] Though a beneficial joint tenancy possesses economic value, it would be a very rash person who took a lease of the right or a mortgage over it: the benefits might well prove illusory. The cases reveal that, though these dispositions are not uncommon, they occur unintentionally. Three types of case can be identified. The first is where the signature of one joint tenant has been forged by another or has been obtained by undue influence affecting a chargee: the disposition takes effect against the beneficial right of the 'guilty' co-owner.[98] The second type of case similarly involves a disponee who believes that there is an effective disposition over the entire property. It applies where the disponee is unaware of a joint tenancy which has arisen under a constructive or resulting trust[99] or is unable to take advantage of a disclaimer by a joint tenant because of undue influence (usually exerted by the other joint tenant).[100] In such cases there is normally a valid legal disposition, but it is subject to the equitable rights of the other joint tenant. The third type of case is where there is a charging

[95] See Tromans [1984] CLJ 55, 57–61 and the authors and cases cited there. The strongest authority is probably *Edwards v West* (1878) 7 Ch D 858.

[96] Though that was based, surprisingly, on unity of interest (the option was in favour of another joint tenant) rather than on unity of title. [97] Nield [2001] Conv 462.

[98] LPA, s 63. Any doubt about the operation of this section (*Cedar Holdings Ltd v Green* [1981] Ch 129, rejected in *Ahmed v Kendrick* (1987) 56 P&CR 120) has evaporated following the abolition of the doctrine of conversion (in trusts for sale) by TLATA, s 3. Recent examples are *Abbey National plc v Moss* (1993) 26 HLR 249; *Mortgage Corpn v Shaire* [2001] Ch 743; *Bank of Ireland Home Mortgages Ltd v Bell* [2001] 2 FLR 809; *First National Bank plc v Achampong* [2004] 1 FCR 18; [2003] EWCA Civ 487, [54]; *Edwards v Lloyds TSB Bank plc* [2004] EWHC 1745 (Ch), [16]–[22].

[99] Usually binding on the disponee because the claimant is in actual occupation of the land (*Williams & Glyn's Bank Ltd v Boland* [1981] AC 487; Land Registration Act 2002, Sched 3, para 2). See eg *Bank of Baroda v Dhillon* [1998] 1 FLR 524.

[100] Following the principles in *Barclays Bank plc v O'Brien* [1994] 1 AC 180 and *Royal Bank of Scotland plc v Etridge (No 2)* [2002] 2 AC 773.

order to secure an otherwise unsecured obligation.[101] Here the chargee did not set out to take security: the charge is subsequently imposed by a court.

Although there are many examples of these unintentional dispositions of equitable joint tenancies (virtually all by way of charge, rather than lease) none has raised severance issues. Almost invariably, the question has been whether the chargee can have the land sold. When assessing the rules, how relevant is it that almost all dispositions are unintentional? Crown[102] has argued that 'There is a simple remedy for this problem and that is to require the borrower to sever the joint tenancy . . . '. This argument is flawed, as the lender is invariably unaware that the security is over one beneficial joint tenant's interest. It is therefore tempting to say that severance should be widely recognized in order to protect the disponee; however, that might be too generous. The disponee is fortunate that the disponor has any beneficial interest on which the disposition can bite: it is unclear why the law should extend legal principles to improve the protection.

We can now investigate specific dispositions. The first is the mortgage or charge. Prior to 1925 a typical mortgage would take the form of a conveyance of the property, with a right for the mortgagor to redeem. It is not difficult to see that this gives rise to severance: the conveyance attracts the rules applying to transfers.[103] So much is uncontroversial (it may be an example of less obvious transfers) but what is the effect of a charge? Since 1925, of course, mortgages of legal estates can take effect as only as long leases or charges. Indeed, since the Land Registration Act 2002[104] the charge is the only vehicle for registered estates. However, we are dealing with mortgages of equitable interests (only an equitable joint tenancy can be severed) and the above rules are inapplicable to equitable interests: these can still be mortgaged by outright transfer. Nevertheless, we have just seen that mortgages of equitable interests normally take effect unintentionally, as a consequence of a failed attempt to mortgage the legal estate. Given that the attempted mortgage of the legal estate is invariably by way of charge, it follows that there will be a charge (and not a transfer) of the equitable estate.[105]

As a matter of principle, there is a strong argument that a charge should not effect a severance; there is no transfer and the charge may be seen as a encumbrance similar to a rentcharge or profit (neither of which severs).[106] Unfortunately, the authorities provide a confused picture. In England the cases uniformly support severance,[107] though the contrast between charges and mortgages

---

[101] See eg *Lloyds Bank plc v Byrne & Byrne* [1993] 1 FLR 369.
[102] (2001) 117 LQR 477, 484.     [103] *York v Stone* (1709) 1 Salk 158.     [104] S 23(1)(a).
[105] A charging order clearly gives rise to charge: Charging Orders Act 1979, s 3(4).
[106] Clearly expressed by McClean (1979) 57 Can BR 1, 12–13: 'correct application of the common law rules based on the destruction of one of the four unities'.
[107] *Bedson v Bedson* [1965] 2 QB 666, 690; *Cedar Holdings Ltd v Green* [1981] Ch 129, 138; *First National Securities Ltd v Hegerty* [1985] QB 850, 854 (Bingham J, upheld by the Court of Appeal). See also *Re Sharer* (1912) 57 SJ 60; *Midland Bank plc v Pike* [1988] 2 All ER 434; *Monarch Aluminium v Rickman* [1989] CLY 1526; *First National Bank plc v Achampong* [2004] 1 FCR 18; [2003] EWCA Civ 487, [54].

has never been raised. It seems to have been assumed that the same principles apply to both. Indeed, the severance issue has virtually never been relevant on the facts of the cases. In Commonwealth Torrens jurisdictions, awareness that mortgages take effect by way of charge has long been the basis for doubts as to severance.[108] Although there is no great weight of case-law, the issue was fully considered in *Lyons v Lyons* and severance was rejected.[109] Prima facie, principle supports the Commonwealth analysis. This is buttressed by a feeling that severance should not be expanded where the other joint tenant is ignorant of it.[110]

Are there arguments in favour of the English cases? Perhaps the strongest point is that the use of charges is commonly a technical substitution for the pre-1925 transfer of the interest: the reforms were not intended to disadvantage the mortgagee.[111] There is also the practical point that a security over an interest liable to disappear on death is a patently weak security. This has led to arguments that the parties must have intended severance,[112] but this is difficult to comprehend. Whilst the joint tenants can sever by agreement, there is no way in which the intention of one joint tenant and a third party can sever.[113] Nevertheless, an argument remains that the law should not provide a trap for chargees. In policy terms, the challenge is to resolve the reasonable expectations of chargees with the desire to limit severance where the other joint tenant may be unaware of it. Given the doctrinal arguments against severance and the fact that these charges are almost invariably created unintentionally, it is suggested that *Lyons v Lyons* is correct and severance should be denied.

This leaves open the argument in favour of some form of suspension of survivorship. Though this has been supported by some authors[114] it does not gain support from any of the cases. Given that it is controversial even in the context of leases in which it has arisen, there are obvious difficulties in extending it to charges.

We now turn to leases. Why should anybody take a lease from a beneficial joint tenant? One possibility is that the lease may be unintentional, as is so often the case for mortgages. In practice, this is relatively unlikely: entry into a lease does not usually give rise to sufficient benefits to encourage the lessor to indulge in the misconduct by chargors seen in many of the mortgage cases.[115] This is reflected in

---

[108] Wells (1936) ALJ 322; Baird (1936) 9 ALJ 431.

[109] [1967] VR 169, accepted in *Re Shannon's Transfer* [1967] Tas SR 245 and *Rogers v Resi-Statewide Corporation Ltd* (1991) 105 ALR 145. See also *Re Young* (1968) 70 DLR 2d 594; *Re Sorensen and Sorensen* (1977) 90 DLR 3d 26, 36.      [110] Crown (2001) 117 LQR 477, 483.

[111] See Mendes da Costa (1962) 3 Melb ULR 433, 447–454. Cf LPA, s 87 on the effect of legal charges. These arguments were considered and rejected in *Lyons v Lyons* [1967] VR 169.

[112] *Re Sharer* (1912) 57 SJ 60; Nield [2001] Conv 462, 465–6, 474.

[113] *Lyons v Lyons* [1967] VR 169, 179; *Greenfield v Greenfield* (1979) 38 P&CR 570, 578. Severance by unilateral declaration is considered below, but this (if available at all) requires at a minimum that the other joint tenant should be notified.

[114] Most recently, see Nield [2001] Conv 462, 472–3 and 474: 'tantalising compromises'. It was briefly considered and rejected in *Lyons v Lyons* [1967] VR 169, 181.

[115] *Boland* cases (constructive and resulting trusts) are unlikely to arise, in part because of the inconsistency between possession by the lessee and the actual occupation of the other joint tenant.

the lack of modern cases on leases by co-owners, whether in the severance context or other contexts. Few tenants knowingly take a lease from a single joint tenant. With an intentional lease, the lessee might in the past have expected to step into the shoes of the lessor and enjoy possession whilst the joint tenancy continued, but today even this is less clear in the light of TLATA, section 12. The principal utility of leases may well be to give a lease to one of the joint tenants. Though each is likely to be entitled to possess, a lease by one (of two joint tenants) will ensure that the other can enjoy sole possession for the duration of the lease. Today, this lease may be by all the joint tenants acting together,[116] in which case there will be no shattering of unities[117] (though the lease will obviously continue regardless of the death of either). The problem we are considering applies only where the lease is by one joint tenant to the other.

It will be seen below that this area is encrusted with much difficult and old learning, with puzzling distinctions being drawn. One complicating factor is that, as we have just seen, some of the cases involve a lease to one joint tenant. This opens up an argument that the intention of the parties may effectuate a severance, without recourse to shattering any of the unities. The cases are often silent as to the basis for severance, but their authority on shattering the unities is weakened by this factor. However, we might start with two propositions (applicable to leases to a joint tenant and leases to a third party) which appear to be accepted by all authorities and authors. Each involves a lease by one joint tenant, which in any event is binding on the other only in the sense that the tenant can exercise the same rights as the grantor. The first is that the lease remains effective despite the death of the joint tenant grantor.[118] This leaves open the question whether there is any effect as between the original joint tenants. The second proposition is that, where there is a joint tenancy *of a lease*, a sublease by a joint tenant operates as a full severance of the original joint tenancy.

The controversial question has been whether there is a full severance on a lease by a joint tenant of the fee simple. Full severance would ensure that there cannot be survivorship as between the joint tenants. The alternative is temporary severance, which merely protects the lessee against the risk of the grantor joint tenant dying during the term of the lease. The early cases appear to deny full severance[119] and this is supported by Coke.[120] However, more recent cases tend to support it, though sometimes no distinction is made as to the nature of the severance involved.[121] Dicta in *Napier v Williams*[122] are symptomatic of the difficulties

---

[116] LPA, s 72(4). Previously, a lease by all was treated as a lease of the individual rights of those other than the grantee: *Cowper v Fletcher* (1865) 6 B&S 464.

[117] *Palmer v Rich* [1897] 1 Ch 134.

[118] *Anon* (1560) 2 Dyer 187a; *Harbin v Barton* (1595) Moo KB 395.

[119] *Harbin v Loby* (1629) Noy 157.          [120] Co Litt 185a.

[121] *Gould v Kemp* (1834) 2 My&K 304 (not clear whether directed towards full severance); *Cowper v Fletcher* (1865) 13 WR 739, 740 (fuller on this point than 6 B&S 464), though involving a lease to another joint tenant. An Irish case provides the clearest authority: *Re Armstrong* [1920] 1 IR 239.

[122] [1911] 1 Ch 361, 368.

in interpreting what is intended: 'they would thereby sever the joint tenancy. I think that the effect must be that the joint tenancy is severed during the term . . .' As with charges, we find that Australian cases take a more sceptical approach. In *Wright v Gibbons* Dixon J is clear that 'during the lease the jointure is severed and there is a temporary severance'.[123] Probably the fullest review of the material is undertaken by Sholl J in the Victorian case of *Frieze v Unger*,[124] unsurprisingly adopting the analysis of Dixon J. The same approach appears to be accepted in Canada.[125] Megarry and Wade[126] consider that principle and authority point in favour of full severance, though other recent commentators are less convinced.[127]

So far, we have been concentrating upon the state of the authorities. Does principle indicate that any of the solutions is to be preferred? Megarry and Wade[128] suggest that the test is whether the acts are consistent with the right of survivorship. Yet it is unclear that this provides an adequate basis for distinguishing between (for example) leases and rentcharges. Both may be effective whilst the grantor is alive, but both are at risk on the grantor's death. The same is true if we attempt a literal interpretation of the phrase employed in *Williams v Hensman*: 'an act of any one of the persons interested operating upon his own share'. A more promising analysis is that the lessee may be regarded as a tenant in common with the other (original) joint tenant.[129] It is readily apparent that these two persons cannot be joint tenants: there is no unity of interest or title. At the same time, the original joint tenants may be viewed as remaining joint tenants of the fee simple. It seems improbable that an estate subject to a lease is properly treated as a different estate to an unencumbered fee, so as to deny unity of interest. Subject to the following point, there appears to be no reason to recognize a full severance.

The arguments above have to overcome the objection that the lease depends upon the grantor's estate. If that estate terminates (as a joint tenancy does on death) then the lease terminates with it.[130] Whatever the relationship of the lessee with the other joint tenant, this represents a fundamental problem. A sale of part of a joint tenant's interest (say, of one of two houses held by joint tenancy) would, of course, be an effective alienation and severance of that part. Can the same analysis be used as regards a temporal split, as encountered with the lease? It is difficult to see how this argument can succeed, simply because the subject matter of the joint tenancy is the fee simple and this outlives the lease.

---

[123] (1949) 78 CLR 313, 330, accepted by Deane J in *Corin v Patton* (1990) 169 CLR 540, 573.
[124] [1960] VR 230.
[125] *Power v Grace* [1932] 2 DLR 793, 796; cf *Re Sorensen and Sorensen* (1977) 90 DLR 3d 26, 34–5. [126] *Law of Real Property* (6th edn), para 9-040.
[127] Fox [2000] Conv 208; Crown (2001) 117 LQR 477, 484–90.
[128] Note 126 above, para 9-040.
[129] Note the careful description by Sholl J in *Frieze v Unger* [1960] VR 230, 243: 'hold as would tenants in common'.
[130] Cf *Barrett v Morgan* [2000] 2 AC 264 in the context of a sublease.

It is difficult to avoid the conclusion that the courts have striven to protect the tenant without a sufficiently principled explanation as to how this is achieved. If the purpose is simply to protect the tenant, then perhaps the temporary severance analysis can be defended as the minimum necessary to achieve that purpose. Yet the idea of temporary severance adds an awkward conceptual twist to an already highly complex area. Once it is accepted that some form of severance is effected by a lease (as is inevitable on the state of the authorities) this may lead to the conclusion that the English favouring of full severance is justified.[131]

We have observed that a joint tenancy of a lease is fully severed when one of the parties enters into a lease.[132] It is very difficult to explain why there should be any difference between joint tenancies of fees simple and joint tenancies of leases. Again this is a pointer towards a wide view of severance as regards joint tenancy of fees simple, despite the danger of arguing from anomalous examples.

Analogous questions arise if a life interest is created in a joint tenant's interest, though this has received less attention. Insofar as life interest is a freehold interest, one might expect it to have a greater effect than a term of years: the immediate freehold in possession is no longer held by the grantor. Those who argue that a term of years effects a full severance will naturally contend that a life interest has the same effect. However, it is instructive that some who argue for a limited effect for a term of years recognize a wider effect for life interests.[133] On the other hand, there are contrary analyses[134] and these are based on Coke.[135] In the absence of clear authority, it is difficult to reach any firm conclusion. However, it is suggested that in the modern law it would be unduly technical to draw distinctions between life interests and terms of years.

## (ii) Mutual Agreement

This second head of severance (like the third) has a very different basis. Instead of a doctrinal analysis based on the four unities, we now encounter the operation of

---

[131] A conclusion supported by McClean (1979) 57 Can BR 1. It also avoids difficult questions as to the nature and effect of the temporary severance. For example, if the grantor dies during the lease, is the grantor's estate entitled to the rent? Does this severance terminate when the lease comes to an end? These issues are explored by Fox [2000] Conv 208, who prefers a solution based on temporary severance (thus enabling the grantor's estate to recover rent) to one based on suspending survivorship which would merely postpone the survivor's claim to the land (see esp pp 212–13 and 228).

[132] In addition to Co Litt 192a, see *Sym's Case* (1584) Cro Eliz 33; *Pleadal's Case* (1579) 2 Leon 159; *Connolly v Connolly* (1866) 17 Ir Ch R 208. The point is recognized in many more recent cases.

[133] *Wright v Gibbons* (1949) 78 CLR 313, 330 (Dixon J); *Frieze v Unger* [1960] VR 230, 242; Challis, *The Law of Real Property* (3rd edn), p 367; Cheshire, *Modern Law of Real Property* (7th edn), p 329 (cited in, *inter alia, Frieze*; the current (16th) edition does not discuss the point).

[134] *Halsbury's Laws of England* (4th edn), vol 39, para 535, n 5; *Power v Grace* [1932] 2 DLR 793; McClean (1979) 57 Can BR 1, 7–8. *Re Sorensen and Sorensen* (1977) 90 DLR 3d 26, 35 is commonly quoted for this proposition, but the fact that the life interest would end on the death of either joint tenant adds a peculiar dimension to the case. Otherwise, it seems to be the only authority suggesting a lesser effect for life interests than leases.

[135] Co Litt 191b. Co Litt 193a is less compelling, as it is based on an analysis which Coke has just doubted.

equitable principles: a world in which intentions are central. It follows that the questions are less analytically difficult than for acts operating on a share. On the other hand, the question whether there is severance frequently involves extensive assessment of the facts of each case. This assessment leaves much scope for different approaches to be taken by different judges. Severance by agreement was certainly not invented by Page Wood V-C: over a century earlier Lord Hardwicke LC had treated it as being an obvious form of severance, alongside alienation.[136]

Given that we are in the realm of intentions, there are relatively few bright line principles. Two points, however, should be stressed. The first concerns whose agreement is required: an issue not considered by Page Wood V-C. If there are two joint tenants, then it is clear that their agreement is required (as we are dealing with severance in equity, there is no need to involve the holders of the legal estate, who might be different persons). More difficult is the case where there are three or more joint tenants. Does the agreement of any two of them suffice? It seems that the answer must be in the negative. As we saw in the context of acts operating on a share,[137] it appears logically impossible to have a situation where A holds as joint tenant with B and C who, as between themselves, are tenants in common. It follows that, where A, B, and C are joint tenants, B and C cannot agree to sever as between themselves.[138] Nor would one expect that an agreement between B and C would be effective to sever A's interest as well as that of B and C. Two reasons justify this. The first is that the analogous third head in *Williams v Hensman* clearly requires the involvement of all the parties. The second reason is that it would be illogical for B and C to be able to sever A's interest when a single joint tenant acting alone cannot sever if there are two joint tenants.

Yet the position is not entirely straightforward. The facts of *Williams v Hensman* are significant. There was agreement between the eight joint tenants that an unauthorized investment be made, though three of them were infants and accordingly not bound by the agreement. This was treated as severing the interests of the adults from those of the infants. However, severance was not based on agreement (otherwise the interests of the adults would have been severed *inter se*, which they were not) but on a dealing with the shares of the adults. What was this dealing? It appears to be that their shares were bound by the investment, whereas those of the infants were not so bound.[139] This is difficult to explain in terms of the unities. It may best be seen as shattering the unity of interest, though it will be recalled that creating rights such as rentcharges does not sever. Yet there are continued suggestions that agreement does not require the participation of all the joint tenants. One example has been already observed in *Re Sharer*;[140] others appear in academic writing.[141] These suggestions are best treated as inconsistent with principle and misconceived.

---

[136] *Partriche v Powlet* (1740) 2 Atk 54. Luther (1995) 15 LS 219, 228, observes that the aim of Page Wood V-C 'was clearly to facilitate claims of severance'.     [137] See p 56 above.
[138] *Wright v Gibbons* (1949) 78 CLR 313, 322 (Latham CJ); *Lyons v Lyons* [1967] VR 169, 172.
[139] See (1861) 1 J&H 546, 558.     [140] (1912) 57 SJ 60, see p 63 above.
[141] Fox [2000] Conv 208, 212; Nield [2001] Conv 462, 466.

The second point concerns formalities. Does the agreement require writing as a 'contract for the sale or other disposition of an interest in land'?[142] It has been said that an agreement to sever 'clearly falls within the terms' of the legislation.[143] But is this so? It is certainly an agreement affecting an interest in land, but it is by no means obvious that it constitutes a 'sale or other disposition'. What it does is to change the nature of the parties' rights, rather than dispose of them. On this basis, one would not expect it to be caught. However, in Australia writing has been said to be required[144] and it is fair to add that some comments in earlier English cases lend support to that approach.[145] Although this ties in with generally stricter Australian approaches to severance, it is not clear that it is well rooted in principle. We will see that the third head covers courses of dealing sufficient to intimate that there is a tenancy in common. This clearly does not require writing:[146] it would be inexplicable if the factually clearer agreement to sever did require writing. The modern English approach clearly denies the need for writing. In *Burgess v Rawnsley*[147] the Court of Appeal was faced with an agreement between two beneficial joint tenants for one to sell to the other. This agreement was unenforceable for lack of writing, meaning that there could be no severance under the first head. However, the court had no hesitation in holding that a necessary inference was that the parties had agreed to sever their joint tenancy and that an oral agreement was effective for that purpose.

*Burgess* shows that an agreement to sever need not be express: it can be inferred from the conduct of the parties. However, it then tends to merge into the third head, to which we must now turn.

## (iii)  Course of Dealing

There are obvious similarities between the second and third heads: both look to the intention of the parties. However, it is the third head which has been employed to test the limits of severance in equity. We might split the issues into three categories. The first concerns the relationship between the second and third heads. The second is whether any form of 'unilateral' severance is permitted by the third head. Finally, there is the important but essentially factual question of what amounts to a sufficient course of conduct.

On the first question, it is sometimes suggested that the third head is essentially a sub-division of the second: it is an implied agreement to sever.[148] However, this

---

[142]  Law of Property (Miscellaneous Provisions) Act 1989, s 2.
[143]  Butt (1982) 9 Syd LR 568, 575–6; see also McClean (1979) 57 Can BR 1, 17.
[144]  *Lyons v Lyons* [1967] VR 169, 171. The authorities relied upon are few and far from convincing.
[145]  *Frewen v Relfe* (1787) 2 Bro CC 220; *Wilson v Bell* (1843) 5 Ir Eq R 501, 507; *Re Wilford's Estate* (1879) 11 Ch D 267, 279 (mutual wills; might be based upon the first head).
[146]  *Szabo v Boros* (1967) 64 DLR 2d 48, 49; this is less tenable if the course of dealing is regarded as an implied agreement (discussed immediately below).                    [147]  [1975] Ch 429.
[148]  *Nielson-Jones v Fedden* [1975] Ch 222 appears to accept this proposition (adopting *Re Wilks* [1891] 3 Ch 59, 64). See also *Re Denny* (1947) 199 LT 291, 293; *Tan Chew Hoe Neo v Chee Swee Cheng* (1928) LR 56 Ind App 112, 116; and *Lyons v Lyons* [1967] VR 169, 171.

was explicitly rejected in *Burgess v Rawnsley*.[149] Although it is easy to see that a course of dealing will frequently amount to an implied agreement, two initial points may be made as to the significance of this wider view of course of dealing. Firstly, the nature of what is happening is not so much that parties agree to do something (an agreement to sever is fully effective without anything further) but rather that they agree that there is henceforth a tenancy in common. The term 'course of dealing' encapsulates this point better than the language of agreement: it suffices if the parties treat the situation as if there were a tenancy in common.[150] The second point (stressed by Sir John Pennycuick) is that that negotiations may suffice for a course of dealing: there is no need for a final agreement. These negotiations will relate to the future of the property, not severance. This wider view of the third head, adopted in *Burgess*, seems to have been accepted.[151] A consequential question is whether it suffices if the joint tenants treat the situation as if there is a tenancy in common, without being aware that the others are doing so. For example, if there is a joint tenancy between A, B, C, and D, does it suffice if there is course of dealing between A and B and a separate course of dealing between C and D? Here there is no overall course of dealing, yet all treat the situation as if there is a severance. The less we treat this head as being separate from mutual agreement,[152] the more attractive becomes the argument for severance.

A highly controversial question is whether a unilateral declaration of severance falls within *Williams v Hensman*. We have seen that the court in *Nielson-Jones v Fedden*[153] held, quite correctly, that a unilateral declaration does not fall within the first head. Walton J also had to deal with an argument that it could fall within the course of dealing head. The language employed by Page Wood V-C ('the interests of all were mutually treated') is not encouraging to such an idea. The idea (still current when *Nielson-Jones* was decided) that the third head is a form of agreement is also, of course, opposed to it. In a thoroughly convincing analysis, Walton J rejected such unilateral declarations.[154] As he observed, such declarations would leave no sensible role for the more narrowly circumscribed severance by written notice introduced in 1925, nor does it fit the pre-1925 use of assignments as the standard method to sever unilaterally.

---

[149] [1975] Ch 429, Lord Denning MR, 439; Browne LJ, 447; Sir John Pennycuick, 447. See also *Greenfield v Greenfield* (1979) 38 P&CR 570, 577.

[150] The language used here is close to the language of estoppel, though without requiring detriment.

[151] In England, see *Greenfield v Greenfield* (1979) 38 P&CR 570, 577; *Gore and Snell v Carpenter* (1990) 60 P&CR 456, 462; *Hunter v Babbage* [1994] 2 FLR 806, 812. In Australia: *Abela v Public Trustee* [1983] 1 NSWLR 308, 315; *Berdal v Burns* [1990] WAR 140, 144; *Slater v Slater* (1987) 12 Fam LR 1. However, Deane J in *Corin v Patton* (1990) 169 CLR 540, 574 has continued to use the language of implied agreement (see also Toohey J, ibid, 587).

[152] When analogies from common intention for the acquisition of interests point against severance: 'Our trust law does not allow property rights to be affected by telepathy' (*Springette v Defoe* (1992) 65 P&CR 1, 8, Steyn LJ).    [153] [1975] Ch 222; see p 58 above.

[154] *Partriche v Powlet* (1740) 2 Atk 54 provides good authority. *Re Wilks* [1891] 3 Ch 59 is also strongly relied upon and is generally thought to point against unilateral declaration. However, the fact that two of the joint tenants were infants must raise doubts about its application as between adults.

The issue was soon before the Court of Appeal in *Burgess v Rawnsley*.[155] As the court rejected the proposition that the third head requires implied agreement, the unilateral declaration route became more viable. However, the case was decided on the basis of an agreement to sever, so the dicta on unilateral declarations appear to be obiter. The greatest interest centres on the following statement by Lord Denning MR: 'It is sufficient if there is a course of dealing in which one party makes clear to the other that he desires that their shares should no longer be held jointly but be held in common'.[156] Although Lord Denning MR uses dicta in *Williams v Hensman* as authority,[157] the full dicta of Page Wood V-C point in the opposite direction. It should be added that we have seen that Lord Denning MR also supported his analysis by relying on the words of LPA, section 36(2):[158] another dubious argument! It is revealing that both Sir John Pennycuick and Browne LJ[159] regard section 36(2) as effecting a 'radical alteration' and Sir John Pennycuick also stated that a 'mere verbal notice by one party to another clearly cannot operate as a severance'. Commentators have also been hostile to Lord Denning's analysis.[160] Subsequent cases have not sought to resolve the problem directly, but either imply that the approach of Sir John Pennycuick is to be preferred or draw attention to the shortcomings of Lord Denning's analysis.[161]

In other Commonwealth countries there has been widespread rejection of severance by unilateral declaration. Although several of these cases pre-date *Burgess* (or do not deal with it)[162] there are also strong direct rejections of it.[163] The rejection of *Burgess* is made easier because of the absence of severance by written notice (section 36(2)) in these countries: the reasoning of Lord Denning MR was based partly on section 36(2) and partly on the old equitable severance principles. Although some cases are thought to point in favour of unilateral declarations,[164] they suffer from weak citation of relevant authorities and, in any

---

[155] [1975] Ch 429.        [156] Ibid, 439.

[157] Specifically 'it will not suffice to rely on an intention, with respect to the particular share, declared only behind the backs of the other persons interested'. Although all agree that an uncommunicated intention will be ineffective, it is doubtful whether Page Wood V-C intended that a *unilateral* communicated intention suffices: this would go much further than his previous sentence (quoted in the previous paragraph of the text) recognized.                    [158] See p 54 above.

[159] [1975] Ch 429, at 444, 447.

[160] Hayton [1976] CLJ 243; Butt (1976) 50 ALJ 246; and (1979) 9 Syd LR 568, 581–7; Megarry and Wade, *Law of Real Property* (6th edn), para 9–043; Bandali [1977] Conv 243, 252; MacCallum (1980) 7 Monash ULR 17.

[161] *Harris v Goddard* [1983] 1 WLR 1203, 1209 (Lawton LJ: 'Unilateral action to sever a joint tenancy is now [following s 36(2)] possible'); *Gore and Snell v Carpenter* (1990) 60 P&CR 456, 462; *Hunter v Babbage* [1994] 2 FLR 806.

[162] In Australia: *Freed v Taffel* [1984] 2 NSWLR 322, 324. In Canada: *Golding v Hands* [1969] WAR 121; *Munroe v Carlson* (1975) 59 DLR 3d 763; *Gillette v Cotton* [1979] 4 WWR 515. In New Zealand: *Austin v Austin* (1908) 27 NZLR 1099.

[163] In Australia: *Marriage of Pertsoulis* (1980) 6 Fam LR 39, 47; *Davies v Davies* [1983] WAR 305, 308; *Slater v Slater* (1987) 12 Fam LR 1, 4; *Corin v Patton* (1990) 169 CLR 540, 548 (Mason CJ, McHugh J, and Toohey J agreeing, 591), 584 (Deane J). In Canada: *Re Sorensen and Sorensen* (1977) 90 DLR 3d 26, 39.

[164] In Australia: *Marriage of Badcock* (1979) 5 Fam LR 672, 681 (but see Butt (1979) 9 Syd LR 568, 586). In Canada: *Ginn v Armstrong* (1969) 3 DLR 3d 285.

event, are somewhat ambivalent. It is quite clear that they have no authority in the light of the strong and more recent rejection of unilateral declarations in the same countries.

The conclusion must be that Lord Denning MR embarked on a frolic of his own. Nevertheless that leaves open the question whether the law should move in the direction he espoused. This represents a far more difficult question, which is considered later in this Chapter.

The third and final issue concerns the type of circumstances which will persuade the courts that there is a course of dealing whereby the interests are treated as severed.[165] This is ultimately a question of fact, but certain types of situation tend to recur and these provide the greatest interest. In recent decades the great majority of disputes have involved parties who have been living together, but whose relationship (usually marriage) has broken down. Perhaps the most common argument has been that negotiations to terminate the relationship and distribute property show a common intention that there should be severance. This provided the background to both *Nielson-Jones v Fedden* and *Burgess v Rawnsley*.

*Burgess* may be regarded as exceptional because there was a final agreement to sell a beneficial interest: the fact that it was unenforceable as not being in writing did not preclude a finding that there was an intention to sever. Most cases involve death before final agreement is reached, *Nielson-Jones* being an example. Walton J summarily rejected the severance claim: 'It appears to me that when parties are negotiating to reach an agreement, and never do reach any final agreement, it is quite impossible to say that they have reached any agreement at all'.[166] This obviously ties in with the idea (rejected in *Burgess*) that the third head involves an implied agreement. In *Burgess*, Lord Denning MR clearly regarded *Nielson-Jones* as wrongly decided on this point.[167] However, neither Browne LJ nor Sir John Pennycuick (the latter recognizing that some of the analysis of Walton J was flawed) wished to go into that question.[168] Sir John Pennycuick provides the most useful analysis:

I do not doubt myself that where one tenant negotiates with another for some rearrangement of interest, it may be possible to infer from the particular facts a common intention to sever even though the negotiations break down. Whether such an inference can be drawn must I think depend upon the particular facts. In the present case the negotiations between Mr Honick and Mrs Rawnsley, if they can be properly described as negotiations at all, fall, it seems to me, far short of warranting an inference. One could not ascribe to joint tenants an intention to sever merely because one offers to buy out the other for £X and the other makes a counter-offer of £Y.[169]

Given that separation negotiations are likely to involve extensive discussions, with long-term continuation of co-ownership very rarely regarded as an option by

---

[165] Unsurprisingly, sufficient evidence may also give rise to a finding that there is an agreement to sever.                                                              [166] [1975] Ch 222, 230.

[167] [1975] Ch 429, 443.      [168] Ibid, 444, 448.

[169] Ibid, 447. He was considering what the position would be if (contrary to his finding) there had been no agreement to sell the interest.

either party, one would expect that severance would readily be recognized. This is enhanced by a generally held perception that survivorship is inappropriate for husband and wife on breakdown of the marriage (or for partners on the breakdown of their relationship) and that this should colour the inferences which should be drawn as to their intentions.[170] The argument that an agreement to sever (or course of dealing) should not be found whilst the parties are still negotiating is singularly unconvincing once one recognizes that either party could sever unilaterally (by written notice or alienation): refusal to sever cannot be a bargaining ploy. It would be wholly exceptional for the parties not to accept that, whatever the details of the outcome, the joint tenancy must come to an end. This renders it surprising that more recent English cases have generally refused to accept severance arising from negotiations. Thus the court in *Gore and Snell v Carpenter*[171] displayed a marked reluctance to treat negotiations as a course of dealing. This is surely difficult to reconcile with *Burgess*, especially in the light of the finding that there had been agreement in principle. Meanwhile, *McDowell v Hirschfield Lipson and Rumsey*[172] appeared to regard a joint tenancy as entirely appropriate in these circumstances, requiring that the parties 'firmly evince' an intention to sever. Severance was recognized in *Hunter v Babbage*,[173] though there the parties had reached agreement subject to a consent order.

Given that Commonwealth courts have generally taken a much stricter view as to severance principles, it is paradoxical that they have been more welcoming towards arguments based on the third head. This has been the experience of most cases in Australia[174] and Canada.[175] This chimes well with the view urged above that the necessary intention can be more readily found following a relationship breakdown. These cases involved (as did *McDowell*) negotiations to buy out the interest of one of the joint tenants, though their reasoning seems equally applicable if the negotiations contemplate the sale of the property and sharing out the proceeds.

A specific context in which Commonwealth courts have generally denied severance is where one of the parties has made a court application. Unsurprisingly, this has been the context of many of the cases on unilateral declarations.[176] It can readily be seen that the rejection of unilateral declaration operates to deny severance.

---

[170]   *Harris v Goddard* [1983] 1 WLR 1203, 1208; *Abela v Public Trustee* [1983] 1 NSWLR 308.
[171]   (1990) 60 P&CR 456, 462 (Judge Blackett-Ord; Ch D).
[172]   [1992] 2 FLR 126 (Judge Stockdale; QBD). It was stressed that severance was not mentioned in the negotiations. However, this is not surprising given that either part could sever at will and any conceivable outcome would terminate the joint tenancy.          [173]   [1994] 2 FLR 806.
[174]   *Public Trustee v Grivas* [1974] 2 NSWLR 316, 322 (the parties had agreed on a court application); *Re Pozzi* [1982] Qd R 499; *Abela v Public Trustee* [1983] 1 NSWLR 308. Contrast the early New Zealand case of *Austin v Austin* (1908) 27 NZLR 1099 (mother and daughter) and, more recently, *Slater v Slater* (1987) 12 Fam LR 1. *Slater* employs an analysis which is much closer to the English cases.
[175]   *Ginn v Armstrong* (1969) 3 DLR 3d 285; *Re Walters and Walters* (1977) 79 DLR 3d 122 (upheld (1978) 84 DLR 3d 416n); *Robichaud v Watson* (1983) 147 DLR 3d 626.
[176]   Going back to *Re Wilks* [1891] 3 Ch 59.

It is no different if both parties apply to court,[177] at least where it is not a joint application indicating agreement between them.[178] One suspects that some of the cases may have involved some form of negotiation between the parties, but this has received little attention. If discussed at all, an agreement or bilateral course of dealing has been quickly rejected. In England, this context has generally given rise to analyses based on LPA, section 36(2).[179] Where no notice of severance can be spelt out of the application, it would be very surprising if there were a viable argument of a course of dealing pointing to a tenancy in common.

One type of negotiation must, however, be considered. Even a concluded agreement that the property (as opposed to a share in it) should be sold is not inconsistent with the joint tenancy: the joint tenancy can readily take effect against the proceeds of sale. It follows that negotiations as to the future of the property possess a very different character from negotiations about the parties' interests. Thus in *Nielson-Jones v Fedden* Walton J held it immaterial that the parties had agreed that the former matrimonial home should be sold, though it would have been different if (as was unsuccessfully argued) the agreement had been that one of the parties should be entitled to all the proceeds. This is clearly correct: numerous cases provide good authority.[180] However, an agreement for sale is often part of a larger negotiation and then it may be a relevant factor pointing to severance. In particular, it is very common for negotiations to relate to distribution of the proceeds.[181] Of course, if the negotiations are incomplete then courts (at least in England) may display a greater reluctance to sever. The principal point being urged in this paragraph is that an agreement to sell the property is not, taken in isolation, an indication of severance.

So far we have been concentrating on joint tenancies between spouses or couples once the relationship has broken down. It should be noted that the principles being applied are the same whatever the factual setting,[182] though the nature of the negotiations is likely to be different. Where a relationship has broken down, a wider range of issues is likely to be subject to negotiation, against the background that the court often has extensive powers to adjust property rights. In other contexts the negotiations are more likely to be limited to the future of the

---

[177] *Marriage of Pertsoulis* (1980) 6 Fam LR 39; *Patzak v Lytton* [1984] WAR 353.

[178] *Hunter v Babbage* [1994] 2 FLR 806; *Public Trustee v Grivas* [1974] 2 NSWLR 316.

[179] See p 53 above.

[180] *Re Haye's Estate* [1920] 1 IR 207 (explaining *Kingsford v Ball* (1852) 2 Giff (App) i); *Re Allingham* [1932] VLR 469; *Abela v Public Trustee* [1983] 1 NSWLR 308, 314; *Flannigan v Wotherspoon* [1953] 1 DLR 768, 773; *Bank of British Columbia v Nelson* (1979) 17 BCLR 223; *Palmer v Rich* [1897] 1 Ch 134 (lease). *Paterson v Paterson* (1979) 108 DLR 3d 234 appears contrary, but confuses dealing with an interest and dealing with the land (it is criticized by Butt (1982) 9 Syd LR 568, 575).

[181] See *Hunter v Babbage* [1994] 2 FLR 806; *Re Pozzi* [1982] Qd R 499; *Flannigan v Wotherspoon* [1953] 1 DLR 768; *Schofield v Graham* (1969) 6 DLR 3d 88. *Bank of British Columbia v Nelson* (1979) 17 BCLR 223 displays a rather puzzling refusal to recognize severance when it had been agreed that the proceeds should go to the wife (Butt (1982) 9 Syd LR 568, 574–5).

[182] A few of the cases relied on above did not involve relationship breakdown.

property. It is unlikely that they will relate to severance alone, given that it is easy for either party to sever by taking the appropriate steps. Accordingly, the question will be whether a common intention to sever can be inferred from the circumstances. Nearly all the factors discussed above will be relevant. For example, an agreement to sell the property and divide the proceeds is likely to sever.[183] On the other hand, it may well be less appropriate to spell an agreement or course of dealing out of negotiations. Suppose a house is held on trust for two brothers as joint tenants. One might suggest that the house (used as a source of income) be sold and the proceeds divided amongst them. The reason may be that he believes that property prices are high and it is an opportune time to get a good price. If the other brother persuades him that sale is not a good idea (or they are divided and neither wishes to go to court) these discussions certainly do not prove that the brothers do not want survivorship. Although sale and division of the proceeds would necessarily sever, this is far more an incidental consequence of sale than the objective of either party. On the other hand, different circumstances might point the other way. If both were originally unmarried, then the subsequent marriage of one (coupled with discussions as to sale) might signal that survivorship has become inappropriate: the married brother might well wish his share to go to his widow on his death rather than to his brother.[184] Discussions as to sale might then be regarded differently.

What agreements might joint tenants make apart from sale and division of the proceeds? One obvious possibility is that they might agree as to benefits from the property and expenses of maintaining it. The courts are reluctant to see this sort of agreement as severing. It is entirely consistent with a joint tenancy that the parties should agree that one should occupy the premises. In many of the marriage breakdown cases one of the parties has continued to reside in the premises: this by itself has been an insufficient pointer to severance. A variation on this theme is provided by *Greenfield v Greenfield*,[185] in which two brothers split a jointly owned house into two maisonettes. Fox J was convinced that the reality was that both brothers wished survivorship to operate. Although the facts might be consistent with a tenancy in common, they were nowhere near sufficient to overturn the clear opinion of the court that the brothers desired survivorship. It appears that an agreement that income should be paid is similarly irrelevant.[186] After all, in a joint tenancy one expects trustees to pay the income to the joint tenants. It should make no difference if, for some reason, it is agreed that all the income should for the time being be paid to one of them. It is the same as regards expenditure on the premises. In *Greenfield*, it was irrelevant that one of the joint tenants had made improvements to

---

[183] *Flannigan v Wotherspoon* [1953] 1 DLR 768 (sisters).

[184] Cf the facts of *Greenfield v Greenfield* (1979) 38 P&CR 570 (not involving a request for sale). The court refused to find an agreement to sever: the brothers had an unusually close relationship.

[185] (1979) 38 P&CR 570.

[186] *Ex p Railway Commissioners for New South Wales* (1941) 41 SR NSW 92; *Flannigan v Wotherspoon* [1953] 1 DLR 768, 775–6.

his maisonette. Similarly, an agreement as to maintenance costs (to be shared by both joint tenants) has been held not to sever.[187] To avoid any ambiguity, it should be stressed that these principles as to income and expenditure apply just as readily whether or not the facts involve relationship breakdown.

A rather different question has sometimes arisen where a joint tenancy covers several properties. Does conduct in relation to some of them display an intention to sever as regards the others? There is old authority on this. In *Crooke v de Vandes*, Lord Eldon LC stated: 'It is not necessary to shew a specific act of division of each part of the property, if there has been a general dealing, sufficient to manifest the intention to divide the whole. The acts, done as to parts, may be evidence as to the rest; as to which no act has been done.'[188] Accordingly, the fact that as property was sold it was divided between the joint tenants showed an intention that they should be tenants in common of the remaining properties. Romilly MR reached a different result in *Leak v Macdowall*: 'But I do not think this inference is to be drawn, merely from the circumstance that a trustee, having realised part of the estate, has paid the money received, in certain proportions, to the parties in severalty'.[189] However, *Re Denny*[190] reveals a relatively modern application of the *Crooke* principle. Jenkins J explained *Leak* on the basis that no inference can be drawn from a dealing with a small part of the property:[191] it was certainly not seen as overturning *Crooke*. One might add that it may well make a difference whether the sale and division is undertaken or sought by the joint tenants or is the decision of the trustees. In the latter setting (as in *Leak*) one can see that it is more difficult to find the necessary agreement or course of dealing between the joint tenants.

*Re Denny* illustrates a further point. On the initial creation of concurrent interests, particular phrases and words are treated as 'words of severance' pointing towards a tenancy in common. Similarly, after the interests have come into existence, language employed by joint tenants can be treated as showing that they treat themselves as tenants in common. This was relevant in *Re Denny* because of the form of the accounts and the language of receipts signed by the joint tenants. It may also arise in the course of negotiations, especially where there is discussion as to the proceeds of sale of the land. In difficult cases we often have to consider the conduct of the parties, but it should not be forgotten that what they have said or, most strongly, committed to writing is the best evidence of whether severance is intended.

The very old and settled principle that joint tenants cannot transfer their interests by will has already been noted.[192] However, it is widely recognized that mutual wills may sever. If joint tenants agree to make mutual wills, then it is

---

[187] *Re McKee and National Trust Co Ltd* (1975) 56 DLR 3d 190, 194.
[188] (1805) 11 Ves 330, 333.        [189] (1862) 32 Beav 28, 29.        [190] (1947) 177 LT 291.
[191] About two-thirds had been distributed in *Re Denny*; property was distributed as it became available on the death of annuitants, helping to show the intention to sever.
[192] See p 49 above.

treated as a necessary inference that they intend severance so that the property can pass on death and be bound by the mutual will obligation.[193] It is the agreement rather than the will which severs. Two cases illustrate this well. In *Re Wilford's Estate*[194] two sisters agreed to make wills leaving property to each other for life, with remainder to their nieces. It was found that the sisters intended the wills to cover the jointly held property: this made sense only if their interests were severed so that they could pass under the wills. In *Re Bryan and Heath*[195] husband and wife (joint tenants) each had children from earlier relationships. They made mutual wills whereby the deceased's interest would pass to the survivor and to the deceased's children. This scheme could work only if there were severance, otherwise the children of the first to die would lose out completely.

Yet it would be wrong to assume that mutual wills always necessitate severance. Suppose the joint tenants agree to make wills whereby each leaves their property to the other, if living, with identical gifts over if the other is dead. This can work perfectly well without severance, whether the survivor is given a life interest or an absolute interest. Survivorship will in any event ensure that the survivor gets the jointly held property and then the mutual wills agreement will bite on the survivor's property.[196] Proof that the parties intended that the joint held property should pass under the will (rather than merely be the subject matter of the gift over) will show an intention to sever, but this is not a necessary part of their scheme.

Part of the problem is that *Re Wilford's Estate* treats it as essential that there be a severance in order to avoid the survivor's receiving an unintended windfall. But other cases show that (provided it is the intention of the parties) the obligation on the survivor is not limited to property passing under the will of the first to die.[197] This makes it less important[198] whether or not there is severance: the mutual will obligation will operate in both settings.[199] However, specific agreements may make severance essential. One example is *Re Bryan and Heath*, as explained above.

A rather different point is whether there is severance before the making of the mutual wills. In principle there should be, as the basis for severance is the agreement of the parties, rather than their putting it into effect. However, the cases do tend to stress that mutual wills have in fact been made. This may be because it is

---

[193] *Re Wilford's Estate* (1879) 11 Ch D 267; *Re Heys' Estate* [1914] P 192, 195–6; *Re Hagger* [1930] 2 Ch 190, 195 (joint will); *Szabo v Boros* (1967) 64 DLR 2d 48; *Re Bryan and Heath* (1979) 108 DLR 3d 245; *Re Sorensen and Sorensen* (1977) 90 DLR 3d 26, 38.          [194] (1879) 11 Ch D 267.

[195] (1979) 108 DLR 3d 245.

[196] *University of Manitoba v Sanderson Estate* (1998) 155 DLR 4th 40.

[197] *Re Hagger* [1930] 2 Ch 190 and *Re Cleaver* [1981] 1 WLR 939 provide examples.

[198] Unless there is severance, the share of the first to die will not pass to a third party until the survivor dies.

[199] It is no objection that the survivor has not received the jointly held property *under the will*, partly because other property will nearly always pass under the will and partly because it is never necessary for the survivor to have received property: *Re Dale* [1994] Ch 31; *University of Manitoba v Sanderson Estate* (1998) 155 DLR 4th 40 (*Re Dale* was not cited).

thought that mutual wills (actual or prospective) can be repudiated whilst both are still alive provided that notice is given.[200] *A fortiori*, before the wills are made either party can resile. However, it does not follow that they have not agreed to sever.[201] This situation is analogous to *Burgess v Rawnsley*,[202] where the agreement to purchase the other's interest was unenforceable, but still gave rise to severance.

## C. Public Policy?

A very different possibility is that severance may operate by virtue of public policy. The context involves one joint tenant unlawfully killing another. A general principle, operating well beyond joint tenancies, is that public policy prevents a person who unlawfully kills somebody from benefiting as a result. One obvious example, unrelated to co-ownership, is that a murderer cannot receive a benefit under the will of the victim.[203] Nobody doubts that public policy will prevent one joint tenant who murders another joint tenant from benefiting by survivorship. It may technically be the case that each joint tenant already owns the whole, but no legal system is likely to allow the murderer to walk off with the entire property.

The difficulty lies in identifying how this public policy operates. There are two principal analyses available. The first is that the law treats the victim's share as being severed, so that it goes to the victim's estate. The second is that survivorship operates, but equity imposes a constructive trust on the murderer so as to prevent any benefit being asserted. The choice has caused some difficulty for Commonwealth courts. Although there has been some support for severance in Australia,[204] a significant majority of cases have rejected this in favour of the constructive trust.[205] In part, this was based upon a reluctance to recognize a new form of severance of the legal estate, which might cause problems as regards the devolution of the legal estate.[206]

In England, the problem had apparently not been litigated prior to *Re K*,[207] a case primarily centred on the statutory discretion[208] to relieve against forfeiture. Vinelott J agreed with counsel's concession that the forfeiture rule 'applies in effect to sever the joint tenancy'. He mentioned some of the Commonwealth cases,

---

[200] Pettit, *Equity and the Law of Trusts* (9th edn), p 132, citing *Dufour v Pereira* (1769) Dick 419; this avoids unconscionable conduct.

[201] Severance is supported by *Re Woolnough* [2002] WTLR 595 (Master Moncaston) in which a common intention to sever was found even though the wills were not mutual (and therefore revocable). The point was that the joint tenants acted together on the basis that their interests would pass by will.                                                                        [202] [1975] Ch 429.

[203] If authority is needed, see *Re Hall's Estate* [1914] P 1 (manslaughter).

[204] *Re Barrowcliff* [1927] SASR 147; *Kemp v Public Curator of Queensland* [1969] Qd R 145.

[205] In Australia: *Re Thorp and the Real Property Act* (1963) 80 WN NSW 61; *Rasmanis v Jurewitsch* (1970) 70 SR NSW 407 (these cases are followed in *Public Trustee v Evans* (1985) 2 NSWLR 188, 193); *Re Stone* [1989] 1 Qd R 351. In New Zealand: *Re Pechar (deceased)* [1969] NZLR 574. In Canada: *Schobelt v Barber* (1966) 60 DLR 2d 519.

[206] See especially *Re Thorp and the Real Property Act* (1963) 80 WN NSW 61, 63; *Re Stone* [1989] 1 Qd R 351, 353.                                                      [207] [1985] Ch 85; relief against forfeiture was given.

[208] Forfeiture Act 1982.

concluding: 'Under English law since 1925 the result is more simply reached by treating the beneficial interest as vesting in the deceased and the survivor as tenants in common'.[209] It is, of course, true that English law is concerned only with severing the equitable estate, so that problems relating to devolution of the legal estate are out of place. The severance analysis was approved by the Court of Appeal in *Dunbar v Plant*,[210] though without mention of any alternative analysis.

However, it is incorrect to assume that severance and the constructive trust produce the same result for equitable interests. As had been recognized at least since Mendes da Costa raised the point in 1962,[211] the position of three joint tenants poses special problems. Suppose that A, B, and C are joint tenants and A murders B. A severance analysis means that B's one-third share is held by B's estate. Nobody will be troubled by A's inability to benefit from his crime. But why should C not benefit by survivorship? After all, survivorship would have operated if B had been murdered by X, a stranger. Mendes da Costa urged that the result (where A murders B) should be that C obtains a half share: the same result as if anybody else had killed B. A would retain a one-third share[212] and B's estate would have the remaining one-sixth under a constructive trust. This looks convincing, as it concentrates on the benefit which A would have obtained from his crime. The issue arose in *Rasmanis v Jurewitsch*,[213] seemingly the only Commonwealth case to consider it. The rather puzzling response was to say that A and C remained joint tenants as to two-thirds (an unexceptional proposition) but that C should be tenant in common of the remaining one-third. One may criticize the severance analysis as being too generous in giving B's estate a full one-third share, but *Rasmanis* does not adequately explain why the estate should get nothing.[214]

Two final elements may be mentioned. Now that the Forfeiture Act 1982 confers power on English courts to grant relief, it has been observed that the exact scope of the forfeiture rule is less significant: the courts will focus on when relief should be given.[215] However, this does not mean that the questions considered above lose their significance.[216] First, we will assume that B's share is severed, as

[209]  [1985] Ch 85, at 100.        [210]  [1998] Ch 412, 418.

[211]  (1962) 3 Melb ULR 433, 438–9; see also Youdan (1974) 89 LQR 235, 254–5; and Thompson [1987] Conv 29, 34.

[212]  The forfeiture rule has never operated in Commonwealth countries to deprive the wrongdoer of existing property rights. In the United States, A may keep only a life interest in the original share (see Youdan (1973) 89 LQR 235, 249) but Commonwealth courts have uniformly rejected this approach: see esp *Re Pechar (deceased)* [1969] NZLR 574; and *Rasmanis v Jurewitsch* (1970) 70 SR NSW 407.                                                    [213]  (1970) 70 SR NSW 407.

[214]  Perhaps the fear was that if C were next to die then the one-sixth share derived from B would pass to A by survivorship, so A would then receive a reward from his own crime. But surely the solution of Mendes de Costa avoids this. There cannot be a joint tenancy of more than the original two-thirds held by A and C: beyond this there would be no unity of interest. The remaining one-sixth share held by C (giving C a half share overall) either has to be held outside the joint tenancy or (more likely) causes unity of title to be shattered so that A and C hold as tenants in common.

[215]  *Dunbar v Plant* [1998] Ch 412, 436–7; Bridge [1998] CLJ 31.

[216]  It is too alarmist, however, to suggest (Thompson [1987] Conv 29, 34) that the Forfeiture Act 1982 may not apply if the severance route is adopted. That contention is difficult to square with either *Re K* or *Dunbar v Plant*.

stated in *Re K*. The exercise of discretion operates 'by excluding the application of the rule'.[217] This means that if the court wishes to benefit A in whole or in part then the tenancy in common is correspondingly avoided. In turn this means that survivorship operates so that C will benefit from B's death. It looks odd that a jurisdiction designed to benefit A will have as great a beneficial effect on C! On the other hand, if there is a constructive trust then the jurisdiction will extend only to the one-sixth share of which A has been deprived.[218] The second element is that there is a huge body of law relating to when forfeiture operates. Much of our discussion has centred on murder, but there is much debate as to the application of forfeiture to manslaughter. This is not an issue specific to co-ownership and is accordingly not discussed in this book.[219]

## D. Policy perspectives

So far, we have concentrated on the existing rules. However, we also need to consider the extent to which the rules are justified as a coherent whole.[220] This may assist in assessing how the courts should proceed in developing legal principles, as well as identifying needs for statutory reform. Severance based on public policy raises distinct factors and is not further discussed here.

There is much to be said for the proposition that severance by written notice is the primary route in the modern law. It provides greater formality and clarity than the equitable bases for severance. As shown above, however, it suffers from two major defects. The first is that it applies only to real property: such a useful form of severance needs to be available for all forms of property, particularly bearing in mind that many trusts involve both realty and personalty. There is also, apparently, a requirement that the same persons be both trustees and beneficiaries: this seems unnecessary provided that notice is given to all concerned. More troublesome (in the sense that it is less susceptible to statutory reform) is the question of what will be recognized as a notice of severance, particularly as regards applications to court and negotiations. It would be unduly technical for a notice to have to declare itself as a notice of intention to sever, but the inevitable consequence of a more lax approach is that many grey cases will arise. It may be insufficiently precise, but courts should be slow to deny an effective notice in situations where survivorship is generally perceived as being inappropriate, whilst not encouraging highly speculative claims.

The equitable routes to severance provide greater difficulty. Two central problems are here addressed. The first concerns the first head in *Williams v Hensman*: acts operating on a joint tenant's share. Although the first head is well

---

[217] Forfeiture Act 1982, s 2(5). *Re K* interprets this as widening rather than narrowing the powers of the court, though this does not appear to affect the way relief operates.
[218] For these purposes, it matters not whether this share is beneficially held by B's estate or by C.
[219] See Buckley (1995) 111 LQR 196; also *Dunbar v Plant* [1998] Ch 412.
[220] See Tee [1995] Conv 105, considering reform possibilities discussed in Law Com WP No 94 (the area was not considered by the final report: Law Com No 181, para 1.3).

grounded in the four unities and traditional legal methods of severance, it must be questioned whether it is justified in the modern law. This ties in with the doubts expressed in the previous Chapter regarding the role of the four unities and the suggestion that they should be relaxed. The principal question is whether it is acceptable to allow severance where the other joint tenants have not been given notice and therefore assume that survivorship will continue to operate. The arguments already seen in the context of charges and leases apply more generally here. If there is no severance, then the purchaser has a very uncertain right: it will disappear if the seller is the first joint tenant to die. On the other hand, we have seen that today very few people deliberately deal with a single joint tenant. The only person likely to be interested in purchasing is another joint tenant, when questions of hidden severance are less troublesome. It is far more likely that transactions will arise when the purchaser (or chargee or lessee) believes they are getting a legal interest. One's sympathy for the purchaser becomes much weaker in these circumstances, especially bearing in mind that survivorship can operate in their favour.

Nevertheless, stepping back from these points it is apparent that survivorship is plainly an inappropriate feature of the new relationship. It can make excellent sense between spouses and other partners (the focus of most modern joint tenancies) and sometimes as regards close relatives, such as unmarried siblings (most commonly seen in older settlements). It makes no sense at all between a purchaser and the other joint tenant or tenants. One may doubt whether any prejudice to the non-notified joint tenant is significant enough[221] to outweigh the long-established hostility towards survivorship. If we were developing a severance structure from scratch, perhaps this method of severance would not be included. But it is well entrenched in our thinking and has sufficient arguments in its favour to rebut arguments that it should be jettisoned.

Unilateral declarations have been supported by Lord Denning MR, but otherwise generally rejected. As a matter of law, this rejection seems inevitable. However, it is interesting that several commentators have expressed the opinion that there are good policy reasons to recognize such declarations, at least if communicated to the other party (as required by Lord Denning MR).[222] This is largely based upon the perception that there is no justification for maintaining a joint tenancy in the face of a communicated desire to sever: the context is usually that of a failed relationship, for which survivorship is patently unsuited. Technical rules should not stand in the way of substantive justice, especially when a well advised joint tenant can unilaterally sever by a transfer. There is much to be said in favour of this argument, though it has been most strongly put forward

---

[221] Reliance on there being no severance (giving rise to estoppel based arguments) is unlikely, given that there can be severance by notice at any time.

[222] Most strongly articulated by Tooher (1998) 24 Monash ULR 422, 448: 'sound in policy and logic'. Whilst criticizing Lord Denning MR as regards authority, McClean describes his analysis as 'fair and simple': (1979) 57 Can BR 1, 31.

in jurisdictions which no equivalent to severance by written notice under LPA, section 36(2). In England, it is far from clear that unilateral declarations of severance should be encouraged. Such a development would permit oral declarations to be effective, which would introduce much more uncertainty and subvert the statutory writing requirement. The deficiencies in section 36(2) of course lend some support for a wider equitable rule (a factor powerfully influencing Lord Denning MR) but the preferable response is legislation to remedy those deficiencies, rather than introducing even greater uncertainty. Of course, an oral agreement or course of conduct can still be relied upon to sever.

Leaving aside unilateral declarations, the second and third heads of equitable severance seem appropriate. The major problem is discovering whether there is in fact a sufficient course of dealing. The courts have been unduly restrictive in this context, at least in the relationship breakdown context. This is an area in which one may hope for further development through court decisions.

Two radical proposals were suggested by the Law Commission in 1985.[223] One was that written notice should be the only form of severance. Although there is good reason to restrict severance where there is no written notice, the Law Commission considers that this proposal goes too far. To deny effect to severance when it has been agreed by the parties is to invite disputes and injustice. Although the proposal is not dissimilar to requiring writing for agreements to sever (as some jurisdictions may do)[224] it fails to take account of the arguments of justice in not restricting severance on purely technical grounds. We might wish to distinguish here unilateral declarations (where section 36(2) does require writing) from bilateral agreements. It is more likely in the latter situation that one party will rely on the agreement by not employing a more formal method of severance.

The second proposal was to allow severance by explicit provision in a will. This enables either party to make it clear (retrospectively, anyway) that they wish to sever, without involving a possibly confrontational notice to the other party. As Tee has convincingly demonstrated,[225] this proposal suffers from two major disadvantages. The first is whether it is acceptable for one party, having made such a will, to be in a position (a) to protect his or her interest if the first to die, and at the same time (b) to take advantage of survivorship if the other is the first to die. Though either party can engineer that position, its inherent inequality is difficult to accept. The proposal is also likely to raise acutely difficult questions as to whether there is a sufficiently explicit provision in the will.

What conclusions can be drawn? Apart from remedying the defects of written notice, it is difficult to envisage significant reforms of the severance rules. Few would argue that the present rules produce ideal results, but any change runs the risk of producing unwelcome or uncertain results. Moving a long way from

---

[223] Law Com WP 94, paras 16.12–14 (see n 220 above).
[224] See p 68 above. However, part performance provides flexibility in these jurisdictions: it is no longer available in England (*United Bank of Kuwait plc v Sahib* [1997] Ch 107, esp 139–40).
[225] [1995] Conv 105, 111–13. See also Thompson [1987] Conv 275, 277.

the present rules, one might ask whether the courts should be given a statutory discretion to exclude survivorship (at least where the relationship between the parties no longer makes it appropriate). This would solve many of the problems. However, it would introduce much uncertainty and be an exceptional court intrusion into the sphere of private property rights. It seems improbable! Perhaps the problems identified in this Chapter are the inevitable consequence of having a survivorship structure.

# 5

# Joint Tenancy and Tenancy in Common Reviewed

That it is somewhat odd to recognize two forms of co-ownership has not escaped the attention of commentators. We have observed above that, prior to 1925, tenancies by entireties and coparcenary were recognized as additional forms of co-ownership. The question asked in this short Chapter is whether we should take the process of simplification further and recognize only one form of co-ownership in the modern law.

There are of, course, several special rules for joint tenancies, but its one practical difference is survivorship. The policy question is whether it is worth preserving two forms of co-ownership when survivorship is the single substantial difference between them. The tenancy in common is obviously the more flexible variant: it does not require all four unities and, crucially, allows property to be held in unequal shares and to pass on a co-owner's death to the deceased's estate. If one were to be abolished, it could only be the joint tenancy. Since 1925, of course, the legal estate must be held by joint tenants: a change designed to render tracing the devolution of the legal estate less troublesome. This is a sound policy (even if not adopted by many common law jurisdictions) and reform of co-ownership need not challenge it. Accordingly, the question may be narrowed to whether the *beneficial* joint tenancy should be retained.

An obvious initial question from those sceptical of reform is why we should limit the choice of purchasers and settlor, an inevitable consequence of abolishing the beneficial joint tenancy. Their scepticism is enhanced by the fact that beneficial joint tenancies are widely used: it is not as if the idea is to get rid of a device which is rarely used. The answer is largely that the joint tenancy frequently frustrates the intentions of the parties, either because the joint tenancy was inappropriate in the first place or because it becomes inappropriate (generally following a relationship breakdown) and the parties have not undertaken the necessary steps to sever.[1] It must be remembered that survivorship is not the only means of giving effect to the intentions of joint tenants: they can leave property to each other by will.

---

[1] The arguments are well put by Thompson [1987] Conv 29 and 275, but see the response by Pritchard [1987] Conv 273. Their analyses form the basis of many of the points made in this Chapter. Bandali [1977] Conv 243 also attacks the joint tenancy.

In addition, one should not overlook the benefits of a simple legal structure: a single form of co-ownership would render almost all of the two preceding Chapters otiose. Apart from the uncertainty of application of many of the rules, their very existence adds complexity and therefore expense for many co-owners. Of course, the law is always willing to accept complexity if it provides freedom of choice and facilitates the implementation of parties' wishes. The question is whether the joint tenancy in practice provides benefits (without greater disadvantages) which justify the legal complexity. One observation is that, though reform of individual rules of the joint tenancy may be urged, it is difficult to contemplate radical reforms which would simplify the structure and improve its operation. This is reflected in the difficulty in advancing reforms of the severance rules, considered at the end of the previous Chapter. Accordingly, abolition of the beneficial joint tenancy is the only reform which could bring about real simplification.

In assessing the joint tenancy, we consider its alleged drawbacks and advantages. First, how severe are the problems caused by joint tenancies? The first problem is that a joint tenancy may be created when a tenancy in common would be more appropriate. In the context of property purchase, modern transfers identify the beneficial interests.[2] This has two consequences. First, we rarely employ the law's preference for a joint tenancy: we look to what the transfer provides. Secondly, it means that, provided the parties have been properly advised, all joint tenancies reflect the wishes of the purchasers. However, this solution does not operate where an interest derives from common intention (giving rise to a constructive or resulting trust) rather than the terms of the transfer. In this context it may be difficult to work out both what is intended and what is the most appropriate outcome. We have seen that it is unclear whether joint tenancy or tenancy in common is the most likely outcome.[3] Though it is difficult to say that the 'wrong' outcome is reached, there is obvious and undesirable uncertainty. So far we have considered purchase, but co-ownership may also be created by gifts and settlements. Here, there is a greater risk that a joint tenancy will be created when it is inappropriate. Thus a trust in favour of X's children will, without more, create a joint tenancy. If the children are unmarried, this may well make sense. But if they are married with children of their own, it is less likely that survivorship will be what they want or what the settlor intended.[4] Some jurisdictions[5] have reversed the presumption of joint tenancy and there is much to be said for this where settlements are concerned.[6] Though survivorship may be intended on occasion, today it is less likely to be desired.

---

[2] See p 40 above.    [3] See p 41 above.

[4] For the analogous issue of lapse in legacies, see p 32 above.

[5] In Australia: New South Wales, Queensland, and ACT (Sackville and Neave: *Property Law: Cases and Materials* (6th edn), para 7.4.5). Most Canadian provinces adopt this reform: *Thom's Canadian Torrens System* (2nd edn), p 349.

[6] Its application in the common intention trust context is less likely to be beneficial: *Delehunt v Carmody* (1986) 161 CLR 464 (p 86 below).

The second problem is that survivorship may cease to be appropriate. This applies most obviously to relationships which have broken down: the context of the great majority of modern severance cases. It is difficult to avoid the conclusion that survivorship is entirely inappropriate in this context: in the normal case neither party would expect to benefit from the other's death, especially if the deceased was in a new relationship. Yet the cases show example after example where there is no severance. Some of these cases could be corrected by the courts' adopting approaches more favourable towards severance. However, it seems impossible to contemplate a reform which would effect a severance in all these cases, certainly not one which bears any relationship to the present rules. Could there be a novel rule that a relationship breakdown itself severs? This would raise huge difficulties of definition, quite apart from the problem of on-off relationships; it seems wildly implausible. This indictment of the joint tenancy appears well justified.

Given that joint tenancy can produce the wrong result, how valuable is it in producing the right result? This involves consideration of the popularity of the joint tenancy and how far it is necessary in order to give effect to a desire for the survivor to take the property. The evidence indicates that a joint tenancy is commonly chosen where a couple purchase their home.[7] This is replicated in recent material from Australia, where one might expect similar property owning intentions as in England.[8] Two main doubts may be voiced. The first is that the joint tenancy may be chosen because the solicitors involved state that it is usual; the parties may not give the question full consideration or understand what they are doing.[9] It is unlikely that there is a lawyers' conspiracy against the tenancy in common! However, it is more likely that they correctly identify that most purchasers do desire survivorship, but that their advice causes a minority to take the easy way out of saying 'yes' when a fuller assessment of the situation might cause them to prefer a tenancy in common. This may indeed happen in some cases, though it seems safe to believe that the joint tenancy does usually represent their intentions. This fits the ideas of 'trust and collaboration' and 'communality' espoused by Simon Gardner in the context of recognising property rights in the first place.[10] The second doubt concerns the structure of relationships. Those who are married (or plan marriage) or are in long-term relationships, especially where there are children, are likely to desire survivorship. However, shorter-term relationships need not give rise to this inference. Just as one might expect two or

---

[7] Todd and Jones, *Matrimonial Property* (1972), p 78. This is equally true in the United States: Hines (1966) 51 Iowa LR 582.

[8] In New South Wales it is said that over 91% of co-owned titles are joint tenancies: New South Wales Law Reform Commission Report No 73 (1994), para 2.14. In Victoria the figure has been estimated at 80%: Tooher (1998) 24 Monash ULR 399, 399.

[9] See Bandali [1977] Conv 243, 243–4.

[10] (1993) 109 LQR 263, 287: 'They do not keep separate accounts . . . , but trust and collaborate with one another for the good of both. In a nutshell, restitution is about "mine or yours"; communality is about "ours".' His stress is on the move away from proving intention: our investigation is not into the proved intention of individual purchasers but on what best fits the intentions of most purchasers.

three friends buying a house together not to want survivorship, so the same may true of two persons who are living together and who view the purchase as a way of getting onto the housing ladder, rather than as a home for the two of them together on a long-term basis. A further factor which may operate in a some relationships is that it may be tax efficient (as regards inheritance tax)[11] to use the tax-free allowance and give one's share in the property to, say, children, rather than to the survivor.[12] This will apply only where the couple's assets exceed £263,000.[13] Whilst this figure is readily reached where there are high property values, it is still far more than the average property price. In any event, this is most likely to be part of a tax-planning strategy for the wealthy and elderly: younger people are likely to have mortgages which reduce the value of their net assets and have a greater incentive (for non-financial reasons) for wanting the survivor to own the property outright. It would be rare for it to affect the parties' intentions at the time of purchasing the home.

We might conclude that the joint tenancy does fit the needs of a large proportion of purchasers of houses. But how far is it needed? Turning first to settlements, the settlor could readily create joint life interests with remainder to the survivor: this has much the same effect as a joint tenancy. Purchasers of houses could readily make wills leaving property to each other,[14] but it is here that the argument begins to break down. Especially where relatively young people are involved and death is unexpected, wills are commonly not made. It would be ideal if there were a will, but we have to accept a world where this cannot be assumed. If the parties are married, then the intestacy rules are likely to provide a satisfactory outcome, sharing the property between the survivor and children in the typical case.[15] However, an unmarried partner faces the prospect of the deceased's family (or worse, an estranged spouse) claiming part of the home. This problem is greatest, of course, where there are no children of the relationship.[16] The risks are graphically illustrated by the Australian case of *Delehunt v Carmody*.[17] The husband lived with his wife for four years. Following their separation, he lived with the defendant for over thirty years. As a consequence of New South Wales legislation,[18] the husband and the defendant owned their home as beneficial tenants in common. When the husband died intestate his wife was granted administration of the estate and was held to be entitled to his share. In practical terms this is a horrendous result, far worse than any of the English

[11] There may be also be advantages in reducing the assets which have to be sold to pay for care costs of the survivor in old age.

[12] This may carry its own risks, including bankruptcy of the children. Cf De Souza [2003] PCB 57.

[13] For 2004–2005. In 2004, the average house value was £166,000: Land Registry *Residential Property Price Report*.

[14] This option can also apply to interests under settlements, though many beneficiaries will not think about making or amending a will. [15] Administration of Estates Act 1925, s 46.

[16] Otherwise they would be able to claim under the intestacy. They are unlikely to be hostile towards one of their parents. [17] (1986) 161 CLR 464.

[18] Conveyancing Act 1919, s 26. The case turned on the application of this provision.

severance cases. This shows that there is a real danger of expectations being disappointed in a large number of cases if a tenancy in common is employed. These may well exceed the numbers of cases in which a relationship has broken down but there has not been severance.

The critics of the joint tenancy can still, of course, make the point that survivorship is inappropriate for relationships which have broken down. We now need to investigate the broken down relationship in more detail. This context is the major source of concern so far as the operation of the joint tenancy is concerned. How well would the law operate if there were no joint tenancy? Obviously, if the parties never wanted survivorship, then the tenancy in common works well. However, in most relationships the parties are likely to want the survivor to get the property. We have just seen that this can cause problems if one dies during the relationship without making a will. The tenancy in common demands that wills be made in order to that the parties' intentions are fulfilled. What happens if a will has been made and then the relationship breaks down? In theory, the answer is simple: a new will should be made. In practice, the obvious danger is that this will be overlooked (as with joint tenancies, unexpected deaths pose the greatest problems) so that on death the property passes to the estranged spouse or partner. This is exactly the same outcome as with an unsevered joint tenancy. The lawyer who sees the problem is as likely to sever a joint tenancy as to urge the making of a new will.[19] In other words, the problems will be just as severe whether a joint tenancy or tenancy in common is employed. Any legal structure which provides for property to go a particular person is apt to malfunction if the relationship with that person has broken down. It is difficult to avoid the conclusion that positive steps must be taken to change the destination of the property and that those steps are in fact not taken in many cases. Indeed, one may argue that joint tenancy is much more likely to produce the correct result because of the court's ability to find a sufficient agreement or course of dealing to achieve severance; implying terms into wills is far more difficult.

Accordingly, similar problems arise whatever legal structure is employed. When assessing whether abolition of the beneficial joint tenancy is justified, three elements are crucial. The first is the question, already discussed, of how many co-owners actually want their spouse or partner to take on their death. If that proportion is high, then the joint tenancy possesses advantages. Consider first the situation where the relationship continues until death. The joint tenancy has the advantage that it operates even if no will has been made, thus avoiding unintended results which may follow if there is a tenancy in common. Where the relationship has broken down, both joint tenancy and tenancy in common can cause problems. However, the joint tenancy still enjoys the advantage that less formality is required to ensure that the property does not go to the survivor.

---

[19] Provisions in favour of a former spouse are ineffective after divorce (Wills Act 1837, s 18A) but it is highly unlikely that a joint tenancy will not have been severed by that stage.

The second element concerns the incidence of relationship breakdown. The main advantages of joint tenancies lie in fulfilling the wishes of co-owners when one dies during the relationship. Both joint tenancy and tenancies in common can cause inappropriate results once the relationship breaks down. It seems likely that breakdown of relationships has become more common. This is reflected in the growth of divorce rates[20] and is likely to be related to greater numbers living together outside marriage.[21] These changes tend to reduce the advantages of the joint tenancy.

The third element concerns the extent to which wills would in fact be made and amended by those who (at the time of purchase) wish their property to go to the survivor. Given that the joint tenancy achieves the desired result whilst the relationship continues, this may help to explain why wills are often not made. It is difficult to assess how many more people (especially those relatively young) would make wills if this were the only way of ensuring that their house passed to the survivor. Equally difficult to assess is whether wills are in fact amended when relationships break down. The problem of the unamended will is not something which features in litigation. However, this is probably because there is no doubt as to the outcome, rather than because that the problem does not exist.

So far, the conclusion appears to be that the joint tenancy possesses advantages which militate against its abolition. This is supported by the argument that it would be odd to abolish a form of property holding which is the choice of most purchasers, even if that choice is based only on the recommendations of their lawyers. However, we need to recall that maintaining both joint tenancy and tenancy in common leads to complexity in the law, and any complexity leads to added expense. This is most obviously seen in the cases on severance, which also demonstrate a lamentable lack of certainty for potential litigants. Nevertheless, the number of reported cases is small. Considering both the question whether there is initially a joint tenancy or tenancy in common, and severance, the cases scarcely get beyond the fingers on one hand for the past quarter of a century! There are certainly some difficult questions involved, but the evidence does not point to a mountain of expensive litigation. Of course, one should not overlook the fact that a very much larger number of cases will have arisen over that period; even without litigation, time and money will have been spent on resolving them. What this complexity shows is that the joint tenancy needs to demonstrate distinct advantages to be worth keeping: a conclusion that it is 'no worse' than the tenancy in common is not enough to defend it.

---

[20] *Social Trends 34* (2004), figure 2.11. There has been a reduction in more recent years, but the number of marriages has also dropped. It has been observed that 'Among those who were married in the latter half of the 1980s, around one in eight men and one in six women had separated within the first five years': *Social Trends 32* (2002), p 44.

[21] *Social Trends 32*, p 42. Of those cohabiting (not followed by marriage) about 1 in 5 relationships survives 5 years: *Duration of past cohabitations which did not end in marriage by number of past cohabitations and sex: Living in Britain 2002* (Dataset LIB0515). It is, of course, possible that the figures are different for those purchasing a home together.

These questions necessarily involve judgements about the strengths of the arguments in each direction and there is ample scope for disagreement as to the outcome. However, this author believes that the case for abolition is not made out. That position could, however, change. Further evidence as to the true intentions of house purchasers, the incidence of relationship breakdown, and the use of wills could paint a quite different picture.

# PART III

# REGULATION OF PLURAL OWNERSHIP OF LAND

# 6

# Regulation: Introduction and Scope

This Chapter considers the general role and scope of statutory regulation of both concurrent and successive interests, from the nineteenth century through to the Trusts of Land and Appointment of Trustees Act 1996 (hereafter TLATA). Subsequent Chapters deal with regulation of occupation, powers of the trustees (coupled with their regulation by the courts), and protection of purchasers and others taking dispositions of the land.

The area involves much learning and history. This book makes no attempt to go fully into these elements, which involve extensive economic and social analyses of land ownership, especially in the nineteenth century. We are studying the modern law of plural ownership, today based on TLATA. However, we must understand the forces that have moulded the law: these are crucial to our modern structures. It may be that we would choose very different structures if we were starting from scratch and, indeed, other common law jurisdictions (with different land ownership traditions) have not thought it necessary to develop as comprehensive a regulatory structure as was adopted in the 1925 legislation.

## 1. The Need for Regulation

An introductory comment on terminology is needed. 'Regulation' is not meant to signify any external body overseeing the operation of successive and concurrent interests, though we shall see that courts have extensive powers to resolve disputes. Rather, we are dealing with the provision of structures by which such interests can, indeed must, be held. These structures are intended to cover three principal (and interwoven) concerns. The first is that the land can be efficiently managed (for example, that money can be raised to undertake desirable repairs). The second is to ensure that those acquiring interests in the land (usually as purchasers, chargees, or lessees) can acquire safe titles without undue delay or expensive enquiries. The third is to establish the relationship between the holders of the successive and concurrent interests on one side and those managing the land on the other. At least since 1925, the response to these concerns has been the placing of legal title and management powers in one small body of

persons[1] and recognizing the successive and concurrent interests as being beneficial interests under a trust.

## A. Successive Interests

The development of regulation of successive interests cannot be understood without appreciating the nature and role of settlements of land in past centuries. Three
factors dominate. First, land constituted the major asset class prior to the growth
in importance of shares in companies in the nineteenth century:[2] it is therefore
not surprising that it attracted more attention than it does today. Secondly, land
ownership was concentrated in a relatively small number of wealthy families: a far
cry from the spread of property ownership encountered today. The final factor was
that the property-owning families tied up their ownership in complex trusts,
designed to keep the land in the family over many generations, generally in the
hands of the eldest male member of the family (primogeniture).

   Accordingly, the principal assets of the country were subject to such settlements,
an issue of interest to historians, economists, and politicians, as well as lawyers.[3] If
these settlements failed to operate effectively, this was a matter of great concern.
Today land is much less important as an element of national wealth, ownership is
significantly more widely spread through the population, and complex trusts are
less popular, even for wealthy families. The nineteenth-century concerns may be
difficult to relate to modern conditions, but that does not mean that they were any
less important at the time.

   We need not consider in detail the evidence for the importance of land and
the concentration of ownership.[4] However, it is worth considering the characteristics and effect of the standard form of settlement, usually described as a strict
settlement.[5] This was refined over the years, but generally adopted the following
form. It would start with a life interest for the head of the family (X), followed by
an entail to the life tenant's eldest son (Y). There would be a remainder interest
in fee simple, though this could operate only if the family died out and would
not normally become important. Although the entail apparently provides for the

---

   [1] Settled land uses the tenant for life as a single trustee-manager. Anomalously, the trustees of the
settlement do not hold any interest in the land.
   [2] The nineteenth-century developments are mirrored by the contemporaneous growth of the
trust for sale (the 'trader's settlement'): Lightwood (1927) 3 CLJ 59. However, note that land constitutes some 77% of UK net capital stock: National Statistics, *Capital Stocks, Capital Consumption and
Non-Financial Balance Sheets* (2003), Table 1.1.1.
   [3] It should be remembered that the 1925 legislation was the product of a number of different
forces. Anderson observes in Bright and Dewar (eds), *Land Law: Themes and Perspectives*, chapter 4,
how much depended on compromise.
   [4] It is estimated that between half and three-quarters of land was settled in the nineteenth century:
Chesterman in Rubin and Sugarman (eds), *Law, Economy and Society, 1750–1914*, p 130. By the
mid-twentieth century, land represented only 7% of assets in settlements (ibid, pp 125–6).
   [5] Well described by Megarry and Wade, *Law of Real Property* (5th edn), pp 312–13 in a section
revealingly headed 'Evils of settlements'. See also Simpson, *A History of the Land Law*, pp 233–41.

passing through generations,[6] the position was complicated by the possibility of barring the entail.[7] Barring an entail (by Y, in the example above) would terminate the entail and create a fee simple in its place. However, without the consent of the life tenant, only a base fee would be created: an interest which would not defeat the ultimate fee simple remainder. Such an interest holds limited attraction. To defeat the remainder, barring an entail needed to be undertaken either by a tenant in tail whose interest was in possession or with the agreement of the prior life interest holder.

How does this relate to the form of the settlement? First, it explains why the life interest is created: it ensures that X cannot bar the entail. Y could do so, but he could create only the unattractive base fee. It might be thought that Y need only wait until X dies, but this would be likely to occur quite late in Y's life, long after Y needed the income. The likelihood was that X would agree to a resettlement whereby Y, the holder of the entail, became a life interest holder, in return for an immediate share in the income from the settled property. X would have the motive of ensuring that the property remained within the family, whilst Y would be under pressure to agree in order to receive income. The resettlement would include an entail in favour of Y's eldest son. Such resettlements would continue generation by generation. Could not the outcome be reached much more simply by creating a series of life interests? The answer is that the rules against perpetuities are liable to invalidate gifts which vest more than one generation distant, so that little could be achieved that way.

The resultant settlements are obviously complex.[8] Indeed, they are likely to be far more complicated than this summary indicates. There are likely to be alternative trusts to cover the situation if an heir dies without children.[9] Furthermore, the settlement provides only for the eldest male in each generation. The reason is to keep the settled estate as a single unit (usually with a mansion house at its heart). Yet settlors did not wish their widows and other children to go unprovided for. Accordingly, they would usually be given monetary rights charged on the land.

So far, we have seen that there was a complex settlement structure affecting much land. This is doubtless of great interest to historians, but why (leaving aside issues of inequality) was it thought to cause problems which required a statutory response?[10] The earliest responses reveal that problems in land management were crucial: not so much problems regarding sale, but problems in ensuring that the land was properly maintained (a prime example was adequate land drainage). A number of factors combined to explain these problems. Most obviously, the land was managed by a life interest holder; why should the holder of a life interest

---

[6] It might be added that descent was to male heirs before female heirs.

[7] See also p 13 above.

[8] The issues following resettlement continue to complicate the law: Megarry and Wade, *Law of Real Property* (6th edn), paras 8-069–8.070.

[9] In the original example, Y might predecease X. If Y had no children, the settlor would wish the property to go to X's next eldest son (Z) and there would need to be an additional remainder in tail in favour of Z.     [10] See Simpson, *A History of the Land Law* (2nd edn), pp 239–40.

spend money on long-term improvements which would only marginally benefit his own interest? Yet this obvious point is rather shallow: in the great majority of cases[11] the children of the life interest holder would benefit and he therefore has every incentive to improve the land. It is more likely that the life interest holder would not have the resources to undertake the work. This could be because of a profligate life style, but a major role was played by the financial claims of widows and other children.

What was needed was a recognition that the cost should be borne, not by the life tenant, but by the capital of the trust. There were usually no liquid funds for this purpose, so a charge on the land was the way to raise money for improvements. This was recognized by legislation in the 1840s.[12] The life tenant obtains the benefit of the higher yield from the land following the work, but has to make payments under the loan which is charged on the land. Other problems might be encountered by the tenant for life in using the land effectively. The rules of waste[13] would prohibit actions such as opening new mines: the value of minerals was thought to attach to the capital rather than justifying income for the life tenant.

Modern lawyers tend to place most stress on alienability of the land. This may not have been a major concern prior to the industrial revolution. Thereafter, it became increasingly necessary to be able to sell or lease in order to take advantage of demands on land for industrial use and the housing which accompanied it. Another obvious point is that it might be desirable to sell land in order to finance improvements to what is left: problems in selling added to the need for the statutory reforms noted above. Nor was this simply a matter of the family being unable to realize potential wealth: when so much land was held under trusts there was a risk that national economic development would be impeded. On the other hand, it is easy to exaggerate the problems. Well drafted settlements could confer powers on the tenant for life[14] and for the larger settlements a private Act of Parliament might be obtained to authorize transactions.[15]

## B. Concurrent Interests

It seems that, prior to discussions leading to the 1925 legislation, concurrent interests were not thought to raise major concerns.[16] However, it was then perceived that tenancies in common could pose considerable problems. Take the simple case of A and B being co-owners. If they are joint tenants, then on A's death (easily

---

[11] There are exceptions, especially where there are no heirs and the fee simple remainder will pass the land to a distant branch of the family.

[12] Settled Estates Drainage Act 1840; approval of the court was required. Repayment had to be made over 12–18 years out of income. Over the years other types of improvement were added and the procedures made simpler.

[13] Megarry and Wade, *Law of Real Property* (6th edn), paras 3-098 *et seq*; *Saunders's Case* (1599) 5 Co Rep 12a.          [14] A pointer to the reforms later found in the settled land legislation.

[15] Scamell [1957] CLP 152, 157 (700 in the first half of the nineteenth century, but at a considerable cost).          [16] Anderson, *Lawyers and the Making of English Land Law 1832–1940*, pp 286–8.

proved by a death certificate) B becomes the owner. A purchaser dealing with B faces no particular problems. However, suppose that there is a tenancy in common and A leaves his share to his four children. In this situation, the purchaser faces two problems. First, the devolution of A's interest has to be traced: perhaps not all that difficult, but still an extra burden. Secondly, the purchaser has to deal with B and the four children. Not only does this complicate the process of buying the land, it makes it less likely that the land can be sold at all. If one of the five tenants in common is reluctant to sell (or cannot be traced) then any transaction could be blocked. The only recourse was an application to court for partition or sale. If all but one of them wished to charge or lease the land, it might be difficult to find any useful resolution of their disagreement.

In the example above, the problems may be regarded as acceptable with just five co-owners. However, the shares might be divided far more dramatically. If A and B each leave their interests to their six grandchildren, we have twelve owners. If the grandchildren each leave their interests to numerous relatives, then we might easily end up with over fifty owners. At that stage matters get out of hand. Not only are the numbers of dispositions high,[17] but the practicalities of dealing with so many owners become horrendous. Indeed, Underhill went so far as to describe this as a 'far worse impediment to "free trade in land" than settlements'.[18] The solution in the 1925 legislation is for the legal estate to be held by a small number (up to four) of joint tenants, with the tenants in common having beneficial interests. The joint tenants are given power to deal with the land and they are the only persons with whom a purchaser (or other disponee) has to deal.[19] This trust is also applied to joint tenancies, which might of course become tenancies in common by severance.

Was this change necessary? Whilst it seems clear that problems did arise in tenancies in common, one may doubt whether they were sufficiently frequent to require such a radical change. It is instructive that most other jurisdictions declined to adopt these changes, even where other aspects of the 1925 legislation have been adopted.[20] There is no reason to think that social or economic factors elsewhere operate to diminish the use of tenancies in common or their potential problems.[21] The trust may be seen as artificial and to give rise to rather pointless

---

[17] A factor which can be greatly reduced in importance by registration of title.

[18] (1920) 36 LQR 107, 116 (see also 108). Underhill was a significant figure in the proposals leading to the 1925 legislation: Anderson, *Lawyers and the Making of English Land Law 1832–1940*, pp 283 *et seq.*

[19] Anderson observes, ibid at p 288, that the trustees still have to identify the tenants in common. For other responses to the problem, see Rowton Simpson, *Land Law and Registration* (2nd edn, book 1), paras 13.4, 13.6.7–13.6.8.

[20] This is true of most Australian states: Sackville and Neave, *Property Law: Cases and Materials* (6th edn), paras 7.4.9, 8.4.6–8.4.7.

[21] It was otherwise for successive interests: complex and long-lasting settlements were far more common in England than elsewhere. Accordingly, it is paradoxical that some jurisdictions have adopted the English reforms of successive interests (at least in part) but not the reforms of concurrent interests.

questions as to the extent to which old rules are changed by the introduction of the trust.[22] Today the trust is so firmly established in our thinking and legislation that it would be difficult to eradicate. As later Chapters show, a substantial edifice of control over co-owners is established by TLATA.[23] Whilst not impossible, it might be difficult to replicate this without a trust.[24]

## 2. The 1925 Legislation: Settled Land

The scheme established by the Settled Land Act 1925 (hereafter SLA) still operates today, though only for settlements created before TLATA.[25] It should not be thought that reform commenced in 1925. The basic scheme was established by the Settled Land Act 1882, following initial and more limited reforms a few decades earlier. What was new in 1925 was the concentration on the location of the legal estate and detailed rules for dealing with it. This, in part, followed upon the basic principle established by the Law of Property Act 1925 (hereafter LPA), section 1 that the only legal freehold estate is the fee simple absolute in possession. Both the 1882 and 1925 Acts conferred powers of sale and general management on the tenant for life, but only since 1925 has the legal fee simple been vested in the tenant for life.

It is central to the settled land structure that powers are vested in the tenant for life: typically (for the traditional large landed settlement) the eldest male member of the family. As a counterbalance, there are trustees of the settlement, who may be seen as playing an overseeing role. Unlike normal trustees, the trust property is not normally vested in them. However, any capital money arising on sale (or other transactions) has to be paid to the trustees. This is to avoid the danger of misappropriation, a real risk for money.

Why should the tenant for life play such a significant role? The answer is to be found in the history of settlements. The life estate in a typical nineteenth-century (or earlier) family settlement would result in management by the tenant for life, who would occupy the mansion house and be responsible for leasing parts of the estate to tenant farmers.[26] Although this management could not bind other beneficiaries (so no long-term dealings were feasible), well drafted settlements would confer powers on the tenant for life. This process was continued in, for example, the earlier statutory reforms relating to improvements. In other words, the legislation

---

[22] This has been tied in with the use of the trust for sale and the doctrine of conversion (that the interests were in the proceeds of sale from the outset). Conversion in this context was so troublesome that it was abolished by TLATA, s 3 (see p 182 below).

[23] The comparison with pre-1925 common law principles can still cause problems, perhaps best shown in debates regarding occupation: p 128 below.

[24] See Proposal IV in Law Com WP 94; it was not pursued in Law Com No 181.

[25] TLATA, s 2.

[26] These were not long-term leases; the fact that the tenant for life might be able to bind only his life estate was of minimal importance.

chose to give powers to the person most closely concerned with the land, who might well already have been given similar powers by the settlement.

There follows a brief outline of the major aspects of settled land. The purpose is not to provide a comprehensive analysis of the operation of settled land,[27] but to enable comparisons to be made with the modern trust of land under TLATA. The settled land scheme is a complex one, but with few exceptions the legislation operates as intended. As will be seen later,[28] one the main reasons for its being dropped by TLATA was the extensive decline in the use of the type of settlement for which it was designed.

## A. When is There a Settlement?

Because no new SLA settlements can be created after TLATA, this can be looked at quickly. SLA, section 1 identifies a number of cases. Most obviously, successive interests under trusts are included. This covers the very standard settlement 'to A for life, remainder to B in fee simple'.[29] More specific provisions cover entails, interests capable of being defeated, determinable interests, and contingent interests.[30] Somewhat less obvious cases are where an infant would otherwise own the land,[31] and where the land is charged with the payment of money as part of a family settlement.[32] In both these last two cases, it is thought necessary to establish powers to manage the land. These quite complex provisions in SLA, section 1 may be contrasted with the simpler ones in TLATA.[33]

## B. The Tenant for Life; Powers

Given the central role played by the tenant for life, identifying the holder of this position is crucial. Apart from those with life interests in possession, there is an extensive list of others who may be tenants for life.[34] By and large, anyone entitled (under the settlement)[35] to an interest in possession in the land qualifies. If there is more than one, then they jointly constitute the tenant for life if they are joint tenants. A rather curious rule applies if they are tenants in common:[36] the settled land becomes a trust of land (trust for sale until TLATA)[37] whilst the

---

[27] See Megarry and Wade, *Law of Real Property* (6th edn), chapter 8 for more detail.
[28] Page 108 below.
[29] SLA, s 1(1)(i). It will be remembered that life and remainder interests can exist only in equity: LPA, s 1.
[30] SLA, s 1(1)(ii)(a), (b), (c), and (iii) respectively. Determinable interests include conditional interests: s 117(1)(iv).                                                    [31] Ibid, s 1(1)(ii)(d).
[32] This does not apply to commercial charges: SLA, s 1(1)(v). Even if settled land, it could be sold subject to the charge: Law of Property (Amendment) Act 1926, s 1.        [33] See pp 114–15 below.
[34] SLA, ss 19, 20(1). Technically, s 20 confers the powers on the extended list; they are then deemed to be tenants for life for the purposes of the Act: s 117(1)(xxviii).
[35] A tenant under a lease is not included if the freehold is settled.
[36] SLA, s 36. This avoids possible problems, discussed above, where the legal estate is held by tenants in common.                                                    [37] Schedule 3, para 2(11).

tenancy in common continues. The trustees of the settlement are then entitled to the legal estate.

In some situations there will be no tenant for life according to these provisions. One is where the person who would otherwise be tenant for life is not of full age.[38] Other examples are where there is a contingent claim to the land (to the first of my children to obtain a university degree) or a discretionary trust. Special provision is made for such cases: the default position is that the trustees of the settlement have the powers of the tenant for life.[39] Provision is made for trustees to apply to take over powers if the tenant for life has parted with his or her beneficial interest.[40]

There are complex and lengthy rules relating to powers of the tenant for life.[41] We consider here some of the most important powers. There is a wide power of sale, though there are special rules for the 'principal mansion house:[42] a provision which betrays the sort of settlement the scheme was designed for! There are powers of leasing, though for maximum periods; thus a standard lease cannot exceed fifty years.[43] The land can be mortgaged to secure a debt, though the purposes for which the money is raised are restricted.[44] To take an obvious example, the tenant for life cannot mortgage the land to secure a debt to be used for her business. It can be seen, therefore, that anybody dealing with the tenant for life needs to take great care to ensure that the powers are not exceeded.

The tenant for life is deemed to be in the position of a trustee when exercising powers.[45] Plainly, there is a risk that, because the trustee is a beneficiary, powers will be exercised in such a way as to benefit the tenant for life rather than the beneficiaries as a whole.[46] For the same reason, there is the more insidious danger that the tenant for life may allow personal opinions to outweigh the interests of the beneficiaries. This is well illustrated by *Re Earl Somers*,[47] in which the tenant for life (because of her views on the number of public houses in the vicinity) sought to sell a public house subject to a covenant that intoxicating liquor should not be sold. Unsurprisingly, the other beneficiaries and the court considered that this was likely to reduce the purchase price! That the tenant for life held her views could not be criticized, but she was not entitled to apply them so as to damage the interests of other beneficiaries.

---

[38] SLA, ss 19(1), 20(1).         [39] Ibid, ss 23 (no tenant for life), 26 (infants).

[40] Ibid, s 24. The powers do not pass to an assignee of the beneficial interest: ss 19(4), 104.

[41] Ibid, ss 38–72. Additional powers are conferred where the tenant for life cannot so act on account of infancy: s 102.

[42] Ibid, ss 38, 65 (a principal mansion house has grounds exceeding 25 acres).

[43] Ibid, s 41 (building and forestry leases 999 years; mining leases 100 years).

[44] Ibid, s 71. Mortgagees are protected against the possibility that money is not wanted for the restricted purposes: s 95.                                               [45] Ibid, s 107.

[46] *Middlemas v Stevens* [1901] 1 Ch 574 provides an example. The beneficial interest of the tenant for life would terminate on re-marriage. She intended to remarry, but first proposed to lease the land to her intended husband. This lease was designed to ensure that she could continue to live in the house regardless of remarriage, but the court granted an injunction to stop it. It might be otherwise if the lease were an entirely proper investment: *Cardigan v Curzon-Howe* (1885) 30 Ch D 531, 539–40.

[47] (1895) 11 TLR 567.

A final point is that SLA, section 106 strictly prohibits any attempt to exclude or limit the powers. The background, of course, lies in the policy behind the legislation: to ensure that land can be sold and managed. If the settlor could exclude powers, then this policy might come to nothing. Although the policy may be out of date today,[48] this was no idle point in the early years of the reform. The legislation was controversial and settlors frequently wished to ensure that the land should remain within the family indefinitely. It must be remembered that section 106 invalidates provisions which prevent the exercise of powers or induce the tenant for life not to exercise them.[49] A good example is a provision that the beneficial interest terminates if the tenant for life ceases to reside. Insofar as this operates to inhibit sale or leasing, it is void: the tenant for life can sell or lease and retain the beneficial interest.[50]

## C. Trustees of the Settlement

The trustees of the settlement have been seen to be somewhat anomalous. In the normal course of events, they do not hold property on trust. However, they play a number of roles. As has been seen, they receive capital money:[51] a reaction to the danger of dissipation by the tenant for life. At that stage, they can be seen as more like conventional trustees.[52]

Although it is not spelt out by the legislation, they also play a more general role: '[The tenant for life] acts, as it were, under the real if somewhat remote supervision of the settlement trustees whose primary duty is to conserve the settled property for the remaindermen but who are also concerned to secure fair dealing to the tenant for life'.[53] This explains the requirement that notice shall be given to them before most powers are exercised.[54] It is intended to give the trustees the opportunity to check that the transaction is appropriate, as well as helping to ensure that capital monies are paid to them.

Thirdly, trustees have a number of additional and more specific roles. These may be explained on the basis that the existence of an independent body of persons provides a convenient way of dealing with disparate issues. Thus we have seen that they may exercise the powers of the tenant for life in certain cases. They are also given powers in certain potentially troublesome situations: notably disposal of a principal mansion house and transactions in which the tenant for life

---

[48] TLATA powers can be excluded: p 144 below.

[49] Substantial difficulties are caused by funds which are provided for the upkeep of the settled property until it is disposed of: see eg *Re Aberconway's ST* [1953] Ch 647.

[50] *Re Acklom* [1929] 1 Ch 195. However, the provision remains valid if the tenant for life gives up residence for reasons unrelated to the exercise of statutory powers: *Re Haynes* (1887) 37 Ch D 306 (North J treating it as 'a condition of residence while the property is undisposed of'). These are just two of a number of cases on such terms. [51] SLA, ss 18(1)(b), 75(1).

[52] Save that they act under the direction of tenant for life as regards investment or application of the proceeds: ibid, s 75(2). [53] *Re Boston's WT* [1956] Ch 395, 405.

[54] SLA, s 101. Purchasers need not investigate this: s 105(5).

is personally interested, as where he wishes to buy the settled land.[55] They also execute certain documents.[56]

Who are the trustees? Normally, they will be appointed by the settlor. However, a settlor who is unaware of the niceties of the legislation may well not appoint trustees. There are then complex statutory rules on the topic as to who are trustees.[57] Now that new settlements cannot be created, it suffices to say that, in default, the court may appoint trustees.[58]

## D. Documentation and the Protection of Purchasers

One fundamentally important point is that a disposition by the tenant for life (or persons having the powers of the tenant for life) overreaches the beneficial interests under the trusts.[59] Overreaching is described more fully below in the context of trusts of land.[60] However, its essence is that the purchaser is not bound by the beneficial interests. This does not, of course, mean that the beneficial interests are defeated; after sale they take effect against the proceeds of sale (or investments purchased with the proceeds). In a settlement to A for life remainder to B, after sale A will receive the income from the proceeds of sale and B will obtain the capital on A's death.

Overreaching depends upon there being a proper exercise of powers, including the payment of capital monies to the trustees. It is therefore essential that the disponee is able to rely on the information available from the documents. At the same time, that information needs to be capable of quick assimilation: too much information will increase delays, expense, and the risk of error. It is for these reasons that rules relating to documentation form a major element of the legislation. Although designed to ensure simplicity for purchasers, they are highly complex and contribute significantly to the unsuitability of settled land for all save large settlements.

There are two main interlinking principles. The first is that every settlement must be created by two deeds. One (the trust instrument) contains all the details of the trusts.[61] The second (the vesting deed), conveys the land to the tenant for life and identifies the trustees.[62] The requirement of two deeds is based on the complexity of nineteenth-century settlements. If a purchaser had to read them, this would be time consuming and expensive, quite apart from the risk of missing

---

[55] Ibid, ss 65, 68.

[56] See eg ibid, ss 9(2) (vesting deeds); 7(2); 8(4) (vesting deeds on the death of a tenant for life: the trustees may be special executors under Administration of Estates Act 1925, s 22); 17 (deeds of discharge at the end of the settlement).                                    [57] SLA, ss 30–3.

[58] Ibid, s 34. For settlements created by will, the personal representatives are the default trustees: s 30(3).

[59] Ibid, s 72. There are complex rules governing precisely what interests are overreached, though their general effect is to exclude commercial rights created under the settlement.

[60] See p 184 below.        [61] Ibid, s 4(3) states what it shall contain.

[62] Ibid, s 5 provides more detail.

or misinterpreting some significant information. To take a simple example: suppose the interest of the tenant for life were to terminate on remarriage. The purchaser would, absent statutory protection, have to discover this provision and then make enquiries as to whether it had been activated. These are exactly the sorts of enquiries that the 1925 legislation set out to abolish.

Accordingly, the second principle[63] is that a purchaser can rely upon the vesting deed and has no right to see the trust instrument. As well as providing the necessary purchaser protection, this has the added advantage of keeping the detailed trusts a private matter for the trustees and beneficiaries. The need for two deeds is emphasized by SLA, section 13, which enacts that transactions do not take effect until a vesting deed is executed.[64] A premature disposition by the tenant for life takes effect merely as a contract. There is, however, protection for a bona fide purchaser of a legal estate without notice.

Once the vesting deed is executed then two main consequences follow as regards the validity of dispositions. The first has already been observed: a purchaser can rely on the information within the vesting deed.[65] Take the example considered above, where a life interest terminated on the remarriage of the tenant for life. So long as the vesting deed identifies the individual as tenant for life, the purchaser can rely upon this. The fact that the land should have been transferred to a new tenant for life[66] is immaterial. Yet not all doubts have been laid to rest. The language of the Act is that the purchaser is 'bound and entitled' to assume the vesting deed is accurate. It is not, unfortunately, stated explicitly that this provides protection against beneficiaries, though this appears to be both intended and preferable.[67] Again, the section applies to 'settled land'. If the settlement terminates on the remarriage (so that some person becomes absolutely entitled)[68] does the land remain settled land? There is evidence to support the argument that 'settled land' includes land which was formerly settled.[69] However, where title is registered a purchaser is able to rely on the normal principle for registered land that a good title is obtained unless a claim is protected on the register.[70]

The second consequence operates where a purchaser fails to comply with the requirements of the Act, especially the payment of the purchase money to two trustees.[71] Such a purchaser will obtain a bad title. Indeed, SLA, section 18 goes so

---

[63] It is not completely new: 2 deeds were already commonly employed where land was vested in trustees: Harpum [1990] CLJ 277, 285–6.

[64] Unless the settlement has terminated before the disposition: *Re Alefounder's WT* [1927] 1 Ch 360.

[65] SLA, s 110(2). There are some exclusions, notably a vesting deed executed after a settlement has been improperly executed by a single deed.   [66] Ibid, s 7(4).

[67] Stone [1984] Conv 354, 356–7; cf Megarry and Wade, *Law of Real Property* (5th edn), p 335 (less fully discussed in 6th edn, para 8–029).   [68] SLA, s 7(5) establishes a right to the legal estate.

[69] Megarry and Wade, *Law of Real Property* (6th edn), para 8-029. A narrower view is taken by Stone [1984] Conv 354 (arguing that the purchaser is instead protected by the doctrine of notice).

[70] Land Registration Act 2002, s 29. In settled land, there is no scope for actual occupation overriding interests: Sched 3, para 2(a).

[71] SLA, s 18(1)(b), (c). Alternatively, payment may be made to a trust corporation (p 186 below) or into court.

far as to state that unauthorized dispositions are void. This means that no legal estate is acquired and the purchaser cannot rely on the defence of bona fide purchaser without notice. In virtually every case, the purchaser should be aware that the land is settled and, accordingly, that the statutory rules must be complied with. Unfortunately, exceptional cases arise where the purchaser is justifiably unaware of the settlement and it seems probable that a bad title will result.[72] For registered land, purchasers dealing with the registered proprietor will again be protected, provided any restrictions are complied with.

How do the documentation rules apply following the ending of a settlement? In particular, how can a purchaser be sure that the settlement really has ended, so that it is no longer necessary to pay capital money to the trustees? There are two protections. First, if a conveyance or assent does not state who are the trustees (as is required for a vesting instrument) then a purchaser can assume that the settlement has ended.[73] Thus in a simple settlement of A for life, remainder to B, suppose that A's personal representatives transfer the fee simple to B. Because this transfer does not identify trustees, a purchaser from B need not (and is not entitled to) ask whether B is in fact absolutely entitled according to the settlement. This protects the purchaser if, say, a life interest vested in C has been overlooked by the trustees. In a minority of cases the tenant for life becomes the absolute owner, typically where a condition subsequent cannot come into force.[74] In such cases (which require no transfer of the legal estate) the trustees must execute a 'deed of discharge'. Purchasers can presume that the settlement has ended.[75]

It should be added that there are several other protections for purchasers. We have already seen some specific instances,[76] but a more general protection is provided by SLA, section 110(1). A purchaser in good faith is deemed to have given the best price[77] and 'to have complied with all the requirements' of the Act. A longstanding puzzle is how to relate this last protection to SLA, section 18, which invalidates unauthorized transactions.[78] *Weston v Henshaw*[79] took the view that section 110(1) would not assist a person who did not know that the transaction was with a tenant for life. However, this was widely criticized and was not followed by Ungoed-Thomas J in

[72] *Weston v Henshaw* [1950] Ch 510 provides a notorious example. The tenant for life had previously held the property absolutely. The later vesting deed was not disclosed to a mortgagee, who thought from the earlier deeds that he was dealing with an absolute owner. The problem would not have arisen if the trustees had exercised their power (SLA, s 98(3)) to endorse the earlier deeds with a note of the vesting deed.
[73] SLA, s 110(5), employing the words 'bound and entitled'.
[74] An example would be 'To A, but if A fails to obtain a law degree by the age of 23 then to B'. If A is awarded a law degree at the age of 21, then A is absolutely entitled.
[75] SLA, s 17. The deed of discharge is adopted in TLATA (s 16(4), (5)) to prove that the trust has terminated. There is no equivalent to the transfer not identifying trustees (the other route to SLA protection): trusts of land have no equivalent to the vesting deed which identifies trustees.
[76] SLA, ss 95 (for mortgagees, as to whether money needed), 101(5) (whether notice given of intention to exercise powers).
[77] Ibid, s 39 generally requires the best consideration that can reasonably be obtained.
[78] Section 18 was new in the 1925 Act, being introduced to deal with the problem that the legal estate was, for the first time, vested in the tenant for life.         [79] [1950] Ch 510.

*Re Morgan's Lease*.[80] Where does this leave the inter-relationship between the two sections? Although some authors give a very limited role to section 110(1),[81] probably the best view is that it applies to a 'peripheral irregularity'.[82] Accordingly, it cannot apply where there is no power to enter into the transaction.[83]

## 3. The 1925 Legislation: Successive Interests and Trusts for Sale

The legislation permits a trust for sale to be created instead of an SLA settlement. Technically, this is achieved by SLA, section 1(7): 'This section does not apply to land held upon trust for sale'. It should be noted that the default position is that there is a settled land settlement. There are no provisions imposing a trust for sale where there are successive interests:[84] it is up to the settlor expressly to create a trust for sale.

What is a trust for sale? Apart from the obvious element that there must be an underlying obligation to sell (a power to sell certainly does not suffice) the requirement was for an 'immediate binding trust for sale'.[85] If there was a prior life interest before the trust came into effect, then the trust for sale would not be immediate: the land would be settled for the duration of the life interest.[86] The existence of two forms of settlement meant that there were grey areas in which it was unclear which system applied, especially as to when the land ceased to be settled.[87] The question whether land ceases to be settled land can still be relevant after TLATA, but the removal of the requirement that the trust be 'binding' means that the older cases can be put on one side.

Why would a settlor prefer the trust for sale? Many of the answers may be found in the section below on the need for reform. However, there are two main categories of reasons. The first is that the settlor may wish to avoid the complications inherent in settled land settlements. In particular, the complex documentation may make little sense unless substantial assets are involved; there may also be a fear that failure to comply with the statutory requirements could lead to further problems and expense. The second category relates to management of the land. If it is desired that management should be by the tenant for life, then the settled land scheme fits well. If it is intended that independent trustees should be responsible,

---

[80] [1972] Ch 1 (not discussing s 18). This issue is most likely to arise in short leases, as the tenant is unlikely to look at the title deeds or register.

[81] Elliott (1971) 87 LQR 338 (on the basis that there will rarely be good faith); Warrington [1985] Conv 377.

[82] Megarry and Wade, *Law of Real Property* (6th edn), para 8.045; Hill (1991) 107 LQR 59.

[83] *Quaere* whether s 110(1) applies to the specific defect (see s 18(1)(b), (c)) of failure to pay capital monies to two trustees.

[84] Contrast SLA, s 1 (p 99 above); also concurrent interests (pp 106–7, 112 below).

[85] LPA, s 205(1)(xxix), applied by SLA, s 117(1)(xxx). The word 'binding' is removed by TLATA.

[86] The right of the trustees for sale to obtain the legal title after the life interest terminates is recognized by SLA, s 7(5).          [87] See eg Megarry and Wade, *Law of Real Property* (5th edn), pp 386–9.

then a trust for sale would fit much better.[88] Where a settlor wants to benefit all his children, it may well be thought better for independent trustees to exercise powers, rather than relying upon agreement between the children.

Prior to the statutory reforms culminating in the 1925 legislation, it would have been easy to argue that settled land should be used if it is intended to retain land in the family, whereas trusts for sale were suitable if it was contemplated that the land should be sold. However, this distinction had lost much of its force by 1925. Employing settled land is no guarantee that it will not be sold: the tenant for life possesses non-excludable powers. At the same time, a trust for sale does not mean that the land must be sold. A power to postpone sale is implied, which may be exercised for an unlimited period.[89] The management powers are, in fact, borrowed from settled land.[90] Although disagreement between trustees prima facie leads to a sale in a trust for sale,[91] some rules paradoxically enable the settlor to make it more difficult to sell land held on trust for sale. In particular, consents[92] can be required before the land is sold. Accordingly, the choice of which system to use is unlikely to be much affected by questions as to whether the land is intended to be sold.

The operation of the trust for sale is not considered here. Insofar as the cases survive TLATA, they are considered in the following Chapters. Much of the legislation has been overtaken by TLATA (which applies to all trusts of land, including trusts for sale); what survives is also studied below. One point to note, however, is that there have never been any documentation rules. Nevertheless, it has always been common to create successive interest trusts using two deeds and ways were found to protect the purchaser from the unknown contents of the deed declaring the trusts.[93] Although the lack of statutory protection may be a little alarming, this may well be preferable to the excessive complexity of settled land. Today, registered land provides protection for purchasers against any restrictions on the powers of the trustees, unless they are protected by entry on the register.[94]

## 4. The 1925 Legislation: Concurrent Interests and Trusts for Sale

It has been seen that the use of tenancies in common could greatly complicate titles. The opportunity was taken in 1925 to ensure that there is a trust: it is provided that a tenancy in common cannot exist at law.[95] The general scheme is

---

[88] If there is no tenant for life, as with a discretionary trust, then the trustees of the settlement will have the powers of the tenant for life. However, there will generally be few reasons to employ settled land in this context.          [89] LPA, s 25. Since TLATA, the power cannot be excluded: s 4(1).
[90] LPA, s 28. Fresh provision is made by TLATA, s 6.          [91] See p 155 below.
[92] Consents were regulated by LPA, s 26, now replaced by TLATA, s 10.
[93] Underhill and Hayton, *Law Relating to Trusts and Trustees* (16th edn), pp 469–70; Megarry and Wade, *Law of Real Property* (6th edn), para 8.110 ('invariable practice'); Harpum [1990] CLJ 277, 285–6.          [94] Land Registration Act 2002, s 26.
[95] LPA, s 1(6). This is reinforced by s 36(1), which prohibits severance of a legal joint tenancy.

that the former legal tenants in common hold the legal title as joint tenants on trust for themselves as tenants in common.[96] Until TLATA, the trust was a trust for sale. This meant that the beneficial interests could be overreached and need not be investigated by a purchaser.[97] Suppose that land is conveyed to A, B, and C as tenants in common (with shares of 60 per cent, 20 per cent, and 20 per cent respectively). Since 1925 they are joint tenants at law, holding on trust for themselves as beneficial tenants in common. Suppose A dies, leaving all his property to his six children. Survivorship operates on the legal title so that B and C are the trustees. A's beneficial interest will pass to his children (each having a 10 per cent share) whilst the beneficial interests of B and C remain unchanged. A purchaser can safely deal with B and C (as trustees) and is wholly unconcerned with A's share and the destination of the proceeds of the sale. It might be noted that if there are two tenants in common (A and B) then the purchaser has to ensure that a further trustee is appointed following the death of A. This is because the purchaser has to pay the purchase money to at least two trustees in order to take advantage of the overreaching rules and thereby take free from the beneficial interests.[98] Accordingly, it may be vital for the purchaser to know whether there is a beneficial tenancy in common or joint tenancy: if it had been a joint tenancy, then B becomes solely entitled on A's death and can sell the land without a second trustee.[99]

For joint tenancies, a trust for sale was similarly imposed in 1925. It may not be immediately obvious why this should be. After all, if one joint tenant dies then the survivors can deal with the land: there is no danger of increasing numbers of co-owners, whose rights may be difficult to trace. However, there are at least two reasons for the law to impose a trust for sale (today, a trust of land). The first is that that the joint tenancy may subsequently be severed. In that event it will be necessary to have a trust, just as where the tenancy in common exists from the beginning. The legislation might have provided for a trust for sale to arise for the first time on severance, but it may be viewed as more elegant and less confusing to have the trust in existence from the beginning. The second reason is that a number of provisions regulate the operation of the trust. Most obviously, LPA, section 30 gave the court jurisdiction to resolve disputes relating to sale and dispositions. It would be inexplicable for this jurisdiction to apply to tenancies in common but not to joint tenancies. It makes far more sense to ensure that the regulatory regime applies to all forms of co-ownership. This argument is even stronger after TLATA, which considerably develops the regulatory structure.[100] A separate point is that it

---

[96] This is analogous to the outcome in the cases where equity would find a tenancy in common despite the existence of a legal joint tenancy: see p 33 above.

[97] TLATA, s 6 provides trustees with almost unlimited powers, including sale; overreaching still operates.         [98] LPA, ss 2(1)(ii), 27 (amended by TLATA, without affecting their substance).

[99] It is possible that purchasers of registered land are today protected in the absence of a restriction on the powers of the proprietor: Land Registration Act 2002, s 26. However, that protection seems not to apply to payment to a single trustee: p 195 below.

[100] Esp in the context of rights to occupy (TLATA, s 12). The provisions relating to consents, consultation, and powers are of limited relevance when the joint tenants are legal and beneficial owners: they have to act together in any event.

is thought necessary to limit the number of legal owners to four: the trust readily enables this to be done.[101]

The detailed provisions imposing trusts for sale are considered below in the section on TLATA. Today they operate to create trusts of land rather than a trust for sale.

## 5. The Need for Reform of the 1925 Legislation

For decades there had been calls for reform of the area.[102] Criticism concentrated on two principal areas. First, the Settled Land Act 1925 was seen as inappropriate for many settlements, an important point when it was the form of settlement imposed by default by the 1925 legislation.[103] Despite a few flaws,[104] it is generally regarded as a technical masterpiece.

So why was it equally generally spurned by most settlors? There are, perhaps, two or three principal answers. The first is that it was a complex scheme, requiring some expertise in complying with its requirements and, in particular, ensuring that the appropriate documentation was produced. This may be entirely suitable for large settlements, but was far more problematic for the everyday case of a testator wishing to give a life interest to a spouse, with remainders to their children. Indeed, the legislation was based on the archetypal nineteenth-century settlement of extensive family estates, whereby complex trusts centred around a life interest in the oldest (usually male) heir. As this form of settlement, so prevalent during the nineteenth century,[105] became increasingly marginalized,[106] so the role of the SLA settlement waned.

This leads to the second point. The essence of the settlement structure lay in the management of the land (including sale) by the tenant for life. This built on the structure of earlier centuries whereby a life tenant (usually holding a legal estate) would manage the land during his lifetime and would often be granted additional powers. The 1925 legislation (and its precursors in the preceding decades) chose not to interfere with this, but rather to build on it by extending the powers of the tenant for life. Yet these powers are held for the benefit of the beneficiaries as a whole, not just the tenant for life.[107] It is easy to see that the tenant for life can

---

[101]  See LPA, s 36(1) 'in like manner as if the persons beneficially entitled were tenants in common' (the cross-reference here is to s 34(2): see p 112 below); Trustee Act 1925, s 34(2).

[102]  In particular, see Potter (1944) 8 Conv NS 147; Scamell [1957] CLP 152; Grove (1961) 24 MLR 123. The problems are recounted in Law Com WP 94, paras 3.1–3.28 (repeated in Law Com No 181, para 1.3).

[103]  SLA, s 1. Even though Potter (1944) 8 Conv NS 147 is sympathetic towards settled land, he considered that the trust for sale should be the default form of settlement.

[104]  Perhaps best known is the weakness of purchaser protection revealed in *Weston v Henshaw* [1950] Ch 510: p 104, n 72 above.                                        [105]  Law Com WP 94, para 3.16.

[106]  Leaving aside questions of social change, the impact of taxation and the death of so many male heirs in the First World War were major contributory factors.                                        [107]  SLA, s 107.

often be in a position of conflict of interests. Unsurprisingly, the cases show that on occasion the tenant for life has pursued his or own interests (not necessarily financial) to the detriment of others.[108] Additionally, an individual tenant for life may be incompetent to manage a sizeable estate. It may make sense for such individuals to have beneficial life interests, but not to manage the land. Of course, there are contrary arguments. The tenant for life is the person with the greatest interest in the land's being put to its best use; he or she may be more willing than anyone else to spend time and energy managing it.[109] As in so many areas, there is no single 'right' answer. In some cases, beneficiary management may be the most efficient as well as fitting the settlor's wishes as to who should be charge of the land. Indeed, the settlor may be more than willing to run the risk of prejudicing the interests of remaindermen in order to ensure that the tenant for life exercises control. In other cases, it may be a recipe for disaster for all concerned.

The third point is not dissimilar. Many modern trusts have features which make the settled land structures less attractive. Although control of the tenant for life fits the old idea of the land descending to the eldest male heir, it is less suited where all the children are to take interests: joint management by them (the effect of the settled land provisions) may well be a source of disagreement or inefficiency. Still less is settled land suitable where there is a discretionary trust; here it is inevitable that the land will be managed by trustees whatever the form of trust[110] and the simpler trust for sale was usually most appropriate. Taxation considerations led to the extensive use of discretionary trusts, especially in the period before the Finance Acts of 1969, 1973, and 1975 removed (or limited) their advantages. Rather differently, the assets may include property other than land.[111] Unless there were to be two separate settlements, settled land was inappropriate.

The result of these points was that settled land settlements were rarely created. A very real danger was that they might be created inadvertently; simply creating a life interest was likely to have that effect.[112] Pressure mounted for the Settled Land Act 1925 to be repealed, at least for future settlements.[113] In practice, trusts for sale were normally employed by those drafting trusts.

However, the trust for sale itself was far from ideal and this provided the second area of criticism. A trust for sale may be appropriate where it is intended that the land will be sold. However, in a very large number of trusts sale is seen only as a distant prospect, especially in the concurrent interests context. Most obviously,

---

[108] See p 100.

[109] The earlier literature questioned the suitability of trustee management: Potter (1944) 8 Conv NS 147, 163. Yet the trustees could appoint professional managers or delegate management to the tenant for life. [110] SLA, s 23.

[111] Settled land could include heirlooms; see the cumbersome provisions in SLA, s 67 (court approval required for sale).

[112] The courts frequently attempted to find other solutions: Lord Denning MR in *Binions v Evans* [1972] Ch 359, 366 (though Megaw LJ, 370, regarded the settled land consequences as 'odd', Lord Denning's reasoning failed to convince Megaw and Stephenson LJJ); *Dodsworth v Dodsworth* (1973) 228 EG 1115; *Griffiths v Williams* [1978] 2 EGLR 121.

[113] Scamell [1957] CLP 152; Grove (1961) 24 MLR 123.

many couples who purchased land as their family home would be nonplussed to be told that they held it on trust to sell it! This would be enhanced if they were given the more technical information that the trust is immediate and binding. As we have seen, a trust for sale was the only way in which beneficial concurrent interests could be held.[114]

In practical terms, it can be argued that little damage was done. There would be a power to postpone sale,[115] so that the existence of a trust (rather than power) to sell would be important only if the trustees disagreed. For trustees who are not also beneficiaries, this is unusual: trustees usually manage the land on a consensual basis. Where they are also beneficiaries disagreement is more common. However, this often resulted in an application to court and the judges decided the case by reference to the purposes for the acquisition of the land: the existence of a trust for sale was rarely determinative of the outcome.[116] The trust for sale also caused problems with the notorious doctrine of conversion, but this could be jettisoned whilst keeping the trust for sale.[117] Unsurprisingly, one can point to many desirable changes to trusts for sale (covering topics as diverse as occupation, consultation, delegation, and trustees' powers) but these have little bearing on the essential nature of the trust for sale.

The general structure of the 1925 legislation involved the trust with a power of sale as the territory of the Settled Land Act settlement. The contrasting and alternative trust was that involving a trust for sale. The paradox is that the trust with a power of sale became almost obsolescent, whilst the trust for sale became almost universal. Given that the most natural analysis (for both successive and concurrent interests) is that of a power of sale, this placed the cart distinctly ahead of the horse. Now that TLATA has abolished the Settled Land Act settlement (for future settlements) it becomes trivially easy to characterize all standard trusts of land as trusts with a power to sell (as part of almost unlimited management powers).

## 6. Trusts of Land and Appointment of Trustees Act 1996

As observed above, Settled Land Act settlements can no longer be created, though existing settlements continue as before.[118] All future concurrent and successive interests take effect as trusts of land, governed by TLATA.

### A. General structure

Today we have a single settlement structure: the trust of land, which is governed by TLATA. Leaving aside old SLA settlements, gone are the problems which used to

---

[114] With the exception of joint tenants for life: SLA, s 19(2).

[115] LPA, s 25. The power could be excluded, no longer the position since TLATA.

[116] See pp 160, 182 below.

[117] TLATA, s 3 achieves this for those trusts which remain trusts for sale: see p 183 below.

[118] TLATA, s 2. Section 2(2), (3) makes provision where there is alteration in the beneficial interests in a pre-TLATA settlement.

exist in distinguishing between settled land and trusts for sale.[119] One aspect of settled land that was sometimes very useful was beneficiary management. The new trust of land involves extended powers to delegate management to beneficiaries, clearly designed to replicate that advantage of settled land.[120] Otherwise, little survives from the old settled land scheme.[121] For concurrent interests there is the more limited change from trust for sale to trust of land.

As well as these broad structural changes, fresh (or, in some contexts, initial) provision is made for a host of issues relating to the operation of trusts for land. Later Chapters deal with occupation, powers of trustees (including their control by the beneficiaries and the court), and purchaser protection. This Chapter considers the general structure and application of TLATA.

TLATA governs trusts of land, including both successive and concurrent interests in land. This single structure cannot hide the fact that some of its provisions may be more important for one or other type of interest. For example, delegation is most important in the successive interest trust. Most concurrent interests involve the same persons being both trustees and beneficiaries, rendering delegation irrelevant. Trusts for sale are expressly included as trusts of land:[122] there is no separate regulatory regime. Their operation may be somewhat different from other trusts of land in practice, given that a disagreement between the trustees leads to an initial inference that the land should be sold. In addition, a real intention that the land should be sold is relevant to decisions by the court as to sale and as to rights to occupy. Nevertheless, it is concluded below[123] that the differences are marginal, often depending more on intentions than on the label of trust for sale.

The new regime also applies to pre-TLATA trusts.[124] Given that it has been seen that old SLA settlements are not affected, this means old trusts for sale. Old express trusts for sale remain trusts for sale. Necessarily, in these cases the use of a trust for sale by itself says nothing about the parties' intentions regarding sale or use of the land: a trust for sale was usually employed because it was the only form of ownership (concurrent interests) or there was a desire not to bring the SLA into operation. However, many trusts for sale were implied by statute, most obviously where there was concurrent ownership (but no express trust for sale) or intestacy. These implied trusts for sale are converted into what may be described as 'simple' trusts of land, whether arising before or after TLATA.[125] For the future, trusts for sale will never be statutorily implied.

## B. Scope of Application

When is there a trust of land within TLATA? This may be said to involve two major situations. The first is where the legislation explicitly applies, either providing directly

---

[119] Stressed by those urging reform, especially Grove (1961) 24 MLR 123.
[120] See p 153 below.
[121] Exceptions are some of the definitions of trusts of land (p 114 below) and the deed of discharge.
[122] TLATA, s 1(2)(a).      [123] See pp 181–3      [124] TLATA, s 1(2)(b).
[125] Section 5(1) and Sched 2, expressly operating retrospectively.

that TLATA operates or simply providing that there is a trust. The second concerns the general meaning of trust of land, where there is no such explicit provision.

Turning to the first issue, a number of provisions in the 1925 legislation created trusts for sale, now amended by TLATA to refer to trusts of land. One example is intestacy,[126] but of greater interest are the provisions dealing with tenancies in common and joint tenancies: LPA, sections 34 and 36 respectively. Apart from these sections, the position is that tenancies in common cannot exist at law,[127] but there is no restriction on the holding of joint tenancies. It has been seen that the 1925 policy was to ensure that the land could be sold by a small number of trustees and that joint tenancies should be treated in a similar way.

As for tenancies in common, the very existence of a tenancy in common means that the land is held on trust.[128] However, in 1925 that was not enough. The legislation needed to identify who held the legal estate and, most obviously, there needed to be a trust for sale: a simple trust of land subject to concurrent interests did not feature in the 1925 scheme.[129] For joint tenancies there would, in the absence of specific provision, have been a legal joint tenancy and nothing more. A trust for sale was required in order that the statutory policies could operate.

As will be seen shortly below, the drafting of LPA, sections 34 and 36 has proved to be one the few weaknesses of the 1925 legislation. Following the introduction of the trust of land, some of the old complexities about trusts for sale have fallen away. In particular, for tenancies in common we need only establish the location of the legal estate: we no longer need to establish a trust for sale. However, TLATA failed to address the weaknesses: it simply changed references in the old provisions from trusts for sale to trusts of land. Its failure to undertake a more radical overhaul has the consequence that we remain prisoners of the history of these provisions.

The greatest problems lie with the tenancy in common. In 1925 the legislative objective was to ensure that there was always a trust for sale, with the persons who would otherwise be legal tenants in common holding on trust as joint tenants. Thus LPA, section 34(2) provides that a conveyance to persons as tenants in common takes effect as a conveyance to them (or the first four of them) as joint tenants on trust for all of them as tenants in common in equity. Section 34(3) makes similar provision for testamentary gifts, with the personal representatives being the initial trustees.[130] A devise to trustees is caught by this, with the personal representatives again being the initial trustees. These provisions are sensible enough, but section 34(1) provides that 'An undivided share in land shall not be capable of being created except . . . as hereinafter mentioned'. It is glaringly obvious

---

[126] Administration of Estates Act 1925, s 33. Other examples from TLATA, Sched 2 include mortgaged property held by trustees after redemption barred (LPA, s 31) and rights of reverter (Reverter of Sites Act 1987, s 1).                                                      [127] LPA, s 1(6).

[128] Just as where there are successive interests, which must necessarily be equitable (LPA, s 1(1), (3)). The SLA, being somewhat narrower in scope, made detailed provision (s 1) for the situations it covered.                                         [129] Harpum [1990] CLJ 297, 301.

[130] This applies even if there is a devise to trustees: *Re House* [1929] 2 Ch 166. Section 34(3A) includes trustees within the 'persons interested' in (2) and (3), for whom the land is held on trust.

that tenancies in common may be created in other ways than those identified by subsections (2) and (3).[131] Even an express trust for beneficial tenants in common appears to be precluded, though doubtless section 34(1) could be interpreted so as to avoid this.[132] The example most frequently discussed[133] involves a conveyance to X, where by virtue of their common intention (often based on contribution)[134] Y has a beneficial interest as tenant in common. Absent section 34(1), it is plain that X holds on trust for X and Y as beneficial tenants in common: a clear example of a trust of land.[135] Yet section 34(1) contemplates that subsections (2) and (3) are the exclusive methods of creating tenancies in common. Such a result would be highly inconvenient and, indeed, absurd.

It therefore came as no surprise that the courts held that there can be a beneficial tenancy in common in these cases. *Bull v Bull*[136] is the leading authority, though Denning LJ puzzled commentators by relying on settled land material.[137] Now that settled land is no longer relevant for new trusts, this argument can be ignored. Whatever the reasoning, the result fits what was previously thought to be the law[138] and has been accepted by the House of Lords.[139] Following TLATA, this might be justified by interpreting section 34(1) as applying only where there is an attempt to create a legal tenancy in common,[140] but it would have been preferable for that subsection to have been repealed.[141] In any event, it seems inconceivable that the defects in the drafting of the section will be allowed to deny a beneficial tenancy in common.

Turning to joint tenancies, the starting point is that joint tenancies can be legal estates. Accordingly, it is essential that a trust is imposed by the legislation. This is achieved by LPA, section 36(1), whenever a legal estate is 'beneficially limited to or held in trust for' joint tenants.[142] The effect of the words 'beneficially limited' is

---

[131] Problems had been apparent at least from 1944: 9 Conv NS 37. The issues are well discussed by Harpum [1990] CLJ 277, 297–303.     [132] Harpum [1990] CLJ 277, 299.

[133] Other examples are found in Megarry and Wade, *Law of Real Property* (6th edn), para 9-052: they include (i) conveyance to X, who holds on trust for the tenants in common; (ii) declaration of trust by a proprietor; (iii) spouses acquiring additional shares by virtue of improvements. These are likely to be dealt with in the same way as the example considered in the text.

[134] This is the constructive or resulting trust based on *Gissing v Gissing* [1971] AC 886.

[135] The position before TLATA was more difficult because of the need to find a trust for sale.

[136] [1955] 1 QB 234, 237.

[137] SLA s 36(4). LPA s 34(1) allows for the operation of settled land rules, but its relevance in *Bull* is far from obvious.     [138] Rudden (1973) 27 Conv 51.

[139] *Williams & Glyn's Bank Ltd v Boland* [1981] AC 487 and *City of London BS v Flegg* [1988] AC 54, 77–78.

[140] Before TLATA, this would have not have produced the essential trust for sale.

[141] LPA, s 1(6) establishes that there cannot be a legal tenancy in common.

[142] The trust is applied 'in like manner as if the persons beneficially entitled were tenants in common'. This may have little scope today, though in 1925 it applied the 'statutory trusts' (ie trust for sale) spelt out by s 35 (repealed by TLATA). There has been some suggestion that s 36 supported the trust for sale in tenancies in common in the *Bull v Bull* scenario: *Re Buchanan-Wollaston's Conveyance* [1939] Ch 738 (relied upon by Ormrod LJ in *Williams & Glyn's Bank Ltd v Boland* [1979] Ch 312, 333) and Lord Denning MR in *Jackson v Jackson* [1971] 1 WLR 1539, 1542. However, it is not entirely clear that any of the judges intended to go this far.

to catch the case where there is a simple conveyance to joint tenants; there is no need for beneficial interests to be held by other persons. The odd wording (for example, it imposes a trust when land is held on trust) is explicable by the fact that it imposed a trust for sale prior to TLATA. The provision appears to work without difficulty.

A different point is that TLATA covers a range of situations where it is thought desirable that the trust for land regime should operate. These are mostly modelled on SLA, section 1, which specified in some detail the situations to which that legislation applied, beyond the normal successive interest trust. Today they are found in TLATA, Schedule 1. Paragraph 1 makes provision for purported conveyances to infants.[143] An infant cannot hold a legal estate, so it comes as no surprise that the land is held by the transferor or (where the conveyance is to a mixture of infants and persons of full age) the other transferees on trust. This triggers the TLATA regime, ensuring that the land can be effectively managed. Paragraph 3 covers rentcharges or other annual payments charged on land, if created voluntarily (or by marriage settlement or family arrangement): it imposes a trust to give effect to the charge. The point is that land may be left to X, subject to an annual payment of £20,000 a year to Y. In practical terms it is difficult to sell the land without the participation of Y: few will want to buy land affected by such a burden.[144] Given that it is contrary to modern thinking to require purchasers to investigate beneficial interests, there is a strong case for extending the trust of land regime to this context.[145] It is, perhaps, the one example which does not really look like a trust. Next,[146] provision is made by paragraph 5 for entails, the creation of which is now precluded.[147] Paragraph 5 provides that the land is held on trust for the person to whom the entail is purported to be given. In other words, the tenant in tail is treated as holding the beneficial fee simple (under a bare trust) but the grant of an entail does not itself amount to a grant of the legal fee simple. This ensures that there is unambiguous documentary proof of the passing of the legal fee simple.

We can now turn to the second issue regarding the scope of trusts of land: the general meaning of 'trust of land'. A small initial point is that TLATA, section 1(2)(a) explicitly provides that express, implied, resulting, and bare trusts are all included. This, of course, indicates the broad intended scope of TLATA.

---

[143] Also replacing LPA, s 19. Para 2 covers minors' rights on intestacy.

[144] It is not similar to a normal mortgage, in which the loan is paid off out of the proceeds. In our example, Y is entitled to an annual payment, not an identifiable capital sum.

[145] Prior to TLATA there was an option to deal with the land free from settled land procedures; that is, to sell the land subject to the liability (Law of Property (Amendment) Act 1926, s 1). Under TLATA there is no such option. Although the Law Commission (Law Com No 181, para 15.1) rightly observes that a sale by a single trustee might have the same effect, it remains a breach of trust unless Y has agreed to it.

[146] The Schedule also makes provision for charitable, ecclesiastical, and public trusts (para 4) and property accruing to a SLA settlement which has ceased to operate (para 6).

[147] No provision explicitly so states, though it is clearly intended (Law Com No 181, para 16.1) and is almost certainly the effect of para 5. Pascoe [2001] Conv 396 argues that it may remain possible to create entails, but this seems highly improbable.

A new departure is the inclusion of bare trusts. In the past these could operate outside the settled land and trust for sale regimes, being essentially unregulated. Problems could arise for those dealing with bare trustees, as it was questionable whether overreaching powers existed.[148] Today it is clear that bare trusts are treated in the same way as any other trust. Bare trusts provide few problems. Sometimes the trust may be imposed by statute (a purported transfer to an infant is one example) but it may equally be express or imposed by equity as a resulting or constructive trust. An example is where X purchases land with her own capital, but the legal estate is vested in her solicitor Y: Y will hold it on resulting trust for X.

When will there be a trust in cases of plural ownership? For concurrent interests, there are no problems insofar as LPA, sections 34 and 36 impose trusts: these sections were discussed above. One example which may not be immediately obvious involves unincorporated associations. The legal estate will usually be vested in trustees, with a trust for the members.[149] This will generally be an express trust.[150] There appear to be no cases dealing with trust aspects of disagreements regarding the use or disposition of the property. The reason is probably that decisions will be taken according to the rules of the association,[151] with a vote of the members (or management committee) settling any disagreement. The court would be very reluctant to interfere with such decisions. On the other hand, the wide powers of management provided by TLATA may be useful.

For successive interests, it is inevitable that there must be a trust. Freehold estates other than the fee simple absolute in possession must, according to LPA, section 1(3) 'take effect as equitable interests'. This inevitably means that the legal estate is held on trust to give effect to them: a trust of land. Accordingly, the creation of life estates and remainders will necessarily activate TLATA. The same is true of future rights (to the first of my children to obtain a law degree) or shifting rights (to my children, but if any of them should be convicted of an offence involving dishonesty then their interest is to go to Y).[152]

Outside these contexts there may be more difficulty. In a large number of situations, equitable claims to land are recognized. Many of these claims are sufficiently proprietary to bind purchasers. More difficult is the question whether the land is held on trust. To get one point out of the way, it is obvious that not every equitable claim gives rise to a trust. Thus a restrictive covenant (an equitable interest binding purchasers for over a century and a half)[153] plainly does not involve a trust.

---

[148] Law Com WP 94, para 3.27; Harpum [1990] CLJ 277, 299, 302–4, 310.

[149] Emmet, *Title* (19th edn), para 11.121.

[150] Though the cases (eg *Re Recher's WT* [1972] Ch 526; *Re Lipinski's WT* [1976] Ch 235) reveal that the objects of the trust may not be specified.

[151] Insofar as the powers of the trustees are limited, this needs to be reflected by a restriction on the registered title: Form R, Sched 4, Land Registration Rules 2003.

[152] This also applies to rights of entry (unless legal under LPA, s 1(2)(e)) and possibilities of reverter. Because SLA, s 1 did not employ the simple requirement of a trust of land, all these examples had to be spelt out: see p 99 above. They all required land to be 'limited in trust' (save for rentcharges and other annual payments).   [153] *Tulk v Moxhay* (1848) 2 Ph 774.

A number of problem cases come to mind, in most of which it would be inappropriate for the TLATA regime to operate. One example is the ubiquitous estate contract, such as a contract to buy the freehold. To quote Barnsley, 'It is a settled doctrine of the Court of Equity that, the moment there is a valid contract of sale, the vendor becomes in equity a trustee for the purchaser of the estate sold'.[154] It would be quite unacceptable for TLATA to operate: it would enable sellers (at least where there are two of them) to overreach the purchaser's interest, notwithstanding its being protected by notice on the register and its being unsuitable for taking effect against the proceeds of sale. The entire structure of post-1925 land law is that certain interests bind purchasers if protected on the register, whilst others may be overreached. Whilst these categories are not necessarily comprehensive,[155] it would be wholly wrong for them to overlap.[156] We must ensure that TLATA operates so as to recognize this.

Further problems may be found in the areas of licences and estoppel. Whilst a contractual licence is not currently viewed as a proprietary interest, constructive trusts may be imposed on purchasers to counter unconscionable conduct on their part.[157] Is this a trust that will attract TLATA, remembering that constructive trusts are expressly included? Again, it would be odd if the constructive trustee could defeat the licence.[158] The answer may be that this constructive trust binds the purchaser personally, rather than being a trust over the land.[159] As such, it would not bind those subsequently dealing with the purchaser trustee (though if they too acted unconscionably a further constructive trust could arise). Estoppels cause yet more difficulty. There is some analysis that estoppels may take effect by way of a constructive trust, though the authority is limited in extent.[160] Just as with licences, it is difficult to see how it could be sensible for TLATA to apply to estoppels generally.[161] However, we may need to be more discriminating in this context. It has become very common in recent years to comment on the

[154] *Conveyancing Law and Practice* (4th edn), p 243, citing *Lysaght v Edwards* (1876) 2 Ch D 499, 506 (Jessel MR). See also Megarry and Wade, *Law of Real Property* (6th edn), para 12-052; Farrand, *Contract and Conveyance* (4th edn), chapter 7.

[155] *Shiloh Spinners Ltd v Harding* [1973] AC 691.

[156] This is demonstrated by the exclusion of nearly all protected interests from even the wider overreaching powers under an ad hoc trust of land: LPA, s 2(3). See p 190 below.

[157] *Ashburn Anstalt v Arnold* [1989] Ch 1.

[158] In *Pritchard Englefield v Steinberg* [2004] EWHC 1908 (Ch) a constructive trust was imposed to give effect to a right to reside for life and it bound a subsequent chargee who could not rely on overreaching; TLATA was assumed to apply. This may be justified as the interest was similar to a life interest: an interest which can normally be overreached (see the analysis of estoppel below).

[159] An issue raised by (though not settled in) *Chattey v Farndale Holdings Inc* (1996) 75 P&CR 298, 313–317 (briefly discussed by the author in Smith, *Property Law* (4th edn), at p 472). The personal liability argument is supported by Law Com No 254, para 3.48.

[160] *Timber Top Realty Pty Ltd v Mullens* [1974] VR 312; *Re Sharpe* [1980] 1 WLR 219; *Re Basham* [1986] 1 WLR 1498, 1504; *Joyce v Rigolli* [2004] EWCA Civ 79, [35]; Sir Christopher Slade: 'The Informal Creation of Interests in Land' (Child & Co Oxford Lecture 1984).

[161] It should be remembered that estoppels are today proprietary interests, at least for registered land: Land Registration Act 2002, s 116.

similarities between estoppels and constructive trusts, most commonly in the context of the constructive trust arising from common intention.[162] Such trusts plainly fall within TLATA,[163] but how do we deal with overreaching as regards an equivalent estoppel claim? *Birmingham Midshires Mortgage Services Ltd v Sabherwal*[164] was clear that overreaching could not be avoided by relying upon estoppel rather than constructive trust. The reasoning appears to veer between not allowing estoppel to apply in such cases and enabling such estoppel claims to be overreached. This is a sensible outcome, even if the latter reasoning is not entirely easy to fit into normal principles. Another context in which estoppel and constructive trusts are seen to overlap was illustrated by *Yaxley v Gotts*,[165] involving an estate contract which would otherwise fail for lack of writing. *Sabherwal* recognized that overreaching would not be appropriate for that sort of estoppel claim. Where overreaching is possible, it may well be appropriate to apply all the trust of land rules.

Beyond these examples, there is scope for arguments that there is a trust in many situations where equity intervenes. Examples are provided by equitable remedies such as rectification and rescission[166] and the imposition of liability on fiduciaries who profit from their position.[167] Whether there is a trust in such cases, and whether it is sensible for TLATA to apply, are difficult issues.

It may be concluded that it was unwise for TLATA to place so much emphasis upon there being a trust of land. Although it works well in the standard successive and concurrent interest situations, the courts need to reign in its scope in other contexts if a sensible outcome is to be achieved.

---

[162] *Grant v Edwards* [1986] Ch 638, 656; *Austin v Keele* (1987) 61 ALJR 605, 609; *Lloyds Bank plc v Rosset* [1991] 1 AC 107, 129, 132–3; *Stokes v Anderson* [1991] 1 FLR 391, esp 398–9; *Oxley v Hiscock* [2004] 3 WLR 715.

[163] The leading case is *Williams & Glyn's Bank Ltd v Boland* [1981] AC 487 (trust for sale).

[164] (1999) 80 P&CR 256; Harpum (2000) 116 LQR 341, 343–5.        [165] [2000] Ch 162.

[166] Usefully discussed by Chambers, *Resulting Trusts*, chapter 7.

[167] Note the emphasis on trust in *Att-Gen of Hong Kong v Reid* [1994] 1 AC 324 (PC) in the context of bribes.

# 7

# Occupation: Rights, Control, and Consequences

It is obvious that beneficial co-owners (or life interest holders) under a trust of land may wish to occupy it. Where they have bought the land (most likely for co-owners), this is nearly always their intention. It may also be the intention of a settlor. This is the main source of dispute whilst the land remains unsold, hence it is the first topic we consider in this Chapter. It must be remembered that occupation by the beneficiaries is not a feature of every trust of land. The intention may be for the land to be rented out commercially, with the co-owners or life tenants being entitled to the rent. This is especially the case for farmland included within settlements.

We need to bear in mind that the trust of land provides very different structures than those encountered in past centuries. Take a life interest, for example. Before the 1925 reforms, a legal life tenant might either occupy personally (typically the mansion house at the heart of a large estate) or lease land and take the rent. These would be the natural consequences of having a legal estate in possession. Now that a life interest is a beneficial interest under a trust of land, more sophistic-ated analysis is required. Insofar as the trust is employed to facilitate dispositions of the land, there is no underlying policy reason for occupation rights to be different whilst the land remains unsold. Indeed, this will be seen to be the usual outcome. Obviously, nobody suggests that the trustees can occupy for their own benefit (whatever rights to occupy may flow from possession of the legal estate) and it is the beneficiaries whose rights are under discussion in this Chapter. Management of the land will, however, be different. Whereas the legal tenant for life in the past would lease farmland to tenant farmers, this is today a role of the trustees.[1] Doubtless the beneficiary can create rights out of his or her own interest (creating leases, for example) but such rights can only be equitable and cannot be greater than the rights of that beneficiary.

The issues discussed in this Chapter cause the greatest problems for co-owners. In a successive interest context, it is clear that the life tenant has the right to take rents if not in occupation. Those with interests in remainder usually have no

---

[1] The trustees may, as will be seen in the following Chapter, delegate powers to beneficiaries with interests in possession.

reason to challenge such occupation. There may still, of course, be a question whether there is a right to insist on taking occupation; this is covered by the principles discussed below. Co-owners pose greater problems because the nature of their rights is that that they are all interested: if one takes occupation, then this may well be at the expense of the others. Unsurprisingly, most of the discussion and cases concentrate on co-owners and that forms the focus for most of this Chapter. It might be added that the co-owners may be life tenants; this gives rise to virtually identical problems to those applying to co-owners of the fee simple.

While all the co-owners occupy, there is unlikely to be any dispute. Problems arise where, for whatever reason, one (or more) do not occupy. The problems may be placed in two categories, often intertwined. The first concerns the consequence of occupation in the past: can an action be brought by the non-occupiers to claim an appropriate share of the financial benefits of occupation? The second category concerns rights of future occupation. This second area is relatively modern. Until 1925 co-ownership could be terminated by either party.[2] Originally this would have been by virtue of physical partition,[3] but by the second half of the nineteenth century the courts could instead order sale. Accordingly, disagreement would lead to termination of co-ownership. The Law of Property Act 1925 (hereafter LPA) introduced two major changes. There is no longer any right to partition; indeed, it normally requires the agreement of all the trustees and beneficiaries. Nor is there any right to a sale, although the legislation employed a trust for sale. As we will see in the following Chapter, in practice sale often follows when there is a dispute between co-owners: this is unchanged by the Trusts of Land and Appointment of Trustees Act 1996 (hereafter TLATA). However, there is no rule that sale must take place. Indeed, in the family context it is usual for one co-owner to retain a house as a home for the children. Now that co-ownership may continue against the wishes of one of the co-owners, future rights to occupy take on real importance.

Before considering these two categories, mention should be made of three further general points. The first is that it is common for an occupying beneficiary to make improvements to the land. The cases have considered the extent to which there can be compensation for this, alongside any obligation to compensate for the occupation. Although it might be thought to raise rather different legal questions, the way the issues are intertwined in the cases makes it sensible to study them together. Another point—a large and difficult one—is that it will be necessary to consider the extent to which the imposition of a trust by the 1925 legislation changes the rules. For example, suppose a trustee (also a beneficial co-owner) occupies land. Do the normal fiduciary duties of trustees require the profit to be disgorged? Turning to the beneficiary who is not a trustee, does the common law right to occupy apply to equitable interests? In the common situation where the trustees and beneficiaries are the same persons, does any right to occupy

---

[2] See Cocks [1984] Conv 198.     [3] See p 47 above.

originate from the legal estate or beneficial interest? The third and very significant point is that TLATA, section 12 confers statutory rights of occupation for the first time. This will be particularly important when considering future occupation, where it probably replaces the previous law.

# 1. Rights to Occupy

Today, TLATA, sections 12 and 13 make detailed provision as to occupation and it is necessary to consider them in some depth. However, it is possible that the older law may still have some influence and it is necessary first to consider the pre-1996 principles.

## A. Pre-TLATA Occupation Rights

It will be recalled that every co-ownership (whether joint tenancy or tenancy in common) requires unity of possession. This means that the each co-owner is entitled to occupation of all of the land. It is what distinguishes co-ownership of a plot of land from separate ownership of parts of it. As will be seen below, it has the consequence that no objection can be made to one co-owner's occupation of the whole plot.[4]

Since 1925 every co-ownership takes effect behind a trust.[5] How does this affect rights of occupation? Between 1925 and 1996 the trust would have been a trust for sale. Arguments based on the doctrine of conversion insisted that the beneficial interests were in the proceeds of sale and so could not give rise to occupation rights. Now that TLATA, section 3 has retrospectively abolished the doctrine of conversion in trusts for sale, these arguments cease to be relevant.[6]

However, the abolition of conversion does not necessarily mean that co-owning beneficiaries enjoy rights of occupation. Co-ownership trusts were common in the pre-1925 cases. These were not in the house purchase context encountered so frequently today, but under settlements and wills. Those cases reveal no evidence of occupation rights.[7] Yet Barnsley has argued that every beneficial fee simple co-owner enjoys occupation rights.[8] Although the earlier twentieth-century cases are somewhat mixed (and much influenced by conversion ideas) rights to occupy became firmly established in the forty years preceding TLATA. The difficult question is whether every beneficial co-owner had a right to occupy or whether this depended upon the intention underlying the trust or the purchase. In *Bull v*

---

[4] See p 131 below.     [5] LPA, ss 34–36.

[6] In any event, a trust imposed by LPA, ss 34 and 36 is, with retrospective effect, no longer a trust for sale.

[7] Barnsley [1998] CLJ 123, 128. *Brook v Badley* (1868) LR 3 Ch 672, 674 is hostile to any such right.          [8] Ibid, esp 124–8.

*Bull* Denning LJ unambiguously asserted a right to occupy irrespective of intention.[9] However, later cases placed greater stress on intention. Indeed, when an express trust for sale in a will clearly signified an intention that the property should be sold, Lord Denning MR himself denied any right to occupy:[10] 'I think it is quite distinguishable. In *Bull v Bull* the prime object of the trust was that the parties should occupy the house together. . . . The present case is very different. The prime object of the trust was that the bungalow should be sold. . . . None of them was entitled to the possession of it.' Part of the reasoning was based on the trust for sale, but the underlying stress was on intention. There have been persistent doubts as to whether beneficiaries enjoy a universal right to occupy,[11] whereas a right based on the purpose of the trust has been adopted by the House of Lords.[12]

Barnsley[13] suggests the absence of a universal right to occupy would be inconsistent with the unity of possession. However, concepts such as possession have to be considered according to their context. How does unity of possession operate on equitable interests? It is urged that it signifies more a right of enjoyment of the interest rather than of occupation: a conclusion readily reached if the trust assets are, for example, shares. Indeed, Barnsley recognizes that there is no right of occupation of land for holders of equitable life interests[14] and in certain testamentary dispositions.[15] Any argument that there cannot therefore be co-ownership in such situations is plainly untenable. A stronger argument in favour of a universal right to occupy is that a trust imposed purely for conveyancing reasons should not affect substantive rights of enjoyment; this appears to be the element underpinning Lord Denning's analysis. However, where a trust is deliberately employed we cannot assume that the rights of the beneficiaries are intended to be identical to the situation had their estates been legal. Given the impossibility of working out whether a trust is employed because of the legislation or because it is actively desired by the settlor or purchasers, recourse to intentions as to use of the property appears to be the best way forward.

[9] [1955] 1 QB 234, 236–7; repeated in *Bedson v Bedson* [1965] 2 QB 666, 678 and approved in *Williams & Glyn's Bank Ltd v Boland* [1981] AC 487, 507, 510. See also *Wight v CIR* (1982) 264 EG 935 (Lands Tribunal). Lord Denning MR's analysis that husband and wife cannot sever a joint tenancy of the matrimonial home has been rejected: p 49 above.

[10] *Barclay v Barclay* [1970] 2 QB 677, 684.

[11] In addition to the notes on *Bull* (n 91 below), see *Chhokar v Chhokar* (1983) 5 FLR 313; Megarry (1966) 82 LQR 29, 33; Cretney (1971) 34 MLR 441, 443; Saunders and McGregor [1973] Conv 270, 272 (supporting an acceptably narrow view of occupation rights).

[12] *City of London BS v Flegg* [1988] AC 54, 81 (Lord Oliver). Many cases recognize rights to occupy without making their basis clear. See eg *Kemmis v Kemmis* [1988] 1 WLR 1307, 1325, 1335; *Meyer v Riddick* (1989) 60 P&CR 50. Ross Martyn [1997] Conv 254, 258 concludes that the basis of occupation was never settled.          [13] [1998] CLJ 123, 126–8, 137.

[14] *Re Bagot's Settlement* [1894] 1 Ch 177.

[15] *Barclay v Barclay* [1970] 2 QB 677, though the testamentary aspect is not prominent in the case.

## B. Rights of Occupation Under TLATA

Section 12 confers rights of occupation (subject to important conditions) on beneficiaries with interests in possession.[16] What is an 'interest in possession'? It obviously excludes interests in remainder; this seems appropriate because beneficial enjoyment has been explicitly deferred. What about discretionary beneficiaries? They do not have interests in possession for taxation purposes[17] and the same applies to any interest if there is a power to accumulate income.[18] It seems most likely that the same applies for the purposes of section 12.[19] For discretionary trusts, this should not normally be a problem. If the trustees wish (in accordance with the terms of the trust) to allow a beneficiary into possession then the discretion can be exercised in favour of that beneficiary and from that time on it would appear that there is an interest in possession.[20] Perhaps more problematic is whether powers to accumulate should preclude occupation. If the power extends to all the income then it is difficult to see how occupation can be justified: it precludes future exercise of the power. However, if a trust of land and other assets contains an express occupation purpose, then it might be argued that the land is necessarily freed from the power to accumulate, so that beneficiaries within that purpose have an interest in possession.

Once there is an interest in possession, section 12(1) provides that one of two requirements must be satisfied:

(a) the purposes of the trust include making the land available for his occupation (or for the occupation of beneficiaries of a class of which he is a member or of beneficiaries in general), or

(b) the land is held by the trustees so as to be so available.

Paragraph (a) appears to confirm the law as it operated (according to the arguments above) prior to TLATA. It constitutes a useful clarification rather than a bold departure. The wording covers both settlements (where the purpose is that of the settlor) and joint purchases (where the purpose is that of the purchasing co-owners).[21] Plainly, it applies to the typical family home situation. However, a number of problems emerge. In many cases it will be difficult to assess how far the purpose extends. This is most likely to be when purposes change over the years. Suppose that two brothers purchase and occupy, as beneficial joint tenants, a large house. One later marries and his wife moves in.[22] She acquires an interest because

---

[16] Sections 12 and 13 are considered by Ross Martyn [1997] Conv 254, esp 258–61.
[17] *Gartside v IRC* [1968] AC 553; applied to exhaustive discretionary trusts in *Re Weir's ST* [1969] 1 Ch 657 (reversed on other grounds [1971] Ch 145) and *Sainsbury v IRC* [1970] Ch 712.
[18] *Pearson v IRC* [1981] AC 753.
[19] Megarry and Wade, *Law of Real Property* (6th edn), para 8–127. TLATA, s 22 defines 'beneficiary', but apart from requiring 'an interest' this does not assist.
[20] Law Com No 181, para 13.3, n 147.
[21] These 2 cases are separated out by TLATA, s 15(1)(a), (b) for purposes material to the exercise of court discretions: p 158 below.      [22] The example is used by Barnsley [1998] CLJ 123, 130 *et seq.*

her husband either transfers it to her or, having severed the joint tenancy, leaves it to her by will. Does she fall within paragraph (a)? This is most likely to be a live issue if her husband has died. It may be said that she is intended by both brothers to occupy. However, is this the purpose of the trust? The 'purposes of the trust' may imply some long-term element, whereas the surviving brother may say that he was simply content for her to stay there for the time being. If the interest had been transferred to her *inter vivos* (to the knowledge of the surviving brother) it might be easier to argue that the purpose does exist. It would be more difficult if the severance and gift by will are unknown to him.

This example also demonstrates that timing of events can cause difficulty. It seems clear that the purpose in paragraph (a) must exist at the time occupation is claimed, rather than when the trust is set up.[23] Accordingly, it matters not that the marriage was after the purchase.

This is connected to the question whether we assess rights to occupy once and for all at the time when occupation is first asserted (which may be described as a 'snapshot' approach)[24] or whether the tests are continuing, ie they have to be satisfied later when the occupation is challenged. In general terms, the snapshot approach favours those in occupation at the time of the dispute, a policy seen in the legislation.[25] However, the wording of section 12 points against the snapshot test: 'entitled by reason of his interest to occupy the land *at any time if at that time . . .*' (emphasis added). Indeed, it would be entirely inappropriate to accept a right to occupy after the individual ceases to have an interest in the land: at least in that context, the test must be continuing. Finally, there may be no comprehensive jurisdiction for the court to control rights to occupy.[26] At least if the tests are continuing, this enables a limited degree of control by the trustees and the court. Overall, it seems preferable to reject the snapshot analysis.[27]

In the context of paragraph (a) this means that the purpose of occupation must continue until the dispute arises. The cases on sale demonstrate how purposes may terminate. If a marriage (or other relationship) breaks down, the courts are likely to hold that the family home purpose has terminated and the property should be sold.[28] It seems logical that the same approach should apply as regards occupation

---

[23] At least where it is the purpose of the purchasers that is in issue: see purposes in the context of the court's s 14 discretions, p 164 below.

[24] Apparently favoured by Barnsley in the context of TLATA, s 12(2) and possibly more generally: [1998] CLJ 123, 135, 132–3.  [25] TLATA, s 13(7).

[26] This is most likely to be a problem where there is one person with a right to occupy: multiple rights are covered by s 13. The scope of the s 14 jurisdiction to control the exercise of trustees functions is discussed below, p 156. Multiple rights may also fall within the Family Law Act 1996: p 128 below.

[27] See also p 125 below, in the context of the suitability requirement.

[28] *Jones v Challenger* [1961] 1 QB 176; *Rawlings v Rawlings* [1964] P 398. An exception is provided by *Chan v Leung* [2003] 1 FLR 23, where the court decided that the purchase was to provide a home for a couple and for the woman if the relationship broke down. The facts were most unusual and the result was justified by a clear determination on her part to protect her position in case things went wrong with the relationship: they had agreed that the property would not be sold without the consent of both of them.

purposes. More surprisingly, the courts have suggested that the family home purpose may terminate in a family context when one party parts with his or interest[29] or, more controversially, dies.[30] Even more troublesome are cases where there are multiple purposes.[31] It can be difficult to work out whether the failure of one of the purposes means that the remaining purposes consequentially fails. In the context of sale, these issues today are less vital: purposes constitute just one matter for the court to take into account.[32] However, it is a crucial question for section 12. These difficulties may induce more sympathy for the snapshot approach; at least termination of purposes would then be less important.

So far, we have been considering paragraph (a). Paragraph (b) provides an alternative ground for occupation where 'land is held by the trustees so as to be so available'. The clear intention is to allow trustees to acquire or allocate land for occupation by beneficiaries.[33] This works well if there is a single beneficiary with an interest in possession (usually a life tenant) but poses greater problems for co-ownership. These problems are considered later in this Chapter in the context of compensation payments.[34] Paragraph (b) appears to confer a power on trustees, though it is not expressed in those terms. Generally, trustees powers can be excluded,[35] but there is no provision which enables settlors to exclude the effect of section 12.[36] This is unimportant for paragraph (a) as the settlor determines the purpose of the trust, but it may be significant for paragraph (b). In practice, trustees are unlikely to depart from a clearly stated intention on the part of the settlor.

Although section 12 describes the beneficiary as 'entitled . . . to occupy', any entitlement under paragraph (b) appears precarious. Unless the snapshot analysis is adopted, it appears that land must continue to be 'held by the trustees so as to be so available'; just as the trustees can decide to allow occupation, so they can decide to cease to do so. In this context there seem to be stronger reasons to adopt the snapshot analysis,[37] but it is difficult to justify doing so just for the purposes of section 12(1)(b). It should be added that the words 'so available' in paragraph (b) refer back to the words in paragraph (a) 'for his occupation (or for the occupation of beneficiaries of a class of which he is a member or of beneficiaries in general)'. This indicates that the trustees can determine which beneficiaries are to be entitled: they are not obliged to make the land available for all those with interests in possession.[38]

---

[29] *Re Citro* [1991] Ch 142, 158–9: 'the secondary purpose [use as a family home, as opposed to sale under the then trust for sale] can only exist while the spouses are not only joint occupiers of the home but joint owners of it as well'. This is discussed at pp 174–5 below.          [30] See p 163 below.

[31] Probably the best known case is *Bedson v Bedson* [1965] 2 QB 666: use as family home and drapery business.                                              [32] TLATA, s 15(1).

[33] This appears most clearly in the original and more confined wording in Law Com No 181, draft Bill, cl 7: 'land has been acquired by the trustees for that purpose'.          [34] See p 138 below.

[35] TLATA, s 8 (referring explicitly to powers in ss 6 and 7). See p 154 below for other powers.

[36] Whitehouse and Hassall, *Trusts of Land, Trustee Delegation and the Trustee Act 2000* (2nd edn), para 2.128. Ferris and Battersby [1998] Conv 168, 175 assume that s 12 can be excluded, but without explanation.          [37] Any other approach makes a mockery of the s 12(1) entitlement.

[38] Barnsley [1998] CLJ 123, 134 suggests to the contrary: that under this provision *all* the beneficiaries are entitled to occupy. This does not appear to be the most natural reading of the words of the statute, especially given the link with para (a).

Finally, rights to occupy are disapplied by section 12(2) if the land 'is either unavailable or unsuitable for occupation by him'. Presumably, 'unavailable' covers the situation where there is a lease (or, less likely, a licence) to somebody else. Could it apply where another beneficiary is in occupation and the premises are not suitable for occupation by both beneficiaries? The trustees cannot evict the occupier in the exercise of their section 13 powers to regulate rights of occupation.[39] It seems desirable to hold that the non-occupying beneficiary retains a right to occupy (albeit one that cannot currently be enforced) as this might enable the trustees to require compensation to be paid by the occupying beneficiary.[40] Hopkins[41] argues that the land ceases to be available if the trustees decide to sell. There is some sense in this, as it ensures that the land can be sold if necessary. However, it is far from clear that trustees should be able to limit rights to occupy in this fashion. If the argument were accepted, it follows that the trustees could similarly decide to lease the land and thereby defeat rights of occupation: this seems an unacceptable interference with the section 12 rights. Indeed, the words in section 12 'entitled . . . to occupy' would be almost completely devoid of meaning: the only practical options for the trustees are to sell, lease, or allow the beneficiary to occupy. The question of unsuitability is more difficult. It is most likely to apply where paragraph (a) operates: the trustees are unlikely to hold land available for occupation where it is not suitable. In *Chan v Leung*[42] it was argued that a house was unsuitable for occupation by one of two partners after their relationship had broken down, as it was too large for her and its condition was deteriorating. Jonathan Parker LJ stated that the test requires 'a consideration not only of the general nature and physical characteristics of the particular property but also a consideration of the personal characteristics, circumstances and requirements of the particular beneficiary'.[43] Given the purpose of the trust and the fact that only short-term possession was feasible,[44] it was held that the right to occupy continued. A clearer example of unsuitability is where the land is farmland and the life tenant is incapable because of inexperience or physical disability from farming it. One reason why this area is difficult is that the trustees will be overriding the purpose behind the trust. This is not easy to justify unless circumstances have changed since the trust was set up. Denying occupation may therefore more readily be justified if the land has to remain suitable for occupation (rejecting the snapshot analysis)[45] as this permits changes in circumstances to be taken into account. Thus a large house may, over time, become unsuitable for occupation by an elderly widow or widower. Even here, some very sensitive questions are involved and some would argue that the snapshot analysis is preferable in this context.

---

[39] TLATA, s 13(7).

[40] Ibid, s 13(6). However, the fact that the trustees have not actively restricted the rights of the non-occupier may still preclude compensation: see p 132 below.        [41] [1996] Conv 411, 420.

[42] [2003] 1 FLR 23; note that the occupation purpose was held to include occupation by her after their separation.        [43] Ibid, [101].

[44] The occupier's visa was limited to the duration of her university studies.

[45] It is implicit in *Chan v Leung* [2003] 1 FLR 23 that rights to occupy will terminate on such a change of circumstances. This is also argued by Hopkins [1996] Conv 411, 420 and Megarry and Wade, *Law of Real Property* (6th edn), para 8-149; *contra* Barnsley [1998] CLJ 123, 135.

## C. The Trustees' Discretions

It has already been seen that trustees have discretions under TLATA, section 12: deciding whether land should be held available for occupation and whether it is suitable for occupation by the beneficiary. However, section 13 confers a number of further important powers on the trustees.

Much of section 13 deals with the setting where two or more beneficiaries have rights to occupy. Particularly where a house suitable for a single family is involved, it may be impracticable for all the beneficiaries to occupy. Given that occupation will usually be based on the purpose of the trust, this is likely to be because the circumstances of the beneficiaries have changed so that sharing the property is no longer realistic. This might be because, say, siblings are co-owners and one later marries; or more commonly, because a married or unmarried couple has split up.[46] Section 13(1) enables the trustees to 'exclude or restrict the entitlement of any one or more (but not all) of them'. This power was considered in *Rodway v Landy*,[47] a rather unusual case involving a surgery owned by two medical practitioners. They had fallen out and their partnership had been dissolved. One initial point is that the two parties were also the trustees and plainly could not agree; the case was one where the court was asked, under its section 14 jurisdiction,[48] to make an order within the section 13 powers. *Rodway* demonstrates that the scope of section 13 is important not only for the trustees, but also for the court. What the court wished to do was to divide the premises so that each doctor had part of them. This would be partition if each got the fee simple of their part, but the proposal was merely that each should occupy part. The objection was taken that this would restrict the entitlement of both the beneficiaries, which is prohibited by the words 'but not all'. Although the statutory wording made this a credible argument, it would preclude sensible conclusions in quite a number of cases. The court used an example of a trust of two houses, where an obvious solution would be for each beneficiary to occupy one of the houses. What is prohibited is excluding all the beneficiaries from all (or the same part of) the land or restricting their rights over the same area of land: in *Rodway*, the restrictions related to different parts of the land.

Section 13(7)[49] contains a significant restriction on the freedom of the trustees: they cannot exclude a beneficiary who is already in occupation (not necessarily by virtue of section 12).[50] This evinces a clear intention not to disturb persons in

[46] In the latter case, the purpose of occupation may have terminated.
[47] [2001] Ch 703, [31]-[33].
[48] The court may make orders 'relating to the exercise by the trustees of any of their functions'. Section 14 is fully considered in the context of decisions to sell: p 156 below.
[49] It was not considered in *Rodway*, though it does not preclude the court's making an order. It would fit the court's analysis of s 13 to say that s 13(7) applies only where occupation of *all the land* is prevented.
[50] It does not confer a right to occupy, given that it limits the s 13 powers of the trustees regarding s 12 rights to occupy: *IRC v Eversden* [2002] STC 1109, [25] (upheld on other grounds (2003) 75 TC 340).

their homes, though it is not limited to residential accommodation. It may be noted that the section explicitly provides that the court can approve the exclusion of an occupying beneficiary. This protection of occupiers extends so as to catch decisions of trustees which are likely to result in occupation being given up.[51]

It is unsurprising that, by virtue of section 13(4), the trustees have to consider intentions of the settlor, the purposes for which the property is held, and the circumstances and wishes of the entitled beneficiaries:[52] these are matters that the court is obliged to consider under section 15.[53] These factors are also relevant when the court is asked to approve the removal of the section 13(7) protection.[54] What is odd is that there is no general requirement for the trustees to take such matters into account in exercising other powers, such as sale. As any decision can be challenged under section 14, however, the point lacks ultimate substance.

The exercise of the section 13(1) power inevitably disadvantages the beneficiary whose rights are excluded or restricted. It is therefore, useful that the trustees can require compensation to be paid by the occupier. This ensures that financial justice can be done as between the parties. This is considered below as part of the compensation rules.[55]

The trustees possess a more general power[56] to impose reasonable conditions on the occupying beneficiary, in particular to require the payment of outgoings or expenses relating to the land or the assumption of other obligations. The latter could include keeping the property properly decorated and in repair. The power is applicable to what may be described as preliminary work. Thus it has been held to apply to expenditure required to divide the property, so that the beneficiaries can occupy separate parts;[57] it would seem also to apply to the converse case where expenditure is required to make the land suitable for occupation by a single beneficiary. On the other hand, it seems appropriate that work constituting permanent improvement should be an expense of the trust rather than the occupying beneficiary. It is important to note that, unlike compensation payments, this power to impose conditions is unrelated to the exercise of section 13(1) powers to exclude rights to occupy. Any beneficiary in occupation by virtue of section 12 (including a life tenant) may be made subject to these conditions.

## D. Relationship to Pre-TLATA Rights

The wording of TLATA assumes that the rights conferred by the legislation are exclusive of other rights of beneficiaries to occupy.[58] To give one example,

---

[51] See p 139 below. More generally, trustees must not act unreasonably: s 13(2).

[52] For a comparison with normal consultation rules, see p 151 below.

[53] It is more surprising that they are not obliged, unlike the court, to consider the 'welfare of any minor who occupies or who reasonably be expected to occupy' (s 15(1)(c)).

[54] TLATA, s 13(8). Exceptionally, this is not a s 14 application and therefore does not trigger the s 15 criteria.                                                                      [55] See p 137 below.

[56] TLATA, s 13(3), (5).          [57] *Rodway v Landy* [2001] Ch 703, [41].

[58] At least, rights by virtue of their beneficial interests. A lease by the trustees to a beneficiary would confer rights outside ss 12 and 13.

section 13(3) enables trustees to impose conditions on a beneficiary 'in relation to his occupation of land by reason of his entitlement under section 12'. It would be extraordinary if a beneficiary could reject the conditions on the basis that there was an equitable right to occupy quite apart from section 12 and he or she was occupying by virtue of that right. Similarly, such an analysis might be used to limit the powers of the trustees to exclude or limit rights under section 13(1).[59]

If the pre-TLATA rights of occupation were based on the purpose of the trust (as was argued above) then it is easy to argue that these rights are transcended by TLATA, section 12. Generally speaking, the section 12 rights are more extensive than those recognized by equity, though there may be some cases where the rights are more circumscribed. Land which is not suitable for occupation provides the best example of this. It would be unconvincing to argue that the old rights continue in this situation: it would be odd and contrary to the TLATA scheme.

However, if Barnsley[60] is right to argue that all beneficial co-owners have rights to occupy, then matters become much more difficult. Although the legislation makes sense only as a comprehensive coverage of occupation rights, it nowhere states that it is exclusive of other rights. It could be asserted that to abrogate extensive equitable rights to occupy requires explicit provision. Whilst the force of this argument is recognized, it is submitted that there is a sufficiently strong inference that section 12 is exclusive of other rights of beneficiaries to occupy.[61] This is largely because the legislation has the feel of a comprehensive scheme; it makes sense only if there are no other rights to occupy. If the old rights survive then section 12 itself would be meaningless and the requirement that the land be suitable for occupation could always be avoided! Similarly, as has been stressed, the powers conferred by section 13 could be sidestepped. It may be that the wording of the sections leaves something to be desired, but the outcome seems reasonably clear.

## E. Spouses, Cohabitants, and Associated Persons[62]

This category of persons includes the great majority of co-owners. Their rights to occupy are significantly affected by separate legislation and this is may well

---

[59] Barnsley [1998] CLJ 123, 140 is troubled by the situation when a trustee is also a beneficiary and exercises the discretion in his or her own interests. However, this may be controlled both by the court's general control over trustees and, more specifically, by the powers of review contained in TLATA, s 14.

[60] [1998] Conv 123; see p 120 above. Barnsley argues that the equitable rights to occupy do survive TLATA.

[61] Supported by Lightman J in *IRC v Eversden* [2002] STC 1109, [24] (upheld on other grounds (2003) 75 TC 340).

[62] 'Associated persons' are defined by Family Law Act 1996, s 62(3) to include those living in the same household (excluding those such as lodgers, but including same-sex couples), relatives, parents, children, and parties to family proceedings.

transcend the provisions of TLATA, especially section 13. The Family Law Act 1996[63] contains a number of provisions conferring rights and discretions on the court, limited to property which has been, or is intended to be, used as the family home.[64] Because this area is one of family law rather than general property law, the provisions are not analysed here in detail. It may be noted that some of the rights and discretions extend to cases where only one party has an interest in the land. Thus a spouse with no property interest (or merely an equitable interest) is given a statutory right to retain occupation or, with the leave of the court, to go into occupation.[65] No directly equivalent right is given outside marriage. These extended rights lie outside the scope of plural ownership.

What is most significant for us is that, for all of cohabitants, spouses, and associated persons, the court has power to vary rights to occupation where both parties have a right to occupy, whether based on property rights (including TLATA, section 12) or the special spouses' right to occupy.[66] In essence, when the relationship breaks down, the court can order that either party should occupy the land and that the other should leave, or otherwise regulate occupation.[67] Relevant criteria include the housing needs of the parties and any children, their financial resources, the effect of any order on them, and their conduct. Particularly important is the likelihood of significant harm to a party or the children in the event that an order is either made or refused. The court may make an order for either a specific or an indefinite period. In all cases the court may impose obligations on the parties as to repairs to or discharge of outgoings on the property, or to compensate for loss of occupation.[68] This last point has some similarity to trustees' powers in trusts of land, although there is more stress on financial needs and resources.

In the case of cohabitants[69] where only one has a right to occupy, the court again has discretion to allow the other party to enter and to restrict the respondent's right to occupy.[70] There are additional factors for the court to consider[71] and the order cannot last more than six months; it can be extended once only.[72] This discretion operates, of course, outside the co-ownership context.

Where there is plural ownership, how do these provisions relate to TLATA? The rights to occupy add little in cases of co-ownership: it would be most unusual for co-owners of their family home not to have rights to occupy under TLATA,

---

[63]  Murphy (1996) 59 MLR 845.

[64]  Family Law Act 1996, ss 30(7), 33(1)(b), 35(1)(c), 36(1)(c). Just as bankruptcy triggers special provisions relating to sale (p 167 below) similar provisions apply to occupation: Insolvency Act 1986, ss 336, 337.                              [65]  Family Law Act 1996, s 30.

[66]  Ibid, s 33. For former spouses, slightly different provision is made by s 35.

[67]  Eviction is treated as Draconian and only to be used as a last resort: *Re Y* [2000] 2 FCR 470.

[68]  Family Law Act 1996, s 40.           [69]  Ibid, s 62(1): 'living together as husband and wife'.

[70]  Ibid, s 36.

[71]  Ibid, s 41 (including the nature and length of the relationship and the fact that the parties have not given each other the commitment involved in marriage).

[72]  This is partly a legacy of its origin in domestic violence. *Chalmers v Johns* [1999] 1 FLR 392 requires 'exceptional circumstances' before a property owner will be ordered out.

section 12. Ground is certainly broken in conferring rights to occupy on those without property interests, but this is wholly outside plural ownership.

More difficult are the provisions regulating rights to occupy, as these certainly do overlap with TLATA, section 13. Of course, the trusts of land discretions are conferred on the trustees rather than the court, but the court may be asked to rule on occupation disputes under TLATA, section 14. It follows that the court might be asked to resolve disputes either under TLATA or the Family Law Act. This would not matter if the criteria which the court has to consider were identical in each Act, but this is not so. It is unsurprising that the Family Law Act criteria, applicable to both occupation rights and payment of compensation, are more family-oriented and needs-based. It follows that an application under one Act might well induce a different outcome from an application under the other.[73]

Statutory provision for occupation in trusts of land was introduced for the first time by TLATA, and the earlier cases therefore provide limited assistance. Perhaps the best guide comes from a similar issue which arose regarding applications under the Law of Property Act 1925 for sale of property held on trust for sale (a property-based jurisdiction) when the matrimonial jurisdiction[74] might have produced a different result. It was held by the Court of Appeal in *Williams v Williams*[75] that applications should be made in the Family Division, where the matrimonial legislation would be taken fully into account. This is a possible pointer to the use of the Family Law Act 1996 in preference to the TLATA powers whenever the co-owners are spouses or cohabitants. Two doubts remain. The first is the inelegance of a structure which requires trustees to exercise discretions in a different manner from how the court will operate: only the TLATA provisions apply to trustees. The second is that the issues in occupation claims may not mirror those in sale applications. Of its nature, sale involves a long-term resolution of what is to happen to the land, whether looked at from a trust of land or a family perspective. Occupation rights may be long-term or short-term. In many cases under TLATA, one expects to see a long-term resolution of occupation claims: one appropriate conclusion may be that the land should be sold. However, it is possible that orders under the Family Law Act will be for shorter periods.[76] In other words, where long-term rights are in issue, it may be that recourse to TLATA is preferable. There is the additional point that the matters to be taken into account under TLATA are wider than those applied under the old trust for sale, so the contrasts with the matrimonial jurisdiction are less marked.

Given the absence of authority, it is impossible to reach definitive conclusions. It may be expected that the courts will wish to employ the Family Law Act 1996

---

[73] Though one should not underestimate the likelihood that the court will reach similar results despite differences in the statutory criteria.

[74] Matrimonial Causes Act 1973, s 24 confers jurisdiction to adjust property rights on the breakdown of marriage.                                    [75] [1976] Ch 278; discussed at p 179 below.

[76] Cretney, Masson, and Bailey-Harris, *Principles of Family Law* (7th edn), para 10–012: 'not intended to be permanent'.

jurisdiction whenever they feel that it is most appropriate, in order that its wider criteria can be taken into account. One obvious conclusion is that it is most regrettable that two statutes passed in the same year give rise to these potential conflicts.

## 2. Compensation for Occupation by Other Co-Owners

### A. The General Position

It has been seen above that the common law recognized that each co-owner had a right to occupy the land. The other co-owners could not complain or seek compensation merely because the occupier had in fact enjoyed the entire commercial benefit of the land, as by making profits from farming it.

This is best illustrated by the well known decision in *Jacobs v Seward*.[77] One party entered upon the property (three fields, close to London), put a lock on the gate, cut the grass, and took it away. It was held that the claimant could take no objection to this activity. As will be seen below ouster of other co-owners does give rise to a claim. However, so far as the lock on the gate was concerned, this was intended to keep the public out and there was no proof that the claimant was prevented from obtaining access. Whilst cutting hay was consistent with the claimant's rights of occupation, removal of significant quantities of soil would be seen as partial destruction of the subject matter and a form of ouster.[78] *Jacobs* clearly demonstrates that one co-owner cannot be challenged because he or she has in fact made sole use of the property. Thus the cases seem clear that, as a general principle, no rent (or equivalent payment) is due to the other co-owners.[79]

Before investigating this area further, we need to consider the extent to which it is affected by TLATA. The legislation not only confers rights to occupy, section 13(1) enabling the trustees to decide which beneficiary is to occupy but also (most important at this stage) section 13(6) enables them to require the occupier to pay compensation to other beneficiaries. It appears to be an inescapable inference that such a decision will override the old common law rules as to whether compensation is payable.[80] Section 13 accordingly determines rights to compensation for future occupation, and this is considered in detail below.[81] However, does section 13(6) apply to past occupation? By past occupation is meant occupation predating any determination by the trustees or the court as to rights to occupy (or as to the payment of compensation).

It is likely that the great majority of disputes will arise where there has been no exercise of the section 13 powers: the facts will simply be that one of the co-owners has occupied the premises. Suppose that A and B hold a house on trust for F and

---

[77] (1872) LR 5 HL 464.    [78] *Wilkinson v Haygarth* (1847) 12 QB 837.
[79] *M'Mahon v Burchell* (1846) 2 Ph 127 (house); recently applied in *Re Kostiuk* (2002) 215 DLR 4th 78.    [80] See pp 127–8 above.
[81] Page p 137 below.

G, who live there. F and G are brothers, who later fall out with each other. G finds it intolerable to live in the same house as F and moves out, the trustees being unaware. Two years later, G consults a lawyer and complains to A and B that F has enjoyed exclusive occupation of the house.

A and B may consider that it is best for F continue to live there (maintaining the existing position) but that F should compensate G at the level of half the rental value of the house. This appears to be a proper exercise of discretion for the future, though there is some doubt because the trustees have not acted to exclude G. Even though G has no wish to return, the trustees would need formally to exclude him in order for section 13(6) to apply. Much more difficult is the question whether the trustees can decide that compensation should be paid for the past two years. The problem is that section 13(6) enables compensation for exclusion by the trustees:[82] the trustees did not exclude G for that period. Alternatively, the trustees might decide that the house should be sold. Again, it is dubious whether section 13(6) can apply to F's past occupation.

The examples just considered involve independent trustees. In the great majority of cases the trustees and beneficiaries will be the same persons. If they are in dispute (most commonly because of a breakdown of a relationship) they are unlikely to agree on such an exercise of the statutory powers. However, under section 14 the court may make the same decisions as the trustees could have done as regards compensation. In this context, it would be understandable if the courts were tempted to construe the section 13 jurisdiction widely enough to justify a compensation order covering past occupation. Thus it might be argued that the trustees should have required compensation from the moment one of the beneficiaries left. This failure to act could then be challenged under section 14.[83] However, there must be considerable doubt as to this: it is difficult to get away from the belief that section 13 deals with future occupation from the time the trustees (or the court) act rather than with past occupation. Therefore it seems unlikely that section 13 can apply to past occupation and it remains necessary to consider the older rules.[84] In any event, there may be other limitations on the section 13 powers which might limit their application.[85]

## B. Established Grounds for Payment

There were several situations in which payment was required from the occupier. An agreement between the parties might provide for payment.[86] Further, a statute

---

[82] There may also be a risk of challenge under TLATA, s 13(7): see pp 126 above and 139 below.

[83] This argument would apply just as well if there were independent trustees.

[84] It is even less likely that compensation for past occupation could be ordered under Family Law Act 1996, s 40(1)(b).

[85] An obvious example (though diminishing in application) concerns occupation predating TLATA, to which the statutory powers surely would not apply.

[86] Whether as rent (*Leigh v Dickeson* (1884) 15 QBD 60) or as part of a management agreement (not readily implied: *Kennedy v De Trafford* [1897] AC 180).

of 1705[87] provided that a co-owner was liable 'for receiving more than comes to his just share or proportion', but this applied only to direct financial receipts. It had no operation where a co-owner occupied the land for his or her own benefit as a farmer and thereby made profits.[88] The profits are seen as resulting as much from the farmer's work and money as from the land itself. Although the 1705 statute was repealed by the 1925 legislation, it is thought that there is a similar duty to account today. The receipts will normally accrue to the holder of the legal title, who is a trustee with a duty to ensure that the beneficiaries get their fair shares.[89]

Ouster of the claimant provides another flexible route to payment. Whilst a co-owner is perfectly entitled to occupy the entire land, there is no right to exclude the others. If they are excluded then compensation must be paid.[90] This is further considered below in the matrimonial home context.

## C. The Trust Relationship

Since 1925 a trust has been employed in all cases of co-ownership. Could this lead to a different analysis? Let us consider the following facts. A and B purchase farmland, the land being placed in A's name. A uses the farmland, in a manner similar to the facts in *Jacobs v Seward*. Could B argue that A is occupying *qua* trustee and as such owes a fiduciary duty to account for any benefit? There have been some suggestions that A might owe additional duties, relative to the common law position.[91] However, this overlooks the point that the trust is imposed as a conveyancing device; it may not be appropriate for it to affect substantive rights. Indeed, it may be argued that A has a right to occupy as a beneficiary (whatever analysis is adopted regarding such rights) and in this guise has no obligation to account. It is only where A claims possession by virtue of the legal title that the fiduciary principles might come into play. In any event, any obligation to account would have to be sufficiently flexible to accommodate an understanding between A and B that A would farm the land.[92] Further, it could have no application to occupation by a beneficiary who is not also a trustee. Thus in *Jones v Jones*[93] a claim for rent against an equitable co-owner in sole occupation was rejected on the traditional principle that co-owners are not liable to pay rent. Overall, it seems safe to conclude that only rarely will the trust relationship make any difference.

---

[87] 4 Anne c 16, s 27. There was no common law duty to account: *Wheeler v Horne* (1740) Willes 208.

[88] *Henderson v Eason* (1851) 17 QB 701. See also *M'Mahon v Burchell* (1846) 2 Ph 127.

[89] *Re Landi* [1939] Ch 828.

[90] *Pascoe v Swan* (1859) 27 Beav 508. *Abbott and Barwick v Price* [2003] EWHC 2760 (Ch), [124] provides a recent example.

[91] This has been in the context of the trustee's claim to possession in *Bull v Bull* [1955] 1 QB 234: Wade [1955] CLJ 155; Crane (1955) 18 Conv (NS) 146; Latham (1955) 18 MLR 307. It appears to be hinted at in *Dennis v McDonald* [1982] Fam 63, 73, 80.

[92] In a family setting, a house may be jointly purchased by A and B for exclusive use by A. The context may be that A is the elderly parent of B: nobody would expect A to have to compensate B.

[93] [1977] 1 WLR 438.

## D. Ouster from the Family Home

Most of the modern English cases involve the family home, when a relationship has broken down and one party remains living there. A number of principles might be employed in this context, as will be seen in the following section. However, it seems probable that the ouster principle provides the best route to the most appropriate outcome.

The first significant case is *Dennis v McDonald*,[94] in which a woman left the home because of her partner's violence. This was treated by both Purchas J and the Court of Appeal as a clear case of ouster. This is unsurprising, though the facts are typical of only a minority of failed relationships. The analysis of Purchas J is most interesting as he stressed that rent will be payable unless there has been a voluntary decision not to occupy: equity will act if the occupation is 'to the exclusion of one or more of the other tenants in common' for whatever purpose or by whatever means'.[95] He further suggested that, whenever a relationship has broken down, it is quite unreasonable to expect both parties to continue to live in the house. The one who leaves should not be treated as taking a truly voluntary decision not to occupy and therefore should be entitled to payment. This seems to be a very sensible practical conclusion, even if it is a distinct extension of ouster. It provides an explanation for the assumption in many recent cases that rent is payable from the breakdown of the relationship.[96]

This approach was further considered by Millett J in *Re Pavlou*.[97] Whilst accepting it, he thought that it would not apply if one party left voluntarily and was free to return. There may be good sense in not requiring payment where the claimant left voluntarily, a proposition supported by Purchas J. However, to apply it in the relationship breakdown context in any save the most exceptional circumstances[98] would run the risk of having to investigate responsibility for the breakdown of the relationship, an investigation which may be fraught with difficulty and which would be at odds with much modern analysis of family law.[99] Thus at first sight it might seem that W has voluntarily left M in order to live with T. However, thorough investigation of the facts might disclose earlier infidelity on the part of M, coupled with behaviour (short of violence) which might justify W's leaving. It is not the sort of investigation which the law should encourage. Nevertheless, matters may well be different where the claimant's children are living with the occupier, especially where no objection has been raised to this state of affairs. It is unlikely that rent will be payable.[100]

---

[94] [1982] Fam 63; Martin [1982] Conv 305. Applied in *Biviano v Natoli* (1998) 43 NSWLR 695 to reach the unsurprising result that exclusion by court order does not constitute ouster; see Conway [2000] Conv 49.            [95] Ibid, 71, supported by Schuz (1982) 12 Fam L 108, 112–15.
[96] One example is *Bernard v Josephs* [1982] Ch 391, 400, 405.            [97] [1993] 1 WLR 1046.
[98] An example may be provided by *Chhokar v Chhokar* (1983) 5 FLR 313, where it was not thought fair to order rent against a wife when her husband had left her and sold the house whilst she was in hospital (the purchaser being bound by her interest).
[99] Cretney, Masson, and Bailey-Harris, *Principles of Family Law* (7th edn), para 14–062 (in the context of financial relief); *Suttill v Graham* [1977] 1 WLR 819, 822.
[100] *Wright v Johnson* [2002] 2 P&CR 210, [32]–[33].

## E. A Broader Discretion?

Relying on *Hill v Hickin*[101] and *Dennis*, Millett J held in *Re Pavlou* that equity would order payment 'in any . . . case in which it is necessary in order to do equity between the parties'. Although this appears to be a broad discretion, it seems to be applied in exactly the same fashion as the extended concept of ouster. In *Abbott and Barwick v Price*[102] Etherton J was prepared to order payment by the occupier where property had been purchased as investment property. There seems to be good sense in this, as the intentions of the parties were not for occupation by either.

The idea of jurisdiction to do equity plainly has attractions, but is such a general principle consistent with the cases? It is difficult to square with the more general proposition that rent (or a share in profits) is not payable simply because one has occupied and others have not. It may be appropriate to employ the idea of doing equity to justify a broad approach to ouster, as was undertaken by Purchas J in *Dennis*. This more specific analysis is both better based upon authority and, most importantly, more easily applied in practice.

As noted, Millett J relied upon *Hill v Hickin* to justify the wide equitable jurisdiction. Although the judgment of Stirling J certainly supports this, its failure to accord with earlier authority has been questioned[103] and twentieth-century cases supported the earlier reluctance to allow a claim.[104] Although the wide jurisdiction has received some support,[105] there must still be a question regarding its correctness.

## F. Relationship to Claims for Improvements and Interest Payments

It will be seen that there can be a claim for improvements in circumstances where there is sale or (rarely today) partition.[106] It has long been accepted that a co-owner who makes such a claim for improvements is then liable to pay an occupation rent.[107] The rationale for this is not entirely clear;[108] in one sense it penalizes the occupier who chooses to make improvements.

It seems to have been accepted in more recent cases that a claim can also be made by a co-owner who pays mortgage interest instalments. This may at first

---

[101] [1897] 2 Ch 579.

[102] [2003] EWHC 2760 (Ch), [125]; there may also have been ouster by changing locks. It had been held that the occupier could claim mortgage payments.

[103] *McCormick v McCormick* [1921] NZLR 384 and *Luke v Luke* (1936) 36 SR NSW 310 observe that it is inconsistent with *Griffies v Griffies* (1863) 8 LT NS 758 and *M'Mahon v Burchell* (1846) 2 Ph 127. [104] *Jones v Jones* [1977] 1 WLR 438.

[105] Cooke [1995] Conv 391, 399–403 (the cases relied upon can, however, be explained on other grounds). [106] See p 140 below.

[107] *Att-Gen v Magdalen College, Oxford* (1854) 18 Beav 223, 255 (point not taken on appeal: 6 HLC 189); *Teasdale v Sanderson* (1864) 33 Beav 534; *Williams v Williams* (1899) 81 LT NS 163; *Brickwood v Young* (1905) 2 CLR 387, 398; *Mastron v Cotton* [1926] 1 DLR 767.

[108] It was suggested in *Luke v Luke* (1936) 36 SR NSW 310 that it was based on the maxim that he who comes to equity (to claim for improvements) must do equity. But what is inequitable about declining to pay an occupation rent?

appear surprising, because such payments possess more of an income than a capital nature. However, contribution can sometimes be justified on the principle that the co-owner is incurring expenditure when there is an obligation on both parties.[109] An analysis found in more recent cases[110] is that the interest is generally a charge on the property and therefore payment of interest operates to the benefit of the non-paying co-owner. Even if the non-payer is not a party to the mortgage, the likelihood is that a first mortgagee will have priority over his or her beneficial interest.[111] Accordingly, interest payments will benefit the non-payer by reducing the amount of the charge.

The proposition that an occupier who claims interest must allow a set-off for rent seems inherently just. Both are of an income (as opposed to capital) nature and the justice of allowing an income benefit to off-set an income cost need not be laboured.[112] Indeed, the courts generally hold that the mortgage interest and the value of occupation cancel each other out.[113] In many cases this achieves a fair result without time-consuming and difficult enquiries as to interest paid and the value of occupation. This does not prevent a claim for payment of mortgage capital:[114] this is a capital, rather than an income, payment.

However, more precise investigation of the figures is sometimes called for. This has generally been recognized where one of the parties is bankrupt.[115] The recent decision in *Re Byford*[116] uses the analysis that one who claims mortgage interest must allow a set-off for the value of occupation. This analysis seems well justified by the authorities. Although Lawrence Collins J adopted the 'necessary in order to do equity' test, this was in the context of showing that ouster is not the only basis for an occupation rent being payable. It should be noted that the converse analysis had been adopted in *Re Pavlou*: a co-owner who claims for the value of occupation must allow a claim for mortgage interest.

How important is it whether a precise investigation of the figures is undertaken? It is quite possible for interest and rent to be significantly different sums. This is most obvious if there is no mortgage, or if the loan is for a small amount relative to the value of the property. In this case it will be vital to ascertain whether an occupation rent is payable irrespective of any claim for interest. Very often the expanded meaning of ouster recognized in *Dennis* will justify such liability, but *Byford* illustrates one situation where it would not apply. The bankrupt co-owner

---

[109]  *Leigh v Dickeson* (1884) 15 QBD 60, 66 (Cotton LJ).

[110]  *Re Gorman* [1990] 1 WLR 616, 626; *Re Byford* [2004] 1 P&CR 159, [23], [28]. The liability to contribute to mortgage interest payments is assumed in *Abbott and Barwick v Price* [2003] EWHC 2760 (Ch), [122].                                    [111]  *Abbey National BS v Cann* [1991] 1 AC 56.

[112]  See the majority in *Ryan v Dries* [2002] NSWCA 3; (2002) 76 ALJ 410.

[113]  *Leake v Bruzzi* [1974] 1 WLR 1528; *Suttill v Graham* [1977] 1 WLR 819.

[114]  *Leake v Bruzzi* [1974] 1 WLR 1528, 1532–3 (Stephenson LJ), 1533 (Ormrod LJ).

[115]  *Re Gorman* [1990] 1 WLR 616; *Re Pavlou* [1993] 1 WLR 1046; *Re Byford* [2004] 1 P&CR 159. A business setting is also likely to trigger a precise investigation: *Abbott and Barwick v Price* [2003] EWHC 2760 (Ch).

[116]  [2004] 1 P&CR 159, especially [31], [41]; Conway [2003] Conv 533.

was still living with the other co-owner, so that no argument based on ouster could get off the ground.[117]

What conclusions can be drawn? There appears to be a conflict between two approaches. On one hand there is the traditional principle that no occupation rent is payable. This seems so well established and so central to the idea of unity of possession that it is difficult to contemplate throwing it over. Nor, as we have seen, is it likely that the mere presence of the trust since 1925 changes the fundamental propositions. On the other hand the cases over the past three decades demonstrate that the courts often consider that payments should be made, at least as part of accounting when the property is sold. This might be as a set-off when a claim for interest is made, but the overall message is that courts do not wish to be limited by such technicalities. Perhaps the best compromise is to say that an occupation rent should be payable from the time that the purpose of the purchase (or trust) comes to an end, subject to unqualified approval by the non-occupier of the occupation.[118] This has the merit of maintaining the general principle that no payment is made whilst requiring payment where it is most relevant. Stress on purpose has been a growing factor in the law on concurrent interests, as regards both sale[119] and occupation.[120] This analysis therefore fits much of the modern thinking as to how trusts of land work.[121]

## G. Trusts of Land Legislation

It has been seen that TLATA, section 13 enables the trustees to restrict occupation to one (or more) of the beneficiaries. That jurisdiction is significant in the present context because the trustees can impose conditions on the occupier.[122] These conditions most obviously relate to obligations such as council tax and repairs. More interestingly, however, the trustees may under section 13(6) require the occupier to compensate another beneficiary whose section 12 occupation rights they have excluded or restricted. In many cases the trustees will be unable to reach a decision because they will be the co-owners in dispute. However, an application may be made to the court under section 14[123] and the court will be able to make an order.

This means that, when considering what to do in the future, an occupation rent can be ordered regardless of the problems discussed above. This is a useful additional provision. It has to be considered against the background that, before

---

[117] No claim (for sale, for example) had been made by the trustee in bankruptcy, so that no ouster of the trustee in bankruptcy could be shown. Conway [2003] Conv 533, 539–40 argues for an extended meaning of constructive ouster to be employed in favour of a trustee in bankruptcy. Although ouster provides a sound basis for a claim to rent, her analysis seems far-fetched in this context.   [118] Cf *Wright v Johnson* [2002] 2 P&CR 210; p 134 above.

[119] Eg *Jones v Challenger* [1961] 1 QB 176 (p 161 below); TLATA, s 15(1)(a), (b).

[120] Eg *City of London BS v Flegg* [1988] AC 54, 81 (Lord Oliver); TLATA, ss 12(1)(a), 13(4)(a), (b).

[121] The bankruptcy scenario in *Byford* is covered in that 'the basis for their joint occupation has gone': *Re Citro* [1991] Ch 142, 158–9.   [122] TLATA, s 13(3)–(5).

[123] *Rodway v Landy* [2001] Ch 703.

1925, any co-owner was entitled to either partition or sale. There was simply no possibility of exclusion of a co-owner from future occupation and therefore the old rule that occupation rent was not payable could readily be accepted. Now that partition or sale can no longer be insisted upon, it seems necessary to have power to ensure that one of the parties does not gain an undue financial advantage from being allowed occupation.[124]

However, this does not mean that the application of the jurisdiction is trouble-free.[125] It applies only where the trustees exclude or restrict section 12 rights to occupy. This means that a beneficiary without such a right to occupy cannot be compensated. If the intention is that two out of three beneficiaries should occupy, then it seems consistent with the purpose of the trust not to pay compensation to the third. However, some cases are less straightforward. The facts of *Bedson v Bedson* illustrate one problem which may be significant: what happens if the occupation purpose has terminated as regards one of the parties? In that case, land was purchased as both a home and a drapery business. When the wife left the home the court refused sale because the drapery business purpose survived. Unless the 'snapshot' approach to occupation rights is adopted, it appears that the wife's right to occupy had ended with the ending of the family home purpose.[126] Accordingly, there is no scope for ordering compensation. There appears to be little justification for this result: in *Bedson* itself (pre-dating TLATA) the court ordered rent to be paid. Similar situations might arise in a simpler situation where the relationship has broken down, but it is thought appropriate to delay sale, perhaps because this in the interests of minor children. It makes no sense to limit powers to order compensation to be paid, something which might be a powerful factor if the party with custody of the children is the higher earner of the two. A different problem arises if the land is not available or suitable for occupation. Section 12(2) excludes the right to occupy and hence section 13(6) does not apply.[127] It is far from clear that there should be no power to require compensation in at least some such situations.

There are further problems.[128] Under section 12(1)(b), rights to occupy may arise because 'the land is held by the trustees to be so available [for his occupation (or for the occupation of beneficiaries of a class of which he is a member or of beneficiaries in general)]'.[129] Presuming that there is no occupation purpose, this seems to permit the trustees to allow one of several beneficiaries with interests in possession to occupy without this being one of the purposes of the trust. In that

---

[124]  Prior to TLATA, Purchas J suggested that a very similar result could be achieved by the court's indicating that it would order sale unless the occupier undertook to pay rent: *Dennis v McDonald* [1982] Fam 63, 74.

[125]  Barnsley [1998] CLJ 123, 135–6, 138–42: 'The section raises far more questions than it seeks to resolve'.                              [126]  The termination of purposes is considered above, p 123.

[127]  Ross Martyn [1997] Conv 254, 261; see also p 125 above.

[128]  See also p 132 (need for decision to exclude) above.

[129]  The added words are from para (a).

scenario, the other beneficiaries fall outside paragraph (b),[130] though it is far from clear why there should be no right to require compensation to be payable for their benefit. This may lead to questions as to whether it is ever appropriate to exercise the paragraph (b) power in favour of one of several co-owners and whether an attempt to do so would survive a challenge under section 14.

Just as troublesome could be a case where the land ceases to suitable for occupation. Suppose a trust is set up for the occupation of a house by two brothers. The elder brother becomes disabled in old age and the house is no longer suitable for occupation by him: he moves to a residential home. Can the younger brother be required to pay compensation? The answer appears to be not, even if the younger brother marries so that it would no longer have been feasible for the brothers to share the house in any event. Another case[131] in which section 13(6) does not apply is where a tenant in common assigns, or leaves by will, his or her interest to a third party. The third party may well be outside the occupation purpose and therefore gain no benefit from the interest. This may be an overly harsh outcome for the third party. However, it may be a fair result if the purpose genuinely is for occupation by the other co-owner; in other cases the entire occupation purpose may terminate so that none of the beneficiaries has a right to occupy. Furthermore, in appropriate cases the court may be prepared to order sale if the occupiers refuse to undertake to pay rent.[132]

The next point to note is that the section 13 powers cannot be exercised 'in a manner likely to result in any such person ceasing to occupy'.[133] What happens if the occupier cannot afford to make payments? This seems to preclude any obligation to make payments, though the court is explicitly given jurisdiction to approve action by the trustees which removes the protection of occupiers. If the intended occupier is not yet in occupation, it remains to be seen whether the trustees can properly give occupation when they know that compensation cannot be afforded.

Finally, section 13 provides no enforcement mechanism.[134] In particular, there appears to be no clear right for the beneficiary out of possession to claim the payment, unless the Contracts (Rights of Third Parties) Act 1999 can be made to apply.[135] Otherwise the only sanction appears to be for the trustee to seek an injunction against the occupier or seek to terminate the occupation. The latter course may not be consistent with the provisions in section 13 which protect occupiers (though these can be overridden by the court) and which prevent the exercise of the powers so as to leave nobody in possession.[136]

---

[130]  See p 124 above, though a wider application of s 12 may be desirable in order to trigger the s 13 powers.                                                                [131]  Cf Barnsley [1998] CLJ 123, 130 *et seq*.
[132]  Cf *Mortgage Corpn v Shaire* [2001] Ch 743, though the third party was there a chargee.
[133]  TLATA, s 13(7).          [134]  Barnsley [1998] CLJ 123, 141–2.
[135]  This seems improbable unless the occupying beneficiary has agreed to make the payment.
[136]  TLATA, s 13(7), (1).

## 3. Claims for Improvements

The compensation claims discussed above are claims against the occupying co-owner. The question now to be considered is whether a co-owner (generally the one in occupation) can claim for improvements to the land. The basic position is that the improver cannot recoup the expenditure: it is a voluntary act that benefits another person and as such falls outside restitutionary principles.[137] On the other hand, recovery will be allowed if the improvement has been authorized by the other co-owners[138] or if the expenditure satisfies a legal duty on them.[139]

However, the non-recoupment rule is frequently avoided. Where there is sale (or partition, in the older cases) the courts have long permitted improvements to be brought into account.[140] It is thought that once the value of the improvements is realized it is just that their value should accrue to the person who made them. There is no requirement for the non-occupier to contribute out of his or her own resources. It should be noted that it does not matter whether or not it is the improver who seeks sale[141] and there is no distinction between joint tenancies and tenancies in common.[142] As one would expect, the amount that can be claimed is limited to the amount by which the value of the property has been increased, taken as at the date of the action, and cannot exceed the amount expended.[143] Equally unsurprisingly, no claim can be made if there is an intention to benefit others, rather than to be given credit for the improvements.[144]

Turning to the modern law, improvement claims are relatively uncommon in the family home context. Where the improvement is made during the continuance of the relationship, the courts may be inclined to say that it is not intended to give rise to accounting on future sale.[145] Otherwise, improvement will affect the payment on sale.[146] Most claims will be for mortgage payments made after the relationship has broken down. It has already been seen that improvement claims expose the improver to a claim for rent and that, in the family home context, the courts generally hold that mortgage interest payments and rent cancel each other out.[147]

---

[137] *Leigh v Dickeson* (1884) 15 QBD 60.     [138] *Squire v Rogers* (1979) 27 ALR 330.
[139] *Leigh v Dickeson* (1884) 15 QBD 60 (Cotton LJ, 66); see also p 135 above for interest payments.
[140] *Swan v Swan* (1819) 8 Price 518; *Leigh v Dickeson* (1884) 15 QBD 60; *Re Jones* [1893] 2 Ch 461; *Re Cook's Mortgage* [1896] 1 Ch 923.
[141] *Brickwood v Young* (1905) 2 CLR 387, 395. Mortgagees' sales also trigger recoupment: *Re Cook's Mortgage* [1896] 1 Ch 923.
[142] The equality inherent in joint tenancies is not an overriding consideration: *Re Pavlou* [1993] 1 WLR 1046.     [143] *Re Jones* [1893] 2 Ch 461.
[144] *Wright v Johnson* [2002] 2 P&CR 210: mortgage repayments intended to benefit co-owners' children.     [145] *Noack v Noack* [1959] VR 137.
[146] *Mayes v Mayes* (1969) 210 EG 935. As between husband and wife, Matrimonial Proceedings and Property Act 1970, s 37 makes special provision for improvements.     [147] See p 136 above.

## 4. Conclusions

It is not difficult to conclude that much of this material is unjustifiably complex. Basic rights to occupy are satisfactorily dealt with by TLATA, at least if the statutory rights are exclusive of any other rights based on equity. However, compensation payments and improvement claims still involve far too much reliance on old and uncertain principles which fail to recognize modern needs, especially in the family home context. As regards past occupation, it is regrettable that the opportunity to clarify this area was not taken when TLATA was enacted. Even for future occupation, the powers in section 13 are more limited than is desirable.

# 8

# Powers of Trustees: Extent, Exercise, and Control

## Introduction

Since the property legislation of the nineteenth century[1] it has been regarded as vital to ensure that there are adequate powers in settlements. This has also applied to concurrent interests since the 1925 legislation. The obvious reason has been to ensure the most appropriate management and use of land, in particular the ability to sell it when such is desirable. The modern legislation (Trusts of Land and Appointment of Trustees Act 1996, hereafter TLATA) emphasizes not only the existence of the powers, but also checks and balances to ensure that they are properly exercised. The court possesses a wide discretion to oversee their exercise and much of this Chapter is devoted to the criteria which the court has to take into account and their practical application.

One of the most difficult issues concerns the balance of power between beneficiaries and trustees. This is considered in this Chapter, in terms of how the beneficiaries can limit and control the actions of trustees. It should be borne in mind that this is meaningless for most holders of concurrent interests, who will be both trustees and beneficiaries. Most disputes arise when the relationship between co-owners (usually, though certainly not invariably, spouses or partners in a relationship) has broken down. They are likely to disagree as to what should be done with the land and court control is most important in this context. In many other cases of co-ownership[2] the trustee will be one of the beneficiaries, with a non-trustee beneficiary being in disagreement with the trustee. The danger of a trustee exercising powers for his or her personal benefit is obvious and it comes as no surprise that the court is ready to determine what should happen to the land.

A final point to note is that this Chapter does not purport to cover all the material on trustees' powers. The previous Chapter dealt with powers relating to occupation. In practice, of course, powers relating to occupation cannot be

---

[1] See Chapter 6 above.
[2] Especially where there is a constructive or resulting trust based on the *Gissing v Gissing* [1971] AC 886 line of authority.

separated from other powers.[3] The question may be whether to allow a beneficiary to occupy or, alternatively, to sell the land. Nor does this Chapter deal with the protection of purchasers and other disponees when powers are exercised. This vitally important topic is covered in the following Chapter.

## 1. The Extent of the Trustees' Powers

Prior to TLATA the powers in trusts and settlements were listed in some detail.[4] Although many common transactions were covered, not every lease or mortgage would qualify.[5] The approach taken by TLATA, section 6 is strikingly different: 'For the purpose of exercising their functions as trustees, the trustees of land have in relation to the land subject to the trust all the powers of an absolute owner'.[6] The section originally conferred explicit power to purchase land, but today section 8 of the Trustee Act 2000 confers such a power on all trustees (subject to any contrary provision in the trust) and TLATA section 6(3) merely confirms that this new power applies to trustees of land.

The broad statement of powers in TLATA, section 6 precludes most arguments as to the extent of trustees' powers. In the next section we shall see that there are some restrictions on the exercise of the powers, but we start from the proposition that they are unlimited. This seems a sensible and natural progression from the previous position of conferring wide powers. It should also be noted the powers are 'For the purpose of exercising their functions as trustees'. It should be unnecessary to stress that the trustees have no powers to affect beneficial interests: that is no part of their functions as trustees. What we are dealing with are essentially management powers, albeit that certain management decisions (especially sale) may impact dramatically upon beneficiaries. Other types of powers include powers to delegate functions to beneficiaries, to convey the land to beneficiaries, and to partition the land. These powers are conferred by specific statutory provisions[7] and are dealt with separately later in this Chapter.

[3] Note that court applications under TLATA, s 13(7) (see p 139 above) involve slightly different matters for the court to consider than the more general jurisdiction under s 14, which is considered in this Chapter.

[4] Settled Land Act 1925, ss 38–72, 102 (extension where the tenant for life was an infant). These powers were applied to trustees for sale by Law of Property Act 1925 (hereafter LPA), s 28.

[5] Harpum has argued that the power to charge land should be limited to raising money for the acquisition or improvement of the land: [1990] CLJ 277, 331–3. The cases show that other charges are a frequent source of litigation, usually involving improper conduct by the trustees. It may be observed that charges for other purposes are common and economically important, especially charging homes to secure the business liabilities of one or more of the co-owners. Harpum's argument was not accepted when TLATA was introduced.

[6] Duplicated by Trustee Act 2000, s 8(3), where land is acquired under that section. As observed by Whitehouse and Hassall, *Trusts of Land, Trustee Delegation and the Trustee Act 2000* (2nd edn), para 11.73, s 8(3) appears wholly superfluous (cf Ferris and Battersby (2003) 118 LQR 94, 115–16). The s 8(3) powers are subject to the same constraints as TLATA, s 6: Trustee Act 2000, s 9(2).

[7] TLATA, ss 9, 6(2), and 7 respectively.

A most important point is that TLATA, section 8 permits the settlor to exclude or restrict any (or indeed all) of the section 6 powers. This represents a break with thinking prior to TLATA: section 8 has 'revolutionary effect'.[8] Previously, the objective of ensuring that land could be efficiently managed had been thought so important that legislation rendered void any attempt to limit powers.[9] How can we explain the new provision? It is most unlikely that co-ownership trusts arising on the purchase of land will contain any restrictions: the purchasers will usually be trustees and will maintain sufficient control by virtue of that status. It is where a settlement is set up (whether *inter vivos* or by will) that a settlor may wish to restrict powers. This is most likely if the property is intended to be a home of a beneficiary or, more generally, if it is wished to keep it within the family. Two factors are probably most important in assessing the significance of section 8. First, the amount of property within such trusts is very much less than in the nineteenth century: the days when settlements covered the great majority of valuable land in the country are long past. Accordingly, it matters less that there may be limits on dealing with such land. For a specific plot of land the arguments may not have changed, but their overall economic significance has. The second factor is probably more telling. For well over a century lawyers and landowners have become accustomed to legal structures whereby land can be sold and otherwise dealt with. They do not, of course, mean that land will in fact be sold: it is apparent that wide powers are consistent with long-term property retention, especially where the trustees appreciate that the settlor has such a desire and there is no pressing need to sell.[10] It seems unlikely today that many settlors will wish to exclude the powers, even if they do not wish the land to be sold. To do so would produce inflexibility, especially in the face of unforeseen developments. It is more likely that settlors will qualify the powers, primarily by requiring consents before their exercise.[11]

If the powers are excluded, is there any way to (for example) sell the land if all agree that sale is the only sensible course of action? This is especially problematic if some of the beneficiaries are infants or unascertained[12] and therefore unable to approve a sale. As will be seen below, it is unlikely that the supervisory powers of the court under TLATA, section 14, extend to overriding the terms of the trust.[13] It is sometimes suggested that excluding the power of sale is inconsistent with the principle that a fee simple cannot be rendered inalienable.[14] However, this seems improbable. The principle is that a fee simple cannot be made subject to a

---

[8] Watt [1997] Conv 263, 264. The article contains a useful analysis of possible ways of getting round an exclusion of powers.    [9] Settled Land Act 1925, s 106.

[10] The breaking up of the large estates in the early twentieth century was largely a result of the need to find resources to pay death duties, coupled with the carnage of the First World War and a general decline in the role of land as a source of social and economic power: see Grove (1961) 24 MLR 123, 125.

[11] Specifically authorized by s 8. Consents are considered below, p 147.

[12] Though an application under the Variation of Trusts Act 1958 might succeed.

[13] See p 156 below; also Hopkins [1996] Conv 411, 422; Watt [1997] Conv 263, 266.

[14] Sydenham [1997] Conv 242; a relatively modern application of the principle is found in *Re Brown* [1954] Ch 39.

condition subsequent, so that it terminates on any purported transfer.[15] This is quite different from limiting trustees' powers, as these relate to the scope of authorized transactions which may overreach the beneficial interests. Indeed, if the law were otherwise, many of the nineteenth-century concerns about powers to dispose of land would have been misplaced!

In considering ways to get around a settlor's exclusion of powers, we need to examine principles applicable to trusts generally. The most promising possibility[16] is found in the Trustee Act 1925, section 57. Where a disposition (including a sale) 'is in the opinion of the court expedient, but the same cannot be effected by reason of the absence of any power for that purpose' then the court may confer the necessary power for that purpose. In the trusts of land context, the power is not so much absent as excluded. Nevertheless, it is to be hoped that the courts will still consider section 57 to be applicable. The fact that the power has been deliberately excluded would doubtless be a relevant factor for the court to consider in deciding whether to exercise its jurisdiction.

## 2. Constraints on the Exercise of Powers

### A. Equitable Principles

Giving the trustees the powers of an absolute owner does not mean that they can be exercised with the freedom enjoyed by such an owner. As the Law Commission observes,[17] 'General equitable rules will continue to ensure that these powers can only be properly exercised in the interests of the beneficiaries'. This may be said to have two principle elements. First, the trustees must act with reasonable care and skill.[18] Failure to comply with this standard may lead to liability. Secondly, the courts will be prepared to review decisions by the trustees. However, unanimous decisions[19] by trustees are unlikely to be upset if they were taken *bona fide* and were not perverse.[20] Given that TLATA, section 14 confers a broad discretion to review the exercise of functions of trustees of land, this is likely to overshadow the more general equitable jurisdiction.

[15] Strikingly, it has no application to determinable fees: *Re Leach* [1912] 2 Ch 422.

[16] For other possibilities, see Watt [1997] Conv 263, especially pp 266–70. In addition to the points already considered, note (1) the jurisdiction to sanction compromises on behalf of infants or unascertained persons (restricted to genuine disputes by *Chapman v Chapman* [1954] AC 429); (2) the jurisdiction under Trustee Act 1925, s 63, to authorize conveyances for the maintenance, education, or benefit of infants; and (3) the inherent emergency jurisdiction of the court (*Re New* [1901] 2 Ch 534).     [17] Law Com No 181, para 10.9.

[18] Trustee Act 2000, s 1, applied by TLATA, s 6(9). The standard takes into account any 'special knowledge or experience' of the trustee and whether the trustee acts in the course of a business or profession.

[19] The exercise of powers has to be unanimous. More questionable may be cases where a power is not exercised because the trustees are split on the question.

[20] Law Com No 260, para 3.3; Pettit, *Equity and the Law of Trusts* (9th edn), pp 402–4; Ferris and Battersby (2003) 119 LQR 94, 97.

## B. Statutory Controls Within TLATA, Section 6

Section 6 contains a number of restrictions, most of which have little general impact. However, section 6(5), a provision described as a 'total mystery',[21] provides that the 'trustees shall have regard to the rights of the beneficiaries'. This is puzzling for two reasons. First, it appears to repeat the general equitable principles: it goes almost without saying that trustees have to consider the interests of the beneficiaries in exercising their powers. More worrying, it seems to imply that trustees can override the rights of beneficiaries so long as they have regard to those rights. Such a proposition is very surprising, as one would not expect trustees to defeat rights of beneficiaries.[22]

Perhaps the most credible explanation is that the 'rights' encompass future rights and, perhaps, rights of a non-financial nature.[23] This would make sense, without suggesting that present rights can be overridden. It should also be remembered that, as discussed shortly below, the wishes of beneficiaries with interests in possession are given particular weight.[24] Although there is no requirement to consult other beneficiaries, it seems entirely proper that the trustees should take their rights into account. For example, the trustees may take into account the fact that sale will preclude occupation of a long-term family home by those with interests in remainder.

There are also more specific controls. First, powers cannot be exercised in contravention of enactments or rules of law or equity (or orders made thereunder); these include orders by the court or the Charity Commissioners.[25] Next, where another enactment confers powers subject to some qualification, the trustees must continue to observe that limitation.[26] In other words, if earlier legislation simply fails to confer a power, it is today conferred by section 6. However, if earlier legislation confers explicitly states that there is no power, or power subject (for example) to getting the approval of a Secretary of State, then no wider power results from section 6.

The application of these more specific controls where there is an earlier enactment is moderately straightforward, but what is the meaning of 'any rule of law or equity'? In a similar vein to the comments above on section 6(5), it seems unnecessary to require compliance with rules of law and equity.[27] Indeed, this control may

---

[21] Whitehouse and Hassall, *Trusts of Land, Trustee Delegation and the Trustee Act 2000* (2nd edn), para 2.42. The authors observe that the notes to the Trustee Act 2000 treat it as clarifying the equitable duty, not changing the law.

[22] Unless authorized by the legislation. One example is found in TLATA, s 13 (occupation), in which context s 13(4) lists matters to which the trustees are to have regard.

[23] Ferris and Battersby [1998] Conv 168, 174, (2003) 119 LQR 94, 100–2. However, they rely on the analogous word 'interests', which may possess a different connotation.

[24] TLATA, s 11 requires them to be consulted: their views are to be weighed against the 'general interest of the trust'.                                      [25] Ibid, s 6(6), (7).

[26] Ibid, s 6(8).

[27] Whitehouse and Hassall, n 21 above, para 2.43. See Ferris and Battersby (2003) 119 LQR 94, 102–3 for its effect as regards overreaching; p 196 below.

overlap with section 6(5), though it covers additional cases, such as the exercise of a power, whereby the trustee makes a profit. However, the reference to court orders may make good sense. If a court has ordered that a specific transaction shall not be carried out, then the trustees cannot argue that that this is transcended by TLATA, section 6, even if the order pre-dates TLATA.

## C. Consent Requirements

It has been seen above that section 8 permits the settlor to exclude or restrict powers. One specific example of this is that the exercise of powers can be made subject to obtaining one or more consents. This is made explicit by section 8(2). Consents are dealt with separately in this section as they attract a number of specific rules. They are important because, without consent being given, the power simply cannot be exercised.

Prior to TLATA, consent requirements could be implied in order to give effect to the settlor's intention. Sometimes this was to ensure that occupiers could not have their occupation disturbed by sale. Now that the legislation confers rights to occupy and decisions to sell can be challenged, it no longer seems necessary to imply consent requirements in order to protect present occupation. However, a variant is that the settlement may intend a future beneficiary to have rights which can operate only if the property remains unsold, for example, a future right to purchase the property. The courts reasoned that, in order to prevent those rights from being rendered nugatory, the consent of the future beneficiary was impliedly required.[28] Even though the beneficiary could today employ TLATA, section 14 to challenge a decision to sell, it seems likely that a court would feel that the stronger protection of limiting the power of sale was necessary to give full effect to the settlor's intentions. Indeed, it could be argued that the power of sale might be postponed in such cases (an option not open prior to TLATA) though this may produce too inflexible an outcome: requiring consent provides a more balanced response. Could it be argued that the phrase 'makes provision' in section 8(2) is limited to express provision? This seems improbable. Contracting out of statutory implications into trusts generally does not require express provision[29] and the wording in the trusts for sale legislation prior to TLATA (at a time when implied consents were widely recognized) was not dissimilar to section 8(2).[30]

Several provisions ensure that consent requirements do not operate as an unreasonable bar on sale. If the consent of an infant is required, then the trustees must

---

[28] *Re Herklots' WT* [1964] 1 WLR 583 (right to acquire house in part satisfaction of one-third beneficial share).

[29] See eg *IRC v Bernstein* [1961] Ch 399, 412–13 (Trustee Act 1925, s 69(2), where the wording is 'if a contrary intention is not expressed in the instrument').

[30] LPA, s 26(1) ('by the disposition made requisite') and (2) ('expressed to be required in a disposition').

instead obtain the consent of a parent with parental responsibility or guardian.[31] A more general provision is that the court may relieve the trustees of the obligation to obtain a consent. This forms part of the court jurisdiction, found in TLATA, section 14, over trustees' functions. One can contemplate three types of cases in which it might be useful. The first is where a beneficiary is absent for an extended period and cannot be contacted. If a transaction is urgent, then it is easy to see that a court may be willing to approve the transaction. The second type of case is where the beneficiary is under a mental disability. It would plainly be wrong if this were to preclude necessary dealings with the land.[32] The third type of case is where consent has been refused. One would expect the court to be more reluctant to approve the transaction in this circumstance, given that the settlor's wishes are being defeated. However, consent may be irrationally refused and then the court may be prepared to make an order. In particular, the person who refuses consent may no longer possess any interest requiring protection or other beneficiaries may stand to lose significantly.[33]

In addition, purchasers receive two forms of protection. The first is where the consent of several persons is required. In order to avoid the need for extensive enquiries, the purchaser is protected so long as any two of them consent.[34] However, the trustees receive no such protection and it remains their responsibility to ensure that all consents are required. Given that trustees act very rashly if they fail to obtain all consents, this protection fails to make the sale of land easier; it simply limits the checks the purchaser has to make. The second protection relates to consent requirements unknown to the purchaser. This forms part of a package of protections for purchasers in TLATA, section 16 and is considered in the following Chapter.

## D. Consultation Requirements

Traditionally beneficiaries have been little involved in decisions by trustees, as least as a matter of trusts law. For trusts of land, it is very different. This is readily understandable when the future of beneficiaries' homes is at stake; other cases may involve long-standing family ownership of land which renders beneficiary involvement desirable. In any event, TLATA, section 11 requires consultation 'in the exercise of any function' relating to the land, subject to any contrary provision.[35]

---

[31] TLATA, s 10(3). A literal interpretation discloses no protection to the trustees if the infant's consent is not obtained. However, the provision makes sense only if the parent's consent is sufficient in place of the infant's. The wording of the predecessor provision (LPA, s 26(2)) was very similar and was assumed to protect the trustees: Megarry and Wade, *Law of Real Property* (5th edn), p 394.

[32] Prior to TLATA the consent of the beneficiary's receiver sufficed: LPA, s 26(2).

[33] A simple example is provided by *Re Beale's ST* [1932] 2 Ch 15, in which a bankrupt life interest holder refused consent; see also the older cases in which consent was implied to protect occupation: *Bull v Bull* [1955] 1 QB 234, 238–9.     [34] TLATA, s 10(1).

[35] It appears that the 'uncertainties and limitations' of s 11 are such that it is normally excluded: Haworth (2003) 153 NLJ 1596, 1597. It does not apply (subject to opting in by the settlor: s 11(3)) to trusts or wills predating TLATA: the previous consultation provision (LPA, s 26(3)) did not apply to express trusts.

What is meant by 'function'? It is not defined, though it is encountered in a number of provisions in TLATA. Perhaps the most significant (apart from section 11) are sections 14 (court control over functions) and 9 (delegation of functions).[36] The heading 'Functions of trustees of land' governs sections 6–9A, but this is of limited assistance as trustees have powers under other provisions. The best example concerns the section 13 powers regarding occupation: section 15(2) assumes that these are functions within section 14.[37] In *Notting Hill Housing Trust v Brackley*[38] it was argued that the termination of a joint tenancy of a periodic tenancy by one joint tenant could be attacked on the ground that the other joint tenant had not been consulted. This was against the background that the House of Lords had recently decided that one joint tenant can serve notice to determine a periodic joint tenancy.[39] This notice is likely to have a disastrous effect on the other tenant and the House of Lords' decision has been the subject of much criticism and attempts to get around it. Nevertheless, the Court of Appeal held that no exercise of a function was involved and accordingly refused to interfere with the termination of the tenancy. The underlying reality is that the court was reluctant to allow the trusts of land legislation[40] to negate the clear decision of the House of Lords; this fits with the analysis that the imposition of a trust is not intended to impose radical changes on co-owners.[41]

*Notting Hill* treated functions as meaning the exercise of powers and duties: unproblematic in itself. However, beyond that the reasoning produces difficulties. The main idea[42] appears to be that a positive act is required. What in substance had occurred was that the trustee had withheld his consent to the continuation of the tenancy. This may make sense in the particular setting, but has to overcome one major problem. It is plain beyond doubt that section 14 (court applications) permits challenges to decisions by the trustees not to sell.[43] There is here no requirement of positive action. This may be explained because section 14 brings in 'functions' in providing that the court may make an order 'relating to the exercise by the trustees of any of their functions'.[44] In other words, there need not be an exercise of function prior to the application: the court order that there should be sale clearly does relate to the function of sale. By contrast, section 11 requires consultation in the exercise of a function, which does require the trustees to be

[36] It is also encountered in ss 6 (powers) and 10 (consents).

[37] Another example might be the power to postpone sale where there is a trust for sale: TLATA, s 4(1).          [38] [2002] HLR 212. Cf Ferris and Battersby (2003) 118 LQR 94, 106–7.

[39] *Hammersmith and Fulham LBC v Monk* [1992] 1 AC 478; cf Megarry and Wade, *Law of Real Property* (6th edn), para 9-006.

[40] It was also highly material that the same result had been reached in *Crawley BC v Ure* [1996] QB 13 on the consultation rules prior to TLATA (LPA, s 26(3)).

[41] See eg *Re Warren* [1932] 1 Ch 42, 47 (Maugham J) and *Monk*, 493 (Lord Browne-Wilkinson).

[42] Peter Gibson LJ, [20] (analysing *Ure*) and [23]. The idea that the notice to terminate the periodic tenancy is not a positive act lies at the heart of *Monk*.

[43] Law Com No 181, para 12.6.

[44] But Peter Gibson LJ seems to assume at [25] that s 14 would not apply on the facts of *Notting Hill*.

exercising a function. There is therefore no need to consult where the trustees intend not to do something. But does it make sense to limit section 11 in this manner? If the trustees are considering whether to sell, is it sensible to require consultation only if they are minded to sell? This points to an interpretation of 'function' so as to include decisions whether to act, but that is difficult to reconcile with *Notting Hill*.

Jonathan Parker LJ[45] provided another basis for justifying *Notting Hill*. He suggested that, in giving notice, the joint tenant was not acting as trustee, but rather signifying his 'personal wish and intention'. This is attractive as not establishing any general limitation on section 11. However, it remains the case that it was the legal joint tenancy that was terminated and it is difficult to see how the notice was not an action by the joint tenant as trustee. As suggested above, the underlying problem is that the trust is extremely artificial where the same persons are trustees and beneficiaries. Some provisions, such as section 14 court applications, work well in these cases, but consultation frequently looks inappropriate.

Assuming that positive decisions are required for section 11 to apply, it is easy to see that consultation is required if the trustees wish to sell, mortgage, or lease the land. However, there are many trivial decisions relating to the land. Examples are minor changes to tenancy contracts, appointment of agents, and taking out of property insurance. A strict interpretation of section 11 might suggest that consultation is required in all these cases, though it would seem senseless in such mundane matters and more likely to divert attention away from important decisions. It is unlikely to occur.

Who must be consulted? The requirement is limited to those with interests in possession. It follows that those with interests in remainder or who may benefit under discretionary trusts[46] need not be consulted. In concurrent interests trusts, it will normally be necessary to consult all beneficiaries, though consultation of infants is explicitly not required. In successive interest trusts, those with life interests are to be consulted. For all trusts of land, consultation is required only 'so far as practicable'. This excludes cases where a beneficiary cannot be contacted, at least within a reasonable time span.[47]

What is the effect of consultation? It would be a vacuous exercise if the trustees could ignore what they hear. Section 11(1)(b) requires them to 'so far as consistent with the general interest of the trust give effect to the wishes of those beneficiaries, or (in case of dispute) of the majority (according to the value[48] of their combined interests)'. In considering the effect of this, it is necessary to distinguish concurrent and successive interest trusts. Virtually every dispute in recent decades has

---

[45] At [31]; he also agreed with Peter Gibson LJ. Note the criticism by Pascoe [2004] Conv 370.

[46] See p 122 above in the context of occupation rights; the wording in the 2 contexts is identical.

[47] *Quaere* whether it could justify not consulting as regards trivial decisions: how far does 'practicable' vary in its application according to the significance of the transaction?

[48] Whitehouse and Hassall, n 21 above, at para 2.114 observe that this is not readily applied to life interest holders, the value of whose interests will vary according to age and health.

involved concurrent interests, so these trusts are considered first. The typical case involves the same persons being both trustees and beneficiaries. It takes no great imagination to work out that if they disagree then the consultation principle will fail to advance a solution; an application to court will be necessary. It is important to note that the circumstances and wishes of the beneficiaries with interests in possession are amongst the matters to which the court is to have regard in exercising its section 14 control over trustees' functions.[49] However, in the majority of cases the disputing parties will each have a half share, so their views will cancel each other out. In other cases the views of the majority may be more important, but in practice other matters (in particular, the purpose for which the property is held and the interests of children) are likely to be more compelling. Where a trust has been set up by a settlor with independent trustees (as opposed to arising on the joint purchase of land) the consultation rule is more likely to be significant. It may be the basis for stopping a transaction if there has been no consultation[50] and the views of the majority may be a strong factor in deciding whether a transaction should go ahead.

It might be noted that when the trustees exercise their section 13 powers regarding occupation, they are to have regard to the circumstances and wishes of those who are entitled to possess.[51] At first sight this seems to duplicate the provisions in section 11. However, there are two differences. First, section 13 applies only to those with rights to occupy, not necessarily all the beneficiaries with interests in possession. Secondly, there is no provision for the majority to prevail. In the section 13 context, these changes make sense. Curiously, however, there is no disapplication of section 11,[52] so it might be thought that both provisions operate alongside each other. This somewhat anarchic position matters little. Any dispute is likely to result in a court application under section 14. It is made clear by section 15 that, in occupation disputes, the section 13(4) principles apply in place of the normal section 11 principles.[53]

Successive interest trusts are likely to raise rather different issues. Usually the trustees and beneficiaries will be different persons, so that transactions agreed on by the trustees are likely to go ahead unless section 11 can be used as a basis for a challenge. As with concurrent interests where there are independent trustees, one might expect the views of the life interest holders to carry great weight. Suppose the trustees wish to sell investment property, but the beneficiaries with interests in possession believe that land in the area will increase in value and seek to stop the sale. If those beneficiaries' opinion is perverse or uninformed, it will be easy for the trustees not to accept it. But what if both opinions could rationally be held? The trustees believe that the interests of the trust are best served by sale; not so the

---

[49] TLATA, s 15(3). The wording is very similar to s 11; see p 158, n 95 below.
[50] *Waller v Waller* [1967] 1 WLR 451.    [51] See s 13(4); p 127 above.
[52] Pointedly, s 11 is expressed not to apply to s 6(2) functions (see p 152 below): this is the only limitation on its scope.    [53] See s 15(2) (s 13 functions) and (3) (other functions).

beneficiaries. In this scenario, it seems that the views of the beneficiaries should prevail if the consultation provisions are to be taken seriously. However, it remains an important duty of the trustees to balance the interests of life interest holders and remaindermen.[54] If they believe that the interests of all the beneficiaries are best served by a particular course of action, it may not be too difficult to persuade the court that opposition expressed by the life interest holders is not 'consistent with the general interest of the trust'. This most obviously applies when the remaindermen would be prejudiced by the decision advocated by the life interest holders, perhaps as regards their future occupation. It will be much more difficult to use this analysis if there is no obvious clash between the interests of the two groups of beneficiaries, as in the above example relating to sale of investment property.

## 3. Specific Additional Powers

TLATA confers a number of additional powers upon trustees. As explained below, these may possess different incidents (especially as to whether they can be excluded) than the general powers conferred by section 6. The first such power is conferred by section 4 on trustees for sale: a power to postpone sale. This appears to follow from section 6 in any event, but what is important is that the power to postpone cannot be excluded. Section 4 makes it clear that the trustees can decide indefinitely not to sell. Accordingly, the land may be retained without time limit, despite the terminology of trust for sale. The inability to exclude postponement emphasizes the extent to which we have moved away from the imperative of sale which was so central to the 1925 legislation.[55]

Perhaps more significant is physical partition of the land between the beneficial co-owners. Before 1925 the co-owners had a right to have the land partitioned so that each would become sole owner of part, regardless of the sense of doing so. We have seen[56] that TLATA, section 7 permits partition with the agreement of all the trustees and beneficiaries. The beneficiaries must be 'absolutely entitled': partition is not thought appropriate where there is, for example, a life interest. On the other hand, unanimity between trustees and beneficiaries can justify any outcome.[57]

Somewhat different is the power of the trustees under section 6(2) (introduced for the first time by TLATA) to convey the land to the beneficiaries, if the beneficiaries are of full age and capacity and absolutely entitled. In such cases, co-ownership and the trust of land will continue, but the existing trustees can relieve themselves

---

[54] This is sometimes viewed as a duty to be fair: Hoffmann J in *Nestlé v National Westminster Bank plc* [2000] WTLR 795 (upheld [1993] 1 WLR 1260, though Leggatt LJ, 1284 is lukewarm as to this formulation of the duty).

[55] Under LPA, s 25(1) (repealed by TLATA) a power to postpone was implied, but could be excluded.                                                       [56] Page 48 above.

[57] Underhill and Hayton, *Law of Trusts and Trustees* (15th edn), pp 894 *et seq* (see also pp 710 *et seq*).

of any further role. Just as the beneficiaries can bring the trust to an end,[58] this provision enables the trustees to terminate their involvement.[59] It does not require the agreement of the beneficiaries and, indeed, the usual consultation require-ments are excluded.[60]

Most interesting, however, is the ability of trustees to delegate any of their powers to one or more beneficiaries with interests in possession. This power is most likely to be significant for successive interest trusts, where beneficiaries are less likely to be trustees. In the old Settled Land Act settlements the powers were vested in the tenant for life. Although this is now viewed as far from ideal,[61] there are many sit-uations in which settlors will wish beneficiaries to manage the land. One example is where property is left to a settlor's widow or widower for life. It is quite natural for the settlor to wish their spouse to control the future of their home. The delega-tion provisions in trusts of land enable settlors 'to reproduce the functional equiv-alent of a strict settlement', as expressed by Lord Mackay LC.[62] Although much can be achieved by the consultation provisions and by requiring consents (as well as relying on the good sense of the trustees) these may not give as much positive control as is wished.

Although a power to delegate had existed since 1925[63] it did not extend to sale. Today TLATA, s 9 enables trustees to delegate any of their functions relat-ing to the land to a beneficiary of full age entitled to an interest in possession.[64] It was suggested above that some settlors will wish there to be delegation. Can they (through the terms of the trust) require that the trustees *must* delegate? Section 9(1) itself provides a discretion to delegate, but is it an exhaustive code for delegation? It may be that an obligation to delegate would be upheld.[65] In any event, if the trustees refuse to delegate then an application may be made to court for the exercise of its statutory discretion under TLATA, section 14. The intentions of the settlor will be a relevant consideration, though many beneficiaries, especially if aged, will not wish to undertake the hassle of a court application.

There are rules relating to the exercise of the power and its revocation: these are of particular importance to those dealing with the delegate. Delegation should be

---

[58] *Saunders v Vautier* (1841) 4 Beav 115, affirmed Cr&Ph 240.

[59] The power might be viewed as balancing the greater powers over trustees conferred on benefi-ciaries by TLATA.

[60] TLATA, ss 11(2)(b). In a s 14 application regarding s 6(2) the court does not have to take account of their wishes: s 15(3). The drafting of s 6(2) is a 'nightmare': Whitehouse and Hassall, *Trusts of Land, Trustee Delegation and the Trustee Act 2000* (2nd edn), paras 2.44–2.51.

[61] Law Com WP 94, para 3.16, repeated in Law Com No 181, para 1.3. The tenant for life is frequently in a position involving a conflict of interest.

[62] 570 HL Deb col 1535; see also Law Com No 181, para 1.5.     [63] LPA, s 29.

[64] The meaning of interest in possession was considered in the context of occupation: p 122 above.

[65] Cf Whitehouse and Hassall, *Trusts of Land, Trustee Delegation and the Trustee Act 2000* (2nd edn), para 2.85, though expressing doubts. Perhaps the optimal solution would be for the obligation to apply unless the trustees obtained a court order to the contrary (analogous to the position for consent requirements), but this cannot be spelt out of the present legislation: cf p 156 below.

by power of attorney: a deed executed by all the trustees.[66] The power may be revoked by a single trustee and it terminates automatically on the appointment of a new trustee or on the beneficiary's ceasing to have an interest in possession.[67] The power of attorney may be relied upon by those dealing with the delegate as proof that the trustees were entitled to delegate to that person.[68] Both delegates and persons dealing with them are protected against unknown revocation of the power.[69] This is important given the ease with which revocation can be effected.[70] The beneficiary has the duties and liabilities of a trustee, but does not have powers of sub-delegation and, unsurprisingly, cannot receive capital money.[71]

An important consideration is whether the trustees are liable for the acts and defaults of the beneficiary to whom powers are delegated. Too wide a liability could lead to reluctance to exercise the power to delegate.[72] The original TLATA, section 9(8) went close to the opposite extreme, providing for liability only for the initial decision whether or not to delegate. However, the law relating to the general duty of care of trustees was restructured by the Trustee Act 2000; this legislation repealed section 9(8) and inserted TLATA, section 9A. This section applies the new statutory duty of care to decisions relating to delegation and to keeping it under review: clearly there may now be a breach if trustees ignore warning signs that the beneficiary in question may act improperly. It is in this context significant that any trustee can revoke the delegation. However, it is explicitly provided that there is no liability for default by the beneficiary unless there is a breach of this duty.[73]

Before leaving these specific powers, we must ask whether they can be excluded or made subject to consents. It has already been seen that the power to postpone sale (section 4) cannot be excluded. TLATA, section 8 permits the powers in sections 6 and 7 to be so limited. The powers to convey to the beneficiaries and to partition fall within those sections and therefore section 8 applies to them. As regards partition, excluding the power has limited effect for adult beneficiaries. Partition would require their consent, but if all the trustees and beneficiaries are united in desiring a course of action (of which partition may be an example) then it may be undertaken regardless of the terms of the trust.[74] The only real significance is that the power to partition must exist before the court can override (under section 14) any absence of consent. Turning to the power to delegate, this is conferred by section 9 and therefore may be thought to be mandatory.[75] This would be a

---

[66] TLATA, s 9(1), (3); Powers of Attorney Act 1971, s 1, as amended by Law of Property (Miscellaneous Provisions) Act 1989, Sched 1, para 6.

[67] TLATA, s 9(3), (4) (different rules apply where there is delegation to 2 or more beneficiaries jointly).

[68] Ibid, s 9(2). This is vital in order that the purchaser does not have to investigate the trusts.

[69] Powers of Attorney Act 1971, s 5.

[70] *Quaere* whether a person who is aware of the appointment of a new trustee, but who does not appreciate that this effects a revocation, is protected. Given that revocation would not be expected by those unfamiliar with the legislation, it is to be hoped that the protection continues.       [71] TLATA, s 9(7).

[72] This argument caused the rejection of the Law Commission's proposal (Law Com No 181, para 11.3) of liability for all acts and defaults of the delegate.       [73] TLATA, s 9A(6).

[74] *Brice v Stokes* (1805) 11 Ves 319 and, generally, Pettit, *Equity and the Law of Trusts* (9th edn), pp 509–12.       [75] Cf the question whether occupation rights (s 12) can be excluded: p 124 above.

surprising outcome: there seems little reason to permit the settlor to exclude sale but not delegation.[76] Though the inference from section 8 is that other powers cannot be excluded, the express prohibition on exclusion in the section 4 context points in the opposite direction. The point appears to be unsettled.

## 4. Court Applications

### A. Background

Statutory court control over trustees has long been an important element of trusts of land, originally in their pre-TLATA guise of trusts for sale. This has been especially important where the trustees and beneficiaries are the same persons: the great majority of concurrent interest trusts. Whilst the courts are generally reluctant to interfere with the decisions of independent trustees,[77] it is obvious that trustees who are also beneficiaries may either be unable to reach decisions or (if the dissentient beneficiaries are not trustees) be likely to favour their own interests. Court control is essential in such cases. Because of the prevalence of cases without independent trustees, statutory court control is in practice much more important than equitable principles limiting the exercise of trustees' discretions.[78]

Before TLATA, the formal legal structure was that there was a trust for sale with a power (implied by LPA, section 25) to postpone sale. Trusts are mandatory, whereas powers must be exercised unanimously. It followed that if the trustees disagreed then the power to postpone had not been exercised and the land had to be sold.[79] However, this was only the beginning. Whatever the theory, the land cannot in practice be sold (without a court order) if one of the trustees refuses to participate. The court had jurisdiction to review the decisions of trustees (especially a failure to sell) under LPA, section 30. The courts developed an analysis whereby the purpose for which the land was held would be given great weight. Despite the notional obligation to sell, sale would not usually be ordered if the purpose could still be fulfilled. Beyond that, it was accepted that the court possessed a discretion. The test commonly applied was whether the applicant's 'voice should be allowed to prevail'.[80] As will be seen shortly, TLATA lays down matters to which the court is to have regard. These are similar to the previous law, but not identical. A question considered later below is how far the older cases are still relevant. At this stage, we simply observe that they provide a useful starting

---

[76] The delegation structure proposed by Law Com No 181 (based on Trustee Act 1925, s 25, which s 69(2) permits to be excluded) would have permitted exclusion. It is far from clear that the different structure employed by s 9 was deliberately intended to change this. [77] See p 145 above.

[78] Subject to the point that excluding or qualifying the powers of the trustees may also limit the jurisdiction of the court: p 156 below.

[79] *Re Mayo* [1943] Ch 302 (trustees of a will). With a power for sale (as is usual today) disagreement means that the power has not been exercised: *Re 90 Thornhill Road* [1970] Ch 261 (settled land power).

[80] *Re Buchanan-Wollaston's Conveyance* [1939] Ch 738, 747. A fuller quotation is found on p 160 below.

point, especially in contexts where there are no (or few) cases on the TLATA provisions.[81] However, the new provisions are different and it is unsafe to assume that the same result will be reached in all cases.

## B. Jurisdiction

TLATA provides two bases for court applications. The most general is TLATA, section 14 and that is the subject matter of this section. Section 15 lays down matters for the court to have regard to in section 14 applications. The second basis is provided by TLATA, section 13(7). This very limited jurisdiction to exclude beneficiaries already in occupation has already been considered.[82] Other issues relating to occupation fall within section 14. Somewhat separately, the family law jurisdiction[83] applies to jointly owned property. As will be seen later in this Chapter, at least some of this jurisdiction (with its greater stress on the needs of the family) operates in priority to section 14. It follows that disputes between husband and wife are unlikely to be resolved under TLATA.

First, we must consider the scope of the section 14 jurisdiction. In particular, what sorts of disputes can be resolved under section 14 and who can apply? Section 14(2) states that 'the court may make any such order—(a) relating to the exercise by the trustees of any of their functions . . . as the court thinks fit'. This is deliberately broad[84] so that all disputes can be brought before the court. Conferring such a broad jurisdiction also means that the court has greater choice as to remedy. In the past the court was thought to have power simply to sell or not to sell, but it is now clear that more imaginative solutions are possible, such as one party's remaining in occupation and paying rent to the other.[85]

The crucial phrase is 'exercise . . . of . . . functions'. We have already seen that 'functions' cover powers and duties and that the wording of the section is intended to cover both decisions by the trustees to act and failure to act.[86] To take the most common type of dispute, it means that there can be an application either to enforce a sale or to prevent a sale of the land. A more controversial point is whether the court can do something that the trustees could not. The section explicitly allows the court to override the absence of consent (or consultation), which acts as a pointer to the court's *not* having a general jurisdiction to override terms of the trust. This appears to be confirmed by the Law Commission.[87]

[81] There are important recent cases on applications by creditors, but little guidance in other situations.
[82] See p 127 above.
[83] Matrimonial Causes Act 1973, s 24; Family Law Act 1996, ss 30–41; see p 179 below.
[84] Law Com No 181, paras 12.6–12.7. It may be noted that trusts of land include trusts where not all the assets constitute land. Section 14 can therefore be used in respect of trustees' functions as regards assets other than land.
[85] Law Com No 181, para 12.4–12.5. In practice, the earlier position may not have been much different: Purchas J in *Dennis v McDonald* [1982] Fam 63, 74 (p 138, n 124 above).
[86] See p 149 above.
[87] Law Com No 181, para 12.7: 'if the trustees have more powers, then the court's overall "capacity" will be increased accordingly'.

This is particularly important where the settlor has limited the powers of the trustees. Suppose the settlor provides that the land should not be sold during her widower's lifetime. It follows from the conclusion reached above that the court cannot order sale even if it is convinced that sale is in the best interests of the trust.[88] One can see that a court might be reluctant to see its role fettered in this way, but is there any way of avoiding that result? Perhaps the only possibility is to treat the functions of trustees as being what they are according to TLATA, without regard to the specific trust, but this is by no means a natural reading of the statute. It may be noted that, if sale cannot be ordered, exclusion of powers is far more powerful than requiring consent, as section 14 permits the absence of consent to be overridden. It may be doubted whether this is an entirely sensible structure.

A different sort of case is where a beneficiary enjoys rights of occupation under section 12. Can the trustees ask the court to exclude that beneficiary in order that a sale can go ahead? As a matter of practicality, it will be impossible to sell the land if there is a beneficiary in occupation who refuses to leave.[89] The trustees possess no power to exclude a beneficiary in occupation and the power in section 13(7) for the court to exclude such a beneficiary operates only where it is desired that another beneficiary should occupy. The arguments above suggest that the court possesses no jurisdiction. However, a viable contrary argument is that the trustees can sell even if they cannot exclude the beneficiary; therefore the court can make an order 'relating to' sale.[90] In other words, the relevant function is sale rather than exclusion of the beneficiary; the court may reason that the beneficiary must be excluded in order that a sale can proceed. Yet such an exercise by the trustees of the power of sale would appear to be a breach of trust if it is designed to defeat rights of the beneficiaries: the existence of a power of sale does not mean that it is proper for the trustees to exercise it in these circumstances. The proposition that 'functions' extend to the exercise of powers in breach of trust is unattractive.

The remaining question is: who can apply under section 14? Section 14(1) permits applications by a trustee or a person who 'has an interest in property subject to' the trust. Most obviously, beneficiaries can apply. So also can a trustee in bankruptcy of a beneficiary (in whom the bankrupt's property vests) and, perhaps less obviously, a chargee of a beneficial interest,[91] including the holder of a charging order.[92] The fact that the holder of an interest in the land can apply is

---

[88] There might be some other jurisdiction which could be applied: p 145 above.

[89] That the beneficial interests will be overreached on sale by two trustees (*City of London BS v Flegg* [1988] AC 54) is unlikely to affect this.

[90] At least 2 cases have entertained s 14 applications where it was arguable that there was a s 12 right to occupy: *Mortgage Corpn v Shaire* [2001] Ch 743 and *Chan v Leung* [2003] 1 FLR 23 (no appeal on sale aspect). However, in neither case was the extent of the right to occupy clear and neither addressed the interrelationship between rights to occupy and the s 14 jurisdiction.

[91] A recent example is *First National Bank plc v Achampong* [2004] 1 FCR 18; [2003] EWCA Civ 487.

[92] For an example under the old law, see *Lloyds Bank Plc v Byrne & Byrne* [1993] 1 FLR 369; the wording of s 14(1) was intended to ensure that chargees could apply: 570 HL Deb col 1543 (Lord Mackay LC).

curious, in that the interest apparently need not be related to the trust. Thus a tenant of the trustees might seek to stop them from selling, though it is extremely dubious whether such an application would be taken seriously. The absence of an interest precludes any section 14 application. Thus an unsecured creditor (without a charging order) cannot apply, nor can a settlor. These results are unsurprising; it might be noted that settlors generally possess no standing to enforce trusts.[93]

## C. The Exercise of Discretion

It has been observed above that, prior to TLATA, much stress was placed on the intention underpinning the trust (or more accurately, the purchase of land giving rise to the trust). Today section 15 lists matters the court is to take into account and this provision needs to be considered in some detail. It is desirable that the parties to a trust of land dispute agree a resolution of it and avoid the expense of litigation, but this often requires their knowing the likely outcome of a court application. The great majority of cases have involved sale of the land and the following analyses assume that the question is whether the land should be sold. However, similar principles will apply as regards any function of the trustees.[94]

Section 15(1) includes amongst the matters to which the court is to have regard:

(a) the intentions of the person or persons (if any) who created the trust,
(b) the purposes for which the property subject to the trust is held,
(c) the welfare of any minor who occupies or might reasonably be expected to occupy any land subject to the trust as his home, and
(d) the interests of any secured creditor of any beneficiary.

In addition, section 15(3) requires regard to be had to the 'circumstances and wishes' of beneficiaries of full age who have interests in possession.[95] In case of dispute, it is the majority (by value) who are taken into account. This requirement, which did not exist prior to TLATA, is similar to the consultation provisions operating on the exercise of trustees' powers. Two specific points may be mentioned. First, the circumstances of these beneficiaries may be taken into account: this goes

---

[93] This underpins the right of a beneficiary who is absolutely entitled to terminate the trust, notwithstanding a direction to accumulate income: *Saunders v Vautier* (1841) 4 Beav 115, affirmed Cr&Ph 240.

[94] A recent example is *Rodway v Landy* [2001] Ch 703 on occupation rights; pp 48, 126 above.

[95] Section 15(3) applies to 'any other application'. Section 15(1) refers to s 14 applications generally and s 15(2) (discussed below) deals with wishes of beneficiaries in applications relating to s 13 functions. It is quite clear that s 15(3) does not apply to s 13 functions, but does 'any other application' refer to both (1) and (2) and thereby exclude s 14 applications generally? This question was raised in *Mortgage Corpn v Shaire* [2001] Ch 743, 761, where it was held that s 15(3) does apply to s 14 applications (in other words, 'other' applies to s 15(2) but not s 15(1)). If it were otherwise, then, as Neuberger J commented, it would be 'very difficult to give it [s 15(3)] any meaning at all'.

beyond section 11 on consultation. For example, it enables the court to consider the ill-health of an occupying beneficiary. Secondly, it is unclear whether the circumstances of a minority beneficiary are to be taken into account. It makes sense to say that the wishes of the majority rather than the minority are to be considered, but less sense to say that the circumstances of only the majority must be considered. At the end of the day it probably matters little, as the court can always take into account other material considerations.[96]

It remains to be seen whether section 15(3) will have a significant impact. It is difficult to predict how powerful it will be in comparison with the matters listed in section 15(1). It would be surprising if a person with, say, a 60 per cent share could use this to defeat the purpose of the trust or the welfare of an occupying minor. As regards secured creditors, their interests are likely to be opposed to those of the beneficiaries and the fact that all the beneficiaries are opposed to sale is unlikely to carry much weight. However, the courts will take into account whether the charge is over a majority or minority interest, though without placing much stress on it.[97] Section 15(3) might have more of a role where the section 15(1) criteria point to no obvious answer, for example when land has been purchased as an investment and the majority of the beneficiaries present a considered opinion that it should (or should not) be sold.

Where the application relates to the trustees' functions under section 13 (occupation of the land), then section 15(2) brings in the views of the beneficiaries. The court must consider the circumstances and wishes of the beneficiaries entitled to occupy under section 12. This is a narrower group of beneficiaries than under section 15(3) but this is justified because it is their rights which are at stake. If there are three beneficiaries with interests in possession, but only two with a right to occupy a house, there seems no good reason why the third beneficiary should have a say as to which of the other two should occupy: his or her interests as beneficiary are, at most, only tangentially affected. It should also be noted that there is no provision for majority views to prevail, it is a more open discretion.

## (i) Disputes Involving the Original Beneficiaries

This category of dispute involves the most important general principles. Two other types of dispute are separately dealt with: bankruptcy applications and applications by chargees and other successors in title.

The stress in the pre-TLATA cases on the purpose of the trust is reflected in paragraph (a) and (b) of section 15(1). It follows that these earlier cases may provide a useful guide to the outcome of disputes today. Three qualifications must be made at the outset. First, the role of infant children was never very clear under the old law. It appears that it would not normally be the case that they would

---

[96] Section 15(1) states that the relevant matters 'include' those listed.

[97] *Mortgage Corpn v Shaire* [2001] Ch 743, 762. On the other hand, the value of the debtor's share (the maximum the creditor can claim) relative to that of the other shares may be highly relevant to the viability of other beneficiaries satisfying the debtor's claim: p 177 below.

feature as part of the purpose, though it was generally agreed that that their interests should be taken into account. Today, it is clear from paragraph (c) that their interests are to be considered alongside purposes: they are not subsidiary to purposes. This means that we will rarely need to ask whether the purposes include occupation by children, though it might be relevant in the rare case where the house is purchased (or a trust set up) specifically for occupation by an infant child. The older cases dealing with children are unlikely to be helpful today. The second qualification is that the interests of secured creditors (paragraph (d)) is new and has led to a somewhat different approach in cases involving such creditors.[98] However, this lies outside our immediate concern with the original beneficiaries. The third qualification is more elusive. The older cases involved a trust for sale, where the default position was that there should be sale. This is certainly not the case for the modern trust of land, at least unless a trust for sale has been expressly created by the settlor (or purchasers) However, very few of the older cases placed any stress on the old obligation to sell (at least where there was a purpose for the trust or purchase) so it is unclear how far this change in legal structure will affect the result in a typical case. We return to this issue after considering the cases.

Two early cases illustrate the approach adopted by the courts. In *Re Buchanan-Wollaston's Conveyance*[99] a group of four neighbours bought an adjoining strip of land as co-owners. Their object, as made clear by a written agreement, was to enhance the amenity and value of their houses by ensuring that the strip would not be built upon: unanimity was required for transactions relating to the land (exactly the opposite of the normal trust for sale principles). One of the co-owners had sold his house and now sought to have the strip sold, it no longer being of any benefit to him. The Court of Appeal was clear that sale would not be ordered simply because the trustees disagreed and therefore had not exercised their power to postpone sale. Sir Wilfrid Greene MR stated[100] that the court: 'must look into all the circumstances of the case and consider whether or not, at the particular moment and in the particular circumstances when the application is made to it, it is right and proper that such an order shall be made . . . in circumstances such as these, the Court is bound to look at the contract into which the parties have entered and to ask itself the question whether or not the person applying for execution of the trust for sale is a person whose voice should be allowed to prevail'. On the facts, it was clear that sale should be refused as it would be inconsistent with the agreement, though it was recognized that the result might have been different if the circumstances had changed so that the agreement had ceased to operate as intended.[101]

---

[98] *Mortgage Corpn v Shaire* [2001] Ch 743; p 176 below.

[99] [1939] Ch 738. Contractual restraints on alienation are valid if supporting a valid collateral purpose: *Elton v Cavill (No 2)* (1994) 34 NSWLR 289.       [100] [1939] Ch 738, 747.

[101] An example was given where all the neighbours had died and the houses (but not the strip) had been sold; the owners of the strip would have no reason to retain it.

Such written agreements are rare. More commonly, land is purchased for a purpose which is never articulated in writing. Most obvious is a purchase of a house as a family home. A series of cases has recognized that such unwritten purposes are just as powerful. The seminal case in this series is *Jones v Challenger*.[102] Husband and wife acquired a house as their family home. Following the wife's adultery, they were divorced. The husband remained in occupation and the wife sought sale. Devlin LJ applied the principles in *Re Buchanan-Wollaston's Conveyance*, treating the conventional preference for sale as governing only cases in which there was no collateral purpose: the party seeking sale 'should have good grounds for doing so and, therefore, the court will inquire whether, in all the circumstances, it is right and proper to order the sale'. However, on the facts that purpose had terminated on the breakdown of the marriage and therefore sale should follow, even though the court still possessed a discretion as to the outcome. In other words, a purpose of occupation by husband and wife did not include occupation by just one of them. This analysis was soon applied where a marriage had irretrievably broken down but there had been no divorce.[103] It should be added that purposes apply regardless of marriage. Thus in *Re Evers' Trust*[104] the Court of Appeal applied the collateral purpose principle to an unmarried couple. Similar analyses will apply on the breakdown of other family relationships.[105]

Today, the role of purposes is a central aspect of section 15. As in the past, only if purposes are still subsisting can they be taken into account: spent purposes are not relevant.[106] It is obvious that the collateral purpose will rarely prevent sale in disputes between spouses and partners. If they are happily living together, no question of sale will arise.[107] If they have split up, then the purpose will have come to an end and sale will follow. So when will purposes be relevant in the family home setting? The cases reveal two principal situations. Sometimes (very rarely as between husband and wife or partners)[108] the main purpose will be to provide a

---

[102] [1961] 1 QB 176 (purchase of lease).

[103] *Rawlings v Rawlings* [1964] P 398. Willmer LJ dissented, although his disagreement related more to the marriage relationship rather than to the principles applicable to collateral purposes. See also *Jackson v Jackson* [1971] 1 WLR 1539, in which one relevant factor was that the house was larger than necessary for one person.

[104] [1980] 1 WLR 1327. It will be seen below that disputes between married couples are generally dealt with under discretionary powers in matrimonial legislation. Most s 14 cases are between either unmarried couples or parents and children.

[105] *Rivett v Rivett* (1966) 200 EG 858 (father and son); *Smith v Smith* (1975) 120 SJ 100 (sister and brother).

[106] *Rodway v Landy* [2001] Ch 703, [26] (para (b)); *Bank of Ireland Home Mortgages Ltd v Bell* [2001] 2 FLR 809, [27] (para (a)).

[107] It will be otherwise on bankruptcy or on an application by a secured creditor, but these situations are not presently under discussion.

[108] *Chan v Leung* [2003] 1 FLR 23 (p 123, n 28 above) is one exceptional case, based on purposes in the occupation context. See also *Oke v Rideout* [1998] CLY 4876 (County Court), though the case against sale there was much stronger because it had been agreed that the entire beneficial interest should be held by the occupier.

home for one of the co-owners. This was the case in *Abbey National plc v Moss*.[109] Following her husband's death, the defendant transferred their house into the names of herself and her daughter. The daughter was already living there with her family, but some time later the relationship between mother and daughter broke down and the mother was evicted. The Court of Appeal held that the purpose was to provide a home for the mother alone, rather than mother and daughter.[110] It followed that, although occupation by both was no longer feasible, the purpose of occupation by the mother was continuing and that sale should be refused. This result seems especially appropriate where, as in *Moss*, the mother originally owned the home. However, it may also apply where the property has been jointly purchased. In *Charlton v Lester*[111] the mother was a protected tenant of a house. Her daughter and son-in-law encouraged her to purchase the freehold, to which they contributed, and all three lived in the house. When the daughter and son-in-law purchased a separate house for themselves they wanted the mother's house sold. Oliver J rejected their claim: the purchase had been on the understanding that the mother would be able to keep her existing home. There are many cases in which a house is jointly purchased for occupation by relations (whether parents, children, or others). If the appropriate purpose can be proved, it seems appropriate to refuse sale even where the occupier is not the original owner or occupier. Whilst it is true that the person claiming sale will otherwise receive no immediate benefit from the land, this may be precisely the basis upon which the land was purchased. In any event, there is flexibility: purposes are never conclusive. If the circumstances of the claimant have unforeseeably changed, this may provide a strong reason why the purpose should not prevail, even though it continues.

A different sort of case is where there are multiple purposes. In these circumstances the termination of one of the purposes may not mean that the land should be sold. Perhaps the best example is provided by *Bedson v Bedson*.[112] In this case, a husband and wife owned property consisting of a drapery business and family accommodation. When the marriage broke up the Court of Appeal refused to order sale: the purpose of enabling the husband to conduct the drapery business was still extant. Any unfairness to the wife was countered by ordering rent to be paid.[113] It will readily be appreciated that many cases will involve multiple purposes, though perhaps less distinct purposes than in *Bedson*. It is probably

---

[109] (1993) 26 HLR 249. The case involved a chargee who was held bound by the purpose, but *a fortiori* sale would have been refused if there had been an application by the co-owner chargor.

[110] It was found that the purpose of the transfer was to facilitate succession on the mother's eventual death. The conclusion was buttressed by the stipulation that the mother should consent before any sale.

[111] [1976] 1 EGLR 131; also see *Harris v Harris* (1995) 72 P&CR 408 (father and son). Without special facts, sale is usual when family arrangements break down: *Rivett v Rivett* (1966) 200 EG 858; *Smith v Smith* (1975) 120 SJ 100.

[112] [1965] 2 QB 666. That the husband's money had been used for the purchase was material. The court was also sympathetic to the husband who had been deserted by the wife: a contrast to the approach in *Rawlings v Rawlings* [1964] P 398.

[113] Today, TLATA s 13(6) may provide authority for this: p 131 above.

incorrect to assert that sale will be refused if any purpose still subsists: some
purposes may be secondary and given little weight. However, deciding whether
one of them is dominant will frequently be very difficult. Perhaps the true
explanation of *Moss* and (more clearly) *Charlton* is that providing a home for the
daughter was intended in each case, but was distinctly secondary to the purpose of
providing a home for the mother. Today the idea of dominant purpose is not such
a crucial factor. Purposes form one of the factors for the court to take into account
under section 15: the outcome does not simply follow from whether there is or is
not a surviving purpose.[114] One specific example of multiple purposes is the provision of a home for children. Although it was generally agreed that the position of
children could be taken into account, there were differences of opinion as to
whether there was a purpose of providing a home for them.[115] This seems unlikely
to be a material issue now that section 15(1)(c) specifically mentions the welfare of
minors as a factor to be taken into account. There is no suggestion that this is
more or less important than purposes: all will depend upon the circumstances. As
already observed, it will rarely be relevant to ask whether there is a purpose for
their occupation.[116]

One question remains curiously unanswered. Where a couple purchase a house
as a family home, does that purpose survive the death of one of them? In most
cases the survivor will inherit the entire property (whether by survivorship or
under a will or intestacy) and no problem will arise. However, the deceased's share
in a tenancy in common may pass to a third party who seeks sale. *Jones v
Challenger*[117] supports the idea that the purpose has come to an end. Neuberger J
in *Mortgage Corpn v Shaire* takes the same approach,[118] noting that there was no
evidence as to intention on death. However, the Court of Appeal in *Stott v
Ratcliffe*[119] permitted the survivor to continue to occupy when there was evidence
supporting this. In many respects this seems the most realistic and the preferable
outcome. Especially where a retirement home is purchased, it seems implausible
that the parties intend the survivor to have to leave the home when one of them
dies.[120] Even where a younger couple, who are unlikely to have contemplated
death, are involved, it is far from clear that sale on the death of one of them

---

[114] However, purposes appear to play a stronger role as regards occupation rights (see p 123 above).
This means that the older cases on sale may still be influential in that setting.
[115] *Rawlings v Rawlings* [1964] P 398 (Salmon LJ, 419) and *Re Evers' Trust* [1980] 1 WLR 1327
support such a purpose; *Burke v Burke* [1974] 1 WLR 1063 denies it.          [116] See p 160 above.
[117] [1961] 1 QB 176, 183 (Devlin LJ).
[118] [2001] Ch 743, 762. This fits well with the idea that the purpose ends if one of them parts with
his or her interest (see p 174 below) although the merits of that idea are far from clear.
[119] (1982) 126 SJ 310; see also *Harris v Harris* (1995) 72 P&CR 408 (father and son; the collateral purpose was intended to cover occupation by either and so was not affected when the father
moved elsewhere a year before his death) and *Arkwright v IRC* [2004] WTLR 181 (Special
Commissioners), in which it was assumed that the home could not be sold (reversed [2004] STC
1323 on the ground that valuation issues should be determined by the Lands Tribunal).
[120] The force of this argument may be weakened by their choice not to have a joint tenancy or will
passing the interest to the survivor, but this is likely to be the result of accident rather than design.

represents their intentions.[121] Of course, it may be argued that house is too large for occupation by the survivor,[122] but that factor may be relied upon in any event.

One more general point on purposes concerns timing. It is clear from *Rodway v Landy*[123] that paragraph (b) deals with current purposes: 'the relevant purposes are those subsisting at the time the court is determining the application'. As well as meaning that the court will not consider purposes that have terminated, it accepts that any new (or, more likely, varied) purpose will be taken into account. Plainly, purposes may change over time. Thus if the co-owners agree a use for the land after their relationship (whether personal or business) has broken down, then that use will fall within (b). However, all the co-owners need to agree (or concur in) the new purposes.[124] Are similar rules applied to paragraph (a) and the intention of the settlor? Arden LJ has held that this purpose must exist at the time the trust is set up.[125]

Do the earlier cases reveal much beyond the purpose analysis? Although the general test of 'whose voice should be allowed to prevail' was frequently quoted and it was recognized that the court retained a discretion, in practice sale was generally refused if purposes continued and ordered if the purposes had ended. Unsurprisingly, the courts expressed willingness to take exceptional circumstances, such as illness, into account.[126] Beyond that, there is little to provide guidance.

In a case such as *Bedson*, where just one co-owner is left in occupation, how strong is the argument that the party claiming sale is left with their investment locked into the land, often with no income? In *Bedson* itself the payment of rent went some way to countering this point, but it will not always be viable for rent to be paid. Apart from this, the courts have shown little sympathy for the claimant. In *Browne v Pritchard*[127] Ormrod LJ observed that an interest in the home 'is the least liquid investment that one can possibly make'. That is true, but is it a good reason why one party should be able to obtain the entire benefit of the premises? It seems odd if one of the parties enjoys the luxury of the former family home, whilst the other, deprived of capital resources, has to accept inferior accommodation.[128] *Browne* involved the matrimonial, rather than trusts, jurisdiction. However, a similar approach was taken in *Re Evers' Trust*,[129] in which sale was refused under the trusts jurisdiction where the land was the home of an unmarried couple's children. The refusal to sell can of course be justified where there are children living in the house. Most people would agree that the desire to recover a share in

---

[121] Supported by Barnsley [1998] CLJ 123, 133 in the occupation context.

[122] As was argued in *Shaire*.　　　[123] [2001] Ch 703, [26].

[124] *White v White* [2004] 2 FLR 321, [24]. Section 15(1)(b) refers to the purposes for the property is held, not the purposes for which it is being used.

[125] *White v White* [2004] 2 FLR 321, [23].

[126] *Burke v Burke* [1964] 1 WLR 1063, 1067 (extended to illness of a relative living with the occupying co-owner).　　　[127] [1975] 1 WLR 1366, 1371.

[128] This appears to have been the position in *Browne*. See Gray [1982] CLJ 228.

[129] [1980] 1 WLR 1327, 1334 (2 of 3 children were from the mother's previous marriage).

the value of the house is outweighed by the need to avoid disruption in the housing arrangements for children, especially when sale will result in unsatisfactory accommodation for them.

One solution to this type of case is for the occupying party to buy out the claimant. This ensures that the land remains available for use by the occupier, whilst unlocking the investment of the other. It may be preferable to the alternative of paying rent to the claimant, both because it unlocks the capital and because it produces a more satisfactory clean break. Yet in many cases it is financially unrealistic. It will be unusual for the occupier to have the necessary savings and it may not be feasible to increase the mortgage, especially if the occupier is looking after young children. Where buying out is practicable, the courts encourage the parties to negotiate it. In appropriate cases the court may put pressure on the occupier by indicating that sale will be ordered unless agreement is reached.[130] The party seeking sale will normally be perfectly happy to be bought out by the occupier. The court would almost certainly refuse a sale if a reasonable offer by the occupier were refused: refusal would be little short of malicious and no court would countenance such conduct when exercising a statutory discretion.

So far, the major stress has been on the earlier cases. We must now return to the question of their significance post-TLATA. As will be seen below in the context of charges, Neuberger J has concluded: 'I think it would be wrong to throw over all the earlier cases without paying them any regard. However, they have to be treated with caution, in light of the change in the law, and in many cases they are unlikely to be of great, let alone decisive, assistance.'[131] This has to be accorded the greatest respect, particularly as it followed an extensive review of the changes introduced by TLATA. Although the conclusion will be argued to be fully justified in the context of chargees' applications for sale (where there have been significant statutory developments)[132] does it follow that the earlier cases cease to be of great assistance in disputes between co-owners?

If we consider the terms of section 15, the relevant provisions are (b) (purposes) and (c) (welfare of minors). Paragraph (a) relates to the settlor's intentions and is unlikely to be significant in the typical case of the purchase of a family home. Paragraph (d) relates to charges and is not relevant to the present discussion. It has already been seen that paragraph (c) may give greater prominence to the interests of children[133] than the earlier cases, though their interests were already considered by the courts. Just how much prominence will be accorded to them is unclear from the cases. In a case involving an application by a chargee, it was said: 'it is difficult to attach much if any weight to their position in the absence of any evidence as to how their welfare may be adversely affected if an order for sale is

---

[130] *Bernard v Josephs* [1982] Ch 391.  [131] *Mortgage Corpn v Shaire* [2001] Ch 743, 761.

[132] See p 176 below.

[133] They need not be children of the co-owners: *First National Bank plc v Achampong* [2004] 1 FCR 18; [2003] EWCA Civ 487 (grandchildren).

now made'.[134] This indicates that the courts will require evidence of specific harm to their welfare before paragraph (c) will be engaged. On the other hand, this was in the context of an application by a creditor: it may be expected that the interests of minors will be more significant where sale is sought by one of their parents. Perhaps surprisingly, sale was ordered in *White v White*[135] when the parent caring for two children would have to downsize and the children might have to share a bedroom. On the other hand, Park J was more willing in *Edwards v Lloyds TSB Bank plc*[136] to take children's interests into account, although this was in circumstances in which postponing sale would cause little hardship. It seems that the interests of children can be relevant, though when other factors point towards a sale it will require a very strong case for the court to be persuaded that sale should be refused or significantly postponed. Two other aspects of section 15 should be noted. The first, already discussed,[137] is that the circumstances and wishes of the beneficiaries must be considered. The second aspect is that it must always be remembered that the factors listed in section 15 are not exclusive: the court can take into account any appropriate factors. These might well include the welfare of an adult disabled person (not a co-owner) living with the occupying co-owner.[138]

Leaving aside the welfare of minors, does any of this impact on the general conclusions from the cases that sale will be refused if there is a continuing purpose, but ordered if the purpose has ended? Taking the former first, there appears to be little reason why purposes should be significantly less important.[139] Given that they constitute just one factor today, it is possible that they may be somewhat less powerful. This might be relevant where there are multiple purposes (exemplified by *Bedson*) and would allow other factors, such as the needs of the party seeking sale, to be more prominent. However, any changes as a result of TLATA are likely to be marginal. More problematic is the leaning towards sale where purposes have ended. In the past, the courts reasoned that the trust for sale re-asserted itself in these circumstances, so that the land should be sold. Now that trusts for sale are no longer the normal form of trust of land, this reasoning falls to the ground.[140] However, too much should not be read into this. If land is purchased for a purpose and that purpose fails, then (absent special factors) sale seems the appropriate outcome: the project has been frustrated. Accordingly, the result reached by the cases is appropriate even though the reasoning today would be significantly different: we obviously cannot say today that the law leans towards

---

[134] *First National Bank plc v Achampong* [2004] 1 FCR 18; [2003] EWCA Civ 487, [65] (Blackburne J in the Court of Appeal).                                                  [135] [2004] 2 FLR 321, [14]-[15].

[136] [2004] EWHC 1745 (Ch).              [137] See p 158 above.

[138] Apparently accepted in *First National Bank plc v Achampong* [2004] 1 FCR 18, [2003] EWCA Civ 487, [65]; see also *Mortgage Corpn v Shaire* [2001] Ch 743, 761; and *Edwards v Lloyds TSB Bank plc* [2004] EWHC 1745 (Ch), [33] (adult children in full-time education).

[139] It is very different for applications by secured creditors, but the courts have never allowed purposes to play a significant role in that context.

[140] This was one factor influencing the views of Neuberger J in *Shaire* regarding the relevance of the earlier cases. The other factors in that case were more specific to applications for sale by chargees.

sale. Though other factors may be taken into account, avoidance of sale is likely to require exceptional circumstances, at least where no minors are involved.

Finally, what about trusts where the trustees and beneficiaries are different persons, so that the trustees can be seen as reaching an independent and disinterested conclusion? This structure is most likely where there are successive interests, though it can also apply to concurrent interests created by a settlement. It is in this type of trust that we have seen that the courts would not normally interfere with decisions by trustees.[141] There is no doubt that TLATA, sections 14 and 15 apply to all forms of trusts. It is less clear when the courts will choose to exercise the jurisdiction. The absence of authority means that it is difficult to do more than speculate as to the most likely outcome. It seems most consistent with present practice and the legislation if courts decline to intervene when trustees have considered the relevant factors. The fact that a judge might come to a different conclusion should not by itself be sufficient to justify intervention. However, any one of four factors might point to a contrary outcome. The first, fairly obviously, is where the trustees have not considered the relevant factors (principally those listed in section 15). Indeed, where a judge feels that a plainly incorrect decision has been reached, it may not be too difficult to conclude that the relevant criteria have been overlooked.[142] The second factor concerns giving effect to the views of beneficiaries, as is required by section 11. This requirement is applicable to all types of trustees. Although trustees may be able to justify reaching a conclusion differing from the views of the majority of the beneficiaries, they cannot simply ignore those views.[143] The third and fourth factors are similar: bankruptcy and secured creditors. We will see in the following section that special rules apply on bankruptcy: these rules apply whether or not the trustees are independent. Later, it will be seen that secured creditors are usually able to obtain sale, applying section 15(1)(d). This willingness to order sale is likely to be the same whether or not the trustees are independent. Although the court may allow the trustees to resolve most issues which affect the beneficiaries (the settlor has chosen them to undertake that role) it does not follow that they should be held the scales as between beneficiaries and creditors. It requires little imagination to realize that they are likely to be on the side of the beneficiaries.

### (ii) Disputes Involving a Trustee in Bankruptcy

When one of two beneficial co-owners[144] becomes bankrupt, can the trustee in bankruptcy force sale? This is, of course, likely to be the only way in which the value of the bankrupt's interest in the land can be realized so as to assist in paying

---

[141] See p 145 above.

[142] For a recent discussion of similar principles applicable to the exercise of powers of appointment, see *Abacus Trust Co (Isle of Man) v Barr* [2003] Ch 409; Conaglen [2004] CLJ 283.

[143] See p 150 above.

[144] Similar problems can arise when holders of other beneficial interests become bankrupt, but examples are rare.

the debts owed. To avoid any doubt, it should be stressed that the other co-owner will receive their share of the amount realized if there is a sale. Despite this, few such co-owners will welcome sale: the family home is lost and their share in the proceeds may well be inadequate to fund the purchase of alternative accommodation, at least of the standard of the old home. This applies whether or not the relationship between the co-owners has broken down. It should be noted that the matrimonial jurisdiction cannot be exercised against trustees in bankruptcy. On the other hand, an order made prior to bankruptcy does bind the trustee in bankruptcy.[145]

TLATA, section 15(4) makes it clear that the normal criteria for the exercise of the court's discretion do not apply on bankruptcy. Their place is taken by section 335A of the Insolvency Act 1986.[146] The application for sale is still made under TLATA, section 14, but the application is to the bankruptcy court and the criteria it is to consider are very different. Though the court is given power to make such order as is just and reasonable, an important distinction is drawn according to the time since bankruptcy. For the first year, the court has to consider the interests of the creditors and all the circumstances of the case; for homes, also relevant are the conduct (relative to bankruptcy), needs and financial resources of the spouse (or former spouse), and the needs of any children.[147] It should be noted that the bankrupt's interests are not relevant, though the bankrupt may benefit incidentally if the interests of spouse or children justify refusal of sale. Rather more surprisingly, the interests of cohabitants are not relevant, though they too may benefit if there are children. Sale in that first year will be unlikely in many cases where there is a spouse or child. In any event, most cases have involved applications well after a year. After that year, things change dramatically. The interests of the creditors are to prevail 'unless the circumstances of the case are exceptional'.[148]

The really important question is what counts as exceptional. It is relevant that the test is identical to that developed by the courts prior to the statutory test.[149] This was recognized by the Court of Appeal in the leading case of *Re Citro*.[150] Accordingly, we can look to pre-1986 cases to guide us. The general picture is not encouraging for families of bankrupts. Sale will not be refused merely because of the hardship which

[145] *Mountney v Treharne* [2003] Ch 135.
[146] Inserted by TLATA, though the law had been very similar since 1986. Section 335A applies in cases of co-ownership; ss 336 and 337 apply similar principles to spouses with statutory rights of occupation and minors in occupation.
[147] Without any apparent age limit, though doubtless the significance of adult children or those not living in the home will be minimal.
[148] Richman argues that this could be affected by the Human Rights Act 1998: (2000) 150 NLJ 1102: see p 172 below.
[149] Based on *Re Lowrie* [1983] 3 All ER 353. Earlier cases had shown preference for the trustee in bankruptcy, though without articulating a test of exceptional circumstances. See esp *Re Turner* [1974] 1 WLR 1556; *Re Densham* [1975] 1 WLR 1519; *Re Bailey* [1977] 1 WLR 278.
[150] [1991] Ch 142, 159, 160 (applying the law prior to the Insolvency Act 1986). See Cretney (1991) 107 LQR 177; Brown (1992) 55 MLR 284.

will be found in typical cases of bankruptcy. In *Re Citro* Nourse LJ made it clear that simply having to sell the family home, requiring new schooling arrangements for children, would not suffice: 'the personal circumstances of the two wives and their children, although distressing, are not by themselves exceptional'.[151]

At the time of *Re Citro*, *Re Holliday*[152] was the only fully reported case[153] in which sale had been postponed. There were three children, the youngest aged twelve, and sale was postponed for five years. This was justified in *Re Citro* on the basis that the bankrupt husband had lodged the bankruptcy petition. Not only were the creditors not seeking bankruptcy, but their debts were covered by the bankrupt's assets. True, they would have to wait until the house was sold in order to get their money, but it was entirely safe. This is quite different from the other cases, in which the family can be seen as continuing to occupy the home at the expense of the creditors. The Court of Appeal in *Re Holliday* thought it relevant that the wife would have had difficulty in finding accommodation in the area with her share of the proceeds of sale. However, such factors failed to impress the majority of the Court of Appeal in *Re Citro*. As Nourse LJ put it, the circumstances involved 'the melancholy consequences of debt and improvidence with which every civilised society has been familiar'.[154]

It will be a very unusual case where a co-owner has sought bankruptcy and the debts are likely to be paid. What other circumstances will count as exceptional? Some guidance has been given in dicta in the earlier cases. Sale may be postponed if the period falls within a particularly sensitive part of a child's education leading up to examinations.[155] In *Barca v Mears*[156] special educational needs of a child were considered. However, they were not persuasive given that the needs were not severe and were not shown to be likely to be significantly affected by sale. Another example may be if the home has been specially adapted for a handicapped child.[157] Several more recent cases have shown that severe ill-health of the bankrupt's spouse may justify postponement, especially if the house has been specially adapted. Indefinite postponement was ordered where there was renal failure and chronic osteoarthritis restricting mobility[158] and where chemotherapy treatment required the avoidance of stress (though the outcome was expected to be known within six months).[159] Shorter postponement, for one year, was allowed where there was paranoid schizophrenia which could be seriously affected by a move to smaller accommodation away from the family.[160] One reason for not allowing a

---

[151] Ibid, 159.    [152] [1981] Ch 405.

[153] Cf *Re Mott* [1987] CLY 212: sale refused where the house was the home of an elderly parent in poor health.    [154] *Re Citro* [1991] Ch 142, 157; see also *Re Lowrie* [1981] 3 All ER 353.

[155] *Re Lowrie* [1981] 3 All ER 353, 356. This was before the introduction of special rules for the first year; it may be less important apply today.    [156] [2004] EWHC 2170 (Ch).

[157] *Re Bailey* [1977] 1 WLR 278. Presumably the same would apply to handicapped spouses or partners.    [158] *Claughton v Charalamabous* [1999] 1 FLR 740; a chairlift had been installed.

[159] *Judd v Brown* [1998] 2 FLR 360 (not considered on appeal: [1999] 1 FLR 1191).

[160] *Re Raval* [1998] 2 FLR 718 (it was already 8 years since bankruptcy, so the statutory 1-year period had already been substantially exceeded).

more lengthy postponement was that the creditors could not be sure of being paid. These cases involve severe ill-health. It is unlikely that distress and nervous illness will lead to sale being postponed unless there is a temporary reason for delay.[161] Although the needs of the bankrupt are not relevant[162] they may still impact on the exceptional circumstances test. When an elderly spouse (aged seventy-four) was caring for a terminally ill bankrupt (aged seventy-nine) with a life expectancy of six months, it was held that the spouse had needs in these exceptional circumstances which justified postponing sale for three months after the bankrupt's death.[163]

A recent development is that the residence of the bankrupt (or spouse) goes back to the bankrupt, free from the claims of creditors, after three years.[164] Although the limit does not apply where an application for sale is brought within the three years, the underlying policy is to limit the period during which bankruptcy operates. As was said in *Re Byford*, 'All parties concerned would know where they stand within a reasonable time. . . . the court should take into account that policy in deciding what is equitable.'[165] Although this development generally benefits bankrupts and their families, it might militate against lengthy postponements of sale.[166]

Despite some sympathetic responses in really exceptional cases, it is plain that the interests of creditors are seen as outweighing those of co-owners in the vast majority of cases. Why should this be? One initial point is that the present legislation is based on recommendations made by the Cork Committee on Insolvency Law and Practice,[167] though the Committee had recommended greater court discretion.[168] Although the courts have consistently shown (both before and after the Insolvency Act 1986) an inclination to order sale, some judges have been more ready to postpone sale. We have seen this in *Re Holliday*, but *Re Citro* also contains pointers in that direction. Of the four judges involved, both Hoffmann J at first instance and Sir George Waller (dissenting in the Court of Appeal) wished to postpone sale. Within the majority, Bingham LJ regretted that the authorities compelled an order for sale. He commended the approach of Hoffmann J: 'It is in my view conducive to justice in the broadest sense and it reflects the preference which the law increasingly gives to personal over property interests'.[169] Of course, now that the test has been laid down by statute, the only question for the courts is as to what counts as exceptional circumstances.

None of this answers the question why the trustee in bankruptcy should be able to enforce sale, at least where the bankrupt co-owner would have been

---

[161] *Re Densham* [1975] 1 WLR 1519; *Barclays Bank plc v Hendricks* [1996] 1 FLR 258 (applying the bankruptcy test where there was a charging order).

[162] Even, it seems, in establishing the test of exceptional circumstances: *Re Bremner* [1999] 1 FLR 912, 914.                                                                                          [163] *Re Bremner* [1999] 1 FLR 912.

[164] Insolvency Act 1986, s 283A, inserted by Enterprise Act 2002, s 261.

[165] [2004] 1 P&CR 159, [15] (s 283A was not in force at the relevant time).

[166] The court can extend the 3-year period: s 283A(6).                          [167] (1982) Cmnd 8558.

[168] See esp para 1123; Cretney (1991) 107 LQR 177. Cf Hoffmann J at first instance in *Re Citro*.

[169] At 161.

refused sale. As will shortly be seen, a successor in title to a co-owner cannot defeat a purpose of occupation by another co-owner,[170] so why should the trustee in bankruptcy be in a better position? It may be understandable if a co-owner has enjoyed a profligate lifestyle at the expense of the creditors,[171] but the co-owner may have obtained no benefit at all from debts leading to bankruptcy.[172] On occasion, mortgagees who are subject a beneficial interest of a spouse or partner are still able to enforce sale[173] by invoking the bankruptcy rules.[174] Whilst this is undoubtedly correct on the basis of the present law, it is less clear that it represents sound policy.

On the other hand, it must be remembered that we are not confiscating the co-owner's interest: if the land is sold then half of the net proceeds will go to a co-owner with a 50 per cent share. Unless there is sale, the co-owner is in substance enjoying the benefit of property part owned by creditors. Indeed, those creditors (who may be involuntary creditors) stand to lose the money owed to them if the property cannot be sold. Where significant sums are lent it will be unusual for the co-owner not to be made a party to a charge. Experience shows that co-owners are usually willing to be party to such charges, in which case they are liable to lose their homes.[175] Though this makes the situation technically quite different, it is not obvious that co-owners deserve significantly greater protection as regards other creditors: it is largely fortuitous whether co-owners have been asked to join in a charge. More generally, it may be argued that the co-owners commonly benefit from loans which give rise to bankruptcy,[176] so it is only fair that they share in the pain if things go wrong. Of course, this benefit does not exist in every case. A further point is that TLATA, section 15(1)(d) stresses the interests of secured creditors. As will be seen [177] the courts have interpreted this so as to enable sale to take place where the creditor cannot otherwise be protected. Against this background, it might seem inconsistent not to allow sale where there is bankruptcy, especially as regards involuntary creditors. On the other hand, it can of course be argued that the policies adopted for applications by both trustees in bankruptcy and secured creditors in section 15(1)(d) are misguided.

A further question is whether the interests of children should be more compelling. It is plain that loss of the family home and interruption of children's schooling will not be enough to count as exceptional circumstances.[178] Yet mortgagees can

---

[170] *Abbey National plc v Moss* (1993) 26 HLR 249.    [171] *Re Densham* [1975] 1 WLR 1519.

[172] One example is bankruptcy arising from debts which have been used for gambling.

[173] Because of the priority of the interest of the spouse or partner, the mortgagee is otherwise unable to take possession in order to sell. The situation is usually the result of failure to enquire as to interests of occupiers (*Williams & Glyn's Bank Ltd v Boland* [1981] AC 487) or failure to ensure the absence of undue influence (*Royal Bank of Scotland plc v Etridge (No 2)* [2002] 2 AC 773).

[174] *Alliance and Leicester plc v Slayford* (2000) 33 HLR 743.

[175] Subject to the protection afforded by *Royal Bank of Scotland plc v Etridge (No 2)* [2002] 2 AC 773.

[176] Either because it is used to support a higher standard of living for the family or because it benefits the bankrupt's business, itself a source of wealth for the family.    [177] Pages 176–9 below.

[178] The contrast with TLATA, s 15 is noted in *Pickering v Wells* [2002] 2 FLR 798.

take possession without reference to the interests of children, whether or not there are exceptional circumstances. If we are serious about protecting the interests of children, then providing protection only on bankruptcy seems odd. In any event, sale will not take place immediately and there will be no question of sudden eviction in the midst of GCSE or A-level examinations. Those who wish to be hard-hearted may observe that children frequently have to change school when their parents move houses and doubt whether the families of bankrupts have any better right to continue to live in pleasant houses in attractive neighbourhoods than the less fortunate members of society.

The arguments are finely balanced. In part, the problem lies in failure to think through the issues throughout property law. Do we wish to protect spouses/ partners and children against creditors, whether secured or not? Is it relevant that the spouse/partner is a co-owner? To a large extent, the pressure towards protecting the family home is the same whatever the pattern of ownership. A tentative conclusion might be that it is appropriate to order sale in many cases, but that a more open discretion to postpone sale is justified.

It is possible that *Barca v Mears*[179] heralds a movement towards a greater discretion. For the first time, it was argued that the rules as established by *Re Citro* were inconsistent with the European Convention on Human Rights and, in particular, the Article 8 right to respect for family life and home. Strauss QC (sitting in the Chancery Division) considered it to be 'questionable whether the narrow approach as to what may be "exceptional circumstances" adopted in *Re Citro*, is consistent with the Convention'. He was particularly concerned about cases in which the adverse results of bankruptcy are of a 'usual' nature, but still very severe. He thought that it might be necessary to interpret the Insolvency Act 1986 so that such circumstances did (contrary to *Re Citro*) provide a basis for refusing (or delaying) sale. However, the facts came nowhere close to justifying such an outcome and accordingly no final view was expressed. It remains to be seen whether higher courts will adopt this less strict approach. It must be remembered that the Convention rights are not absolute and have to be balanced against other claims. The real question (as Strauss QC recognized) is whether the law as established in the legislation and *Re Citro* provides a proportionate response to the rival claims of creditors and family.

Some jurisdictions have long had legislation protecting the family home, generally limited to married couples. For example, in New Zealand the Joint Family Homes Act 1964 provides protection on bankruptcy for registered homes up to a specified amount.[180] Any such provision raises obvious questions as to how it

---

[179] [2004] EWHC 2170 (Ch), adopting a suggestion in Rook, *Property Law and Human Rights*, pp 203–5.

[180] Currently NZ$82,000 (approximately £30,000). At least in the UK, this is a relatively small sum in comparison with the average value of houses. As the non-bankrupt spouse would get their share in any event, the real benefit is about £15,000 (assuming equal shares). Nevertheless, where the net value of the share is less than this, being able to keep the home is a valuable benefit.

might reduce the flow of money and credit and thereby inhibit commerce and reduce overall wealth. Whilst these are powerful factors,[181] it may be doubted whether they are of great relevance in the bankruptcy setting. Any creditor who is concerned about payment will seek security: the principal consideration in such cases will be the ability to enforce that security, not the position on bankruptcy. It may be true that awareness of approaches hostile to creditors might inhibit the giving of credit, but it is fanciful to consider that this poses such a significant risk as to deter reform. The Enterprise Act 2002 introduces similar protection[182] in England and Wales for the first time, though it is not limited to the family context and not at all generous. If the value of the bankrupt's interest in his or her residence (or the residence of a spouse) is below £1,000[183] then sale is to be refused. This ensures that sale will follow only if there is a significant benefit to be received by creditors. It is interesting that, unlike section 335A, the emphasis is as much on protecting the bankrupt as on protecting family members.

## (iii) Disputes Involving Successors in Title and Creditors

What happens if one of the co-owners sells or charges his or her interest? Alternatively, what happens if one of the co-owners dies and his or her interest passes to personal representatives? Can the new holders of the beneficial interest seek sale? To get one point out of the way, sale cannot simply be refused on the basis that the transferee is bound by the interest, whether as an overriding[184] or registered[185] interest. The transferee can scarcely be in a worse position than the transferor, who could always apply under section 14. The real question is whether transferees, in the application of the section 15 criteria, are in any different position from the original co-owners.

Most of these issues are not specifically addressed by TLATA. The one exception, fully discussed below, is that section 15(1)(d) requires the court to consider the interests of secured creditors. In fact, nearly all the cases in the area involve secured creditors. It should be stressed that we are dealing with security over a beneficial interest: security over the land binding all beneficiaries (upon which chargees normally insist) can be enforced without recourse to TLATA. The history of the area is intertwined with that of bankruptcy and it is for that reason that bankruptcy has been analysed first. Prior to the Insolvency Act 1986 sale on bankruptcy was based on principles which could be applied to other successors in title; the courts showed a willingness to apply the same principles regardless of whether a trustee in bankruptcy or secured creditor was involved. Before the

---

[181] Recognized by Lord Nicholls in *Etridge*, n 173 above, [34]: 'Their home is their property. The law should not restrict them in the use they may make of it. Bank finance is in fact by far the most important source of external capital for small businesses with fewer than ten employees. These businesses comprise about 95% of all businesses in the country, responsible for nearly one-third of all employment. Finance raised by second mortgages on the principal's home is a significant source of capital for the start-up of small businesses.' [182] Insolvency Act 1986, s 313A.
[183] SI 2004 No 547. [184] *Bank of Baroda v Dhillon* [1998] 1 FLR 524.
[185] *First National Bank plc v Achampong* [2004] 1 FCR 18; [2003] EWCA Civ 487, [60].

adoption of the exceptional circumstances test in *Re Lowrie* and *Re Citro*, this was quite innocuous: the court was simply balancing competing claims under the discretion afforded by LPA, section 30. Now that we have a specific test for bankruptcy, as stipulated by the 1986 Act, the approach of equating bankruptcy and secured creditors has become difficult to maintain. It will be seen that recent cases have rejected that approach, though without significantly weakening the protection of creditors.

First, however, we need to consider the impact of purposes on successors in title. Nothing in section 15 denies the operation of the original purposes where there is a successor in title. This facilitates the continuation of the approach earlier taken in *Abbey National plc v Moss*.[186] There, the purpose of mother and daughter was to provide a home for the mother. When a secured creditor of the daughter sought sale, it was held that the creditor was bound by the purpose: sale was refused. Since TLATA purposes are less determinative of whether or not there should be sale: they constitute one of the matters for the court to consider. Now that the courts are required to consider the interests of secured creditors, it may well be that a different result would follow on the facts of *Moss*. Be that as it may, the important point is that the purpose may survive the transfer or charge of the beneficial interest. It might be added that such transactions are rarely deliberate:[187] there is no scope for any policy to encourage them.

However, the courts have taken a different and more controversial approach where the purpose has been for joint occupation by the co-owners (not the position in *Moss*). The difficulty initially arose because the courts needed to explain how sale could be ordered in favour of a trustee in bankruptcy; this was before the statutory regime in the Insolvency Act 1986. The standard analysis at the time was that a collateral purpose, if continuing, would ordinarily deny sale.[188] In some bankruptcy cases the marriage had broken down, terminating the purpose, but what response could be employed if the marriage was continuing? Nourse LJ observed in *Re Citro* that: 'In none of the decisions [involving a continuing marriage] is there to be found any overt consideration of the argument or any reasoned explanation of its rejection'.[189] In *Re Citro*, as there were two bankrupt brothers and the marriage of one of them was still sound, Nourse LJ thought it necessary to give more consideration to the purpose argument. His analysis was as follows:

As a matter of property law, the basis of their joint occupation is their joint ownership of the beneficial interest in the home. Although the vesting of one of their interests in a trustee for creditors does not in itself destroy the secondary purpose of the trust, the basis for their joint occupation has gone. It must, I think, be implicit in the principle of *Jones v Challenger* that the secondary purpose can only exist while the spouses are not only joint occupiers of the home but joint owners of it as well.[190]

---

[186] (1993) 26 HLR 249; see p 162 above.     [187] See p 61 above.
[188] *Jones v Challenger* [1961] 1 QB 176; p 161 above.     [189] [1991] Ch 142, 158.
[190] Ibid, 158–9.

The intention of this is plainly to ensure that the purpose argument cannot be used where the spouses (or partners) cease to be joint owners. The passage is not entirely easy to interpret. The point appears to be that though, in a general sense, the purpose continues, in *Jones v Challenger* and similar cases the purpose requires the parties to remain joint owners. This may be explained by stressing that the bankrupt party ceases to have a right to occupy: in this sense the basis for *joint* occupation has gone. This interpretation was adopted in *Abbey National plc v Moss*.[191] *Moss* was decided in favour of the mother on the basis that the purpose was for her occupation (rather than joint occupation).

This reasoning appears very artificial. However, despite its origin in bankruptcy, it naturally applies to any successor in title (including secured creditors). Since the Insolvency Act 1986 it has been unnecessary to rely on it in the bankruptcy setting. This is emphasized by TLATA, section 15(4), which explicitly states that the normal section 15 criteria are inapplicable on bankruptcy. This did not stop cases after *Re Citro* from applying the reasoning to secured creditors, so as to justify sale in cases of joint occupation.[192] It may be observed that whether a purpose has terminated is less significant after TLATA. This is because purposes constitute just one of the factors to be considered by the court.

At the same time, these cases also required 'exceptional circumstances' before a sale would be refused. In other words, secured creditors of a co-owner are treated in exactly the same fashion as the trustee in bankruptcy, both so as to defeat purposes and to ensure virtually automatic sale.[193] Whilst it was doubtless entirely proper to take the position of the creditors fully into account, it was less clear that the adoption of the bankruptcy test was justified. These doubts became much stronger after TLATA.[194] Whatever the position before, the test of exceptional circumstances is simply not found in section 15: it is found only in the bankruptcy setting. On the other hand, it may be argued that the same results should follow, on the basis that the secured creditor will seek bankruptcy if sale is not available.[195] However, there may often be disadvantages in choosing the bankruptcy route:[196] it is unsafe to equate the two areas.

---

[191] Note 170 above, at 257. Hopkins (1995) 111 LQR 72 argues that *Moss* erred in thinking that the purpose had come to an end in *Re Citro*. Whilst it is correct that *Re Citro* denies that the purpose has been destroyed, it remains the case that Nourse LJ stressed the role of joint occupation. Accordingly, the result in *Moss* seems correct even if there is something of a short cut in its reasoning.

[192] *Barclays Bank plc v Hendricks* [1996] 1 FLR 258 (see also Pill LJ refusing leave to appeal: 21 March 1996): charging order. This takes the argument a step further because the purpose included occupation by children (the chargor husband had left the family home).

[193] *Lloyds Bank plc v Byrne & Byrne* [1993] 1 FLR 369 (charging order); *Zandfarid v BCCI SA* [1996] 1 WLR 1420; *Halifax Mortgage Services Ltd v Muirhead* (1997) 76 P&CR 418; *Bank of Baroda v Dhillon* [1998] 1 FLR 524 (the last 3 cases involved charges over a beneficial interest).

[194] Though the older material was initially applied in the County Court in *TSB Bank plc v Marshall* [1998] 2 FLR 769.                    [195] Radley-Gardner [2003] 5 Web JCLI.

[196] In particular, the giving up of the security: *Alliance and Leicester plc v Slayford* (2000) 33 HLR 743, [20], [23], [25]. This is explored by Harper [2001] NILQ 318, 324–5.

It was against this background that Neuberger J reviewed the law in *Mortgage Corpn v Shaire*.[197] The case involved a charge by a co-owner who subsequently died. It purported to be a charge over the legal estate, but it was forged and accordingly bound only his share. Because the debt could not be paid by the deceased's estate, the chargee sought sale. It has already been seen[198] that Neuberger J was in principle prepared to depart from the earlier cases in the light of TLATA. He considered a wide range of arguments supporting his conclusion that the bankruptcy cases no longer determine the outcome of creditors' applications. As well as the arguments summarized above, he made the telling point that the interests of secured creditors are today explicitly made material by section 15(1)(d): to give priority to their interests (as an exceptional circumstances test does) is neither necessary nor consistent with the wording of the section. The learned judge also noted that the law is less likely to favour sale now that there is no longer a trust for sale. However, one may doubt how much difference is made by TLATA in this respect, given that the courts did not previously order sale where it was inappropriate to do so.[199] In any event, he concluded:[200]

All these factors,[201] to my mind, when taken together point very strongly to the conclusion that section 15 has changed the law. As a result of section 15, the court has greater flexibility than heretofore, as to how it exercises its jurisdiction on an application for an order for sale on facts such as those in *In re Citro* and *Lloyds Bank plc v Byrne & Byrne* . . . where one has concluded that the law has changed in a significant respect so that the court's discretion is significantly less fettered than it was, there are obvious dangers in relying on authorities which proceeded on the basis that the court's discretion was more fettered than it now is.

However, this is simply the first stage of the analysis. Though we no longer have a test requiring exceptional circumstances, the interests of secured creditors are material under section 15. How will the courts weigh them against purposes and the interests of children? In *Shaire* there were no infant children and the purpose was not seen as strong in the light of the chargor's death, but Mrs Shaire (the surviving co-owner) held a majority 75 per cent share[202] and clearly she did not wish to sell. In these circumstances, Neuberger J sought to achieve a result whereby Mrs Shaire could keep her home, whilst not prejudicing the creditor. He was acutely conscious that, should sale simply be postponed, the creditor would be left with the quarter share of the deceased co-owner.[203] This result was thought inappropriate: it would condemn the chargee to waiting for an indeterminate

---

[197] [2001] Ch 743. The case is criticized by Pascoe [2000] Conv 315, though she appears to overstate its impact.                                                              [198] See p 165 above.
[199] See p 166 above.        [200] [2001] Ch 743, 760–1.
[201] He also considered (1) dicta of Peter Gibson LJ in *Bankers Trust Co v Namdar* (1997) 14 February; (2) statements in textbooks; (3) comments made in Law Com No 181; and (4) the likelihood that the legislature wished to provide a more open discretion in these cases. None of these factors is particularly convincing, though they do add weight to the others.
[202] See TLATA, s 15(3) for the relevance of beneficiaries' wishes: p 158 above.
[203] The charge was for a sum well in excess of the value of the deceased's quarter share, with the result that the chargee could be treated as entitled to the quarter share.

time until sale, without any return in the meantime. Further, the chargee was in the business of lending money, not investing in shares of houses.

Accordingly, he encouraged a solution whereby the chargee's share would be converted into a loan valued at a quarter of the value of the house. If Mrs Shaire was able and willing to afford this commitment, then sale would be refused. Otherwise, sale would probably be ordered. This neat solution enabled her to keep her home, whilst the chargee got what it was in the business for: a loan relationship. However, several factors make *Shaire* an unusual case. Most obviously, Mrs Shaire had a three-quarters share. This meant that it was viable to consider paying interest on the quarter share held by the chargee. If her share had been smaller then this would have been far less likely.[204] On the other hand, her claim to remain was less strong than that of many occupiers: the chargor co-owner had died and there were no infant children. Further, the house was larger than she needed and sale would release a significant sum[205] which would be available for purchase of a new home.

Subsequent cases indicate that the chargee will nearly always succeed. In *Bank of Ireland Home Mortgages Ltd v Bell*[206] the shares were very different: the occupier had a mere 10 per cent beneficial interest and there were debts of £300,000. The Court of Appeal had no hesitation in ordering a sale. The relevant passage reads:

> The 1996 Act . . . appears to me to have given scope for some change in the court's practice. Nevertheless, a powerful consideration is and ought to be whether the creditor is receiving proper recompense for being kept out of his money, repayment of which is overdue (see *The Mortgage Corporation v Shaire*, a decision of Neuberger J on 25th February 2000). In the present case it is plain that by refusing sale the judge has condemned the bank to go on waiting for its money with no prospect of recovery.[207]

It is clear that the interests of the creditor are seen as being most important: the court was not prepared to sacrifice the financial interests of creditors to the natural wish of co-owners to continue living in their homes. It is highly significant that *Shaire* is cited to bolster the case in favour of the creditor, rather than as a pro-occupier case.

Nevertheless, the case of the occupier in *Bell* was unusually weak. Quite apart from the small size of her share and the obvious impossibility of her paying interest on the chargee's share, the case was exceptional in that her interest had been held subordinate to that of the chargee,[208] so that the chargee (whose claim exceeded the value of the house) was entitled to all the proceeds of sale. Furthermore, the purpose of the purchase had ended on the breakdown of the co-owner's marriage. Although there was a minor child, he was very nearly eighteen and could not sway the conclusion. Finally, although Mrs Bell claimed to be in poor health, at most that could affect the timing of sale.

---

[204] Though it should be added that the chargee, on the basis of subrogation, had a separate £34,000 claim against her. The total indebtedness would be in the range £81,000 to £94,000 (or 43%-40% of the value of the house) depending on the value of the house.

[205] Allowing for the subrogated loan, £109,000–£146,000.

[206] [2001] 2 FLR 809; Probert [2002] Conv 61.     [207] At [31], Peter Gibson LJ.

[208] At [26]; doubts were expressed at [21] as to how this was justified.

The facts in *First National Bank plc v Achampong*[209] were slightly more compelling. There were children in occupation, as well as an adult handicapped person. As has already been seen[210] the court refused to place weight on the interests of the children in the absence of evidence of how sale might affect them adversely. As in *Bell*, the marriage (and the purposes related to it) had come to an end. The Court of Appeal followed *Bell* and ordered sale. It may be noted that the occupying wife had a beneficial half share so that, unlike the wife in *Bell*, she had a substantial interest in the house. This element received no stress in *Achampong*[211] so it would be optimistic to think that future cases may distinguish *Bell* on that ground.

On the other hand, Park J took a more generous approach in *Edwards v Lloyds TSB Bank plc.*[212] The facts were different in that the value of the debtor's share comfortably exceeded the debt. It followed that the creditors would not, at the end of the day, lose money if sale were delayed. They might have to wait for their money, but it would be relatively safe. On the other side, sale would result in the occupying wife's having insufficient resources to purchase another home, as well as prejudice to the interests of minor children. Sale was postponed for five years (until the children ceased to be minors) with the possibility of further postponement. Interestingly, there was no requirement that interest be paid on the debt. This outcome may be seen to mirror rules applied in the law relating to mortgages when mortgagees seek possession.[213]

At least in the typical case where the debts exceed the value of the debtor's share, it is apparent from the cases that the success of the secured creditors is virtually complete. Without any formal requirement of 'exceptional circumstances', the courts are concluding that the interests of the creditors require sale. It remains to be seen whether convincing arguments could be made that children's interests (especially regarding continuity of education) require sale to be refused. It seems likely that the courts would be no more generous than on bankruptcy: a delay for a short period such as a year may be ordered in appropriate cases.[214] Another point is that both *Bell* and *Achampong* stress that the marriage in each case had broken down, bringing to an end purposes connected with it. This ensured that section 15(1)(a) and (b) did not apply. Whilst one can appreciate that this was correct in each case, it seems unlikely that there would be any difference if the relationship with the chargor was still intact. The status of the relationship is

[209] [2004] 1 FCR 18; [2003] EWCA Civ 487; Thompson [2003] Conv 314; Radley-Gardner [2003] 5 Web JCLI. [210] See pp 165–6 above.
[211] Except for an observation that it was not feasible for her to buy out the creditor's share. Presumably, payment of interest on it as a loan (the result in *Shaire*) was equally unrealistic.
[212] [2004] EWHC 1745 (Ch).
[213] *National & Provincial BS v Lloyd* [1996] 1 All ER 630; *Bristol & West BS v Ellis* (1996) 73 P&CR 158.
[214] Thompson [2003] Conv 314, 325 notes the oddity that the bankruptcy protection for one year is not replicated in s 15. In practice, possession applications most frequently reach the courts after a lengthy period of default. In *Pritchard Englefield v Steinberg* [2004] EWHC 1908 (Ch) sale was postponed for 2 months to see if the occupying life interest holder could find somebody willing to purchase subject to her interest.

obviously a vitally significant factor as between the parties to it, but its relevance as regards creditors is far from clear. If the relationship has terminated, then the case for refusing sale is weak even without section 15(1)(d). However, it appears to be of limited relevance that the relationship continues:[215] the most that can be said is that it is more likely that the house is of an appropriate size for the occupants. This argument reflects the position on bankruptcy prior to the Insolvency Act 1986, where it has been seen that the status of the relationship was of marginal significance.[216]

## D. Interplay with Family Law Discretions

So far we have considered the principles generally applied under TLATA, sections 14 and 15. The most common example of concurrent ownership involves, of course, the family home. Yet in this context there are other discretions possessed by the courts and it seems likely that at least some of these discretions usually operate to the exclusion of the TLATA jurisdiction. One initial qualification should be added. The discretions cover disputes between the co-owners. The TLATA jurisdiction will continue to operate where third parties (most obviously secured creditors or a trustee in bankruptcy) are involved, as well as where the co-owners are not subject to the discretions.

The family law discretions may operate both as regards ownership of the property and occupation of it. As regards husband and wife, the court has since the Matrimonial Causes Act 1973[217] possessed a wide discretion to vary property rights on divorce. This valuable matrimonial jurisdiction is frequently used to ensure that the party looking after the children can keep occupation of the home, at least until the children leave home.[218] The rights of the other party may (where appropriate) be recognized by the payment of some form of rent.[219] The exercise of this jurisdiction does not depend upon both parties having property rights and it enables the court to take a realistic view of their needs. The criteria are much wider than those in TLATA, section 15. In particular, they include the resources and needs of the parties. Of particular importance to us is that, prior to TLATA, applications in the Chancery Division under LPA, section 30 were not entertained when the Family Division possessed the matrimonial jurisdiction, as was firmly held by the Court of Appeal in *Williams v Williams*.[220] This ensured

---

[215] Supported by the statement in *Achampong* at [65] that any purpose of use as a family home was not a factor to which 'much if any weight should be attached'.

[216] See p 174 above. The artificiality of the reasoning that the purpose had terminated should not mask the underlying approach that the status of the marriage is immaterial.

[217] Section 24; s 25 lists criteria to be considered by the court. Rights of third parties, esp secured creditors of property-owning spouses, cannot be varied: *Edwards v Lloyds TSB Bank plc* [2004] EWHC 1745 (Ch), [24].

[218] The more recent cases show a greater reluctance to order such a delayed sale and seek a clearer resolution of the property issues: Cretney, Masson, and Bailey-Harris, *Principles of Family Law* (7th edn), paras 14.092–14.098.     [219] *Harvey v Harvey* [1982] Fam 83.

[220] [1976] Ch 278.

that the wider family law criteria were applied by judges familiar with the needs of family members. However, the matrimonial jurisdiction does not apply to unmarried couples, for whom the older collateral purposes principles continued to operate. Has TLATA changed this interplay between the principles? Despite the greater breadth of the section 15 criteria, *Laird v Laird*[221] and *Tee v Tee & Hamilton*[222] are emphatic that cases should still be decided under the matrimonial jurisdiction, though neither case mentions the difference in the legislation.

It is unfortunate that that these two jurisdictions operate without any statutory clarification of the relationship between them. The preference for the family law jurisdiction is justified (especially by virtue of the wider range of factors to be taken into account) but it may be regretted that litigation was required for it to be established. Yet the differences should not be exaggerated. Although the TLATA criteria are narrower, it is likely that the courts will exercise their discretion so as to come to similar results for both married and unmarried couples. This has been exemplified in disputes between unmarried couples. Although the family law discretion is here inapplicable, the courts strived to reach comparable results under section 30 and the same will surely apply under TLATA. In *Re Evers' Trust*[223] the Court of Appeal recognized that section 30 applications involve principles different from those operating under the Matrimonial Causes Act 1973. Nevertheless, the court was plainly striving to develop section 30 so as to reach much the same result in each area. Yet there are limits as to what can be done, not least because section 30 (like TLATA, section 14) operated only if the cohabitants were co-owners and did not allow the adjustment of property rights.

There are other family law discretions which may come into operation. First, the Family Law Act 1996 contains discretions directed specifically at occupation of the family home. These have a wider application than the Matrimonial Causes Act discretion in that they can apply as between cohabitants and between non-divorcing married couples. When considering the relationship with TLATA, the application to cohabitants is likely to prove most interesting.[224] It has already been seen in the occupation context that the Family Law Act jurisdiction may well be operated in preference to TLATA.[225] It may be added that many applications for sale under TLATA, section 14 involve the question whether the respondent should remain in occupation. That question brings the Family Law Act 1996 into play.

Secondly, there are powers in the Children Act 1989 (including powers to adjust property rights, thus going beyond TLATA).[226] In *White v White*[227] it was held that it was wrong for the court to resolve the issues by a simple application

---

[221] [1999] 1 FLR 791.     [222] [1999] 2 FLR 613.
[223] [1980] 1 WLR 1327 (esp 1332–3); Thompson [1984] Conv 103.
[224] Conflicts between spouses will usually be in a context where divorce is likely.
[225] See pp 128–31 above.     [226] Sched 1, para 1(2)(d)(e); for relevant criteria, see para 4.
[227] [2004] 2 FLR 321. Thorpe LJ considered (at [5]) that the Children Act jurisdiction should be given primacy if either should; Arden LJ considered (at [27] that both should be considered together.

under TLATA. As Thorpe LJ observed (in terms equally applicable to the Matrimonial Causes Act and Family Law Act): 'Each regime imports different statutory checklists and the resolution of different considerations. Each invests the court with different powers.'[228]


# 5. Trusts for Sale

In this section, an analysis is made of the modern role of the trust for sale. It will be recalled that, until 1996, there was a trust for sale whenever there were concurrent interests in land. In addition, very many successive interests employed a trust for sale, given that settlements under the Settled Land Act 1925 (the only alternative) were rarely suitable for modern conditions.

When will there be a trust for sale today? Before 1996 a trust for sale was implied whenever there were concurrent interests.[229] These trusts are converted into trusts of land (without a trust for sale) by TLATA[230] and therefore lie outside the scope of this section. Both before and after 1996 it is possible to create a trust for sale expressly. Before 1996 these express trusts were very common; they remain trusts for sale.

It follows that there will be numerous trusts for sale dating from before TLATA, as well as those created more recently. They all constitute trusts of land[231] and are therefore subject to the principles discussed in this Chapter. There are two special statutory provisions which are specific to trusts for sale. The first is that TLATA, section 4(1) implies a power to postpone in all such trusts, a power which cannot be excluded.[232] Secondly, we will see shortly that the doctrine of conversion is abolished. However, the first question is whether the operation of TLATA is affected by the existence of a trust for sale.

If a settlor today creates a trust for sale, this is likely to signify that sale really is intended, albeit not necessarily an immediate sale. This may have several consequences. First, it has been seen[233] that powers are discretionary, whereas trusts are mandatory. This (coupled with the principle that powers must be exercised unanimously) means that the land should be sold if the trustees for sale disagree on the question of sale. Conversely, there will be no sale if there is a similar disagreement in any other trust of land. Obviously these consequences may be overturned by an application to court. However, even then sale may be more likely if there is a trust for sale. Quite apart from any reluctance to interfere with the decision of the trustees (if they are not also beneficiaries) the court is likely to stress the settlor's intention that the land should be sold.[234] So far we have considered

---

[228] At [15].
[229] Where there were successive interests, trusts for sale were not implied: a Settled Land Act settlement arose unless there was a trust for sale (Settled Land Act 1925, s 1(7)).
[230] Sched 2, paras 3(6), 4(4).     [231] Section 1(2)(a).     [232] Discussed above, p 152.
[233] See p 155 above.     [234] TLATA, s 15(1)(a).

questions of sale, but other aspects of TLATA are also likely to be affected. If the intention is that the land should be sold, then proving that the purposes of the trust include occupation[235] is likely to be difficult. Accordingly, the choice of a trust for sale is likely to carry real consequences. On the other hand, it may be speculated that there will be relatively few such trusts for sale: it will be rare for early sale to be intended when land is either transferred to trustees[236] or purchased by co-owners.

When we consider pre-TLATA trusts, it is inappropriate to draw any inference that sale is intended merely from the presence of an express trust for sale. In concurrent interest trusts a trust for sale had to be employed pre-TLATA. Its use does nothing to indicate that sale was intended. In successive interest trusts the use of a trust for sale is slightly more deliberate. However, the real purpose would have been to avoid a Settled Land Act settlement, not to ensure early sale.[237] Accordingly nothing can be implied, either as to sale or use of the property, simply from the existence of a trust for sale. It may be that early sale was intended in a few cases, but this will have to be proved by factors other than the legal form. On the other hand, the effect of disagreement between the trustees is the same as in post-TLATA trusts: prima facie the land should be sold, at least if there are independent trustees. In any event disagreement between trustees appears to be relatively uncommon, at least where they are not also beneficiaries.

One of the most curious (and criticized) aspects of the pre-TLATA trust for sale was the doctrine of conversion. On the basis that the settlor intended the land to be sold, equity treated the beneficial interests as being in the proceeds of sale (ie money) from the beginning. The beneficial interests were converted from land into money, even while the property remained unsold. In some cases this would work justice. If the settlor in an *inter vivos* trust for sale wants the land sold quickly and a beneficiary makes a will giving all his personalty to X, it may make sense to say that the trust assets should go to X, regardless of whether the land had in fact been sold by the time of the beneficiary's death. However, two major problems dogged conversion. Perhaps most obviously, the trust for sale was used in situations where nobody imagined that sale would take place quickly. To treat a couple's interest in their family home as being in money makes virtually no sense. The doctrine also led to great uncertainty. Many cases involved construction of legislation and the courts were called upon to decide whether the doctrine applied to a wide variety of statutes. Whilst it can be argued that the courts never adopted

---

[235] TLATA, s 12(1)(a).

[236] Sale may well be intended where a trust is set up by will: the testator may intend that the trust should be of the proceeds of sale. In *inter vivos* trusts a settlor with a similar intention is more likely to sell first and then create a settlement with the proceeds.

[237] Indeed, early sale was not intended in most pre-1925 uses of the trust for sale: Lightwood (1929) 3 CLJ 59, 69. It may be that an early sale will similarly not be intended in some post-TLATA trusts for sale. However, some evidence of this (for example, use of a trust for sale in ignorance of TLATA) is likely to be needed.

a doctrinaire approach[238] and that most of the results made practical sense,[239] the doctrine appeared artificial and the litigation unnecessary.

TLATA, section 3 abolished conversion in trusts of land. It is perhaps odd that the doctrine was abolished for future trusts for sale, given that early sale will generally be intended. However, the complexity of the previous authorities was such that the radical reform introduced by section 3 can readily be justified. One notable consequence is that all legislation applying to land will be interpreted as applying to beneficial interests in land held on trust for sale.[240] Given that it will apply anyway to other trusts of land, this will rarely be problematic. With the exception of trusts created by wills of those dying before the Act,[241] the abolition is retrospective. This means that there is little point in considering how the doctrine operated.

To avoid any doubt, it should be stressed that conversion and sale are two quite different matters. Nothing in section 3 stops the land from being sold. From that time on, the beneficial interests will be in the proceeds of sale and not in the land.

The final question to consider is whether modern settlors should be advised to create trusts for sale. The practical consequences appear relatively small. So long as it is made clear, an intention that the land should be sold can be given effect without creating a trust for sale. Although there is little, if any, disadvantage in creating a trust for sale, it will be rare that positive advantages justify its use.

---

[238] They recognized purposes justifying postponement of sale, as well as rights of beneficiaries to occupy the land.

[239] Anderson (1984) 100 LQR 86. See also Warburton [1986] Conv 415.

[240] For one exception established by TLATA, see Sched 3, para 12(3) (registration of writs and orders affecting land under the Land Charges Act 1972).

[241] The absence of any statutory trust for sale in such cases (contrast Administration of Estates Act 1925, s 33 for deaths intestate) means that testators using a trust for sale were likely to have contemplated immediate sale. Even so, it is an odd exception.

# 9

# Protection of Purchasers

The origins of the modern law of trusts of land lie in the need to ensure that, where the trustees think fit, land can readily be sold and otherwise dealt with. This has already been seen in the context of the regulation of plural ownership and the powers of trustees of land.[1] It is obvious that purchasers (a term which will be used to include mortgagees and lessees) have to be confident that, when dealing with trustees of land,[2] they will obtain a good title to the land. If that were not so, then it would become difficult to sell or otherwise deal with trust land: an outcome likely to be detrimental to beneficiaries and to the economy as a whole.

The fundamental proposition is that where land is dealt with pursuant to powers vested in the trustees, the purchaser or other disponee is not affected by the trusts. Instead of having interests in land, the beneficiaries have a claim to the proceeds of sale (or other disposition). This is the principle described as overreaching: the transfer of the interests from land to money. It is crucial because it means that the purchaser does not need to investigate the beneficial interests and discover whether the beneficiaries approve of the disposition. In this Chapter the operation of overreaching is considered. The most awkward questions arise when there is some irregularity in the transaction: can the purchaser still rely on overreaching? This is an important question, as it determines what sort of problems the purchaser has to look out for and whether trusts of land are truly purchaser friendly.

## 1. Overreaching

### A. The Operation of Overreaching

First, we consider the basic overreaching principles, assuming no irregularity.[3] Charles Harpum has demonstrated[4] that overreaching occurs as a result of

---

[1] See Chapter 6 and p 142 above. To aid this objective, the number of trustees is limited to 4: Trustee Act 1925, s 34 (limited to trusts of land).

[2] There may also be problems where it is wrongly thought that the trust has terminated, so that the purchaser believes that he or she is dealing with an absolute owner. This problem and the statutory response are considered at p 200 below.

[3] Few cases involve no irregularity: it is rare for sale to be challenged simply because a beneficiary does not want the land to be sold. Most litigation involves some breach of trust, being the cause of loss to the beneficiaries.

[4] [1990] CLJ 277, approved by Peter Gibson LJ in *State Bank of India v Sood* [1997] Ch 276, 281; see also Ferris and Battersby (2002) 118 LQR 270 and (2003) 119 LQR 94.

trustees[5] acting within their powers. Previously, some had argued[6] that overreaching depended upon the conversion of assets into personalty effected by the trust for sale. This conversion no longer operates (Trusts of Land and Appointment of Trustees Act 1996 (hereafter TLATA), section 3) but overreaching continues unaffected.[7] Although overreaching is frequently thought of as an important plank of the 1925 legislation, it is really a case of the legislation's taking advantage of an idea that was already present in legal analysis. Indeed, it applies generally to the exercise of powers and is not limited to trusts or to land. What did occur in 1925 was that the range of situations covered by trusts of land was considerably widened. In these trusts there would nearly always be either a trust for sale or power of sale.[8] It follows that there is a very wide scope for overreaching.

## B. Overreaching and the Need to Pay to Two Trustees

Section 2 of the Law of Property Act 1925 (hereafter LPA) makes provision for overreaching in a range of circumstances not restricted to trusts of land. In some of these circumstances it is doubtless correct that overreaching is a direct effect of section 2. For trusts of land, however, matters are more complex. Overreaching is unhelpfully stated to be available where the interest is 'capable of being over-reached'. The now conventional approach is that overreaching operates by virtue of the powers of trustees rather than any specific statutory provision on overreach-ing.[9] This fits the thesis that overreaching depends upon an exercise of authority: it is a concept that can apply just as readily to trusts of personalty, where there is no equivalent to section 2. It is, then, surprising that Morritt V-C adopted a contrary approach in *National Westminster Bank plc v Malhan*,[10] stating that overreaching is based on the 'terms and operation of Part I, Law of Property Act 1925'. It is hard to discover any provisions in Part I which provide for overreaching. Apart from section 2 itself, section 27(1) is the only possible contender and that may have a more limited effect.[11] Given the brevity of the analysis and the fact that it was obiter, it seems best put on one side.

Overreaching reveals a number of policy issues. At an obvious level, the rights of the beneficiaries to the land are sacrificed in favour of ease of sale. This represented a significant change, introduced in statutory form in the nineteenth century and reaching its zenith in 1925. The fact that the settlor and beneficiaries prefer the property not to be sold is of secondary importance.[12] We consider

---

[5]  Or others acting within their powers, such as mortgagees.

[6]  Harpum, n 4 above, 278–9 demonstrates the fallacy of the argument.

[7]  *Birmingham Midshires Mortgage Services Ltd v Sabherwal* (1999) 80 P&CR 256.

[8]  The bare trust constituted an exception until TLATA.

[9]  Harpum [1990] CLJ 123, esp 293–4; Ferris and Battersby (2002) 118 LQR 270, 272. A contrary argument by Hopkins [1997] Conv 81 is firmly rebutted by Harpum (2000) 116 LQR 341, 343.

[10]  [2004] EWHC 847 (Ch), [42].          [11]  See p 189 below.

[12]  Failure to consult the beneficiaries and take account of their wishes would contravene TLATA, s 11, though this is unlikely to affect purchasers. The point at this stage is that decisions can properly be made by the trustees despite opposition from some beneficiaries.

below whether this is appropriate for modern land law. Another obvious problem is that sale enhances the risk of fraud. Trustees cannot make off with the land, but they can do so with money (in particular, the purchase price or mortgage loan). To limit this risk, LPA, section 27(2) requires capital money to be paid to at least two trustees; the danger of two trustees both being fraudulent is plainly less. Alternatively, payment may be to a trust corporation (principally companies formed to act as trustees and with substantial financial backing).[13] The central role of the two-trustee requirement in protecting purchasers is emphasized by a statutory prohibition on excluding it.

In practice, examples of two or more trustees misappropriating proceeds are quite rare. At least, this is the case where the trustees are independent of the beneficiaries, the traditional form of trust. Problems are more likely to arise where a couple hold land on trust for themselves and other family members.[14] In these cases the close relationship (personal and financial) of the trustees makes it more likely that they will together act improperly. This may be intentional or in ignorance of the beneficial interests of the other family members.

The two-trustee rule is vitally important for purchasers. If it is not complied with, then section 2 is explicit that overreaching will not take place.[15] It will be very rare for a purchaser knowingly to pay a single trustee. It is far more likely that the purchaser will be ignorant of the trust, which will not appear on the title deeds or register of title. Nearly always, the trust will have arisen by virtue of a constructive or resulting trust. Indeed, the trustee is likely to be unaware of it in many cases: the breach of trust may well be innocent.

If the purchaser does pay a single trustee, then all may not be lost. The purchaser can fall back on general priority rules to claim that the beneficial interests are not binding. In registered land, this means that the purchaser will be protected if there is no entry on the register and no overriding interest.[16] Such a claim gave rise to the seminal case of *Williams & Glyn's Bank Ltd v Boland*.[17] A husband held on trust for himself and his wife. The trust arose because of the wife's contribution, but the register contained no hint that the husband was not the sole beneficial owner. The House of Lords held that the wife, living in the house with her husband, was in actual occupation and that her interest was binding on a registered chargee.[18] This made it very clear that purchasers must take steps to

---

[13] LPA, s 205(1)(xxviii); Law of Property (Amendment) Act 1926, s 3; SI 1975 No 1189. Pettit, *Equity and the Law of Trusts* (9th edn), pp 370–3.

[14] Examples are the leading cases of *City of London BS v Flegg* [1988] AC 54 (husband and wife holding on trust for themselves and the wife's parents) and *State Bank of India v Sood* [1997] Ch 276 (all members of the Sood family, occupying the land).

[15] The beneficiary can obtain an injunction prohibiting payment to a single trustee: *Waller v Waller* [1967] 1 WLR 451.

[16] Land Registration Act 2002 (hereafter LRA), s 29. For unregistered land, the doctrine of notice is applied: *Caunce v Caunce* [1969] 1 WLR 286.                    [17] [1981] AC 487.

[18] The question whether interests under trusts could be overriding interests was more controversial in the 1980s than it is today. At the time of *Boland* it could be argued that, by virtue of the doctrine of conversion operating on a trust for sale, the beneficiary had no interest in the land. This argument

investigate any possible rights of occupiers, even in circumstances which do not appear suspicious. Little was said about overreaching: it appeared implicit that overreaching could not operate where there was a payment of capital monies to a single trustee. Although the meaning of actual occupation has been refined in later cases, it has never since been doubted that purchasers paying a single trustee are bound by the interests of beneficiaries in actual occupation. It may be observed that the ultimate effect of *Boland* is to protect only the financial interest of the beneficiary against a chargee from a single trustee. The home is likely to be sold, either because a TLATA, section 14 application by a secured creditor of a beneficiary usually succeeds[19] or because the debtor is likely to be bankrupt if the house cannot be sold; we have seen that the trustee in bankruptcy can nearly always obtain an order for sale.[20]

More troublesome has been the question whether a beneficiary in actual occupation can defeat a purchaser where the purchase money is paid to two trustees. This, of course, is the context in which one expects overreaching to operate. In *City of London BS v Flegg*[21] the Court of Appeal applied *Boland* to conclude that overriding interests could again operate to bind the purchaser. This was swiftly reversed by the House of Lords, but the arguments require some consideration. A house was purchased by the Mr and Mrs Maxwell-Brown, with part of the cost being met by Mrs Maxwell-Brown's parents, the Fleggs. Accordingly the land was held on trust for all four of them; all four occupied the house. Mr and Mrs Maxwell-Brown charged the house to obtain funds, part of which were used to pay off their debts. That ploy was only partly successful: they were now bankrupt. The facts reveal an improper decision to charge (certainly for the full sum borrowed) and an improper application of the proceeds, although little was made of these factors.[22] If overreaching operated so that no overriding interest could be asserted, this would simply destroy the Fleggs' interests: the money had gone, so that any right to the loan monies was valueless.

One argument put forward was that *Boland* placed no emphasis on there being a single trustee, so that the same result (chargee bound by the beneficial interest) should follow. This was rejected, surely correctly, because *Boland* was throughout based on the fact that overreaching was impossible. Accordingly, it was not necessary for the House of Lords in *Boland* to deal with overreaching

---

(rejected in *Boland*) was rendered irrelevant by the abolition of conversion in trusts for sale by TLATA, s 3. It was also unsuccessfully argued that the beneficial interest, being explicitly a minor interest (Land Registration Act 1925, s 3(xv)) could not also be an overriding interest. Today, Land Registration Act 2002 does not employ the category of minor interests, though beneficial interests can be protected by restrictions (LRA, ss 42–4, Land Registration Rules 2003, rr 93, 94).

[19] See eg *First National Bank plc v Achampong* [2004] 1 FCR 18; [2003] EWCA Civ 487 (p 178 above). [20] *Alliance and Leicester plc v Slayford* (2000) 33 HLR 743 (p 171 above).

[21] [1986] Ch 605; [1988] AC 54.

[22] Trustee Act 1925, s 17 protects chargees, who are not 'concerned to see that such money is wanted, or that no more than is wanted is raised'. For application of the proceeds, see LPA, s 27, p 189 below.

at all. Indeed, whether overreaching takes place does not always depend entirely upon the number of trustees. Overreaching is possible if there is a single trustee and no capital money,[23] whilst even two trustees cannot overreach if they have limited powers.[24] As *Boland* did not constitute contrary authority, the result that the Fleggs' interests were overreached followed as a matter of ineluctable logic. In the words of Lord Oliver, 'Once the beneficiary's rights have been shifted from the land to capital moneys in the hands of the trustees, there is no longer an interest in the land to which the occupation can be referred or which it can protect'.[25]

Perhaps more difficult was an argument based on LPA, section 14. This states that: 'This Part of this Act shall not prejudicially affect the interest of any person in possession . . .' Although section 14 'has puzzled conveyancers ever since' 1925,[26] it looks a more promising route for the Fleggs to promote their case. It applies (unlike the overriding interest argument) to both registered and unregistered land and appears to be applicable because the relevant sections (section 2 on overreaching, sections 34–6 on concurrent interests) are in LPA, Part I ('This Part').[27] It has never been clear what the purpose or effect of section 14 is, though courts had on occasion relied upon it to advance the interests of occupiers. The most prominent example is provided by *Bull v Bull*,[28] in the context of beneficiaries' rights to occupy. However, the House of Lords in *Flegg* was plainly reluctant to allow it to interfere with overreaching. The ability of two trustees to deal with the land was seen as so central to the structure of the 1925 legislation that it could not be destroyed by an unheralded effect of an ambiguous provision like section 14. As a matter of logic from the drafting of the legislation, it is certainly possible to argue that section 14 trumps conveyancing, but such a startling result was unacceptable to House of Lords.

A further minor point is that the charge in *Flegg* had not been registered. This did not affect overreaching: there was still a conveyance within section 2.[29] This seems correct: the chargees were not relying on having a registered or legal estate. It would have been different in a priorities dispute based on registration rules, of which *Boland* is an example. An argument that an interest is defeated because it is not entered on the register is viable only if the charge is registered.[30]

A quite different issue was faced by the Court of Appeal in *State Bank of India v Sood*.[31] The facts were similar to those in *Flegg*, but with one novel feature. There was no 'capital money', as the charge was to provide security for existing debts. As in *Flegg*, it appears that there was a breach of trust, given that the debts were

[23] *State Bank of India v Sood* [1997] Ch 276 (though there were 2 trustees); discussed below.
[24] Trustees' powers were not unlimited prior to TLATA. Both before and since TLATA consent can be required for the exercise of powers.                                    [25] [1988] AC 54, 91.
[26] Lord Oliver in *Flegg*, 80. See the analysis by Harpum [1990] CLJ 277, 316–20.
[27] *Quaere* whether overreaching today is more a result of the powers in TLATA, s 6.
[28] [1955] 1 QB 234.          [29] Lord Oliver: [1988] AC 54, 91.          [30] LRA, ss 28–9.
[31] [1997] Ch 276; Thompson [1997] Conv 134.

personal debts of the trustees, unrelated to the land.[32] Again, this factor received minimal attention. The question was whether overreaching could take place in the absence of capital money. From the beneficiaries' point of view, such an outcome would be disastrous: they would lose out to the chargee, without anything being received to which their interests could attach.

With some unease, the court held in favour of the chargees. Two background factors need to be recognized. First, a gratuitous transaction entered into by trustees must plainly be a breach of trust and chargees who are aware of the circumstances are likely to find that a personal remedy can be pursued against them.[33] The second factor is that there may be a good reason why capital money is not received: the transaction may not be gratuitous and may be entirely proper for trustees to enter into it. One very good example is a lease at a full rent: the absence of any capital sum is no reason to challenge the exercise of the power to lease. In the context of charges, the most likely scenario (as in *Sood*) is that a loan precedes the charge. The charge may be justified on the basis either that it means that the loan is not called in immediately, or that better terms (for the borrower) are available for secured loans. It remains the case that the beneficiaries lose out if the charge has to be enforced, but the transaction looks entirely proper from the perspective of the chargee.[34]

The problem facing the beneficiaries was simple: the legislation contains no requirement that there be capital monies. Rather, it makes provision where there are capital monies. Although it was argued that the legislation could be interpreted so as to require capital monies,[35] this involved a significant amount of ingenuity and was not backed up by any authority. The beneficiaries' argument was further weakened because they accepted that even a nominal payment would validate the charge, which would then cover earlier debts. Given that it is common for charges to be entered into with two trustees[36] to cover past and future debts (often with no contemporaneous payment) it would have been surprising if the court had reached any other conclusion. *Sood* itself involved two trustees, but it should be remembered that two trustees are required only where capital monies are paid. It follows that overreaching would have occurred had there been only one trustee.[37]

Although section 2 is the principal provision dealing with overreaching, mention should also be made of section 27(1). As Harpum has demonstrated,[38] the

[32] Oddly, Peter Gibson LJ indicates that the beneficiaries' right to redress against the trustees was based on failure to consult them (at 290).       [33] Receipt-based liability is discussed at p 194 below.

[34] On the face of it, the transaction in *Sood* was with 2 trustees who were the sole beneficial owners; there was nothing to arouse suspicion.

[35] On the basis that LPA, s 2(1)(ii), unlike (iii) or (iv) (or the 1922 Act), does not refer to 'any' capital money. Peter Gibson LJ thought the point a strained one; the difference in wording could be explained on other grounds.

[36] Typically, the family home is used to secure the business debts of one or both spouses or partners: the context of *Barclays Bank plc v O'Brien* [1994] 1 AC 180.

[37] Any subsequent capital payment would require payment to 2 trustees for a good receipt to be given, although this would not affect overreaching: Peter Gibson LJ, 289.

[38] [1990] CLJ 277, 284–5, 296.

purpose of this provision is to protect purchasers against any requirement to ensure that the money is correctly applied by the trustees, a requirement which would be very onerous and destroy much of the protection of purchasers. However, as redrafted by TLATA, it appears to give more general protection.[39] Indeed, if read literally it might protect purchasers even if trustees' powers are limited: a proposition which does not sit easily with specific and detailed statutory protection for this eventuality.[40]

A different sort of question is what rights can be overreached. Unsurprisingly, the basic answer is that beneficial interests under the trust can be overreached. Any rights having priority to the trust are unaffected. However, special provision is made for 'ad hoc trusts of land'. These are trusts where the trustees are either court appointed or approved or a trust corporation. The trustees can then overreach earlier equitable interests, though exceptions are made for rights which cannot sensibly take effect against money (a restrictive covenant is one example) and for most rights protected as land charges.[41]

## C. Reform

Overreaching may be seen as a product of its age, the late nineteenth and early twentieth centuries. At that time the major concern was to allow land to be dealt with readily and to ensure that purchasers could deal with trustees without making onerous enquiries and without fearing that they would obtain bad titles. Given that so much land was tied up in settlements, often with inadequate powers of disposition, this was good for the financial interests of beneficiaries and the broader national economic interest in efficient land utilization. Approaching the question from the twenty-first century perspective, much has changed. The prevalence of such large trusts is much reduced, so the national interest is markedly less involved. This may explain the lack of controversy surrounding the freedom to exclude trustees' powers.[42] At the same time, protection of homes has become a dominant feature of the legal landscape. Examples are the protection of tenants (even if significantly diminished over the past twenty years) as well as limitations on the use of licences to conceal exclusive possession and leases, the protection of the possession of mortgagors in default, and the development, charted in Chapter 7, of beneficiaries' rights of occupation.

In the light of these changes, it is unsurprising that overreaching has come under attack. One argument is that it leaves beneficiaries open to too great a risk of financial loss, the context of most cases. Of course, any structure which enables

---

[39] Note the criticism by Harpum (2000) 116 LQR 341, 343; see also Ferris and Battersby (2002) 118 LQR 270, 292–3.

[40] TLATA, s 16(3). But see *National Westminster Bank plc v Malhan* [2004] EWHC 847 (Ch), [43]: p 185 above and p 193 below.

[41] LPA, 2(2), (3) and (for pre-1925 interests) (5). Megarry and Wade, *Law of Real Property* (6th edn), para 8-168 describe the provisions as being 'in practice, obsolete'.

[42] TLATA, s 8; see p 144 above.

transactions in land opens up a risk of loss; some risk is inevitable. More tellingly, the powers of trustees may be regarded as too extensive to establish a correct balance. Thus they can sell trust property even though it constitutes the home of some of the beneficiaries. TLATA responds to this by beefing up provisions protecting beneficiaries against high-handed actions by trustees.[43] However, these provisions (subject to what will be said below about dispositions tainted by irregularity) leave the protection of purchasers untouched. Indeed, the broadening of trustees powers by section 6 moves further in the direction of protecting purchasers.

Two ideas have been propounded to confer greater protection upon beneficiaries. In 1989, the Law Commission[44] proposed, in the light of *Flegg*, that beneficiaries in actual occupation should be protected against dispositions unless they had given their consent. It will be noted that this is directed only at occupying beneficiaries and leaves untouched the financial risks for others. Interesting as it is, it fits uneasily with usual approaches towards occupation. Occupation generally protects existing rights (as in *Boland*) rather than conferring additional rights.[45] Although the government has announced that this reform will not be implemented,[46] it remains one way of dealing with the problem. Would the requirement to contact occupiers be unduly onerous, where there are two trustees? Although purchasers assume that overreaching will operate where there are two trustees,[47] this already seems short-sighted. Other occupiers could have interests outside the trust, for example under estoppels or equitable leases. Given that *Boland* has not caused undue difficulty in requiring enquiries where there is a single trustee, it is difficult to see that enquiries where there are two trustees would be much more troublesome. In reality, it will be a small minority of cases where there are occupiers other than the trustees.[48]

Charles Harpum has suggested an alternative approach: limiting the powers of trustees to enter into charges other than for purchasing or improving (or repairing) land.[49] This provides protection for both financial and occupation interests of beneficiaries. In reality, a beneficiary in occupation has little to fear from a sale: buyers simply will not buy from trustees if other beneficiaries are in possession and are unwilling to move out. It may be true that the beneficiaries' interests would be overreached and that an action by the purchaser to evict them would succeed, but no purchaser wishes to take the risks of litigation. In practical terms, no sale will go ahead unless the trustees evict the beneficiaries, which provides

---

[43] See pp 146–52 above.

[44] Law Com No 188; see esp paras 3.5, 4.1–4.3. Only those with a right to occupy would be protected and they must be of full age and capacity: paras 4.8–4.11. The proposals are criticized by Harpum [1990] CLJ 277, 328 *et seq*.

[45] The orthodox approach is clearly seen in *Flegg* (n 21 above). See also *Paddington BS v Mendelsohn* (1985) 50 P&CR 244, 248.          [46] (1998) 587 HL Deb WA213.

[47] *Flegg* (n 21 above) at 76 (Lord Oliver); *Sood* (n 31 above) at 285.

[48] Children form the most obvious category, though occupation by minor children does not count: *Hypo-Mortgage Services Ltd v Robinson* [1997] 2 FLR 71.          [49] [1990] CLJ 277, 331–3.

ample scope for the exercise of the court discretion under TLATA, section 14. It is with mortgages that the risk is greater, simply because there is no change in occupation. In particular, second mortgages both provide a temptation for the trustees to raise money from the property for their personal benefit and contain little obvious benefit to the beneficiaries. The risks for beneficiaries are present whether or not they are in occupation. The principal reason for doubting Harpum's approach is that second mortgages are very common: they are especially important in the context of providing security for loans to the businesses of one or both trustees. If there is no power to charge then this could have far-reaching economic effects and damage the interests of co-owners even where there are no other beneficiaries. If such a reform were to be introduced (it possesses obvious attractions) then it would seem necessary (even if there is a restriction on the register)[50] to protect chargees unless the beneficiaries are in actual occupation; otherwise it could prove impossible to work out who, if anybody, needs to be consulted. This would be a hybrid of the two sets of reform proposals. However, TLATA moves in the opposite direction to what Harpum proposed. Rather than restricting powers, it removes all limits (though express restrictions are permitted and duties are imposed on the trustees).

It therefore appears that overreaching will reign supreme for the foreseeable future. A purchaser from two trustees is entitled to assume that they can take decisions binding the beneficiaries and need make no enquiry of the latter.

## 2. Dispositions Tainted by Irregularity

In practice it is unusual for beneficiaries to object merely because they disagree with the decision of the trustees. The cases involving purchasers have invariably involved some form of breach of duty on the part of the trustees, even where this is not relied upon to attack the purchaser. We must now consider how far trustees' breaches of duty affect purchasers. At the outset, two points should be emphasized. First, the question has featured in very few modern cases, so we are forced to consider legal principle against a background of nineteenth-century authorities. Secondly, the area is significantly affected by legislation. Unfortunately, the wording and effect of this legislation (mainly TLATA) are all too often unclear, sometimes upsetting conclusions that otherwise seem rational.

### A. *Ultra Vires* Transactions: Limits on Scope of Powers (TLATA, Section 8)

This is the easiest category. We have seen that TLATA, section 8 permits settlors to limit the powers of trustees; this includes requiring consent before exercising

---

[50] The restriction may simply record the limit on powers, without identifying the beneficiaries.

powers. Let us suppose that the power to charge is excluded. Overreaching depends upon the existence of a power or trust; it cannot operate in their absence. Originally argued by Harpum,[51] this seems widely accepted today.[52] The contrary view was expressed by Morritt V-C in *National Westminster Bank plc v Malhan*.[53] However, this was largely unreasoned and seems impossible to square with the provisions protecting purchasers in TLATA, section 16 which are discussed below. Accordingly it may be concluded that any purported charge will fail to overreach, just as we have seen that sale by a single trustee fails to overreach. However, where title is registered a chargee can rely on registration of the charge as providing priority in the absence of any entry on the register or actual occupation overriding interest.[54]

It is immediately obvious that such absence of overreaching is viable only if the chargee is aware of the limitation on the powers. Otherwise, any person dealing with the trustees would have to investigate the trusts (whether or not they are to be found in the title deeds or register of title). This would be quite inconsistent with the object of the 1925 legislation of placing a 'curtain' between trusts and purchasers. Even though purchaser protection arguably went too far in 1925, bringing trusts back on to the title would be a thoroughly retrograde step.[55]

Fortunately, there is legislative protection for purchasers,[56] though there are differing rules for unregistered and registered land. For unregistered land TLATA, section 16(3) protects a purchaser who does not have actual notice of any limitation on powers (the trustee is obliged to communicate any limit). This seems an entirely appropriate way of dealing with the issue. For registered land section 16(7) disapplies all the protections in the section. It is surprising that TLATA is silent as to the position resulting from this. It may have been assumed that the matter would be resolved by the presence or absence of a restriction on the register.[57] Unfortunately, this overlooks the possibility that the objecting beneficiary may be in actual occupation and therefore able to assert a claim by way of overriding interest.[58] Another possibility is that it was assumed that authority to deal with the land is conferred by LRA, section 23.[59] Although this has been

---

[51] [1990] CLJ 277. It would be wrong to imply that the thesis was invented by him: he demonstrates that it is firmly rooted in equity jurisprudence.

[52] It was approved by Peter Gibson LJ in *State Bank of India v Sood* [1997] Ch 276, 281. Although Ferris and Battersby in their contributions to the literature have criticized some of Harpum's analysis, they have warmly endorsed his central thesis: see esp (2000) 118 LQR 270, 270–2.

[53] [2004] EWHC 847 (Ch), [43]: see p 185 above. The judge's specific concern about the extent of powers to charge is partly answered by Trustee Act 1925, s 17 (n 22 above).

[54] LRA, s 29. Chargees of unregistered land would have to argue that they do not have notice of the irregularity.

[55] In particular, it would be quite inconsistent with the thinking behind electronic conveyancing: Law Com No 271, para 2.41–2.68 and part XIII.

[56] We have already seen that TLATA, s 10 provides protection as regards selected elements of consent requirements (if more than 2 are required, or children are involved): pp 147–8 above.

[57] No equivalent entry can be made if title is unregistered.

[58] Ferris and Battersby [1998] Conv 168, 185–6; (2003) 119 LQR 94, 119.

[59] Harpum [1977] CLJ 277, 304–9 (based on s 18 of the Land Registration Act 1925); Morritt V-C in *National Westminster Bank plc v Malhan* [2004] EWHC 847 (Ch), [44].

thoroughly and convincingly criticized,[60] recent changes to the registration legislation render it unnecessary to consider the point further.

Today, LRA, section 26[61] provides that 'a person's right to exercise owner's powers . . . is to be taken to be free from any limitation affecting the validity of a disposition'. The powers referred to are those conferred by section 23, which cover virtually any disposition. It seems clear that a restriction on trustees' powers falls within section 26: it is the very case used by the Law Commission to explain the role and effect of the section.[62] Section 26 exempts limitations protected by an entry on the register and those imposed by the Land Registration Act 2002 itself.[63] It is intended that limitations should be protected by entry of a restriction on the register, in which case the disponee cannot object to being affected. What is very important is that, unlike other provisions protecting purchasers, there is no exception for overriding interests. This means that the purchaser is protected even though a beneficiary is in actual occupation.

It should be noted that section 26 appears wider in scope than the normal protections conferred on purchasers by section 29. Not only are overriding interests irrelevant for section 26, but there is no requirement of registration of the person dealing with a trustee. A person entering into a contract to purchase, for example, would be protected. More puzzling is that no mention is made of consideration: volunteers are not normally given priority over unprotected interests. There seems to be no good reason for protecting volunteers dealing with trustees (gratuitous dispositions by trustees will almost invariably be in breach of trust) and Ferris argues that the correct interpretation of section 26 is such that it confers no protection against such equitable liability.[64]

When we compare the protection conferred by TLATA, section 16 and LRA, section 26, a contrast between registered and unregistered land emerges. For unregistered land, a purchaser who is aware of the limitation will not succeed, whereas section 26 contains no such qualification. Although the different structure of the two systems might explain this (actual notice has to be used in unregistered land, as there is no equivalent to the entry of a restriction) it remains somewhat strange. The Law Commission, however, suggests that a purchaser of registered land who is aware of an unprotected limitation may be liable for knowing receipt of trust property.[65] This is a personal liability based upon

---

[60]  Ferris and Battersby [1998] Conv 168, 180–3; [2001] Conv 221; (2002) 118 LQR 270, 281–3. They stress the difference between the ability to act (LRA, s 23) and the authority to act (TLATA, s 6).

[61]  Section 26 is fully considered by Ferris, *Modern Studies in Property Law, vol 2* (ed Cooke), chapter 6. See also s 52 as regards exercise of mortgagees' powers, though this is not relevant for the forms of irregularity presently under discussion.

[62]  Law Com No 271, paras 4.8–4.11 (employing an example involving a consent requirement).

[63]  Simple examples of the latter are that registration is essential for many interests to exist at law and that, in due course, electronic entry will be essential to the validity of many dispositions. See also the provisions on bankrupt proprietors: LRA, s 86.

[64]  *Modern Studies in Property Law, vol 2* (ed Cooke), pp 112, 117.

[65]  Law Com No 171, para 4.11. Ferris and Battersby (2003) 119 LQR 94, 122, note that the wording of s 26(3) ('has effect only for the purpose of preventing the title of a disponee being questioned') preserves this personal liability, though describing it as 'express preservation' may go too far.

unconscionable conduct of the purchaser and, in the opinion of the Law Commission, does not affect the title of the purchaser. Nevertheless, the effect on the purchaser is much the same:[66] it is certainly unsafe for a purchaser to ignore the limitation. This area of equitable liability is notoriously difficult and fluid.[67] It is questionable how far it is appropriate to leave the position of the purchaser so unsettled: the explicit test of actual notice for unregistered land in TLATA, section 16 appears preferable.

One final point may be made. Because LRA, section 26 operates only in favour of the disponee,[68] the trustees are still under an obligation to comply with any limitation on their powers. A beneficiary will be able to prevent a future transaction exceeding powers and to sue trustees for any loss arising from breach.

## B. *Ultra Vires* Transactions: Limits on Powers other than Section 8

Under this heading two matters are considered. The first is receipt of capital money by a single trustee. Thereafter, other restrictions on trustees' powers of disposition are reviewed.

### (i) *Payment to a Single Trustee*

It is plain that overreaching does not operate where capital money is paid to a single trustee.[69] This is the clear result of LPA, sections 2 and 27(2), but is it a limitation of the powers of a registered proprietor against which LRA, section 26 protects a disponee? It seems very clear that the Law Commission intended that no protection should be accorded to a purchaser who pays a single trustee. How is this to be explained in terms of the drafting of section 26? That the limitation is statutory in origin seems an insufficient response, as the section itself excludes limitations within the Land Registration Act 2002, the inference being that other statutory limitations are within section 26. Commentators concur that section 26 does not apply. Ferris and Battersby[70] argue that 'validity' in the section means 'capable of overreaching the equitable interests under the trust'. This would be a convenient result, though apparently rewriting the section to a limited extent; it should be remembered that section 26 is not limited to dispositions by trustees. This was further refined by Ferris.[71] Whilst he concedes that an 'unnatural' construction is called for, he interprets 'right' (in the phrase 'right to exercise owner's powers') as meaning authority granted by the trust instrument, legislation, or

---

[66] Law Com No 254, para 3.48 states that the liability is to make restitution for loss. This makes sense where the property is no longer held by the constructive trustee. The Law Commission recognizes that, in other forms of the constructive trust as a personal remedy, the rights of the beneficiary are given effect to.
[67] For the current test, see *Bank of Credit and Commerce International (Overseas) Ltd v Akindele* [2001] Ch 437.                        [68] LRA, s 26(3); cf n 65 above.
[69] *Williams & Glyn's Bank Ltd v Boland* [1981] AC 487; p 186 above.
[70] (2003) 119 LQR 94, 121.
[71] *Modern Studies in Property Law, vol 2* (ed Cooke), p 113. His construction avoids the unnecessary protection of volunteers: p 194 above.

other sources such as the constitution of a company. Cooke[72] agrees with the result, but on the basis that the trustee 'is not exercising the power in the manner prescribed for overreaching to take effect'. Superficially, this is more attractive: it is based on a narrow (but entirely credible) construction of 'limitation'. However it does appear to limit the utility of section 26 outside the single trustee context, a topic to which we now turn.

### (ii)   Other Limits on Powers

This is a difficult and controversial area. The modern analysis, following the approach of Harpum, is that the scope of overreaching depends on the powers of the trustees. However, it is not a simple matter of determining what the powers are and then saying that everything done within those powers is properly done. Take the facts of *Flegg*. The trustees charged land partly in order to raise money for their own benefit. This seems a very plain breach of trust on their part. However, it did not affect the validity of the charge; in other words, it was not rendered *ultra vires* by the manner of its exercise.[73]

Ferris and Battersby have argued that TLATA has caused a wider range of circumstances to render trustees' dispositions *ultra vires*: 'by its own provisions section 6 purports to limit the exercise of the generous powers it grants to trustees of land . . . . a conveyance is *ultra vires* when it is made in breach of a provision of TLATA, breach of which prevents the general grant of powers by section 6(1) from applying'.[74] If this is correct then the legislation has reduced the protection given to purchasers. This seems unintended and is one reason to be sceptical regarding their argument.

They consider that the restrictions on the exercise of powers fit into two groups. Some irregularities do not affect the existence of power: failure to consider beneficiaries' rights (section 6(5)) and failure to exercise due care (section 6(9)).[75] Other irregularities, they argue, will take away the power: exercise in contravention of an enactment or of the rules of law or equity (section 6(6));[76] powers conferred by other enactments subject to some restriction (section 6(8)); and failure to consult beneficiaries and give effect to their wishes (section 11).[77] With the exception of section 6(8)[78] the problem with most of these provisions is that they relate to the way in which decisions are reached. Although the mandatory language of some of

---

[72] *The New Law of Land Registration*, p 59, n 34.

[73] See p 187, n 22, above. *Sood* is similar; it is instructive because the Harpum analysis of overreaching was explicitly approved: p 193 above.

[74] (2003) 119 LQR 94, 98; the detailed analysis of breaches is at 100–8. See also their analysis in [1998] Conv 168, though they then came to somewhat different conclusions.

[75] This is largely based on the wording of these provisions. It may be added that these irregularities are difficult for purchasers to discover: they seem wholly unsuitable for determining the scope of overreaching.

[76] The potential breadth of this category leads to difficult questions of overlap with s 6(5), (9): (2003) 119 LQR at 105–6.        [77] This last category (s 11) is later relegated, at 117, to a 'possibility'.

[78] This genuinely does seem to place limits on what can be done.

the provisions in the latter group is relied upon by Ferris and Battersby,[79] this seems to add little to the question. It makes complete sense for a duty as to mode of exercise to be mandatory, whilst not taking away the power. Read naturally, these provisions control the manner of the exercise of powers rather than determining whether there is a power in the first place.

If we stopped there we might well conclude that *ultra vires* extends little further (section 6(8) may be the only example) than the operation of section 8, together with the need for two trustees. Unfortunately, there are further arguments. Section 16 makes provision for protecting purchasers against specific defects. We have already considered this in the context of section 8 limitations, where section 16(3) provides that breach does not (absent actual notice) 'invalidate any conveyance'. Section 16(2) provides similar protection in respects of breaches of section 6(6) and (8). As regards s 6(8), it has been seen that this can readily be treated in the same way as section 8 limitations on powers. However, that leaves open the effect of contravention of an enactment or of the rules of law or equity (section 6(6)). It can be argued that, unless the trustee's breach of duty renders the conveyance invalid (so that overreaching cannot take place) there would be no reason to protect a purchaser: no need to include section 6(6) in section 16(2). Furthermore, the very language 'does not invalidate' implies that the conveyance would otherwise be invalid. This may be an example of an attempt to protect purchasers that has back-fired. If the conveyance is invalid it will be necessary to consider in detail what breaches in fact fall within section 6(6). The words 'contravention of . . . any rule of . . . equity' might in particular be very wide in their operation. Can this result be avoided? A bold interpretation would limit section 16(2) and the inferences from it to those breaches which do invalidate the conveyance.[80] It may be difficult to contemplate cases where breaches of (in particular) legal or equitable duties will render the conveyance void, but on this interpretation the effect of the protection is to guard against any such cases that do arise.[81]

If, contrary to the above arguments, breach of section 6(6) does result in an *ultra vires* transaction, what is the effect of this? For unregistered land, section 16(2) protects innocent purchasers, but is there any protection in registered land? As seen in the context of section 8 limits on powers, section 16 does not apply to registered land and there is a danger of being bound by the rights of those in actual occupation. More specifically, does section 26 apply to protect a

---

[79] (2003) 119 LQR at 120.

[80] But does this give too much protection to those with actual notice of the breach? If s 16(2) applies, they are clearly not protected. It can be replied that, just as with registered land, knowing receipt liability could cover such cases. In any event, the law prior to TLATA operated successfully without any such provision!

[81] This is supported by the obiter assumption in *Birmingham Midshires Mortgage Services Ltd v Sabherwal* (1999) 80 P&CR 256 that TLATA had no effect on overreaching and the cases of *Flegg* and *Sood*. This was in the context of registered land, to which s 16(2) does not apply, and before LRA, s 26 provided a possible alternative protection for purchasers. See Dixon [2000] Conv 267 and the reply of Ferris and Battersby [2001] Conv 221.

disponee, assuming no entry on the register? Many equitable rules (for example, that trustees must not exercise powers for personal benefit) are inappropriate for entry on the register and this causes one to doubt whether section 26 is intended to cover such cases. Yet Ferris and Battersby argue that section 26 does apply, as these rules count as a 'limitation affecting the validity of the transaction'. Instinctively, this does not appear to be a natural reading of section 26, though there may be a pragmatic justification for it if TLATA, section 6(6) does limit what trustees can do.[82]

What about the consultation requirements in section 11, breach of which Ferris and Battersby suggest might also preclude overreaching? In this context, section 16(1) provides simply that purchasers are 'not concerned to see that [such a requirement[83]] has been complied with'. This mirrors the previous wording in LPA, section 26(3). Although an argument can be mounted that the provision is unnecessary if overreaching can take place anyway, the focus is more on emphasizing that there is no need to make enquiries, rather than protection against any irregularity.[84] In any event, failure to consult did not affect purchasers prior to TLATA.[85] The argument that breach of section 11 has no effect on overreaching is a strong one, regardless of the outcome as regards sections 6(6) and 16(2).

## C. *Intra Vires* Decisions

Where the trustees act *intra vires* there can be no challenge to a disposition simply because the beneficiaries do not like it. If authority be needed for such an obvious proposition, then it is provided by *Flegg*. However, in some cases there will be a breach of duty by the trustees. Cases in which the trustees have used their powers for their own financial benefit provide a good example. Many of these cases will fall within the provisions in TLATA (especially section 6(5), (6) which state how trustees are to take decisions: the provisions considered in the previous section. However, there would usually have been a breach of equitable duties prior to TLATA.

Can a purchaser be affected by such a breach of duty, assuming that it is insufficient to render the disposition *ultra vires*? The starting point is that overreaching can take place. Indeed, the cases have held in favour of purchasers even where there has been a breach of duty: *Flegg* and *Sood* are excellent examples. That does not mean that the question of a breach of duty can be ignored: a purchaser who

---

[82] In this context, the interpretation of s 26 by Cooke, p 196 above, becomes problematic. Her construction would leave s 26 inapplicable in such cases, with a serious resulting gap in the protection of purchasers. This is a problem only if Ferris and Battersby are correct as to the scope of *ultra vires* transactions.

[83] Also within the protection of s 16(1) are breaches of ss 6(5) (duty to have regard to beneficiaries' rights) and 7(3) (obtaining consents to partition).

[84] Emphasized by the absence of any provision for actual notice. But as regards consents to partition, do purchasers require more positive protection from s 16(1)?

[85] In *State Bank of India v Sood* [1997] Ch 276, the court protected purchasers whilst stating that the trustees might be liable for failure to consult.

knowingly collaborates in a breach of duty is likely to be liable for unconscionable receipt of trust property.[86]

However, Ferris and Battersby[87] have argued that purchasers are affected by such breaches (even as regards *intra vires* dispositions) but that the legislation contains protections. One point can be quickly noted. We have seen[88] that LPA, section 27(1) protects purchasers as regards any need to ensure the proper application of the proceeds. This fills a gap in purchaser protection identified in the nineteenth century and applies whether title is registered or not. However, we are concerned with breaches at the time of the disposition.[89]

Ferris and Battersby proceed to argue that the principal role of LPA, section 2 is to provide protection to purchasers against such risks. They argue that Harpum's analysis leaves no sensible role for the section and that theirs is a workable and necessary interpretation. Whilst providing such protection for purchasers is in principle unobjectionable, it may be queried how far it is necessary in the first place. Although there are cases in which purchasers have been affected by breaches in the exercise of powers, it seems that involvement in the breach is required; it is not enough to have simple knowledge of the trust.[90] Although some of the cases may be a little harsh, they involve purchasers who knew full well what the trustees were doing:[91]—equity does not protect them merely because they considered (wrongly) that the conduct of the trustees was defensible. Although there was some 'judicial willingness to hold that purchasers were put on inquiry',[92] it may be doubted whether such an approach would be taken by a court today.

Accordingly, it is suggested that there is no need to interpret section 2 in the manner suggested.[93] Admittedly it would do little harm, though it should be remembered that purchasers need not be in good faith for section 2 to apply;[94]

---

[86] Dixon [2000] Conv 267, 269–70. Although this is criticized by Ferris and Battersby [2001] Conv 221, it receives considerable support from the Law Commission's use of knowing receipt liability in the LRA, s 26 context. See also Harpum [1990] CLJ 277, 295.    [87] (2002) 118 LQR 270, 283–94.

[88] See p 189 above.

[89] Most cases of misapplication of proceeds will also involve a tainted disposition, but the trustees might decide on misapplication after a perfectly proper sale.

[90] This is illustrated by the cases quoted by Ferris and Battersby (2002) 118 LQR 270, 287, n 115: *Dance v Goldingham* (1873) LR 8 Ch App 902; *Re Bourne* [1906] 1 Ch 113; and *Watkins v Cheek* (1825) 2 Sim & St 199. It should follow that, for registered land, actual occupation of a beneficiary is insufficient by itself to attack the purchaser.

[91] An example is where a contract contains depreciatory terms: *Dance v Goldingham* (1873) LR 8 Ch App 902. The typical modern scenario is one where, on the face of the documents, trustees are also the beneficial owners. This is very different from virtually all nineteenth-century trusts and leads to quite different inferences as to which transactions appear proper.

[92] Ferris and Battersby (2002) 118 LQR 270, 289. The cases quoted (*Robinson v Briggs* (1853) 1 Sm & Giff 188; *Perham v Kempster* [1907] 1 Ch 373) involve purchasers who were party to the breach or subsequent purchasers from them.

[93] It requires some ingenuity in the context of sales by mortgagees: Ferris and Battersby (2002) 118 LQR 270, 293–4.

[94] LPA, s 205(1)(xxi): the normal requirement of good faith is excluded for Part I of the Act.

this may be thought to go too far in protecting them in respect of improper exercise of powers. If section 2 is left without any significant role then this need not alarm us; it can be seen as a pulling together at the beginning of the legislation of diverse circumstances in which overreaching operates.[95]

## D. Trusts which Appear to have Terminated

A very different problem which purchasers may face is that the trust may appear to have terminated: the land is now held by a person who claims to be the absolute beneficial owner. How can the purchaser be sure that the trust has in fact come to an end? If it has not, then the purchase money would have to be paid to two trustees. It would, of course, be inconsistent with the purposes of the legislation if purchasers had to investigate the beneficial interests in order to be sure that the trust has terminated. There are two statutory provisions operating in this context, both limited to unregistered land. We next consider their effect and the position where title is registered.

### (i)  Law of Property (Joint Tenants) Act 1964

This legislation deals with a specific problem arising from survivorship in joint tenancies. If one of two joint tenants (holding on trust for themselves as beneficial joint tenants) dies then the survivor holds the legal title beneficially and the trust of land has come to an end.[96] How can a purchaser be sure that the deceased joint tenant had not severed the joint tenancy and so created a beneficial tenancy in common? If there had been severance (which the survivor might not know about) then the deceased co-owner's estate would have an interest and the trust would continue: the purchase money would have to be paid to two trustees. In the nature of things, it would be virtually impossible for the survivor to prove the negative proposition that severance had not taken place.

This problem was widely recognized and the solution adopted in 1964 was to protect a purchaser in the absence of a memorandum of the severance being placed on the title deeds (good practice requires such an entry following severance).[97] This produces a reasonable balancing of the interests of purchasers and those taking by severance. One point of contention is how far a purchaser can rely on the protection if actually aware of a severance which is not mentioned on the deeds. Although it was originally thought that the purchaser would still be protected,[98] it has been held that the purchaser is not in good faith and therefore receives no protection.[99]

---

[95]  See Harpum [1990] CLJ 277, 278. The provisions on ad hoc trusts of land (p 190 above) do in any event have real overreaching effect.                                      [96]  *Re Cook* [1948] Ch 212.

[97]  The protection is triggered by the inclusion in the conveyance of a statement that the survivor is solely and beneficially entitled. It is retrospective to 1926: Law of Property (Joint Tenants) Act 1964, s 2.

[98]  Jackson (1966) 30 Conv 27, based on statements in Parliament.

[99]  *Grindal v Hooper* (1999) 96/48 LS Gaz 41, discussed by Gravells [2000] Conv 461.

## (ii) Deeds of Discharge

Trusts of land usually come to an end after a beneficiary becomes absolutely entitled. Take a simple trust for X for life, remainder to Y. On X's death Y has the entire beneficial interest. The trust continues at that stage.[100] Unless the land is sold,[101] the trustees are likely to transfer the legal fee simple to Y and this does terminate the trust.

The problem we need to consider arises when Y later decides to sell. How safe is a purchaser in paying the purchase money to Y? The danger is that if X has not died (or if there are other interests under the trust which have been overlooked by the trustees) then the trust will continue. A purchaser is at risk because overreaching operates only if the proceeds are paid to two trustees. TLATA, section 16(4) and (5) employs the deed of discharge as a solution. The trustees should execute such a deed when they transfer to absolutely entitled beneficiaries,[102] whereupon a later purchaser is entitled to assume that the land is free of the trust.[103] As with other provisions in section 16, there is no protection if the purchaser has actual knowledge of an irregularity.

## (iii) Registered Land

The protections described above do not apply to registered land,[104] so is there any protection for purchasers? Purchasers of registered land are normally given priority unless there is a restriction on the register.[105] It is therefore important that, if there is a severance, a restriction requiring payment to two trustees is entered.[106] Absent any entry on the register, a registered disponee is normally bound only by overriding interests. The risk in the present context is that a beneficiary who claims by severance, or whose interest has been overlooked in a transfer by the trustees to a beneficiary, may be in actual occupation.

It was seen above that LRA, section 26 today protects purchasers in respect of most irregularities, at least where they constitute limitations on the right to exercise an owner's powers. It then does not matter that other protections are inapplicable to registered land. However, we observed that it is generally thought that section 26 confers no protection as regards failure to pay to two trustees. This is the very

[100]  Unless the beneficiary is the sole trustee, as in the joint tenancy context just considered.

[101]  The decision will be taken in consultation with Y. This sale does not cause special problems.

[102]  In the example above, Y was solely entitled. The same principles apply if there is a remainder to Y and Z and the land is transferred to Y and Z. For the power of the trustees to transfer to beneficiaries, see TLATA, s 6(2), p 152 above.

[103]  The protection is modelled on s 17 of the Settled Land Act 1925, which employs much the same terminology. For the interpretation of that Act, see p 104 above.

[104]  Law of Property (Joint Tenants) Act 1964, s 3; TLATA, s 16(7).

[105]  LRA, s 29. A notice is not available for interests under trusts of land: LRA, s 33(a).

[106]  A restriction covering the deed of discharge problem is unlikely; other beneficiaries are unlikely to be aware of an improper transfer to the apparently absolutely entitled beneficiary. There will usually be a restriction while the trustees hold the fee simple, but it is likely to be cancelled when the transfer is registered: Land Registration Rules 2003, r 99.

problem which arises when the purchaser believes the trust has come to an end.[107] This is a thoroughly unpalatable result. It means that a purchaser of registered land needs to make enquiries of occupiers, which may require full investigation of the trusts.[108] Given the overwhelming prevalence of registered conveyancing today, this is a serious shortcoming of the legislation. It is possible that the courts may be tempted to extend the section 26 protection to this situation, though it is difficult to see how this could be achieved whilst maintaining the result in *Boland*.

## E. Timing and Effect of Protection

As regards timing, is there protection for purchasers who have binding contracts to purchase? This is important in determining whether knowledge of an irregularity acquired between contract and conveyance defeats the purchaser. Another point is whether a beneficiary can stop the disposition after the contract.

Some of the protections apply only on conveyance: this is applicable to section 16(2), (3), and to the Law of Property (Joint Tenants) Act 1964. Furthermore, it was assumed in *Waller v Waller*[109] that the protection as regards consultation (now TLATA, section 16(1)) did not operate on contract. This fits quite neatly with the statutory protection of purchasers from mortgagees: it does not apply if the purchaser becomes aware of irregularities after contract.[110]

However, the protection in LRA, section 26 for those dealing with registered proprietors is not limited to any specific type of disposition. It might appear to follow that a purchaser will be protected once there is a contract to purchase: this will defeat the rights of the beneficiaries. On this basis, even a restriction entered on the register after the contract would be ineffective. However, there is still a breach of trust and the better view is that knowing receipt liability may still follow, where the purchaser becomes aware of the irregularity before transfer.[111] Again, this is supported by the mortgage cases, where liability follows despite the contract by the mortgagee being seen as an element of the power of sale and as effective to preclude redemption.[112]

It may be concluded that purchasers remain at risk until conveyance.[113] Although they are protected despite actual occupation or constructive notice,

---

[107] As in the *Boland* context, the problem is that the purchaser does not realize that the vendor is a trustee. It is not a case of a limitation of the overreaching powers of trustees.

[108] See Cooke [2004] Conv 41, advocating statutory reform to protect purchasers.

[109] [1967] 1 WLR 451 (injunction binding purchaser). The point was obiter, as there was only one trustee.

[110] LPA, s 104(2); *Selwyn v Garfit* (1888) 38 Ch D 273; *Bailey v Barnes* [1894] 1 Ch 25; *Waring v London & Manchester Assurance Co Ltd* [1935] Ch 311, 318.

[111] For this liability, see p 194 above.

[112] *Waring v London & Manchester Assurance Co Ltd* [1935] Ch 311, approved by the Court of Appeal in *Property & Bloodstock Ltd v Emerton* [1968] Ch 94 and *National & Provincial BS v Ahmed* [1995] 2 EGLR 127.

[113] Presumably, for deeds of discharge the protection of purchasers will be analogous to either the consultation requirements or LRA, s 26.

actual awareness of an irregularity at any stage before conveyance is likely to lead to liability to the beneficiaries.

A different problem arises for those dealing with the initial purchaser (whether as mortgagee, lessee, or onwards purchaser). Suppose that the initial purchaser was aware of the irregularity, would this affect the subsequent disponee? We may assume that the disponee is unaware of the irregularity, let alone the purchaser's knowledge of it. In registered land, the knowing receipt liability is probably sufficiently personal for the disponee not to be affected, absent unconscionable conduct on the part of the disponee.[114]

For unregistered land there may be less protection. If there is actual notice the initial purchaser will be bound by the irregularities against which section 16(2), (3) normally protects. It appears that the initial purchaser will have the legal title,[115] but that the subsequent disponee will have to rely on being a bona fide purchaser without notice. It is unfortunate that the wording of section 16 protects only the conveyance by the trustees.[116] Although a disponee might be able to show absence of notice, this does seem an unnecessary gap in the statutory protection.

---

[114] Cf the question whether such liability could arise in *Chattey v Farndale Holdings Inc* (1996) 75 P&CR 298, 313–17. However, the constructive trust in *Chattey* was not based on receipt principles.

[115] Ferris and Battersby (2003) 119 LQR 94, 107–15.

[116] For deeds of discharge, s 16(5) is differently worded and does seem to protect the disponee.

# PART IV
# OTHER PROPERTY

# 10

# Plural Ownership of Property
# Other Than Land

The development of plural ownership in other property has been less developed. In part, this is because estates in land were based upon tenures: tenure is applicable only to land. For land, lawyers analysed ownership rights in terms of estates, rather than ownership. This led to significant flexibility as regards the range of rights recognized. For other forms of property it is easier to recognize ownership and this has tended to snuff out the development of other rights. This is especially important as regards successive interests; concurrent ownership of personalty is generally recognized. In the successive interests context, an idea comparable to estates is splitting ownership (future rights) and possession (present enjoyment). Possessory rights to chattels are recognized by bailment. This can be seen as part of the stress placed by the law on possession as a basis for actions to vindicate rights to chattels; it has not proved a promising avenue for developing more sophisticated proprietary interests. As will be seen later in the Chapter, most modern analysis is based on commercial transactions, often of the nature of leases. This is only marginally related to plural ownership as considered in this book. Where plural ownership is recognized (most obviously for concurrent interests and trusts) there is nothing really equivalent to the regulatory regime to be found in the Trusts of Land and Appointment of Trustees Act 1996 (hereafter TLATA). There is some regulation, but of decidedly limited impact; it is studied towards the end of this Chapter.

## 1. Trusts

Trusts form something of an exception to what has just been said. It is possible to create interests under trusts which mirror the concurrent and successive interests which can exist in land; this has long applied to trusts of personalty.[1] Indeed, one of the reasons for using a trust for sale after 1925 was to combine personalty and land in a single settlement.[2] An exception (no longer applicable since TLATA)

---

[1] See eg *Howard v Duke of Norfolk* (1681) 2 Swans 454. Given that equity modelled interests under trusts on interests recognized at law (Megarry and Wade, *Law of Real Property* (6th edn), paras 4-21–4-23) this is a little surprising. However, it is firmly settled.

[2] If an example be needed, see *Brandon v Robinson* (1811) 18 Ves 429.

proves the rule. For very technical reasons[3] it was not possible to create entails in property other than land. Under the 1925 legislation entails might well exist in personalty when there was a trust for sale. Accordingly, it was provided that entails could be created in personalty.[4] The telling point is that it was not thought necessary to provide that other forms of interest could exist in personalty under a trust. When rights equivalent to legal estates existed under a trust, equity adopted virtually all their technical rules. These included the notorious rules on conditional interests.[5]

One very important difference between land and personalty is that it is very unusual[6] for statute to impose trusts over property other than land. Accordingly, trusts of personalty cover only a relatively small part of plural ownership of such property. They are most likely to be found in wills or other settlements, though a declaration of trust may occasionally may be found in circumstances analogous to constructive or resulting trusts of family homes.[7] Even where there is a trust, there is no detailed regulation such as encountered with trusts of land.

## 2. Concurrent Interests

### A. Chattels

It is possible to create joint tenancies and tenancies in common in personalty, just as in land.[8] Joint tenancies, of course, are used where trustees hold personalty on trust: trustees are invariably joint tenants. Tenancies in common[9] are quite common as co-ownership of chattels frequently occurs in a business setting. This may be because property is stored mixed together with identical property of others[10] or because it belongs to partners.[11] Indeed, it is recognized by recent legislation on sale of goods, where part of a bulk is sold.[12]

It appears that the requirements and attributes of these interests follow very closely the rules already discussed for concurrent interests in land. One particular point is that severance operates in just the same manner. *Re Hewett*[13] is commonly

---

[3] Megarry and Wade, *Law of Real Property* (5th edn), p 87.

[4] Law of Property Act 1925 (hereafter LPA), s 130(1); Law of Property (Entailed Interests) Act 1932, s 1 retrospectively covered pre-1926 settlements.

[5] See eg *Re Whiting's Settlement* [1905] 1 Ch 96; *Leong v Chye* [1955] AC 648 (PC). Many of the cases on conditional and determinable interests involved mixed realty and personalty trusts. Equity also adopted words of limitation: Simpson, *A History of the Land Law* (2nd edn), p 206.

[6] One example is intestacy: Administration of Estates Act 1925, s 33.

[7] *Rowe v Prance* [1999] 2 FLR 787 (boat). There may be a resulting trust where a transferee has not given consideration, though this will not normally involve plural ownership.

[8] See, generally, Hill and Bowes-Smith in Palmer and McKendrick (eds), *Interests in Goods* (2nd edn), chapter 10.                    [9] Recognized for chattels by Co Litt 198a.

[10] For example, *Re Stapylton Fletcher Ltd* [1994] 1 WLR 1181, 1197–9.

[11] As in *Mayhew v Herrick* (1849) 7 CB 229.

[12] Sale of Goods (Amendment) Act 1995, inserting ss 20A, 20B Sale of Goods Act 1979.

[13] [1894] 1 Ch 362.

cited in this context, though the joint tenancy appears to be a beneficial interest under a trust of personalty. In any event, the modern rules on severance of joint tenancies in land include 'such other acts or things as would, in the case of personal estate, have been effectual to sever the tenancy in equity'.[14] In other words, the rules for personalty now apply to land, though the rules for all forms of property are thought to be the same.[15] However, two points need to be noted about severance. The first is that LPA, section 36(2) provides for severance by written notice. However, this applies to the 'legal estate' and is therefore limited to land. This represents a serious defect in the current law; its inconvenience has led to suggestions that severance by notice is recognized as a form of equitable severance. Unfortunately for co-owners of personalty, these suggestions have little support.[16] The second point to remember is that the joint tenancy in chattels can exist as a legal interest. It follows that severance of the legal joint tenancy has to follow the rules for legal severance. These are restricted to shattering one of the unities. The equitable severance rules are wider. Before 1925 they led to the joint tenancy being held on trust for the parties as tenants in common; the same principles should apply to personalty today. In practice, however, legal joint tenancies of chattels are rare save for trustees; severance of a legal joint tenancy is not an issue which frequently arises.

Throughout any analysis of co-ownership of chattels, it has to be borne in mind that no trust need be involved. Of course, it may be very wise to have the chattels vested in trustees.[17] This may make it easier to manage the property and to resolve disputes; it is especially common where property is left by will. However, there is no automatic imposition of a trust simply because chattels are co-owned. The distinction between equitable interests under trusts and legal ownership is particularly important when, later in this Chapter, we consider the regulation of plural ownership in personalty.

## B. Choses in Action

It has long been the position that there cannot be a legal tenancy in common over choses in action:[18] the only form of legal co-ownership is joint tenancy. This is confirmed by twentieth-century authority[19] and is accepted by virtually everybody. We need to consider why this rule exists and what its significance is.

The rule is more frequently assumed than justified. One relevant factor is that the assignment of choses in action (and therefore of concurrent interests in choses in action) has long been restricted. Until the Judicature Act 1873 legal assignment was not permitted. Even today a legal assignment has to be an 'absolute' assignment of the chose and this appears not to be satisfied by the assignment of a co-ownership share in a chose in action.[20] Even if legal assignment is not possible, however, could

---

[14] LPA, s 36(2).    [15] See above, p 50.    [16] See pp 54, 70 above.
[17] This applies equally to personalty generally. The use of trusts for choses in action is considered below.                                                    [18] Co Litt 198a.
[19] *Re McKerrell* [1912] 2 Ch 648.    [20] LPA, s 136(1); *Re McKerrell* [1912] 2 Ch 648, 653.

not a tenancy in common (if such were permitted) pass on death? More convincing is the point that a chose in action is at heart an obligation. We should not allow interests in the chose to cause problems for the debtor, who requires clarity as to whom should be paid. The rules of assignment recognize this, insofar as notice of an assignment is required. If there were a tenancy in common there might well be problems in identifying who should be paid, as well as a possible increase in the number of persons to be paid.[21] Accordingly, the restriction to joint tenancy, coupled with the inability to undertake legal assignments of co-ownership shares, may be seen as a necessary protection for debtors. Similarly, it can be stressed that the chose in action is a joint right in the creditors, A and B, to be paid (say) £10,000. Quite different would be a right for A to be paid £4,000 and B to be paid £6,000, a consequence which might follow if there were a tenancy in common. The essential joint nature of the cause of action is therefore inconsistent with a tenancy in common.[22]

As to significance, it is important to remember that the chose in action can be held on trust for tenants in common: it is only the legal title which is restricted to joint tenancy.[23] One might argue that trustees are faced with the same problems as debtors in discovering who should be paid. However, trustees may be expected to discover the location of beneficial interests:[24] the parties are not operating in the commercial environment of most choses in action. Furthermore, the trust would be barely viable for concurrent interests if it did not recognize tenancies in common: Chancery judges were well aware of the deficiencies of the joint tenancy.[25]

So long as the parties set up a trust with a beneficial tenancy in common, therefore, the restriction to a legal joint tenancy will do no harm: the estate of the deceased co-owner will not lose out. Will there be problems if the parties do not think about the need for a trust? It has been seen that there are circumstances in which equity imposes trusts to give effect to beneficial tenancies in common in land: these are designed to give effect to the presumed intention of the parties.[26] It may be confidently expected that this presumption of an equitable tenancy in common, applying for example to partnership and unequal contribution, will be applied in the same way where choses in action are co-owned.[27] The other sort of case giving rise to a tenancy in common is where it is made clear by words of

[21] This was reflected in the rules relating to mortgages of land, where one might expect the creditors to hold the mortgage as tenants in common. To avoid problems for the debtor, the legal title would normally be vested in them as joint tenants, with a 'joint account clause' enabling the money to be paid to the survivor. This is today covered by LPA, s 111.

[22] Crossley Vaines, *Personal Property* (5th edn), p 57. This analysis, following Co Litt 198a, concentrates more on rights of action for wrongs done to co-owners than on rights of action arising from contract or debt. Compare the problems with tenancies in common of leases, though here joint obligations (rather than rights) are more prominent: p 24 above.

[23] Although a right under a trust is a form of chose in action, it is therefore one which can be held in a tenancy in common.

[24] Notice of any assignment must be given: *Dearle v Hall* (1828) 3 Russ 1.

[25] See p 30 above.          [26] Page 33 above.

[27] See *Steeds v Steeds* (1889) 22 QBD 537, 541, in which a beneficial tenancy in common was recognized for a debt secured by a mortgage.

severance that a tenancy in common is desired. Normally, this would create a legal tenancy in common, but this of course is not possible for causes of action. It seems inevitable that the courts will ensure that there is a trust in order to give effect to the parties' intentions.

## 3. Successive Interests

This is the most difficult area, in which the interests recognized for land certainly cannot be assumed to be permitted. We have seen that estates in land enable successive rights to the land to be recognized. As a matter of history, that structure is based on the doctrine of tenures. Tenures and estates do not apply to personalty. In the words of Crossley Vaines:[28] 'Chattels are the subject of absolute ownership, and you are either an owner or you are not: a life estate in a chattel is an idea incompatible with ownership'. We may need to question some aspects of this assessment, but the general proposition of absolute ownership is clear enough.

It is not only in the area of plural ownership covered by this book that problems arise. It is common to create successive rights to chattels in commercial settings, analogous to leases of land. Hire provides the best example. The traditional approach has been to recognize possessory rights in goods as creating a bailment. Bailment can cover a wide range of situations, ranging from leaving a car at a garage to be serviced, to leaving coats in a cloakroom, or hiring aircraft for an extended period.[29] The bailee is recognized as having rights in the property (often described as 'special property') which justify actions against third parties who take or damage the property. The entire picture is greatly affected by the manner in which these rights are protected. The bailee's action is based on the interference with his or her possession. It is possession rather than any property right in the goods which is protected.[30] The bailor, described as having the 'general property', can recover if there is permanent damage affecting his or her reversionary interest.[31]

This recognition of a right against third parties certainly imparts a proprietary flavour to the rights of the bailee. For true proprietary status,[32] however, the question is whether the bailment binds successors in title from the bailor.[33] This is perhaps most likely to be an issue on bankruptcy of the bailor.[34] Curiously, there is

---

[28] *Personal Property* (5th edn), p 43.

[29] McMeel [2003] LMCLQ 169 considers that the use of bailment in such diverse contexts has inhibited development of rational personal property principles.

[30] A well known principle is that the bailee can recover for the entire value of the property, though there is likely to be liability to account to the bailor: *The Winkfield* [1902] P 42.

[31] *Mears v LSW Ry Co* (1862) 11 CBNS 850.

[32] The point is well explained by Worthington, *Personal Property Law: Text and Materials*, para 2.3.4.

[33] In the land context, this was the question raised in *National Provincial Bank Ltd v Ainsworth* [1965] AC 1175 regarding the deserted wife's equity. When the proprietary status of licences over land is discussed, it is generally regarded as the crucial issue.

[34] Few people are interested in purchasing from bailors out of possession. There is a greater chance that mortgages may include goods subject to bailment.

no clear answer to the question.[35] It is not seriously argued that every bailment is binding on successors in title: a gratuitous loan of a car for a year has a weak claim to take priority over a purchaser or creditors on bankruptcy. However, it is common for there to be 'leases' of chattels. Long-term hiring contracts are a common way of acquiring cars, ships, and aircraft. In many respects the owner is financing something equivalent to purchase. This is most obviously seen in hire purchase transactions, but the contract is commonly a simple one of hire. The use of the language of leasing in such transactions is calculated to make us think about leases of land, where such arrangements have for centuries bound successors in title.

Most authors consider that such chattel leases do bind successors in title[36] and there is some authority to support that.[37] Furthermore, some forms of bailment are generally recognized as binding successors, pledge being the best example.[38] This is best explained as an application to chattels of the same principles as apply to leases. This seems a safer basis than relying on equitable rights as between bailor and bailee.[39] However, the authorities are inconclusive and it has been argued that there is no property right as the law presently stands.[40] The point must still be considered as undecided, though proprietary status seems likely.

Chattel leases, being analogous to leases of land, do not fall within the categories of plural ownership considered in this book. However, the fact that they cause us such difficulty demonstrates that we cannot automatically apply land law interests, even when there seems to be a sound case for doing so. Chattel leases demonstrate that the difficulties are not based solely on the concepts of freehold tenures and estates: there is more than this technical objection to accepting a wide range of interests in personalty.

Part of the problem, especially in the chattel lease context, lies in the lack of cases: the area is simply under-developed. This is equally the case for claims equivalent to freehold estates, but in this context the problems are much greater. Freehold estates are seen as an alternative to absolute ownership, or as a slicing of such ownership by time. Either way, there may be no individual who can be described as owner of land. For personalty, however, there can be ownership. The

---

[35]  See the careful analysis by Oditah and Zacaroli (1997) 1 CFILR 29, esp 31–34, 42.

[36]  Palmer, *Bailment* (2nd edn), pp 81–99; Worthington, *Personal Property Law: Text and Materials*, para 2.3.4; Lawson and Rudden, *The Law of Property* (3rd edn), p 116; Hill in *Modern Studies in Property Law, vol 1* (ed Cooke), pp 35–9; Bridge, *Personal Property Law* (3rd edn), pp 26–8; Watt [2003] Conv 61 (though the reasoning is suspect: see n 39 below); McMeel [2003] LMCLQ 169. Cf Goode, *Hire Purchase* (2nd edn), pp 34–6.

[37]  *Bristol Airport plc v Powdrill* [1990] Ch 744, 759 (ultimately the case was one of construction of specific legislation); *On Demand Information plc v Michael Gerson (Finance) plc* [2003] 1 AC 368, [29]. The early dicta of Holt CJ in *Rich v Aldred* (1705) 6 Mod 216 also provide support.

[38]  Palmer, *Bailment* (2nd edn), p 1383; *Halliday v Holgate* (1868) LR 3 Ex 299; see also *Franklin v Neate* (1844) 13 M&W 481, 486.

[39]  The latter analysis was used by Sir Nicolas Browne-Wilkinson in *Powdrill* and supported by Watt [2003] Conv 61. However, there is devastating criticism of it by Swadling in Palmer and McKendrick (eds), *Interests in Goods* (2nd edn), chapter 20 and McFarlane [2003] Conv 473.

[40]  Swadling in Palmer and McKendrick (eds), *Interests in Goods* (2nd edn), chapter 20; note the more cautious approach of Sir Anthony Mason in his Foreword (ibid, p vi).

quotation from Crossley Vaines at the beginning of this section demonstrates that this is regarded as inconsistent with any idea of splitting ownership.

Nevertheless, this need not be the end of the matter. An obvious comparison may be made with Roman law, which recognized ownership in the form of *dominium*.[41] This could not be split in the manner recognized by freehold estates. As a result, Roman law was less flexible than the common law in its acceptance of rights in land, though much closer to the common law regarding personalty. Yet Roman law fully recognized that one person may have rights in another's property (*iura in re aliena*). Amongst these rights was usufruct,[42] the right to use property for life. This may be regarded as extremely close to the life estate of English law. In other words, there is nothing in the concept of ownership which necessarily precludes the development of rights such as life interests. However, it may not be so easy to contemplate the full range of estates in land. Take the gift 'my paintings to Emily, but if she sells the family home, then the paintings are to go to Catriona'. If there had been a gift of land, Emily would have had a form of conditional fee simple and Catriona a contingent right to the fee. But who is the owner of the paintings? We might be forced to say that there has to be an owner and the first ownership gift, to Emily, gives her absolute ownership.[43]

A further and rather curious element is that some form of successive interests is recognized when they are created by will.[44] It is clear that this can be achieved by setting up a trust,[45] but what is instructive is that a trust is not required for gifts by will. These successive interests have been accepted in many cases and appear to be unchallenged.[46] Nevertheless, there is great disagreement as to how they operate. Holdsworth observed[47] that this is a 'little explored backwater of the law'; nothing has changed since he wrote.

The main possibilities[48] appear to be as follows, taking A as the person given a right to use for life and B as the person entitled thereafter:

(1) ownership in B, subject to a right of use in A;
(2) ownership in A, subject to an executory gift to B (a chose in action); or
(3) ownership in A, subject to a trust to give effect to B's claim.

Most commentators consider that the cases[49] provide greatest support for the executory gift analysis. This gives ownership to A subject to a cause of action. This is,

---

[41] Buckland, *Textbook of Roman Law* (3rd edn), pp 187–9. I am grateful for the advice of Professor DJ Ibbetson on the Roman law comparisons. [42] J.2.4.

[43] But compare the Roman law solution (for gifts on death) of *fideicommissum*: n 55 below.

[44] Oliver (1908) 24 LQR 431. There have been few developments since that time, but modern authors still mention this 'obscure topic': Bell, *Modern Law of Personal Property in England and Ireland*, p 74. [45] See p 207 above.

[46] In addition to the cases cited below, see also *Foley v Burnell* (1789) 4 Bro PC 34, 319 and *Re Hill* [1902] 1 Ch 807. [47] *History of English Law*, vol 7, p 477.

[48] Taken from Oliver (1908) 24 LQR 431, 432. See also *Re Swan* [1915] 1 Ch 829, 833–4 (the executors being trustees is added as a fourth possibility, but we are interested with legal ownership in A or B).

[49] Especially *Re Tritton* (1889) 61 LT 301, followed in *Re Thynne* [1911] 1 Ch 282 (though the interests were there held under a trust); *Re Backhouse* [1921] 2 Ch 51.

essentially, a non-proprietary analysis in the sense that B's rights are not recognized as a proprietary interest in the assets. At least to the present author, it seems odd to confer ownership on a person to whom a life interest is purportedly given.[50]

The third (trust) analysis is one which gains some limited support from *Re Swan*,[51] though Sargant J thought it preferable to say that there was trust 'as to his possession'. The third analysis is easily explicable as a matter of principle: there is no difficulty with successive interests being held under a trust. However, it remains wholly unclear where this trust comes from, unless it be an extension of the principle in *Re Rose*.[52]

There is much to be said for the first analysis, giving ownership to B subject to a interest in A of the nature of a usufruct. It is similar to the chattel lease analysis in that the person ultimately entitled is the owner and the person given the life interest is a bailee with rights recognized by law.[53] It is the approach espoused by commentators considering the issue over the past century.[54] However, this analysis may be applicable only to life interests. As has been observed, conditional and contingent interests are much more difficult to explain.[55] In such cases, some form of trust or personal obligation may be the only way forward.

The foregoing discussion applies only to gifts by will. Despite some hesitant suggestions to the contrary,[56] it seems generally agreed that *inter vivos* gifts must take effect by way of trust if successive interests are to be created. There is no guidance as to whether equity will imply a trust if an attempt is made to create successive interests. If that were the case, then the outcome would be tolerable.[57] More generally, the possibility of creating rights by trust is doubtless the reason why the question of legal ownership has remained so obscure.[58] It would be surprising if this unhappy state were to change.

[50] Though that proposition seems consistent with long-standing thinking: Crossley Vaines, *Personal Property* (5th edn), p 43, n (p).

[51] [1915] 1 Ch 829, 834 (considering possibilities suggested by Fearne, *Contingent Remainders* (10th edn), p 414). The issue turned on the nature of A's duties.

[52] [1952] Ch 499: equity will give effect to a gift if the donor has done all in his her power to transfer the property. If this is the analysis, it would be inexplicable if it did not also apply to *inter vivos* transfers.

[53] The bailment analysis appears to be the preferred approach of Sargant J in *Re Swan* [1915] 1 Ch 829, 834: any trust is 'preferably perhaps as to his possession of the property'.

[54] Oliver (1908) 24 LQR 431 (observing that the earlier cases, especially *Hyde v Parrat* (1695) 1 P Wms 1; 2 Vern 331, provide support); Holdsworth, *History of English Law*, vol 7, p 477.

[55] Such claims were recognized in Roman law, subject to restrictions on gifts to unascertained persons, by the *fideicommissum*: Johnston, *Roman Law of Trusts*, especially chapter 4 and (more briefly) *Trusts and Trust-like Devices in Roman Law* in Helmholz and Zimmermann (eds), *Itinera Fiduciae*. This applied only to gifts on death. Although this limitation provides an interesting parallel to English law, the English trust (with which *fideicommissum* is compared) permits *inter vivos* gifts to create successive interests.

[56] Oliver (1908) 24 LQR 431, 432, citing Blackstone, *Commentaries on the Laws of England*, Book II, p 398.

[57] We would still need to consider who has the legal ownership. It is most consistent with the cases that this should be the life interest holder, who has possession of the property.

[58] Holdsworth, *History of English Law*, vol 7, p 477; Worthington, *Personal Property Law: Text and Materials*, para 2.2.1.

This area cannot be left without considering whether there are policy reasons inhibiting the development of successive interests. It is a commonplace that the courts are wary of creating new rights in property because this is likely to increase risks and complications for purchasers. For property other than land, this debate has largely been conducted in the context of the recognition of equitable interests in goods.[59] Plainly, the risk to purchasers is greatest where the possessor is not also the owner.[60] It might then follow that we should be reluctant to adopt the usufruct analysis, as that does divorce ownership and possession. Yet it must be remembered that it is very common for the owner of goods to be out of possession; every case of bailment provides an example. Similarly, successive interests can be created under a trust, with the life interest holder being allowed possession of the property. It is unclear that the recognition of a right equivalent to usufruct would cause significant additional problems. In any event, the existence of differing rules for *inter vivos* gifts and those by will seems almost impossible to justify in terms either of modern property theory or policy considerations.

## 4. Regulation

When studying plural ownership of land, it was seen that there is extensive regulation through the trust of land. This is particularly important as regards occupation, powers to deal with the land, and protection of purchasers. Overarching much of this area is the existence of a broad court discretion to resolve disputes. When we turn to personalty we find that virtually none of this regulation applies. In many cases we are thrown back on a rather arid landscape of limited common law rules. However, a distinction must be drawn as to whether or not a trust was employed to give effect to the interests.

### A. Plural Ownership Existing Behind a Trust

Trusts operate subject to both control by the courts and statutory provisions;[61] it follows that there is some measure of regulation. TLATA, of course, does not apply to trusts of property other than land. However, the operation of TLATA requires further examination. Trusts of land are defined to cover trusts which include land,[62] so that a mixed trust of chattels and land is a trust of land. However, the significance of this is very limited. Nearly all the powers (whether general powers, partition, or delegation) are applicable only to land; the provisions relating to consultation, occupation, and purchaser protection are

---

[59] Eg Worthington, *Personal Property Law: Text and Materials*, para 4.10.2.
[60] Note the protection of purchasers from possessors in certain specific instances: Sale of Goods Act 1979, ss 24, 25 (sellers and buyers in possession).     [61] Esp the Trustee Acts 1925 and 2000.
[62] TLATA, s 1(1)(a).

similarly limited. However, the court's jurisdiction (TLATA, section 14) to review the exercise of trustees' functions is applicable to functions relating to all forms of assets.

Let us take the following example. A and B hold land and paintings on trust for X, Y, and Z as beneficial joint tenants. X and Y would like all these assets to be sold and the proceeds invested in shares, but Z disagrees and the trustees decline to sell. X and Y could apply under section 14 for an order that the assets be sold. This application could extend to both the land and the paintings. Of course, the court might agree with the trustees, but the majority opinion of X and Y will carry some weight.[63]

We can now turn to trusts where no land is involved. In all trusts the court possesses power to control the trustees: the beneficiaries have the right to bring the administration of the trust to the court. However, it is unusual for the court to intervene unless trustees have acted improperly in some way.[64] It seems that this is a less active interventionalist role than is encountered in trusts of land. However, virtually all the cases on trusts of land involve trustees and beneficiaries who are the same persons (or at least trustees who have beneficial interests) whereas the basic trusts principles have been forged in cases where trustees are not beneficiaries and may be regarded as taking independent decisions.[65] It is possible that the differences between general trusts principles and the section 14 jurisdiction are less marked than at first sight appears.

What are the powers of the trustees regarding disposition of non-land assets? For land, of course, TLATA, section 6 confers almost unlimited powers. Suppose a settlor leaves a block of shares and a set of paintings (which have been owned by the family for generations) on trust for Rose for life, remainder to Simon. Can the trustees sell the shares or paintings? A well drafted trust will clarify the powers of the trustees, but what is the fall-back position? As regards the shares, it seems quite clear that these are held as an investment and the trustees have virtually unlimited powers of investment.[66] Necessarily, this involves selling existing investments, such as the shares.[67]

Could the paintings be sold and the proceeds invested in, say, shares? This is slightly more difficult. The paintings themselves do not appear to be investments: it is thought that the power in the Trustee Act 2000, section 3 does not permit items to be purchased for enjoyment.[68] If investments cannot be turned into

---

[63] TLATA, s 15(3). Although there is no requirement under s 11 for trustees to consult beneficiaries as regards the pictures, the court is required to have regard to their wishes.

[64] See p 145 above.     [65] See p 167 above.

[66] Trustee Act 2000, s 3. As one might expect, the power is subject to 'standard investment criteria' being considered (s 4) and advice must usually be sought (s 5).

[67] Highlighted by the duty to keep investments under review: s 4(2).

[68] Whitehouse and Hassall, *Trusts of Land, Trustee Delegation and the Trustee Act 2000* (2nd edn), para 11.24. Items such as paintings can be purchased on the basis that they will provide capital growth and therefore be a good investment: Law Com No 260, para 2.28, n 56. There is an express power to purchase land for use: Trustee Act 2000, s 8.

paintings for enjoyment, can the reverse be undertaken, can paintings be turned into investments? In our example, there is unlikely to be a problem if Rose and Simon agree. It is where they disagree (or if Simon is under eighteen) that the issue becomes significant. It could be argued that the Trustee Act 2000 is about investments and the paintings are plainly not held as an investment.[69] On the other hand, this would reduce the powers of the trustees and it seems to adopt a narrower approach than under the previous legislation.[70] It seems preferable to give section 3 the broader interpretation to permit the sale of property held for its use, for the purpose of investing the proceeds. Of course, it does not follow that the trustees should adopt such a course of action. Especially where the settlor has made it clear that it is intended that the paintings should go to Simon, it may be difficult to justify selling.[71]

It might be added that there is a special provision applicable to heirlooms in a Settled Land Act settlement.[72] The tenant for life is given power to sell them, though the consent of the court must be obtained. It has been seen that no new Settled Land Act settlements can be created, so this provision is obsolescent. No equivalent exists in TLATA.

All trusts are subject to the provisions of the Trustee Acts 1925 and 2000 and other provisions relating to trusts. These confer powers (for example to insure the property and to delegate to agents[73]). However, these powers apply to all trustees and mostly fall more within a general assessment of the law of trusts than within our investigation of plural ownership. It is worth noting, though that the Trustee Act 1925, section 57 gives the court power to approve any disposition (including sale) of the trust assets where such would be 'expedient'. This is obviously valuable where there would otherwise be no such power.[74]

## B. Plural Ownership Without a Trust

It has been seen that this is possible for joint tenancies and tenancies in common and also (occasionally) for successive interests created by will. So far as regulation is concerned, there is virtually none.

As observed above, the rules applicable to joint tenancies and tenancies in common are the same as those developed for land. Unsurprisingly, the nature of

---

[69] In our example, their sentimental value appears dominant; other cases could be different.

[70] Trustee Investments Act 1961, s 1(1) applied to 'any property in his [the trustee's] hands, whether at the time in a statement of investment or not'. The Trustee Act 2000 is overtly designed to broaden the powers of trustees.

[71] Indeed, it might be possible to imply that the power to sell the paintings has been excluded. In the land context, cf *Re Herklots' WT* [1964] 1 WLR 583, p 147 above (consent of beneficiary impliedly required).

[72] Settled Land Act 1925, s 67; applicable to chattels settled so as to devolve with the land.

[73] There cannot be delegation to beneficiaries (Trustee Act 2000, s 12(3)); contrast the power in TLATA, s 9 to delegate to beneficiaries.

[74] *Re Hope's WT* [1929] 2 Ch 136 provides an example (successive interests in personalty).

the assets may mean that problems arise in a slightly different form where chattels are involved. It has been seen that every joint tenant and tenant of land has a right to the use of the entirety of co-owned land, but that there will be liability where other co-owners are excluded.[75] This applies also to personalty,[76] though the law gives great freedom to co-owners in their use of co-owned goods.[77] Particular problems have arisen where a co-owner sells chattels (as opposed to his or her share). Although the courts generally held that this was not a wrong because it had no effect on the other co-owners,[78] this has been reversed by the Torts (Interference with Goods) Act 1977, s 10(1)(b). For land it is usually impossible for a single co-owner to attempt to sell. This is because the title deeds will reveal the co-ownership: the only likely exception is where the other co-owner's signature to a transfer has been forged.[79]

Perhaps the only regulatory provision is section 188 of the Law of Property Act 1925, which permits a person holding at least a half share to apply to the court for an order for the division of the chattels. This is a very limited provision. A person with less than a half share has no right even to apply to court. It appears applicable only to co-ownership of chattels capable of division: it offers nothing for example, to co-owners of a single valuable painting. This is high-lighted by the absence of a power to order sale.[80] Although the court may make 'such order . . . as it thinks fit', this is against the background that the application is for division: a quite different order such as sale is not contemplated.[81] It should be added that many cases of co-ownership of chattels involve partnership. In that scenario, there is clear jurisdiction to order sale,[82] but that is part of partnership law, rather than an aspect of plural ownership.

[75] See Chapter 7 above, esp p 131.        [76] *Baker v Barclays Bank Ltd* [1955] 1 WLR 822, 827.

[77] *Fraser v Kershaw* (1856) 2 K&J 496; Clerk and Lindsell, Torts (18th edn), para 14.73; Law Reform Committee, *Eighteenth Report* (Cmd 4774), para 35.

[78] *Mayhew v Herrick* (1849) 7 CB 229; see Hill and Bowes-Smith in Palmer and McKendrick (eds), *Interests in Goods* (2nd edn), pp 257–8.

[79] We are not here concerned with defeating beneficial co-ownership interests: that is the realm of breach of trust rather than ouster.

[80] Wolstenholme and Cherry, *Conveyancing Statutes* (13th edn), vol 1, p 312.

[81] The contrary is argued by Hill and Bowes-Smith in Palmer and McKendrick (eds), *Interests in Goods* (2nd edn), p 255, on the basis that 'the court's discretion is extremely wide'.

[82] See eg *Taylor v Neate* (1888) 39 Ch D 538.

# Index

Bailment 211–13
Bankruptcy, *see* Court applications
Base fees 13

Chattels
  chattel leases 212
  division if co-owned 218
  *see also* Non-land plural ownership
Children
  consent requirements 147–8
  family law discretions 129, 179, 180–1
  joint tenancy 32
  sale decisions 159–60, 163, 165–6, 171–2,
    177–8
Choses in action
  no tenancy in common 209–11
  *see also* Non-land plural ownership
Commonhold 7–8
Commorientes 26
Compensation for occupation and
    improvements 131–40
  agreement 132
  broad discretion? 135
  compensation and improvements
    linked 135–7
    interest payments 135–6
  equitable duty since1925? 133
  future occupation 127, 131–2, 137–9
  improvements 140
  family home 134
  mortgage payments 135–6
  no general right 131
  ouster 133, 134
  past occupation 131–2
  receipts 132–3
  TLATA 127, 131–2, 137–9
  *see also* Occupation, Regulation of plural
    ownership, Severance, Tenancy in
    common, Trusts of land
Contractual licences 116
Conversion, doctrine of *see* Trusts of land
Co-ownership
  1925 scheme 97, 106–8, 109–10
  application to family home
    express provisions 38–41
    *Gissing* trusts 41–3
    reforms 44, 83–9
    suitability of survivorship? 44, 85–6
  forms of 26–7, 46, 48–9
  meaning 22–6

nature of rights and obligations 45–6
need for regulation 96–8
old forms 46, 48–9
partition 47–8
party walls 23
property other than land *see* Non-land
    plural ownership
reform 83–9
*see also* Joint tenancy, Occupation,
    Compensation for occupation and
    improvements
Coparcenary 46
Court applications 155–81
  bankruptcy 167–73
    children 171–2
    exceptional circumstances 168–70
    first year 168
    homestead legislation 172–3
    human rights 172
    normal matters for consideration
      inapplicable 168
    other protections defeated 168
    policy 170–2
    three-year limit 170
  family law jurisdiction 168, 179–81
  independent trustees 167
  jurisdiction 156–8
    defeating occupation? 157
    excluded powers 144, 156–7
  matters for consideration
    buying applicant out 165
    children 159–60, 163, 165–6,
      171–2
    different after TLATA? 159–60, 165–7,
      175–6
    discretion 164–5, 166, 176–7
    earlier cases 160–5
    purposes 159–66, 178–9
      multiple purposes 161–3
      survive death? 163–4
      termination 161
      timing 164
    secured creditors 160, 173–9
      change after TLATA 175–6
      children's interests 177–8
      exceptional circumstances 175
      joint occupation purposes end 174
      remain well protected 176–8
    statutory criteria 158, 159–60, 163,
      165–7

statutory criteria *(Cont.)*
   successors in title 174–5
   wishes of beneficiaries 158–9
   successors in title 174–5
   trusts for sale 155, 160, 181–3
   who can apply? 157–8
   willingness to intervene 155, 167

Determinable fees *see* Freehold estates
Discretionary trusts 122
Donor doing all in power 214

Entails 12–13, 114, 208
Equitable remedies and proprietary status
   212
Estate contracts 58, 116
Estates *see* Entails, Freehold estates, Leases
Estoppel 116–17

Family home
   accounting 133–7
   acquiring interests 4
   declarations of beneficial interest 38–41
   joint tenancy or tenancy in common 41–3,
      83–9
   survivorship 44, 85–8
Fee simple *see* Freehold estates
Fee tail 12–13, 114, 208
Formalities 68
Freehold estates
   absolute and qualified interests 13–15
   applicable only to land 211
   contingent 14
   enjoyment of the estates 20–1
   fee simple 11–12
      equivalent to ownership 11
   fee tail 12–13, 114, 208
   importance 11
   in possession 12, 14
   in remainder 12
   in reversion 12
   leases contrasted 15–16
   life estates
      leases compared 5
      *pur autre vie* 12
      waste 12, 20–1
   trusts of land 114–15
   vesting 14
   words of limitation 19
   *see also* Successive interests

Joint tenancy
   1925 legislation 107, 113–14
   four unities 27–30, 44–6
      unity of interest 28–9, 57
      unity of possession 22–6, 28
         leases 23–6
      unity of time 29–30, 57

unity of title 29, 55–6
nature of 27
necessary today? 83–9
presumed 30
problems caused by 83–5
survivorship 26–7, 44–6, 83
use today and suitability 85–6
*see also* Co-ownership, Non-land plural
   ownership, Tenancy in common,
   Severance

Land companies 6–7
Land registration *see* Registration of title
Leases
   chattel leases 212
   contrasted with plural ownership 3, 4–6,
      15–16
   leases for life 5, 16
   unity of possession 23–6
Licences 116
Life estates *see* Freehold estates, Non-land
   plural ownership
Limitation, words of 19

Mutual wills 75–7

Non-land plural ownership 207–18
   concurrent interests 208–11
      choses in action 209–11
      severance of joint tenancy 209
   regulation 215–18
      no trust 217–18
         division of chattels 218
      trusts 215–17
         land included 215–16
         no land included 216–17
   successive interests 211–15
      chattel leases 212
      *inter vivos* creation? 214
      life interests? 212–15
      no estates 211
      policy aspects 215
      wills 213–14
   trusts 207–8, 210–11, 214, 215–17

Occupation 118–31
   before 1925 118, 120
   before TLATA 118–21
   effect of trust 118–21
   spouses and cohabitants 128–31
      relationship with TLATA 129–31
   TLATA 122–8
      continuing requirements? 123–4
      interest in possession 122
      land unavailable or unsuitable 125
      relationship between TLATA and
         earlier rights 127–8
      right to occupy 122–8

decision by trustees  124
termination of purpose  123–4
timing  123
role of court  127, 157, 158–9
trustees' discretions  126–7
beneficiaries in occupation  126–7
cannot exclude all  126
compensation  127, 131–2
conditions on beneficiaries  127
consultation  127, 158–9
relevant criteria  127
*see also* **Compensation for occupation and
improvements**
**Overreaching**  184–92
ad hoc trust of land  190
application of proceeds  189–90
based on exercise of powers  184–5, 193
capital money  186–8
overriding interests  186–8
reform  190–2
rights overreached  190
single trustee  186–7, 195–6
summarized  16, 184–5
two trustees  186, 187–8
without capital money  188–9
**Overriding interests** *see* **Registration of title**
**Ownership**,
effect for property other than land  208,
209, 211–15
compatible with successive interests?
212–15

**Partition**  47–8, 152, 218
**Party walls**  23
**Perpetuity rules**  17–19
class gifts  18
reform  18–19
wait and see  17–18
**Personal property** *see* **Non-land plural
ownership**
**Plural Ownership**
acquiring interests in the family home  4
commercial and family interests  5–6
leases contrasted  3, 15–16
other forms of multiple ownership  4–8
commonhold  7–8
land companies  6–7
leases  4–6
timesharing  7
unincorporated associations  8
property other than land *see* **Non-land
plural ownership**
scope  3–4
statutory regulation summarized  4
**Powers of trustees**  143–55
consent requirements  147–8
implied  147
infants  147–8

relief from  148
purchasers  148
consultation requirements  148–52
effect  150–1
occupation  151
successive interests  151–2
delegation to beneficiaries  153–5
liability of trustees  154
refusal to delegate  153
revocation  153–4
equitable constraints  145
exclusion of  144–5, 154–5
functions, meaning of  149–50, 156–7
implied by statute  143, 152–5
partition  47–8, 152
postponing sale  152
purchase of land  143
statutory constraints  146–7
transfer to beneficiaries  152–3
*see also* **Occupation**
**Purchaser protection**
consent requirements  148, 192–3, 194
consultation requirements  196, 198
effect of  203
importance of  184
*intra vires* transactions  198–200
irregularities causing *ultra vires*  195–8
limitations on powers  192–5
overreaching *see* **Overreaching**
**payments to single trustee**  195–6
registered land  193–6, 201–2
powers of proprietors  193–5
subsequent purchasers  203
termination of trust  200–2
death of joint tenant  200
deeds of discharge  201
time of protection  202–3
*ultra vires* transactions  192–8

**Registration of title**
irregularities in dispositions  193–6
payment to single trustee  186–7,
195–6
payment to two trustees  187–8
powers of trustees as proprietors  193–5
termination of trust  201–2
**Regulation of plural ownership**  4,
93–117
need for reform after 1925  108–10
need for regulation  93–8
concurrent interests  96–8
successive interests  94–6
property other than land *see* **Non-land
plural ownership**
settled land *see* **Settled Land Act
settlements**
TLATA  110–17
general structure  110–11

TLATA (*Cont.*)
　　scope of application 111–17
　　　bare trusts 114–15
　　　concurrent interests 112–14
　　　extended application 114
　　　trust of land 114–17
　　trusts for sale 111, 181
　　trusts for sale 105–8
　　　concurrent interests 106–8
　　　modern role 181–3
　　　need for reform 109–10
　　　successive interests 105–6
　　*see also* **Compensation for occupation and
　　　improvements, Court control,
　　　Occupation, Powers of trustees,
　　　Purchaser protection, Trusts of land**

**Secured creditors** *see* **Court Applications**
**Settled Land Act settlements** 98–106
　　documentation 102–4
　　general scheme 98–9
　　heirlooms 217
　　need for reform 108–9
　　purchaser protection 102–5
　　　deed of discharge 104
　　　payment to two trustees essential 103
　　tenant for life 98–101, 108–9
　　　powers 100
　　　powers cannot be excluded 101
　　trust for sale compared 105–6
　　trustees of settlement 98, 101–2
　　when applicable? 99
**Severance** 48–82
　　acts operating on share 55–66
　　　contracts 58
　　　dispositions other than transfers 60–6
　　　　charges 62–3
　　　　leases 63–6
　　　less obvious transfers 59–60
　　　multiple joint tenants 56
　　course of dealing 68–77
　　　family disputes 71–3
　　　multiple properties 75
　　　mutual wills 75–7
　　　need for agreement? 68–9
　　　selling the land 74
　　　unilateral? 69–71
　　exclusion of 49
　　mutual agreement 66–8
　　　unanimity required? 67
　　　formalities 68
　　not by will 49–50, 75–7, 81
　　not of legal joint tenancy 50
　　notice in writing 51–5
　　　delivery 51–3

　　effect 54
　　personalty? 53–4, 209
　　reform 55, 79
　　statutory restrictions 53–4
　　wording required 53
　　personalty 50, 53–4, 209
　　policy perspectives 79–82
　　public policy 77–9
　　reform 79–82
　　related to unities 55–6, 57, 58–9
　　unilateral? 51, 58, 69–71, 80–1
**Successive interests,**
　　beneficiary control over management 98
　　history and problems 94–6
　　property other than land *see* **Non-land
　　　plural ownership**
　　Settled Land Act 1925 *see* **Settled Land Act
　　　settlements**
　　strict settlements 94–5
　　trusts for sale 105–6
　　trusts of land 115
　　*see also* **Freehold estates, Perpetuity rules,
　　　Regulation of plural ownership**

**Tenancy by entireties** 46, 48–9
**Tenancy in common**
　　1925 legislation 106–7, 112–13
　　cannot be legal 27, 106
　　contrast with joint tenancy 26–7
　　described 26–7
　　equitable presumption 33–8
　　　executory trusts 38
　　　mortgagees 33–4
　　　partners 34–6
　　　unequal purchase 36–8
　　express survivorship 46
　　leases 24–6
　　parties' intentions in creation 30, 33
　　problems for purchasers 97
　　property other than land 208–11
　　　not choses in action 209–11
　　words of severance 30–3
　　　inconsistent wording 32
**Timesharing** 7
**Trusts (other than of land)** 207–8, 210–11,
　　215–17
**Trusts for sale** *see* **Court applications,
　　Regulation of plural ownership,
　　Successive interests, Trusts
　　of land**
**Trusts of land**
　　ad hoc trust of land 190
　　application 111–17
　　　bare trusts 114–15
　　　extended by TLATA 114

concurrent interests 112–14
property other than land 215–16
successive interests 115
trusts for sale 111, 181
undesired cases? 115–17
beneficiary control *see* **Powers of trustees**
consent and consultation requirements *see*
**Powers of trustees**
general structure 110–11
improvements 140
partition 47–8, 152
termination of trusteeship 152–3, 200–2
trusts for sale 105–8, 181–3
concurrent interests 106–8
conversion 182–3
abolished by TLATA 183
how special today 181–2
modern use of 181–3
need for TLATA reforms 109–10
power to postpone sale 152
successive interests 105–6
TLATA 111, 181
*see also* **Compensation for occupation and**
**improvements, Court applications,**
**Occupation, Overreaching, Powers**
**of trustees, Purchaser protection**

**Unincorporated associations** 7, 115

**Vesting in interest and in possession** 14

**Waste** 12, 20–1
**Wills** 213–14
**Words of limitation** 19